The Parties Respond

CHANGES IN AMERICAN PARTIES AND CAMPAIGNS

FOURTH EDITION

L. Sandy Maisel
Colby College

Westview
PRESS

A Member of the Perseus Books Group

TRANSFORMING AMERICAN POLITICS

Lawrence C. Dodd, Series Editor

Dramatic changes in political institutions and behavior over the past three decades have underscored the dynamic nature of American politics, confronting political scientists with a new and pressing intellectual agenda. The pioneering work of early postwar scholars, while laying a firm empirical foundation for contemporary scholarship, failed to consider how American politics might change or recognize the forces that would make fundamental change inevitable. In reassessing the static interpretations fostered by these classic studies, political scientists are now examining the underlying dynamics that generate transformational change.

Transforming American Politics brings together texts that address four closely related aspects of change. A first concern is documenting and explaining recent changes in American politics—in institutions, processes, behavior, and policymaking. A second is reinterpreting classic studies and theories to provide a more accurate perspective on postwar politics. The series looks at historical change to identify recurring patterns of political transformation with in and across the distinctive eras of American politics. Last and perhaps most important, the series presents new theories and interpretations that explain the dynamic processes at work and thus clarify the direction of contemporary politics. All of the books focus on the central theme of transformation—transformation in both the conduct of American politics and in the way we study and understand its many aspects.

BOOKS IN THIS SERIES

Copyright © 2002 by Westview Press, A Member of the Perseus Books Group

Westview Press books are available at special discounts for bulk purchases in the United States by corporations, institutions, and other organizations. For more information, please contact the Special Markets Department at the Perseus Books Group, 11 Cambridge Center, Cambridge MA 02142, or call (617)252–5298.

Published in 2002 in the United States of America by Westview Press, 5500 Central Avenue, Boulder, Colorado 80301–2877, and in the United Kingdom by Westview Press, 12 Hid's Copse Road, Cumnor Hill, Oxford OX2 9JJ

Find us on the World Wide Web at www.westviewpress.com

Library of Congress Cataloging-in-Publication Data

The parties respond : changes in American parties and campaigns /
[edited by] L. Sandy Maisel. — 4th ed.
    p.   cm. — (Transforming American politics)
  Includes bibliographical references and index.
  ISBN 0-8133-4022-5 (hc: acid-free); ISBN 0-8133-6455-8 (pb: acid-free)
  1. Political parties—United States.   I. Maisel, Louis Sandy, 1945–   .   II. Series.
JK2261 .P29   2002
324.273—dc21
                                                                2002002566

10   9   8   7   6   5   4   3   2   1

To the memory of
Warren E. Miller,
scholar, mentor, and friend

Contents

List of Tables and Figures

Tables

ix

Figures

Prologue

When the first edition of this book was conceived, the authors were asked to comment on the election of 1988, including the election of George H.W. Bush to the presidency, as they examined how parties were responding to various challenges to their role in American politics. The presidential election that preceded the second edition saw Bill Clinton defeat President Bush, and the parties seemed to face a new set of challenges. As the scholars whose chapters comprise this volume thought about the fourth edition, many were concerned with the irony implicit in the American citizenry's expressing dissatisfaction with the two major parties in poll after poll while at the same time seemingly rejecting the Reform party, founded by Ross Perot, in the presidential election and supporting Democratic or Republican candidates for virtually every office on the ballot.

How should one describe the state of political parties following the election of 2000? On the eve of the 1996 election, Americans were having second thoughts about our two-party system. Certainly much the same can be said of the 2000 election. During the fall of 2000, citizens across the country were unhappy with the choice between the Republican candidate, the then Texas governor, George W. Bush, and his Democratic opponent, Vice President Albert Gore. One seemed intellectually unprepared to assume our nation's highest office; the other seemed incapable of finding his true self, many thought because he wanted that office too much. But the same citizens who were lukewarm to the major-party presidential candidates and who were less and less inclined to align themselves with one or the other of the major parties continued to vote for major-party candidates.

The Reform party, whose future had seemed so bright in 1992, was in shambles. The very openness of the party that had seemed so welcoming to those disaffected with the Democrats and the Republicans led to internal strife as Pat Buchanan, whose views were anathema to many of the original Reform party members, used the rules to capture the party nomination, over the objection of many who had been in the party since the visionary days of Ross Perot. The resulting court fight led to further dissension; Buchanan's campaign went nowhere, and the party now seems all but dead.

The new rising star among nonmajor parties is clearly the Green party, whose standard was carried by Ralph Nader in the 2000 election. But the Greens failed to meet the threshold needed to gain federal funding for the 2004 presidential election, one of their stated goals. Worse still, in the eyes of many this "third" party's fate was the one foretold by many critics: enabling George Bush's election despite the fact that Al Gore's views more closely paralleled those of Green party members. Some Greens say that Gore's loss is a small price to pay for building a viable alternative party, but whether the Greens become viable or not remains in serious question.

Now, as they look back on the 2000 election, scholars again are attempting to ascertain how the two major parties are being challenged and how well they are responding.

Despite Americans' dissatisfaction with the two-party system in the United States and a yearning for alternatives, the system remains intact. And in this irony we see continuity. Americans love to hate political parties. But the two-party system has been a constant feature of this polity. The persistence of American political parties despite two centuries of criticism stands as testimony to the importance of their role in our system of government. Although they are never mentioned in the Constitution, parties have had an impact on virtually every aspect of American political life.

Think of the environment in which political parties operate. In the broadest terms, parties seek to attract votes to support their candidates for office on the basis of allegiance to the party label and agreement with the policy positions supported by the party. They do so within a legal and political context that is constantly changing because of world events, a context that varies from state to state and even from community to community within a single state. And they do so without the power to control which candidates carry their banner or what specific positions those candidates espouse.

In the earlier editions of this anthology, I outlined marked changes in the political environment faced by parties over recent decades. Political parties had to reexamine and redefine their roles as the nation responded to the civil rights movement of the 1950s and 1960s, with its profound impact on all aspects of American society and on political processes throughout the nation. The parties had to fashion a response to the Vietnam War and to its legacy—a generation of citizens uncertain whether the traditional political process could answer fundamental dissatisfaction with our nation's foreign policy. The role of the parties was challenged by the women's movement of the 1970s, with the expansion of the politically active electorate and the emergence of new, cross-cutting issues. And in the current post-9/11 context, the parties must respond to the changes wrought by the events of September 11, 2001.

This list of legal, political, and societal changes that challenge the ability of parties to perform their role could be expanded without difficulty to include Supreme Court decisions requiring apportionment schemes that, to the extent possible, equalized the value of votes; an increase in the number of Hispanic and Asian American voters and concern over immigration patterns; increased public concern over the ethics of those in government, from Watergate to Whitewater, with many stops in between; the movement of the nation's population from the Snowbelt to the Sunbelt, with consequent problems for each area; the ending of the Cold War and the search for America's role in the emerging world order; the imposition of term limits on many state legislators. But the lessons remain the same: As the nation has undergone dramatic changes, the political parties have had to function within this changing context, have had to respond.

And there is no doubt that both the parties and the politicians who run for election under party labels and the institutions in which they serve have responded. Some of the responses have been abrupt and some have been subtle. Some have succeeded and some have failed. Some have been welcomed and some, criticized. The Democrats and Republicans have not always responded in the same ways. But the parties have been involved in all of these societal changes, and as organizations and as symbols to the nation, they are not the same now as they were decades ago, nor even 16 years ago, when this book first appeared. Like its predecessors, this volume examines the responses of parties to changes in American society and politics.

The chapters written for this volume examine contemporary political parties, but the historical context of that examination is also significant. As Joel Silbey persuasively argues in the opening chapter, the centrality of the party role has varied significantly over time. Not only the intensity of that role but also the locus of its impact has shifted.

In the two chapters that follow, John Bibby and Paul Herrnson discuss changes in party organization at the state and national levels, respectively. Bibby examines state parties' responses to the nationalization of party politics as well as to the continued trend toward candidate-centered campaigns. Herrnson focuses on national parties' responses to changes wrought by technological advances and alterations of the regulatory environment; thus, the party role has evolved even if the organizational structure has remained the same.

Chapter 4 was written by Warren Miller before his untimely death. His article of four years ago has been updated by his stepson Mark Jones and his former colleague Kenneth Goldstein to include material on the 2000 election. Miller's theme is the persistence of party attachment through all of these periods of change, and it remains as important now as it was when he first articulated it many years ago.

In Chapters 5 and 6 the party role in the nominating process is examined. Bruce Cain and Megan Mullin discuss the ways various state parties have responded to the leeway they are given in setting up their own systems for selecting delegates to national nominating conventions. They explore the various motivations behind the actions of state parties and the consequences that follow from having such an open and decentralized system. Sandy Maisel, Cherie Maestas, and Walter Stone draw on the data they have generated in the course of conducting the Candidate Emergence Study to explore the roles that party leaders play in congressional candidate recruitment. They conclude that party leaders clearly see their role as helping their party to maintain (or gain) majority status in Congress; thus they encourage strong candidates to run in seats thought to be competitive. The result is that competition is intense for some seats but nearly or totally lacking in other districts.

Chapters 7, 8, and 9 explore the role of the parties in general elections. Michael Franz and Kenneth Goldstein draw on data on campaign advertising to analyze the role played by soft money in great detail. Their conclusion is that party money is used to win elections, not to state a message or build support for the party in more abstract terms. Winning seems to be all that matters. Ray La Raja traces the growth of soft money and the ways parties have used it to enhance their own role. He also looks at the implications for parties should reformers succeed in banning soft-money donations. Matthew Kerbel explores the role of parties in the media, focusing on party conventions as a way to explore how party structures and functions are portrayed and to assess the content of the messages communicated about the parties to convention viewers.

Chapters 10, 11, and 12 look at various aspects of the party in government and the ways they have responded to recent changes in the political environment. Barbara Sinclair examines the role congressional parties play in the contemporary Congress, focusing on how the parties go about their various functions in the policymaking process. David Brady and Kara Buckley present their findings on coalitions in the Congress and analyze specific instances where median preferences have resulted in winning coalitions. Calvin Mackenzie traces the history of the partisan role in the appointment process from the era of George Washington to that of George Bush.

In the final chapter, the journalist and political observer David Shribman trains his sights on the 2000 election, the election that bored the American people right up to Election Day but kept us rapt for thirty-six days thereafter, and draws insights for the future of American politics. He looks at subtle changes revealed by election data that might tell important tales for the years ahead.

The thirteen contributions that make up this book represent the most recent thinking by leading scholars, yet they have been written with an undergraduate audience in mind. They not only cover the varying aspects of this topic from differing perspectives but also employ a range of research methods so that students can be exposed to the range of modes of analysis used by contemporary researchers. Taken together, they paint a fascinating picture of American political parties. Parties have adapted as the nation has changed over two centuries. Furthermore, the parties vary over place and political level as well as over time, and any analysis must take into account not only their complexity but also the different points at which they intersect with the American polity. The contributors come to the topic from different perspectives—as political scientists, historians, journalists, and activists; and as students not only of parties but of organizations, voting behavior, elections, the press, the Congress, and the presidency. Only by looking at the entire picture can one begin to understand the complexity of American political parties, the ways they have responded to a changing country, and the reasons they have persisted.

L. Sandy Maisel
Rome, Maine
December 2001

Acknowledgments

The editor of any anthology is indebted first to the authors whose work appears in the volume. In my case, I am particularly grateful to the thirteen scholars who have continued to contribute to this work as it has evolved from one edition to the next. Whether chapters have been substantially revised or are totally new, these works constitute the core of this book; I am very thankful for the authors' continued confidence in the value of this book. At the same time, I want to acknowledge and thank five others whose work appears in this book for the first time. New approaches to this topic by leading scholars is what keeps the book fresh and exciting for the classroom. The lasting friendships I have had with all of these men and women makes my job as editor a great joy.

Producing a book like this one requires the assistance of many dedicated professionals. The "team" that has been involved in seeing this work from manuscript to production is a new one. At Colby College, I would like to thank Sarah Ward, our departmental secretary, who has worked with a number of my manuscripts at various stages; her skill is astounding and her patience with me is amazing. I (and all of my colleagues) consider it a privilege to work with her. The third edition of this book was dedicated to the twelve research assistants I had been fortunate enough to work with in the decade prior to its publication. I could continue that tradition—as I have been blessed with wonderful student assistants in the most recent years, Cathy Flemming, Kim Victor, Oliver Sabot, Brooke McNally, Dave Sandak, Abe Summers, and Laura Mistretta. I particularly want to acknowledge the assistance of Brooke McNally, who played a major role in shepherding this book through to completion.

At Westview Press, I am indebted to my new editor, Steve Catalano, who has taken on this project and others in which I am involved with enthusiasm and professionalism; I hope this is the beginning of a long and fruitful relationship: to Katharine Chandler, the project editor, and to Chris Arden, whose copyediting was most important. And as always, I appreciate the confidence of Larry Dodd, the editor of the series in which this book appears, for allowing me to develop this book under his gentle guidance.

I want to add a special note of thanks to my wife, Patrice Franko. In the past eight years, I have learned the joys of sharing not only a life and a home but also a profession with a wonderful mate. Working on building a happy home together is a great joy. That I have and will continue to benefit from her professional support and encouragement, and from her informed criticism and suggestions, creates a dimension to our life together that is difficult to overestimate. I look forward to years—and volumes—of continued collaboration, but mostly of love and friendship.

Finally, this volume is dedicated to the memory of Warren Miller, whose chapters have been an important part of each edition of this book. I was not fortunate enough to have studied under Warren. But I was oh so fortunate to have him as a friend. When, as a much younger scholar, I conceived of this book, I knew I needed one "star" to give it legitimacy among those who study parties. All I had to do was ask Warren; he never knew how to say no to a friend. Warren's contributions to political science, to the American Political Science Association, to the National Elections Studies, to his universities, and to our profession were legion, widely recognized, and now sorely missed. But they were just a small part of Warren Miller. His concern and caring and support, his willingness to give of himself for others, and his deep friendships that were only matched by his familiar deep-throated greeting—"Hey big fella. How are ya?"—remain the lasting memories of all who were fortunate enough to be touched by this wonderful man.

L.S.M.

1

From "Essential to the Existence of Our Institutions" to "Rapacious Enemies of Honest and Responsible Government": The Rise and Fall of American Political Parties, 1790–2000

JOEL H. SILBEY

Since the 1790s, few elections in America have occurred without the involvement of national political parties. From the Jeffersonian Republicans and Federalists in the first years of the new nation to the Democrats and Republicans of the present day, along with a range of third-party movements from the Anti-Masons in the 1820s to the supporters of Ross Perot and Ralph Nader in the 1990s, parties have dominated the American political scene. They have served as the main organizers of social and economic conflict, as the primary mobilizers of voters, and as critical cue givers to legislators and other officeholders.

In the functions they perform and in their outward appearance as they engage in these tasks, parties have seemed to enjoy great stability within the American system for over two hundred years. That appearance of stability is deceptive, however. The role and importance of political parties have significantly varied over time, reflecting major changes in the way Americans live, think, and go about their politics.

Scholars have usually distinguished five distinct party systems in our history: (1) the original Federalist-Republican system, which lasted from the early 1790s until about 1815; (2) a Democratic-Whig system, which arose in the 1820s and lasted until the mid–1850s; (3) the first Republican-Democratic system, which lasted from 1860 to 1896; (4) a second Republican-Democratic system, which held sway from 1896 to 1932; and (5) the New Deal party system, which began in the early 1930s. These analytic distinctions are based on the lineup of the particular interests and social groups that supported each party—distinct voting blocs that existed not occasionally and haphazardly but maintained themselves in a sustained, repetitive fashion in election after election throughout the years of a particular party system. Each system was bounded by an electoral realignment, a powerful overturning surge at the polls in which major shifts in voting choice occurred among some of these groups—shifts powerful enough, and long-lasting enough, to fundamentally change the lineup and the shape of subsequent party warfare (Chambers and Burnham 1975; Kleppner et al. 1981; Shafer et al. 1991).

But this notion of voter commitment to the parties is only one aspect of the story of America's political warfare from the past to the present time. In addition to these electoral shifts, sharp variations and significant changes have also occurred in the reach and importance of political parties throughout our history, changes that have to be taken into account in any analysis of the history of the American party system. Given the attitudes manifested toward parties at different moments in our past, the role they have played, the extent of their power, and, most critically, the centrality of their place in the political world at one time or another, we should consider, I suggest, a somewhat different delineation of the changing shape of the partisan dimension in the American political universe.

I propose that our political history in fact comprises four distinct political eras: (1) a preparty era from the 1790s to the late 1830s; (2) a party era that solidified in the 1830s and lasted to the 1890s; (3) a declining-party era that began in the 1890s and stretched into the 1950s; and (4) an increasingly postparty era in which, while the parties continue to perform certain functions in the political world, their reach, importance, and acceptance have sunk to levels unknown for almost two centuries.

The justification for arranging American party history in this way grows out of an analysis of the different kinds of political institutions, norms, and behavior that have predominated in each era. Thus, although two major parties have always operated on the scene, only once—from 1838 to 1893—did they totally penetrate the entire American political landscape and dominate the political culture in determinative fashion. Before 1838, they were incompletely developed and seen as foreign, unwelcome, and, many hoped, only a very temporary intrusion into public affairs. Since the 1890s, they have been in sharp decline throughout the nation's political system—until, in an increasingly nonparty, candidate-centered age, they have plummeted to their present position of limited relevance to most people (Formisano 1974; Wallace 1968, 1973; Wattenberg 1986).

Preparty Era: Factions Organized
Around Temporary Issues

The 1790s were contentious years in American politics. The recently ratified Constitution had established a new national political arena with a central government of great potential, power, and authority. The efforts of Treasury Secretary Alexander Hamilton to invigorate the federal government were not universally supported, however. Given all that was at stake and the geographic extent of the political battlefield, those opposing the Hamiltonian initiatives as detrimental to their own interests came together under the banner of Jeffersonian Republicanism in time to contest the congressional elections of 1794. Two years later, they bitterly fought to wrest the presidency away from their still-dominant enemies (Chambers 1963). These dramatic contests, occurring early in our history as a nation, were only the forerunners of ever-recurring conflict in American life and the constant need to mobilize in the battle for political power.

But these original attempts to establish political parties were incomplete. The Jeffersonian Republicans and the Federalists were only partially accepted by those involved in American politics, and they ultimately foundered, not just as electoral coalitions but as institutions having any role at all to play in American politics. They were neither deeply rooted in the political soil nor all-encompassing in their influence and importance. To be sure, some coordinated efforts were made to select candidates, manage campaigns, attract voters, and bring legislators and other officeholders under the discipline of a party. From Washington to the state capitals, party labeling and party coordination of political activities took place, as did the polarized articulation of contrasting policies. All of these practices were repeated in successive election campaigns in meetings of Congress and the state legislatures. Federalists and Republicans seemed to be everywhere (Banner 1970; Fischer 1965; Banning 1978; Goodman 1964).

Nevertheless, there was always an intermittent, ad hoc quality to all of these efforts and a casual attitude toward the partisan forms. Although these early combatants had much ideological vigor, they were quite deficient organizationally. There was little coordination between the national level and the political battles in the states of party warfare. The network of institutions needed to mobilize voters and to present each party's policy stances was only partially developed and was erratic in its activities and relevance. In some places, such as New York and North Carolina, these institutions were built quite early and were used extensively. Elsewhere party organization was not even rudimentary (Formisano 1974, 1981). Early political development remained focused on elites rather than on average voters. The voting behavior of the relatively small electorate remained quite volatile and was only occasionally party-oriented throughout the years of Federalist-Republican battles. Not until later years were Election Days characterized by sustained partisan alignments and behavior (Benson, Silbey, and Field 1978; Bohmer 1978; R. P. McCormick 1982).

The full development of political parties in the United States was hampered in this early period by a powerful mind-set against them, combined with little appreciation of their potential usefulness in an expansive, pluralist society. There was profound distrust of any institution that organized and sustained domestic political conflict. Such distrust originated in the still-potent eighteenth-century fear that recurrent internal conflict endangered all republics. Parties, by organizing such conflict, were seen to make matters worse and jeopardize a nation's very survival (Shalope 1972; Watts 1987).

According to some scholars of this early period, therefore, even to label the institutions of the 1790s as parties distorts the record, given the strong evidence of their weakness, incompleteness, and irrelevance, as well as the hostility toward them. Indeed, as one such scholar has written, "[U]ntil the idea exists that parties are legitimate, that there are necessary divisions within a complex society, that there are continuous, enduring group conflicts that can and should be organized in a sustained, partisan political fashion, [it is] anachronistic" to call what existed in the decade and more after the Constitution "anything but factions organized around temporary issues" (Benson 1981, 24). In a preparty era, Federalists and Republicans could be little else but factions.

Party Era: Essential to the Existence of Our Institutions

The failure of political parties to establish themselves as a normal part of American politics lasted for about a half century after the ratification of the Constitution. The era ended because political activities had increased in scope and vigor, thus leading to the need for a more extensive, powerful, and permanent system to deal with the problems of American politics. As the nation continued to grow after 1815, as incipient sectional tensions and regional rivalries became more vocal, as social antagonisms grew along religious and nationality lines, and as different economic interests renewed their battles to control government and its policies, it soon became clear that the pressing political needs of a pluralist nation of great size and many conflicts required political institutions beyond the Constitution and the limited forms of organization that had occasionally been present (Formisano 1971; R. P. McCormick 1967; Shade 1981; Silbey 1991).

The push for parties came out of three streams: the need to manage and guide a rapidly growing electorate; the need to bring together like-minded interests and factions into coalitions in order to win elections;

and the need to enact specific policies in an arena where real differences over public policy existed alongside perceptions of serious public danger if the wrong policies, people, or groups dominated. For ten years after 1815, political excitement increased in intensity in America—initially at the state and local levels, stimulated by battles over economic development and social cohesion, and then in renewed contests over national problems and the presidency. As these conflicts developed, they involved more people than ever before, inasmuch as suffrage requirements for adult white males had eased up dramatically. Political leaders had to give sustained attention to dealing with a larger electorate that had spread much farther geographically than ever before and had been aroused by the renewal of a wide range of bitter policy and group conflicts (Nichols 1967; R. P. McCormick 1967; Benson 1961; Williamson 1960; Watson 1981).

These political leaders were successful in finding a way to deal with their political problem. At first, the impulse toward both mass politics and collective political organization originated with outsider movements such as the Anti-Masons, which took the lead, ahead of the conventional political leadership, in their willingness to mobilize the masses. Their example was not lost for very long on many astute political observers, who were searching for ways to structure the changing political landscape. New York's Martin Van Buren and his well-organized associates, the Albany Regency, learned from what was happening around them, made the case for parties, and acted collectively, accepting the direction and discipline that such action entailed. As Michael Wallace (1973, 138) has argued, "[F]or the individualism so dear to Whig and Republican theory, [they] . . . substituted an almost servile worship of organization." A Van Buren lieutenant, Churchill Chambreleng, set forth the new tone clearly and forcefully in a speech before Congress in 1826: Political parties, he argued, are "indispensable to every Administration [and] essential to the existence of our institutions; and if . . . an evil, [they are ones] we must endure, for the preservation of our civil liberty." But parties "never yet injured any free country. . . . The conflict of parties is a noble conflict—of mind to mind, genius to genius" (*Register of Debates* 1826, 1546; Remini 1951; Benson 1961).

The original organizational impulse and the assault on ideological antipartyism culminated in the election of Andrew Jackson in 1828. But that victory, far from being an end to party development, was in fact the beginning. In the subsequent decade, the intellectual defense of parties and the building up of partisan institutions utterly transformed the political scene into something quite different from anything that had preceded it. The excitement of the process whereby the Jackson administration defined itself, and the persistent battles over the presidential succession and economic policy that followed, completed the movement toward a partisan-dominated nation (Benson 1961; Formisano 1971; Watson 1981).

Whatever hesitancies some politically involved Americans continued to have about these organizations and however intense the organizations' demands for the subordination of the individual in the collective, more and more political leaders played by the new political rules in order to achieve their specific policy goals. The party impulse spread into the camp of Jackson's opponents. Still deeply imbued with the old-style antiparty attitudes of an earlier era, the Whigs (reluctantly at first) adopted the style of, and the argument for, political parties. Ultimately, many of them became powerful articulators of the necessity for party. They built up their organization as well and even celebrated the political parties (Silbey 1991; Holt 1999).

This development involved more than rhetorical acceptance and behavioral exhortation. It meant moving from intermittence, individualism, and voluntarism to persistence, structure, and organized professionalism. Parties sank very deep roots into the system, among leaders and followers alike, and came to shape all but a small part of the American political world. Organizationally, their arrival meant the building of patterned, systematic institutions to do the necessary work. Elections were frequent in nineteenth-century America. Parties were always nominating, running, or preparing to nominate or run some candidate for one or another of the great array of elected offices. As they emerged, parties designated candidates at every level, replacing individual and group freewheeling with disciplined processes of choice. They collectively shaped what they would say and controlled all other aspects of the mobilization of the electorate. Party organizations grew into a regular array of committees, legislative caucuses, and conventions, designed to hammer out decisions about candidates, priorities, and programs, to run the actual campaigns, and to bring the voters to the polling booth on the day appointed. These institutions had a symmetrical shape across time and place. Their organization was decentralized, but they looked, and generally acted, the same everywhere. Wherever parties were present, their constituent elements and responsibilities remained constant from state to state across the country (R. P. McCormick 1967; Gienapp 1982; Silbey 1991).

The heart and soul of nineteenth-century party organization were the conventions that were held at every political level from the local to the national. Conventions had occasionally met earlier in American history, but it was only from the late 1830s onward that they became a widespread and normal part of the political scene. Each level of activity replicated the pattern whereby people were called together to hammer out policy initiatives, choose candidates, and select delegates to the next-highest-level convention. Topping all such activities was the national convention held every four years. All of these meetings, at every level, were cloaked with tremendous power. Their authority in party affairs was considered to be total, as they represented the place where major decisions were made about all things (Thornton 1978; Silbey 1991).

Once the conventions were over and the party's candidates had been chosen, their arguments clarified and formalized, the Whigs and Democrats proceeded to disseminate each campaign's political discourse, using a growing network of partisan newspapers, pamphlets, and organizing mass rallies. The parties' platforms originally codified each party's stance. In the debates that followed the conventions, Whigs and Democrats presented quite polarized images to the voters. They remained forever nose to nose. Party leaders drew on a rich pool of ideas about policies to sharpen differences among the voters overall and to draw together their own tribes. In their platforms, newspaper editorials, and campaign speeches, they enshrined the religious, nationality, sectional, and cultural animosities between groups, reflected the most up-to-date differences over the economic direction of the newly liberated, rapidly developing society, and provided a way for politically involved Americans to understand the world and its problems. The party leaders also became adept at mobilizing the tensions that were present and bringing them together into large policy frameworks. In sorting out the political world, they defined what was at stake and linked the different outlooks and perspectives into a whole (Benson 1961; Howe 1979; Silbey 1991, 1999).

Each political party in this dialogue aggregated society's many interests and social groups in a selective way, reaching out not to everyone but only to a portion of the electorate. The result, in the 1840s, was one party, the Whigs, that stood for social homogeneity and governmental vigor in all things, economic and social. Another party, the Democrats, espoused social and ethnic pluralism and was suspicious of too much government activity in human affairs. Both parties clearly and repeatedly articulated the differences between them. They hammered home, once again, how "utterly irreconcilable" they were—"as opposite to each other as light and darkness, as knowledge and ignorance" (*Louisville Journal* 1852; Benson 1961; M. Holt 1978).

The extent of party organization varied across the country and was never as complete or as tight as party leaders desired. As in most human situations there were holdouts against what was happening as well as incomplete areas of party development (Altshuler and Blumin 2000). But despite all of their reservations and the incompleteness of the structure, the ideal of comprehensiveness was always sought. The many elements constituting an efficient model were present, if not quite as developed as they would later become. More the point, I suggest, was the trajectory of party development and the similarity of party operations across the nation. There was a more widespread commitment than ever before, a movement in a particular direction, and a shift in values toward collectivities as the means to promote and achieve political goals. The atmosphere and mechanics of each campaign became the same everywhere (Shade 1981; Silbey 1991).

More critical still, popular voting behavior had become extremely party driven by the end of the 1830s, as the battles over policies penetrated popular consciousness and the parties' mobilization machinery matured. Turnout at the polls dramatically increased over earlier levels in response to each party's extensive mobilization activities. When voters cast their ballots, their sustained commitment to a party in election after election became the norm in a way that had never been the case before. Each succeeding election was viewed not as a separate contest involving new issues or new personalities but as yet another opportunity for people to vote for, and reaffirm, their support for their party and what it represented. As the editor of the *Albany Argus* put it in the 1840s, "[T]he first duty of a Democrat is to vote; the next to vote the regular ticket." Much more often than not, voters did both (*Albany Argus* 1846; Kleppner 1979; Formisano 1971; Benson 1961).

By the beginning of the 1840s the American people were worshiping more and more at the "shrine of party." Their commitment to the parties moved beyond instrumentalist calculation of the rewards of specific policies or the benefits to be gained from particular candidates. Each party's popular support was rooted in the intense, deep, and persistent loyalty of individual voters to their party home. The electoral pattern furthered such commitment. Party warfare split Americans decisively and evenly. The battles between Whigs and Democrats, and later between the Republicans and Democrats, were highly competitive. Close electoral contests were the rule. Indeed, their closeness reinforced the drive to organize and turn out the vote and to expand even further the commitment to individual parties and to the party system as the preferred mode of organizing the nation's political affairs and settling its major problems (Silbey 1967, 1977, 1985; Gienapp 1982).

As a result, parties had great vitality in the 1840s and thereafter. They were everywhere. For the first time, they were considered both natural and necessary. They came to control all but a small part of American politics, and they staffed the government through their patronage operations. Once in office, the party leaders were expected to carry out the policies their party stood for—as, indeed, they attempted to do. Although elaborate policymaking was unknown in the middle of the nineteenth century, whatever efforts were made occurred in response to party promises and arguments. Finally, both the appeals of the two major parties and the loyalty of voters and leaders to them occurred at a national level. Despite whatever sectional tensions there were in the United States, both the Whigs and the Democrats were able to attract support and make their influence felt as the parties developed, regardless of the pressures to divide along other gradients (Silbey 1967; R. L. McCormick 1986; Formisano 1981; Shade 1981).

Two major disruptions of the political system—first the electoral realignment of the 1850s and then the Civil War—demonstrated that the passionate commitment to one's party had limits. The increase in ideological intensity along sectional lines in the 1850s and 1860s shook the political nation severely. It was a destructive, chastening experience for those in command of the traditional political channels. Nevertheless, when the smoke cleared after a series of intense voter shifts, after the death of one party and the rise of another, the essential structure of American politics remained largely as before. Electoral coalitions were reshaped, sectional tensions became the norm, and one of the parties, the Republican Party, was no longer national in its reach. But the central reality of partisan-defined and partisan-shaped political actives stood firm. The nation's agenda and institutions, as well as the reactions of both leaders and voters to the events of the day, continued to reflect the dominance of existing patterns of two-party politics and the intense loyalties that had been such a crucial aspect of them since the late 1830s (Gienapp 1987; Silbey 1977, 1991).

After the Civil War, the reach of political parties into American life expanded further than ever before as the party era continued. New partisan forms, such as the urban political machine, developed to meet new needs. In general, however, the structures, appeal, and meaning of parties remained much as they had been for the preceding thirty years. Much emphasis was put on reinforcing party loyalty and eliciting automatic partisan responses to new issues and conflicts, whatever their nature. Even as society began to change dramatically from agricultural to industrial-urban, Democrats and Republicans continued to confront each other in the well-disciplined, predictable phalanxes of people deeply committed to powerful, closely competitive institutions designed to fulfill group and individual needs (Kleppner 1979; Jensen 1971; McSeveney 1971; R. L. McCormick 1981).

The extent of the partisan imperative in nineteenth-century American politics was demonstrated, finally, by the behavior of the many challenges to the Democratic-Whig-Republican hegemony. From the beginning of this partisan political era, there were regular protests against the central tenets of the political nation from people ever impatient with or continually frustrated by the national parties, their advocacy, and their command of the system. Yet the way in which these challenges interacted with politics suggests the adherence of the protesters to many of the central political values of their era, despite their persistent outsider questioning, stance, and self-image. Between 1838 and the early 1890s, minor parties organized and campaigned much as the major political parties did; they also nominated candidates, thought about whom they wished to appeal to, and sought to mobilize particular voters behind their policies. Most held national conventions and issued national platforms. Somewhat more sporadically, they called state, district, and local conventions as well. They staged campaign rallies and organized to get out the vote. They issued pamphlets and published party newspapers. In emulating their enemies to the extent that they did, they underscored the power of the partisan impulse on this particular political landscape (M. Holt 1973; Kleppner 1979).

Declining-Party Era: Too Important to Be Left to Politicians

This party era lasted into the 1890s. With the electoral realignment of that decade, the role of the parties began to shift dramatically. Launched against them was a full-scale assault that included shrewd (and ultimately successful) legislative efforts to weaken their organizations, their command of the landscape, and the powerful partisanship that had made the system what it was. Parties found themselves less able than before to resist the reformist onslaught. As a result, the equilibrium between them and their challengers was upset. The churning and destabilization of the electoral landscape led to profound systemic disintegration. From the 1890s on, the nation's politics started to become nonpartisan. The vigor of American electoral politics, rooted in the passionate confrontations between two well-developed and dominant parties, gave way to an antiparty, and ultimately nonparty, way of carrying on political activities. America's political ways went from focusing specifically on the ceremonies and rituals of partisan polarization to appealing, organizing, and working beyond parties. As that happened, Americans moved from strong commitment to one party and angry dissatisfaction with the other to vituperative dissatisfaction with all parties (R. L. McCormick 1981; Burnham 1965, 1970; McGerr 1986).

There was no sudden upheaval or coup d'état. The new era opened with an extended period of transition, during which many of the institutions, values, and approaches of the past continued to be important. At the national level, after 1896 the Democrats vigorously contested the new Republican electoral hegemony in the traditional manner. The two parties' internal processes of defining themselves, resolving their divisions, and choosing their candidates also remained largely as they had been. The same was true of their external behavior during campaigns as well as their approach to government staffing, responsibilities, and policymaking. But with the loss of electoral competitiveness in many parts of the country in the 1890s, the fires of political confrontation cooled. Organizing elements became flabby as the losers in one-sided electoral situations lost workers, coverage, heart, and vigor. As a result, politics shifted into new channels. At the same time, as a major element of the nation's transformation, an alternate vision of political propriety developed and then took firm hold. The basic ambivalence this vision manifested toward the political world evolved into a powerful negativism stimulated by what was seen as excessive political expediency and increasingly sordid partisan manipulation of democratic politics. Coupled with the rise of new, very powerful external forces that were reshaping the society, this negativism eventually imposed its view of prosperity on the American system (Benson 1955; Hays 1957, 1959; R. L. McCormick 1981).

As Richard Jensen has succinctly noted, the Progressives sought, early in the new era, "to banish all forms of traditionalism—boss control, corrupt practices, big business intervention in politics, 'ignorant' voting and excessive power in the hands of hack politicians" (Jensen 1978, 27). For the Progressives, political reform, especially the concerted attack on the parties, was a prerequisite to everything else they wished to accomplish. Party politics was corrupt, irrational, and unprincipled. They thus redefined politics as a detached search for objective, and therefore correct, policies—a search unrelated to the passions, rituals, self-interest, and deception connected with political parties (Hays 1957; Wiebe 1967; Ranney 1975).

In the first decade and a half of the twentieth century, the Progressives and their allies were able to take a series of legislative actions that attacked and ultimately destroyed several of the links between parties and voters. They energized the efforts under way since the 1880s to reform election laws—especially to institute voter registration and government-controlled official ballots. Their successful passage of a large number of such legislative initiatives had a major impact on the political system. Nonpartisan electoral reforms weakened the partisan imperative by challenging, first, the politicians' control of nominations and the election process and, second, the party-dominated, unrestrained wheeling and dealing over policy priorities (Kousser 1974; R. L. McCormick 1981).

At the same time, in the economic realm the Progressives successfully promoted the growth of government power and a shift in focus from generalized, distributive policies to new regulative channels, which demanded technical expertise, well-developed budgeting and financial skills, and an ability to deal with sophisticated control mechanisms—rather than the more generalist negotiating talents of party leaders, which had previously dominated a simpler, more limited government apparatus and its activities. As a result, there was a steady increase in the number of, and the activities engaged in by, specialized nonpartisan interest groups, each of which sought to shape specific government policies without the mediation of political parties. In addition, government eventually took over responsibility of matters the parties had traditionally controlled, social welfare being one prime example. The nonpartisan civil service continued to expand—challenging, and ultimately weakening, the partisan patronage resources that had been so important to party operations (Benson 1955; R. L. McCormick 1981; Wiebe 1967).

All of this indicated the success over several decades of what Daniel T. Rodgers (1982) has called "the explosion of scores of aggressive, politically active pressure groups into the space left by the recession of traditionally political loyalties" (114). This nonpartisan occupation had significant long-range effects on the political nation. The emerging organizational society of technicians, bureaucrats, and impersonal decisionmakers had no faith in or commitment to mass politics—especially as expressed through the parties. Although no one group was solely responsible for the changes that occurred, all reforming groups, whatever their interests, aims, and nature, shared a commitment to move in the same direction. As their numbers and reach increased, their vision grew to be quite popular. The Progressives' political agenda was antipartisan in direction and was vigorously pushed (R. L. McCormick 1981; Hays 1957, 1959).

The many changes taking place slowly worked their way through the political nation. The impact of each of the pressures was cumulative. From the beginning, the reform challenge meant that parties had competition at the center of the political world for the first time since 1830s. For decades to come, however—well into the 1940s—there were different balances between old and new. In some areas, parties retained vestiges of influence and the capacity to shape events, as evidenced by the electoral vigor of the urban political machines and the success of their policy initiatives. For a time during the New Deal years, there was evidence that political parties still had a strong kick, reminiscent of an earlier era and perhaps suggestive of a return to dominance by them. An electoral realignment in the 1930s not only restored the Democrats to power with a new agenda but also invigorated the loyalties of voters fired by the Great Depression and the Rooseveltian response. These loyalties took deep hold and shaped much about electoral politics and some aspects of policy as well for a generation thereafter. The period from the 1890s into the 1950s, therefore, was a mixed, postparty era, and amid the signs of party decay in government affairs, in policymaking, and in the structure of electoral involvement, partisanship still anchored much voter choice as it had in the past (Campbell et al. 1960; Burnham 1970; Andersen 1979; Silbey 1991).

Postparty Era: Anarchy Tempered by Distrust

But the partisan honeymoon of the 1930s and 1940s, however powerful and dramatic, was only a deviation from the long-range pattern of party collapse. The decline of political parties resumed and quickened as the New Deal began to fade from popular memory after World War II. Other, extraparty elements became even more firmly entrenched on the landscape. Over time, parties as organizers and as symbols of the battles over public policies lost more and more of their relevance. Party control of the electoral process continued to weaken. Shifts in the way political information was presented, from partisan to nonpartisan sources, had been under way throughout the twentieth century. Party newspapers, with their relentless, clear, direct, and unambiguous message, gave way to a different journalistic style serving a broader clientele. Newspapers—cheap, sensationalist, nonpartisan, and often cynical about politics—came into their own at the turn of the century. But they failed to provide quick and easily absorbed partisan guides, as their predecessors had done—an oversight that had a long-term effect (McGerr 1986; Burnham 1970, 1982).

This transformation accelerated greatly with television's rise in the 1950s. In its style of presentation and dominance of the scene, television even more sharply curtailed the parties' ability to shape what was at stake; this had been a central factor in mobilizing voters into loyal party channels in the nineteenth century. Parties had once been able to argue that all political legitimacy lay with them. Independent newspapers and television challenged that assumption in both direct and indirect ways. Television, to the parties' detriment, emphasized imagery and personality, in contrast to the allegedly artificial styles and deceptive auras of the political parties; it also ignored or downplayed the distinguishing features of parties that made them important to the political process (Ranney 1983).

A further factor in the post–World War II years was that the size, reach, and influence of the federal government became the central fact of the political nation. With this growth of state power, a partisan-directed model of activities and behavior lost its last vestiges of importance among many Americans. Instead, the interest-group pattern, unmediated by partisan priority setting and influence, finally replaced it. Well-entrenched, nonpartisan, economic interest groups began to forge and make permanent the kinds of links with the legislative and administrative branches that they had been groping toward since the end of the partisan political nation in the 1890s. Their earlier belief that parties were a barrier to their best interests was succeeded by a growing sense of the irrelevance of parties to their activities at any level. From the 1930s on, the expansion of nonpartisan interest groups accelerated, reaching well beyond their original economic base among the new industrial forces to encompass any segment of the society that sought government assistance. By the 1960s, every policy impulse had its own organization that moved readily into the legislative and administrative arenas, largely as if parties did not exist. Many different groups, with many different agendas and enthusiasms, articulated issues, mobilized voters, financed campaigns, and organized legislative and administrative support for their limited goals. These in turn became vested interests in their areas of concern and became dominant as articulators of specific demands. The result was a cacophony of voices, continuous discordant battling, and, often, policy fragmentation (Lowi 1979).

At the same time, in the 1960s, the legitimacy of parties was subjected to a renewed assault, echoing a theme once dominant and now reborn with a virulence and power long forgotten. All of the earlier deficiencies of parties, from corruption to elite manipulation and the denial of democracy, were once again widely rehearsed. Much media commentary took up the assault and gave it a repetitive reality, especially during such unpleasant episodes as the Democratic National Convention of 1968. This unrelenting negative commentary took a toll. Its intellectual offensive against parties, coupled with the massive shifts in communications—both of which rested on the Progressives' changing of the playing field and the rules of the game—added up in such a way as to impel the creation of a new nonparty political nation (Ranney 1975; Burnham 1982).

By the end of the 1950s, all of the antiparty tendencies at play had become quite clear, and these determined the course of the next decade. A *New York Times* reporter later argued that John F. Kennedy, at the outset of the 1960s, was "the last great representative of the politics of loyalty, human intermediation, compromise and tradition" (1980). With Kennedy's death, the parties' last bastion—the electoral arena—gave way. Throughout the 1960s, there was certainly a profound shift in the ways in which mass politics was organized, its rituals displayed, its supporters mobilized. Party-dominated mass meetings, conventions, and campaign rallies continued, but they were in a prolonged state of decay and became increasingly irrelevant to the country's political business. The parties' ability to coalesce a range of interests around themselves significantly ebbed. Although national party conventions still nominated and labeled candidates, they had less and less influence over the actual process of choosing the candidate whom the party would put forward. Delegates were no longer the key players they had once been. They had lost their bargaining, reviewing, and reflecting power. In Richard Jensen's apt summing up, more and more "candidates for office selected themselves" (1981, 219) by mobilizing the nonpartisan resources on the political scene. This situation affected the candidates' subsequent runs for office as well. In many campaigns, party labels became less prevalent than they had previously been. Increasingly, presidential candidates preferred to run as individuals, emphasizing their personal qualities rather than their adherence to party norms.

The impact of the successful century-long assault on parties and on the way the American voter engaged in politics was enormous and emblematic of the whole thrust of the post–1893 American political nation. To begin with, individual involvement in the electoral system changed dramatically over the years. American voters in the 1990s no longer behaved as their ancestors had exactly one century earlier. The size of the electorate grew throughout the twentieth century as various legal and social constraints on the participation of particular social groups fell away. But even while that was happening, popular interest in politics waned. It could be reinvigorated from time to time, as in the New Deal years, but once again the trend line was clear: downward, toward popular nonparticipation. All of the destabilizing elements working against political parties were coterminous with a massive fall-off in other aspects of political involvement, demonstrated most starkly by the steep decline in turnout at the polls over the course of the twentieth century. By the 1990s, in fact, there was a sizable "party of nonvoters" on the American scene. This group was, at best, sporadically mobilized; it consisted of people who were eligible to vote but usually did not do so (Burnham 1965, 1970, 1982).

Added to popular disinvolvement was popular partisan dealignment. When they did come to the polls, the voters demonstrated that they had become increasingly unstuck from party moorings and instead were caught up in what Walter Dean Burnham (1973, 39) has referred to as a "volcanic instability." The all but automatic identification with parties became the minor key in voter behavior. Despite the occasional power of certain economic or other issues to reawaken such party identification for a while, such issues became less and less influential as time passed. Whatever the parties' differences, whatever distinct ideological and policy stances they fostered, parties could no longer draw voters to them as they had once routinely done. Less and less did the electorate consider "voting for 'my party' a sociological or psychological imperative," as Everett Ladd put it (1985, 2). At every level of political activity, each election became a new throw of the dice; the electorate behaved differently each time, and the ordering of choice among many voters between the parties became increasingly unpredictable from contest to contest. "The politics of the 1930s and 1940s resembled a nineteenth-century battle-field, with two opposing armies arrayed against each other in more or less close formation," wrote one scholar, but "politics today is an alto-gether messier affair, with large numbers of small detachments engaged over a vast territory, and with individuals and groups frequently chang-ing sides" (King 1978, 372).

Given all this volatility and the absence of strong, widespread partisan influences across the voting universe, electoral strategy had to shift. Candidates for lesser offices, already themselves free from many party constraints, copied the presidential nominees and no longer ran for office primarily by mobilizing the party faithful, if they did so at all. There were no longer enough of such faithful to be effectively mobilized. Rather, the candidates' effort centered on appealing to uncommitted, or partially committed, voters. Campaign advertising almost never identi-fied candidates with their party, emphasizing their personal attributes in-stead. Who or what an individual was, rather than a party's policy stance or deeply rooted partisan loyalties, became the centerpiece of political af-fairs. In campaigns for offices where incumbents seemed all but immune, such as in the House of Representatives after the 1960s, campaigning turned more and more on emphasizing extreme personal deficiencies in one's opponent (King 1978; Brady 1988; Wattenberg 1991).

All this was of a piece. By the end of the twentieth century it was crystal clear that America's political present was very different from its political past. The contrast is marked indeed. The nineteenth-century political na-tion reflected a culture that sought first to bring people into the system and then to tame them and their desires through disciplined collectivi-ties. America's powerful individualism, it was felt, needed such disci-pline. In the 1890s, it was impossible to think about American politics without paying close attention to the political parties involved at every point. In sharp contrast to this, in "the dealigned political universe of the 1990s," the political process powerfully highlighted that individualism and showed little regard for the political parties—except as conceived negatively. It became a system in which a premium was placed on the seeking of individual, rather than party-defined, objectives. The reputa-tion of political parties continued to plummet—irreversibly, it seemed (Lawrence 1996, 166).

The success of Ross Perot in drawing almost 20 percent of the popular vote in the 1992 presidential election from two candidates perceived as particularly flawed leaders only underscored, once again, how far the party system had fallen (Pomper 1993; Nelson 1993). Perot's 1992 plat-form emphasized highly individualistic, self-centered claims to personal virtue and denounced the normal ways of parties and politicians and their inability to pursue effective policies or discipline themselves to behave responsibly. His less successful third-party effort four years later did not detract from that point, for his weak showing was due more to his personal idiosyncrasies and fall from public grace than to any resurgence of robust two-partyism.

To be sure, there continued to be occasionally intense and often strident shards of partisanship in the political system, also evident among some voters some of the time. Parties continued to serve important purposes in organizing electoral activities. Party identification still mattered, although, as we have seen, among a declining proportion of those who went to the polls on Election Day. And in the late 1990s, analysts discerned a particular strengthening of the parties at the elite level, both generally and especially in Congress after the Republican electoral success in 1994. The newly elected 104th Congress, dominated by militant, ideologically driven freshmen members, was highly partisan both rhetorically and behaviorally. In the early stages, the degree of party unity in roll-call voting for and against the Republicans' "Contract with America" agenda reached levels not seen for a very long time in national politics (Pomper 1996; *Congressional Quarterly Almanacs* 1994, 1995).

But such partisan survivals, and the apparent reinvigoration of partisan power, do not seriously call into question the main trend: the long-range institutional and ideological collapse of the party system. Such survivals never added up to the kind of all-encompassing partisan commitment characteristic of the party era. Whatever many congressmen and other party leaders felt and did, it did not have the reach and power that would have been mediated by fully developed political parties. Partisan decay in the electorate, which had been occurring for so long already, continued throughout the 1990s (Wattenberg 1996). And the high degree of unity manifested in congressional roll-call voting in 1995 did not last, except among the most intense partisans. Others moved away from such commitments, demonstrating instead in their votes a commitment to issue and constituency elements. Significant internal rifts within the legislative parties also led to some fragmenting of the party coalitions, defections from them and repeated challenges to what had once been normally expected partisan commitments.

In the last presidential election of the twentieth century—despite some efforts to influence voters by attaching negative labels of ideological extremism to both of the major parties—neither the candidates themselves nor the voting public showed particular interest in any strategy that emphasized the party label. Quite the contrary, in fact. Some observers were fascinated by the existence of a base of loyal voters committed to each party. But a large and growing middle group continued to be motivated by nonpartisan influences, and they were up for grabs in each election season and cast their ballots for reasons other than the strength of their partisan commitment. And politicians could not even fully count on their party's base come Election Day (Wattenberg 1998).

I will leave it to my colleagues to explore in more detail the current situation of parties in American politics. But a few concluding remarks are in order. First, despite the occasional tightening of party lines in some parts of the public in the 1990s, at the same time the role and relevance of parties continued to weaken elsewhere on the political landscape. Certainly, even though partisan behavior among legislators and voters might at times be extreme, popular attitudes toward the parties continued to range from dismissive to very negative. Whatever the partisan survival and the occasional eruption of partisan perspectives among the extended American public, parties at the outset of the twenty-first century were routinely considered to be "at best interlopers between the sovereign people and their elected officials and, at worst, rapacious enemies of honest and responsible government," irrelevant to, or destructive of, our ability to solve the critical problems facing the nation (Ranney 1978a, 24). Few Americans seem to care whether the parties ever returned to their former position in national affairs (Wattenberg 1998). This indifference, or perhaps it was cynical negativism, was a very far cry from the celebration of the political parties and the widespread appreciation of their critical role that had once filled the American scene so forcefully. At the beginning of a new millennium, the Democratic and Republican parties continue to play a political role in the United States. But without such widespread appreciation among voters, they can hardly be seen as the vigorous, robust, and meaningful players within the nation's political system that they once clearly were.

2

State Party Organizations: Strengthened and Adapting to Candidate-Centered Politics and Nationalization

JOHN F. BIBBY

In the face of a changing and often unfriendly environment, political parties in the American states have demonstrated adaptability and resilience. This capacity to cope with forces of change has meant, of course, that the parties have undergone substantial alteration. Indeed, today's twenty-first-century state party bears scant resemblance to either the old-style organization of the late nineteenth century or the organizations that existed in the 1950s and 1960s.

The state party organization of late nineteenth and early twentieth centuries was often hierarchically run; was closely tied to local machines; was fed by federal, state, and local patronage; and frequently was supported and influenced by corporate interests. In many states, these old-style party organizations were capable of controlling nominations and providing resources needed to conduct general-election campaigns. They were labor-intensive organizations that placed great emphasis on mobilizing their supporters on Election Day. In this they benefited from an absence of popular cultural support for the independent voter. Independents were often called "mugwumps" and were scorned as "traitors" and "corrupt sellers of their votes." Walter Dean Burnham (1970) has characterized the organizations of this era as "militarist," in the sense that they drilled their supporters to turn out and vote a straight party ticket (72–73).

Progressive reformers of the early twentieth century sought to undermine the organizations' bases of power by instituting the direct primary system of nominations to diminish their control over nominations, the civil service system of public employment to severely limit their patronage, and corrupt-practices legislation to cut off some of their sources of financing (Mayhew 1986, 212–237). These reforms, particularly the direct primary and accompanying party regulatory statutes, had their desired effect. Hierarchical state party organization had largely passed from the scene by the 1920s. The Republican and Democratic state organizations that replaced them had vastly reduced influence over nominations and gradually lost their ability to direct state-level campaigns. By the early 1960s, state party organizations were in weakened condition in all but a few states (Key 1956, 271; Epstein 1986, 144–153).

Since the 1960s, state parties have demonstrated their adaptive capacities and have quite literally been reborn in most of the states as well-funded, technologically advanced service agencies to state and federal candidates (Aldrich 2000; Morehouse 2000). The state parties have achieved this status while facing a series of challenges and competitors for influence. These potentially party-damaging influences have included (1) a weakening of partisan ties among the voters; (2) the emergence of candidate-centered campaigns run by the candidates' personal organizations, instead of by party organizations; (3) the growth of PACs as a major source of political money; (4) issue advertising by interest groups; and (5) a strengthening of national party organizations that has resulted in the integration of state parties into national campaign strategies.

After exploring the legal and electoral environment in which parties must operate, this chapter describes the processes of adaptation and change that have occurred within state party organizations since the 1960s. The emergence of professionalized, service-oriented state party organizations operating with substantial budgets is analyzed to demonstrate the remarkable durability of parties. The changing national-state relationship and the implications of heightened levels of intraparty integration and partnership are also explored, along with the implications of issue-oriented activists assuming a larger role within the organizations.

It must be stressed that although the process of adaptation since the 1960s has transformed state parties into agencies providing an array of essential services to candidates and local party units, the parties have not regained control over nominations, nor have they reclaimed the power to run the campaigns of their candidates. A new type of party has emerged at both the state and national levels, a party that operates "in service" to its candidates and officeholders but not in control of them (Aldrich 1995, 273). The state parties also now find themselves in a much closer relationship with national party units, which provide them with funds and essential technical services and have integrated the state units into national campaign strategies. This is a complex relationship characterized by elements of national-state party partnership and of state party autonomy, as well as by state party dependence on national parties.

The Changing Legal Environment of State Parties

In most Western democracies, political parties are considered to be private associations not unlike the Rotarians, Elks, or Sons of Norway and as such have been permitted to conduct business largely unregulated by government. In fact, however, American political parties are quasi-public institutions possessing not only the characteristics and rights of private associations but also a public character while performing essential governmental functions: making nominations, contesting elections, organizing the government. It is this public aspect that has been used to justify state regulation of parties. However, the extent of this regulation has been restricted by the Supreme Court's enforcement of the parties' rights of association under the First Amendment.

State governments' most significant regulatory device has been a requirement that parties nominate their candidates via the direct primary. Before the direct primary was first instituted by Wisconsin in 1903 and then spread to the fifty states, party leaders could exert substantial influence over party nominating caucuses and conventions. By involving ordinary voters in the selection of party nominees, the direct primary has reduced the capacity of party leaders to control nominations; it has also encouraged candidates to form personal campaign organizations in order to contest primary elections.

The state regulatory process goes well beyond party nominating procedures. State laws determine eligibility criteria for parties to be listed on the general election ballot, regulate who can vote in partisan primaries, and regulate campaign finance. State statutes frequently extend to matters of internal organization such as procedures for selecting officers, composition of party committees, dates and locations of meetings, and powers of party committees. Although the content and extent of regulation varies from state to state, the net effect of state regulatory laws is to mold state parties into quasi-public agencies and limit the party leaders' flexibility in devising strategies to achieve organizational goals.

Limiting the State Regulatory Burden on Parties

The status of parties as quasi-public entities that are subject to extensive governmental regulation has been undergoing a process of modification since the mid–1980s as a result of a series of Supreme Court decisions that have extended to parties the rights of free political association protected by the First and Fourteenth Amendments. In according this constitutional protection to parties, the Court has struck down a series of state-imposed restrictions on parties (see Peltason 1999, 16–18; Epstein 1986, 189–199).

In the case of *Tashjian v. Connecticut*, 479 U.S. 208 (1986), the Court ruled that Connecticut could not prevent voters registered as independents from voting in a Republican primary, if the state GOP wanted to allow independents as well as registered Republicans to vote in its primary. Although this decision, with its extension of First Amendment rights to parties, constituted a major step toward freeing parties of burdensome state regulations, its immediate effect was quite limited. Few states took advantage of *Tashjian* to open their parties to independents (Epstein 1989, 239–274). Nor is there much likelihood that Republican and Democratic parties will attempt to use the *Tashjian* precedent to abolish state-mandated primaries, since they are popular with voters and well ingrained in the American political culture.

In 1989, the Supreme Court in *Eu v. San Francisco Democratic Committee*, 489 U.S. 214 (1989), further limited state regulatory authority over parties. Asserting that California statutes violated the political parties' rights of free association, the Court struck down state laws that banned parties from engaging in preprimary endorsements, limited the length of state party chair's terms, and required that the state chairmanships rotate every two years between Northern and Southern California. The Court stated its "compelling state interest" test for determining the constitutionality of state regulatory laws. It said that if a state law "burdens the rights of political parties and their members, it can survive constitutional scrutiny only if the State shows that the law advances a compelling state interest." In this instance, it was held that California had failed to demonstrate a compelling state interest for its restrictions on parties (see Peltason 1999, 10, 16–18).

In 1996, the Court expanded on its doctrine that parties have freedom of association rights in the realm of campaign finance law. In *Colorado Republican Party v. FEC*, 518 U.S. 604 (1996), it freed parties from the spending restrictions imposed by the Federal Election Campaign Act (FECA) to engage in independent expenditures (spending not coordinated with candidates). This decision opened the way for major increases in spending by state and national parties in federal elections.

The most recent instance of the Court limiting state regulatory power came in 2000 when the Republican and Democratic parties of California, plus several minor parties, challenged the constitutionality of the state's blanket primary law, which had been adopted by referendum in 1996. In striking down the law, the Supreme Court declared in *California Democratic Party v. Jones*, 530 U.S. 567 (2000) that California's blanket primary constituted a "stark repudiation of political association" that denied parties the power to control their own nomination processes and define their own identities. Here the Court was adopting the view that parties are mainly private, rather than public, institutions. This decision left open the question of whether or not open primaries are constitutional, although the dissenting justices asserted that the decision cast serious doubt upon various forms of the open primary. It is not clear, however, that the states, the parties, or the Court are prepared to throw out traditional open primary systems that have become established parts of the states' political cultures.

Limiting Party Patronage

Traditionally, party organizations relied upon patronage—government jobs—to provide them with campaign workers and contributors. Civil services laws, public employee unions, and a critical public have severely limited this source of party support. A series of Supreme Court decisions since the 1970s have further undermined large-scale patronage operations. In once patronage-rich Illinois, the Court hit at the heart of the large-scale patronage operations run by both Democrats and Republicans. It ruled that Cook County Democrats could not fire people on the basis of their party affiliation without violating these persons' First Amendment rights (*Eldrod v. Burns*, 427 U.S. 347 [1976]). This decision was followed by one banning the Illinois GOP from using "party affiliation and support" as a basis for filling state jobs unless party affiliation was an "appropriate requirement" (*Rutan v. Republican Party*, 497 U.S. 62 [1990]). As a result of these decisions, government employees or applicants may not be discharged or denied a job, promotion or other benefit of public employment because of failure to belong to the winning party or for expressing views contrary to those of the winning party (see Peltason 1999, 32–37)—except for those jobs for which it can be demonstrated that party membership is relevant.

Today patronage operates primarily in appointments to state boards and commissions controlling gambling, higher education, licensing, state investments, environmental protection, and recreation. These positions are much sought after by persons seeking recognition, policy influence, and material gain. Politics also often intrudes into state decisions regarding state contracts, bank deposits, economic development, and purchase of professional services. These types of preferments are useful to the parties primarily for fundraising, but do not provide large numbers of campaign workers the way old-style patronage operations did. Today the ground troops of the parties are no longer patronage workers and job seekers, but volunteers recruited on the basis of issues and ideology, plus members of organized groups allied with the parties.

The Decline of the Party-Column Ballot

The party-column ballot form, especially when combined with a provision for expedited straight ticket voting by making a single mark, punch, or lever pull, encourages straight ticket voting. By contrast, the office-bloc ballot form facilitates split-ticket voting (Bass 1998, 224, 260; Campbell et al. 1960, 275–276, 285–286; Rusk 1970; Campbell and Miller 1957). The trend in recent decades has been away from the party-column ballot toward office-bloc ballots: the party column ballot was the predominant type in the 1950s, but by the late 1990s the states were divided almost evenly between the two types of ballots. Further reflecting a weakening partisanship in voting has been the decline in the number of states permitting expedited party voting from 30 in 1946 to just 17 in 2000 (Kimball and Owens 2000).

The State Electoral Environment

There is great diversity among the states in terms of election laws; strength of political parties; political traditions; and citizens' partisan, ideological, and policy orientations. This diversity should not, however, obscure common features of the electoral environment within which every state party must operate. Common to all the states are candidate-centered campaigns, an increasing role for political action committees, issue advertising by interest groups and parties, and heightened interparty competition for statewide offices and control of state legislative chambers.

Candidate-Centered Campaigns

Candidates run under party labels that help them attract votes from among party adherents in the electorate, but there is nothing that forces candidates to let the party organizations run or participate in their campaigns. Indeed, there are substantial obstacles to party control of campaigns.

The direct primary system of nominations has had the effect of encouraging candidates to rely upon their own personal campaign organizations. Party organizations can rarely guarantee favored candidates victory in the primaries. The direct primary has severely weakened the party organizations' ability to control nominations, and this has in turn reduced the incentives for individuals to become dues-paying, meeting-attending party members who might be mobilized to support organization-backed candidates in the primaries. The direct primary, therefore, imposes a personal responsibility upon each candidate to create a campaign organization capable of winning the primary (see Epstein 1999, 49–50).

The reduced role that party affiliation plays in voter choices on Election Day has also encouraged candidate independence from party organizations. Voters commonly split their tickets; for example, there were split outcomes in Senate and presidential voting in 10 of 34 races (29 percent) in 1996 and in 9 of 34 contests (26 percent) in 2000. After the 1998 elections, in 22 states the party of the governor did not control at least one house of the state legislature (including in Maine and Minnesota, whose governors were independents). In 2001, 26 states had this type of divided party control of government. In the American political culture, it is frequently advantageous not to be perceived as closely tied to a political party, for many voters glorify a candidate who stands above party.

New Campaign Technologies and Professional Management

Campaigns for major statewide offices, competitive congressional seats, and an expanding number of state legislative seats are directed by professional consultants who utilize the latest and most sophisticated campaign techniques. Many state party organizations can provide candidates with essential campaign services. But these state organizations seldom have sufficient resources to provide all the services a candidate needs, and the parties must assist a wide range of candidates. In addition, 24 states impose limits on party contributions to candidates (Jewell and Morehouse 2001, 65–67). Parties must also set priorities in dispensing their resources, with the result that some candidates receive little or no state party support. As a consequence, candidates find it necessary to secure their own campaign operatives. With adequate financing, candidates can now create personal organizations that employ professionals capable of conducting polls and focus groups, exploiting the persuasive qualities of the electronic media, targeting direct-mail advertising, and getting out the vote.

The candidates' need for surrogates for the old-style machines and face-to-face campaigning has thus spawned a major industry—that of the professional campaign consultants. These so-called "hired guns" often work on several campaigns simultaneously. Frequently, they are from out of state and have few if any ties to the state parties. Most are loosely affiliated with either the Republicans or Democrats, in the sense that they work almost exclusively for only one party's candidates. But they work primarily for candidates, not parties, and hence tend to reduce the party role in campaigns and reinforce the tendency toward candidate-centered politics.

Allied Group Support of Candidates: The Ground War and Issue Advocacy

As the old-style machine type of party with the ability to mobilize voters at the local level has been replaced by a professionally staffed state party headquarters and the personal organizations of candidates, interest groups allied with the parties now play an increasingly important role in getting out the vote for favored candidates and in placing issue ads in the media to assist these candidates. In terms of getting out the vote for Democratic candidates, organized labor, teachers, and minority-group organizations are especially important. Indeed, such organizations have become the party's ground troops. Republican candidates have fewer mass membership groups aligned with them to provide help in getting out the vote, although fundamentalist Christians and anti-abortion groups do engage in this activity.

Increasingly significant forces in state elections are independent expenditures (expenditures made without coordination with the candidate) and issue advocacy advertisements (ads that do not explicitly call for the election or defeat of a candidate), which to the average viewer or listener are virtually indistinguishable from a candidate advertisement. Indeed, in targeted state legislative races where control of the chamber is at stake, it is no longer unusual for special-interest spending on issue ads that support a specific candidate to run into six figures and to exceed the spending of the candidates themselves. The case of Wisconsin is illustrative. In recent elections two clusters of interests have engaged in massive issue advocacy campaigns: supporting GOP candidates are the Wisconsin Manufacturers and Commerce (the state's major business group), the Farm Bureau, the realtors, and builders; and backing Democratic candidates are the teachers unions, the AFL-CIO, and trial lawyers (Ehrenhalt 2000; Walters 2001). This level of spending has meant that the agenda of campaigns can be heavily influenced not by the candidates or parties, but by allied groups.

The Growth of PACs

Most commentary on the role of PACs in campaigns has been focused upon their role in congressional elections and their tendency to support incumbents. The expanding role of PACs is, however, also having a major impact upon races for state offices. All states permit corporations, trade associations, unions, and other organizations to create PACs that can solicit voluntary contributions from employees, stockholders, and members. As is true at the national level, industry and trade association PACs, in particular, have proliferated in the states and their numbers are now an estimated 12,000 nationwide. The extent of PAC activity in the states varies depending upon such factors as the number of organized interests within a particular state and the state laws regulating PACs. For example, thirty-two states impose contribution limits upon PACs, whereas others permit unlimited contributions (Malbin and Gais 1998, 17–18). PACs are contributing an increasing share of campaign dollars in both congressional and state elections. In several states, a majority of funds expended by legislative candidates is provided by PACs. Most state PACs follow the congressional-level pattern of contributing primarily to incumbents in an effort to gain access, thereby tending to foster a candidate-centered type of politics.

Well-financed state-level PACs provide not only contributions to candidates but also in-kind services and they increasingly engage in independent expenditures and issue advocacy designed to benefit specific candidates. In some states, so-called "super-PACs" operate using funds from interest groups, other PACs, and even national-party state legislative campaign committees to pay for massive issue advocacy campaigns in targeted races that hold the promise of being pivotal to gaining party control of legislative chambers.

State-Level Competitiveness and Incumbent Reelection in Congressional and Legislative Races

Interparty Competition in Statewide Races

Across the country, it is now possible for either party to win statewide elections. This is true of even former one-party bastions like the states of the old Confederacy, where since 1966 only Georgia has failed to elect at least one Republican governor and only Louisiana has not elected a GOP U.S. senator. Similarly, in the traditional citadels of Republicanism such as Kansas, Maine, Nebraska, North Dakota, and Vermont, the Democrats have won more governorships since 1966 than the GOP. There is even evidence that in the once solidly Democratic South, electoral competitiveness is seeping into lower-level state constitutional offices. Thus, in 2000, Republicans occupied all of the elective lower-level state constitutional offices in Alabama, Texas, and Virginia; and six lieutenant governors, four attorneys general, and three secretaries of state were Republicans.

Intense Contests for Control of State Legislative Chambers

Bitter struggles for control of legislative chambers are now commonplace in many states. Thus, going into the 2000 elections, party control in 20 chambers hinged on majorities of five seats or less, including three chambers that had equal numbers of Republicans and Democrats. Six chambers changed party control in the election. Changes in party control were a regular occurrence in the 1990s: in 1994, the Republicans gained control of an additional 18 chambers; in 1996, 10 chambers changed hands, and in 1998 8 chambers did so. Because a switch of a few seats can cause a shift in party control with political power, redistricting, and public policy consequences, marginal legislative seats have become major partisan battlegrounds on which the state and national parties and their allied groups focus resources.

Although it is a truism of state legislative politics that an overwhelming proportion of incumbents win reelection through skillful use of the advantages of public office, by building personal organizations and followings, and through generous support of PACs, state legislatures in most of the states have entered the era of competitive politics. As a result, the state parties, their officeholders, and candidates have a major stake in the outcome of races in marginal legislative districts.

The Transformation of the State Party to Service Agency

In the late 1960s and early 1970s, the conventional wisdom among political observers was that parties were in a state of decline (see Broder 1971; Ranney 1978b). The parties' weakened state, however, was not a permanent affliction. Since the 1960s, the American state party organizations have become more professionalized and organizationally stronger in the sense that they can provide campaign services to their candidates. They still do not control nominations because of the direct primary, but many are playing an important supportive role in campaigns. The state parties have also become more closely integrated into national campaign structures.

Party development within the states offers striking parallels to the resurgence of party organizations at the national level (see also Chapter 3, "National Party Organizations at the Dawn of the Twenty-First Century"). The Republican and Democratic national committees have strengthened their fund-raising capacities, built professional staffs, and developed the ability to provide essential services to candidates, and the state parties have done the same.

Powerful state party organizations capable of controlling nominations and based upon patronage continued to operate into the 1960s, particularly in the Mid-Atlantic, New England, and lower Great Lakes states (Mayhew 1986, 205). However, by the mid–1980s this type of organization had almost ceased to exist (Reichley 1992, 383–384). Civil service laws, public employee unions, and public distaste for political cronyism severely weakened patronage-based organizations. In addition, the Supreme Court in a series of previously noted decisions made old-fashioned patronage control of thousands of nonpolicymaking jobs virtually illegal. An Illinois state Democratic chair summed up the situation by observing that "the party no longer functions as an employment agency. More and more, we must rely on the spirit of volunteerism that moves so many other organizations." And even in Indiana, a state never noted for its sensitivity about political favoritism, the GOP state chairman lamented, "It is no longer possible to fire people for political reasons" (quoted by Reichley 1992, 385).

To survive and perform a meaningful role in state politics, the parties have had to adapt to a changed political environment of candidate-centered politics, heightened interparty competition for statewide offices and control of legislative chambers, active involvement of party-allied groups, an absence of patronage, new campaign technologies, and a strengthened national party organizational structure. In adapting to these forces, state party organizations have become service agencies for their candidates and local affiliates.

The Service-Oriented State Party Organization

Indicators of state parties' heightened organizational strength and adoption of a candidate-service orientation include (1) permanent party headquarters; (2) professionalized leadership and staffs; (3) adequate financial resources; and (4) programs to maintain the state party structure, assist local party units, and support candidates and officeholders (Cotter et al. 1984; Aldrich 2000; Appleton and Ward 1996; Reichley 1992, 386–391).

Permanent Headquarters Equipped with Modern Technology. In the 1960s, state party headquarters often had an ad hoc quality and led a transitory existence. State chairs frequently ran the party from their offices or homes, and the headquarters moved from city to city depending upon the residence of its leader. In the mid–1970s, 10 percent of the headquarters still lacked a permanent location (Huckshorn 1976, 254–255), but a 1999 survey found that 98 percent of the parties had a permanent location and 34 percent owned the building where the headquarters were located (Aldrich 2000, 656). The extent to which the headquarters utilizes up-to-date technology depends upon the parties' financial resources. Almost all have some form of computerized voter database that is used for fund-raising, mailings, and voter registration, voter contact, and recruiting volunteers. The national party organizations frequently provided technical assistance in the creation of these databases, especially in the case of the Republicans. There are distinct party differences in how the databases are used. Republican organizations have emphasized direct-mail fund-raising, while Democrats have found the databases most useful for contacting voters, providing Election Day reminders and information to voters, and recruiting volunteers. Most state parties also operate web sites (Goodhart 1999). A notable example of a permanent headquarters well stocked with high-tech equipment is that of the Wisconsin GOP. Its three-story facility in Madison contains a telemarketing center capable of contacting 400,000 persons in a single day, computers that link up with every media outlet in the state (with reporters' names listed by legislative and congressional district), a computer-based research facility, a finance center, and office space for political operatives.

Professional Staffing. In the recent past, it was common for a state headquarters to operate with minimal staff—often just a secretary or executive director, plus volunteers. Twenty-first-century campaigning and party building, however, require more extensive and professionalized staffing. Virtually all state parties now have full-time professional leadership, with 54 percent of the chairs working full time in their positions, compared to approximately one third in 1984 (Aldrich 2000, 656; Reichley 1992, 389). Practically every state organization has a full time executive director and a majority have a field staff, public relations director, research staff, comptroller, and fund-raiser. The average headquarters has a staff of nine in an election year, plus seven part-time employees (Aldrich 2000, 656). The parties in Florida exemplify the trend toward staff professionalism. The state GOP has regularly had a staff of 25 plus several part-time employees and the Democratic party has had a staff of 16 and 4 part-time workers (Appleton and Ward 1996, 62).

Although the state parties have made substantial progress in developing professional staffs, they constantly face the problem of high turnover in leadership and staff positions. The average tenure for state chairs is only two years (Aldrich 2000, 656); and their senior political operatives tend to be transients who move about the country from job to job with party organizations, candidates, and consulting firms, following leads frequently provided to them by Republican and Democratic national party organizations (Reichley 1992, 391–392).

Finances. Operating a professional headquarters capable of providing essential services to candidates and local units requires an ability to raise substantial amounts of money on an ongoing basis. Virtually every state party is now equipped with the technology to operate direct-mail fundraising in addition to more traditional methods such as dinners, large-contributor programs, and contributions from allied groups. Aldrich's 1999 survey found that the average state party election-year budget was $2.8 million. National averages, however, mask the extent to which some state parties are capable of raising prodigious amounts of money. In 1996, the New York state GOP committee raised $25 million (Dao 1998).

The average state party's multimillion-dollar budget, not to mention substantial sums transferred to their accounts by national party committees (see below), stands in contrast to the findings of Alexander Heard in his 1960 classic study of campaign finance. Heard reported that two thirds of Republican state committees had centrally organized fund-raising operations and that the Democrats had generally failed to develop regularized fund-raising programs (1960, 218–220). Although party fund-raising abilities vary from state to state, it is clear from Aldrich's survey (2000) that most state parties have developed substantial revenue sources.

Party Activities: Candidate Support and Party Building

Since the 1960s, state parties have expanded their activities in the spheres of both candidate support and party building. In terms of support for candidates, over 80 percent make financial contributions to gubernatorial, state constitutional, congressional, and legislative candidates (Aldrich 2000, 659). Parties also assist candidates by matching them up with appropriate PAC donors. Thus, the organized groups become partners with the party. State parties also provide an array of campaign services—polling, fund-raising assistance, media consulting, and campaign seminars. There are also the large-scale voter mobilization activities of the state party organizations, including registration drives, voter identification and list maintenance, phone banks, and absentee ballot operations.

In addition to operating regularized fund-raising and voter identification programs, state parties also engage in such party-building activities as publishing newsletters, conducting leadership training sessions, conducting polls, recruiting candidates, sharing mailing lists with local units, and conducting joint county-state fund-raisers and get-out-the-vote drives.

Although the state parties are organizationally stronger and provide a broader array of campaign services than in the past, the key to understanding their role in campaigns is to recognize that they supplement the candidates' own personal campaign organizations. The job of the state party is normally to provide money, voter mobilization activities, technical services (e.g., polls, consultants), and volunteers. Campaigning in the American states is candidate-centered, not party-centered, and consequently party organizations rarely control nominations or run campaigns. Instead, the candidates normally have their own headquarters and organizations.

Party Differences

Studies of state party organizations have consistently shown that on the whole Republicans tend to have stronger, more professionalized, and better financed state organizations than do the Democrats (Aldrich 2000, 655; Reichley 1992, 387–391; Cotter et al. 1984). The Republican operations tend to be less labor-intensive and more capital-intensive than

Democratic organizations. The South is the region with the strongest party organizations, reflecting the impact of growing interparty competition in that region (Aldrich 2000, 655).

The benefits of a Republican organizational strength advantage were demonstrated during the heavily contested postelection recount and challenge phase of the Florida presidential election in 2000: overnight the state party became a full-fledged operative arm of the Bush campaign. The three-story headquarters was turned over to Bush lawyers and strategists; 30 employees scheduled for after-election layoff were put on round-the-clock service to the Bush organization; party workers observed every court clerk's office to act as an early warning system for surprise motions and orders; and state Republicans handed out disposable cameras to document questionable vote counting and evidence bags to gather disputed chads (Nagourney and Barstow 2000).

The tendency of the Republicans to have stronger party organizations than the Democrats reflects a key difference between the parties. Republican party organizations tend to be a more important campaign resource for their candidates than Democratic party organizations. This does not necessarily mean that Democratic candidates are lacking in adequate resources. Rather, it reflects the fact that Democratic organizations and their candidates rely more heavily upon allied groups such as labor unions, teachers, abortion rights advocates, minority groups, environmentalists, and trial lawyers to provide money, manpower, media advertising, and in-kind services, where Republicans pay professional staff members for these services. For example, during the 2000 campaign in Michigan, the United Auto Workers sent out 2 million pieces of campaign literature and had 2,000 poll workers on duty in McComb and Oakland Counties; teachers' unions ran daily shuttles for people wanting absentee ballots and made 1 million get-out-the-vote phone calls; and the National Abortion Rights Action League and the League of Conservation Voters had full-time staff assigned to the state (Hoffman 2000; Traugott 2001, 68). Of course, the GOP parties are not without their allied groups, such as the Christian right and business organizations, that supplement their campaign efforts, but the general pattern is for Democratic parties and candidates to be more dependent upon this type of assistance.

Party Organizational Strength and Election Outcomes

The organizational strength of state parties affects their ability to mobilize voters on Election Day and is a factor in determining the extent of interparty electoral competition (Patterson and Caldeira 1984; Barrilleaux 1986). An analysis of gubernatorial elections has shown that the party that has an organizational strength advantage over the opposition gains an incrementally higher percentage of the vote (Cotter et al. 1984, 100–101). And as Jewell and Morehouse (2001) point out, southern Republican parties were unable to take advantage of gains made by their presidential candidates in the 1950s and 1960s because their organizations were weak. The "spectacular gains of Republican candidates for congressional, state, and local office in more recent years are in large measure a product of much stronger Republican Party organizations" (99). Superior or improved organizational strength does not, however, necessarily bring with it electoral victories. The relationship between party organizational strength and votes is complex and often indirect. In some cases, strong party structures—like those of the Republicans in Florida, Ohio, Pennsylvania, and Texas—have clearly contributed to electoral victories. But in other states in which one party has enjoyed a long history of electoral success, the dominant party may have little incentive to develop or maintain its organization. This was true of the Democratic party in the South until it was seriously challenged by the Republicans in recent decades. It is frequently the electorally weaker party that has the greatest incentive to build an effective organization as a first step toward electoral victories, as did southern Republican parties in the 1960s and 1970s. Thus, party organizational strength can have long-term consequences. A strong party structure can provide the infrastructure for candidates and activists to continue competing until political conditions become more favorable. In most states for the foreseeable future, the level of two-party competition is apt to be sufficiently intense that a party that fails to maintain an effective organization is likely to fall on hard electoral times (Jewell and Morehouse 2001, 99).

Legislative Campaign Committees

The expanding role of state legislative campaign committees parallels the greatly increased involvement of the senatorial and congressional campaign committees at the national level (see Chapter 3). Thus, while the Republican National Committee (RNC) and Democratic National Committee (DNC) focus upon presidential campaigns and working with their constituent state organizations, the congressional and senatorial campaign committees are the principal party support agencies for House and Senate candidates, for whom they provide money (including assistance with PAC financing), polling, campaign management training and consultants, issue ads, media consulting, and a variety of other technical and issue materials.

The division of labor is quite similar at the state level. The state central committees concentrate on statewide races and working with their local affiliates, while the state legislative campaign committees focus upon recruiting and assisting legislative candidates.

Reasons for the Emergence of Legislative Campaign Committees

Legislative campaign committees are composed of incumbent legislators in both the upper and lower houses and are normally headed by the ranking party leaders in each chamber. These committees developed in response to intensified competition for control of legislative chambers, the escalating costs of campaigns ($500,000 expenditures in targeted races are no longer unusual), the inability of state central committees to provide sufficient assistance to legislative candidates, and aggressive legislative leaders determined either to gain or maintain majority party status (Gierzynski 1992, 11–14; Shea 1995, 31–46; Rosenthal and Simon 1995). The development of LCCs is also linked in many states to a heightened level of legislative professionalism: full-time legislators with adequate salaries, per diem allowances, fringe benefits, and ample staff. Professional legislators tend to place a high value on retaining their seats. Fragile party majorities in legislative chambers have dramatically increased the legislators' stakes in elections because the outcomes can either grant or deny the power and perquisites that go with majority status. Legislative leaders have adapted to these conditions by creating LCCs to protect their own interests as well as those of their party colleagues. In addition, professionalized legislatures with abundant staff resources provide essential ingredients for an effective campaign organization—virtually full-time leaders, party caucus staffs with proximity to the process, and computer and media resources (Rosenthal and Simon 1995, 252). Legislative staff in Illinois and New York are especially active in supporting candidates (Stonecash 1988, 484).

Campaign Committee Strength and Autonomy

As they have become the principal party organizations supporting legislative candidates, in some instances—for example, the Ohio and New York Democratic LCCs and the Illinois Republican LCC—LCCs have become their state party's strongest organization (Morehouse 2000, 17–18).

Campaign committees led by legislative leaders tend to operate with considerable autonomy from the state party committees, although there is some cooperation and coordination of activities. In Minnesota, for example, the Democratic-Farmer-Labor party legislative committee occupies space in the state party headquarters, thereby facilitating coordination during the campaign season (Jewell and Morehouse 2001, 212). However, as Frank Sorauf (1992) has observed, LCCs are party organizations built by incumbents and serve "only the agendas and priorities of legislative partisans." This tends to "insulate them from the pressures of their party. Collective action has helped to bring legislative parties freedom from agendas of presidential and gubernatorial parties" (120).

This pattern of LCC autonomy carries over to relations with local party organizations, which have historically been considered important participants in legislative campaigns. Recruitment and campaign priorities tend to be determined on a statewide basis by legislative leaders and not in consultation with local party officials; and since the campaign committees focus their activities on a relatively few competitive districts, most local party leaders have little meaningful contact with LCC personnel. Even in those districts in which the campaign committees are active, they normally engage in little joint activity with local party units. As a result, the development of strong LCCs has brought few benefits to local parties (Shea 1995, Chapter 7).

The GOP state party organizations tend to be organizationally stronger than those of the Democratic party, but Democratic LCCs tend to be stronger than the GOP's. The Democrats have had greater electoral success than the Republicans in controlling legislative chambers, and Democratic LCCs have benefited from the fund-raising advantages that go with incumbency and majority status. In many of the states, alliances with activist groups such as teachers' unions have increased the effectiveness of Democratic legislative campaign committees (Gierzynski 1992, 56).

Campaign Activities

Recruitment. A crucial aspect of LCCs' activity is candidate recruitment. Recruitment activities affect the quality of the party's legislative candidates, which in turn affects the candidates' ability to raise money, recruit workers, establish credibility with the media, and make a competitive run for a legislative seat. Alan Ehrenhalt, a state politics expert, has noted:

> Every year, Democrats and Republicans battle for legislative control . . . in what is advertised as a debate about which party best reflects the views of the electorate. Within the corridors of the state capitol, however, the biennial legislative elections are recognized for what they really are: a competition to attract candidates who have the skills and energy to win and the desire and resourcefulness to say in office. (Ehrenhalt 1991, 29–30)

Full-Service Campaign Agencies. Although they started out as organizations that simply distributed money to candidates, the LCCs, like the state central committees, are increasingly full-service campaign agencies. Especially in states with professional legislatures, some campaign committees with multimillion-dollar budgets, such as those in Illinois and Ohio, have become the dominant players in legislative elections by providing an extensive array of campaign services, candidate training seminars, campaign management, polls, media production, direct mail, computerized voter targeting, phone banks, and opposition and issues research.

Working with PACs. Although PACs were first considered a threat to parties, it is interesting to note that the rise of PACs coincides with the emergence of LCCs as full-service campaign organizations, as well as with the strengthening of state party headquarters operations. Like the state committees, LCCs have learned to adapt to a political environment in which PACs are major participants. The LCCs now work closely with the PACs and seek to channel PAC funds into races where additional money holds the potential to affect the outcome. Party legislative leaders provide PAC directors with political intelligence about where their contributions will have maximum impact. Candidates are also assisted through committees' giving them a mark of legitimacy when they are identified by LCC leaders as candidates that would constitute good investments for PACs. An assistant to the speaker of the Indiana House observed, "[F]or every one dollar we [the LCC] raise, we direct two dollars of interest groups money"; and the president of the Maine Senate stated that his committee performs a "match-making service" by "identifying a candidate's philosophy with the PACs and then connecting them" (Gierzynski 1992, 55).

Electoral Strategies. In an electoral environment of often narrow and fragile majorities within legislative chambers, it is not surprising that LCCs concentrate their resources on competitive races to maintain or win control of chambers (Gierzynski and Breaux 1998, Chapter 10). Two basic decisional rules frequently used in allocating resources to legislative candidates are (1) invest in competitive races; and (2) respond to the activities of the opposition (Stonecash and Keith 1996). The majority parties tend to emphasize aid to endangered incumbents and open seats, whereas the minority parties tend to focus their largesse on competitive challengers and open seats.

Leadership PACs

A further basis for the enhanced role of the state legislative party has been the emergence of so-called leadership PACs, those controlled by legislative leaders who are in a position to raise more money than is required for their own reelection. Leadership PACs transfer funds to needy candidates, whereas LLCs frequently specialize in providing services to candidates. By contributing primarily to marginal races, leadership PACs augment the role of the LCCs. However, there are also instances in which the leaders have used personal PACs to promote their own careers within the legislature rather than attending to their party's electoral goals (Gierzynski 1992, 68). Recently, some of the states have moved to prohibit or restrict contributions from leadership PACs.

National-State Party Relations: Heightened Intraparty Integration and Nationalization

Until the late 1970s, most political scientists stressed the fragmentation and dispersion of power as prominent characteristics of American parties. The postwar era's leading parties scholar, V. O. Key, Jr., described the relationship between the national and state parties as independent and confederative (1964, 334). The RNC and DNC were dependent upon state parties for financing and were so lacking in power that a landmark study characterized them as "politics without power" (Cotter and Hennessy 1964).

Since the 1970s, however, the trend has been toward heightened intraparty integration and nationalization. Through their ability to raise massive amounts of money through direct mail, large-giver programs, and solicitation of unions, corporations, trade associations, and various groups for both hard and soft money, the national committees have been transformed into substantially more powerful institutions capable of exerting considerable—but not overwhelming—influence upon their state and local affiliates. This increased national party influence has resulted in greater integration and interdependence between the national and state party structures. It has also aided state parties as national parties have ploughed resources into their state affiliates and utilized them to achieve national party objectives.

Enforcing National Party Rules upon State Parties

After the 1968 election, the Democratic party intensified its efforts to ensure the loyalty of state parties to the national ticket. Through a series of party reform commissions, the national party developed detailed rules governing how state parties must select their national convention delegates. It has also implemented a national Democratic Charter containing prescriptions for the organization and operation of the state parties. These rules have been vigorously enforced upon the state parties, particularly with regard to procedures for selection of national convention delegates. The national parties' rule-making authority has been backed up by a series of Supreme Court decisions which ruled that national party delegate selection rules take precedence over state laws and state party rules (*Cousins v. Wigoda*, 419 U.S. 450 [1975]; *Democratic Party of the U.S. v. Ex rel. La Follette*, 450 U.S. 107 [1981]).

Unlike the Democrats, the Republicans have not sought to gain influence over their state units through rules enforcement. Instead, the GOP has maintained the confederate legal structure of the party, and the RNC has maintained a relatively permissive posture toward its state parties with regard to delegate selection procedures. Centralization and nationalization, however, have moved forward within the GOP by means other than rules changes and enforcement. They were accomplished through the national party's provision of large-scale assistance to state organizations and their candidates (Bibby 1981); the Democrats then followed the Republicans' example.

Providing Financial and Technical Assistance to State Parties

RNC efforts to provide assistance to state parties started in a modest way when Ray C. Bliss served as national chairman (1965–1969). These efforts were greatly expanded by Chairman Bill Brock (1977–1981) and were further augmented by his successors. The RNC has developed multimillion-dollar programs to provide cash grants, professional staff, data-processing services, consultants for organizational development, fund-raising, campaigning, media, and redistricting. Major investments of money have been made to assist state parties in voter-list development and get-out-the-vote efforts. In 1978, the RNC also launched a program of support for state legislative candidates.

The RNC's fund-raising advantage over the DNC enabled it to begin its program of assisting state parties well before the DNC followed suit under the leadership of national chairmen Paul Kirk (1985–1989) and Ron Brown (1989–1993). The Republican national party's continuing financial advantage over the Democrats has meant that the RNC's efforts have been more extensive than those of the DNC. Beginning with the 1988 elections, the DNC expanded national party support programs by subsidizing the use of "Coordinated Campaign" structures within the states to serve a broad range of candidates. The Coordinated Campaign is geared to provide basic campaign services such as voter registration, voter-list development, get-out-the-vote drives, polling, targeting, media relations, and scheduling to an array of candidates. Coordinated campaigns are funded by the DNC, senatorial and congressional committees, candidates' organizations, key Democratic constituency groups such as organized labor, and in some instances legislative campaign committees. The level of DNC support and state party involvement in coordinated campaigns depends upon the institutional readiness and capacity of the state organization and the priority given to the state's races by national party strategists. Where state parties are deemed incapable of running an effective coordinated operation, the DNC has brought in national party operatives to run the program on a temporary basis.

The Republicans have operated programs similar to the Democrats' coordinated campaign structure in recent elections as the national GOP organizations, state parties, and candidate organizations have run joint voter-identification and get-out-the-vote activities. Through state parties, the RNC invested $40 million in its Victory 2000 programs, which resulted in 110 million pieces of mail and 65 million phone calls to get out the vote (Republican National Committee 2000).

By providing assistance to their state parties, the national party organizations gained leverage and influence with their affiliates. What this means is that conditions can be imposed by the national party upon the state units receiving assistance, including such requirements as hiring qualified consultants, developing approved campaign plans, and cooperating with national party activities.

National-to-State Fund Transfers

As the campaign efforts described here demonstrate, involvement by national parties in state party organizations has become an integral part of national campaign strategies since the 1980s. A critical aspect of this process of integrating state organizations into national campaign efforts has been massive transfers of funds from national party organizations to state and local units. During the 1999–2000 election cycle, the DNC, Democratic Congressional Campaign Committee, and Democratic Senatorial Campaign Committee transferred a total of $226.9 million in both hard and soft money to state parties; and the RNC and the Republican congressional and senatorial campaign committees transferred $184,451,675 to their state affiliates (see Table 2.1).

These transfers are encouraged by the Federal Election Campaign Act, which imposes strict limits on party spending for presidential nominees who accept federal funding of their campaigns, as well as expenditure limits on direct contributions to Senate and House candidates and on coordinated expenditures on behalf of these candidates. At the same time, the FECA does permit state and local party organizations to spend without limit on "party-building activities" such as voter registration, get-out-the-vote drives, phone banks, and facilities. In addition, parties may engage in independent expenditures and issue advocacy advertising that benefits their candidates. Issue advocacy ads, which in reality are thinly disguised candidates' ads, have become a major area of expenditure of state parties utilizing funds transferred to them by the national party committees.

Table 2.1   National-to-State Party Transfers, 1999–2000 Election Cycle

	Republican National Party Transfers	Democratic National Party Transfers
	Republican National Comm.	Democratic National Comm.
Hard $	$33,853,563	$41,892,535
Soft $	93,017,578	73,087,085
Total	$126,871,141	$114,979,620
	National Republican Congressional Comm.	Democratic Congressional Campaign Comm.
Hard $	$10,957,743	$15,383,695
Soft $	15,852,920	34,707,004
Total	$26,810,663	$50,090,699
	National Republican Senatorial Comm.	Democratic Senatorial Campaign Comm.
Hard $	$10,689,700	$24,388,338
Soft $	20,485,179	37,444,869
Total	$31,174,879	$61,833,207
Total Transfers	$184,486,683	$226,903,526

Source: Federal Election Commission, "Party Fundraising Escalates" (Federal Election Commission, Washington, D.C.; January 12, 2001), pp. 8–9.

National party organizations are capable of raising far more money than the FECA spending limits permit them to spend directly in support of their federal candidates, so they have adopted a strategy of transferring their "surplus" funds to state and local parties for party-building and issue advocacy activities that implement national party strategies and priorities. An indicator of the strategic nature of national party fund transfers can be seen in Table 2.2. It shows large-scale transfers by the RNC and DNC in 2000 to battleground states in the presidential election, most notably Florida, Michigan, Ohio, and Pennsylvania, while states having a low priority in the campaign got only token or small transfers. The senatorial and congressional committees similarly directed their transfers to those states with highly competitive races. For example, the Democratic senatorial committee transferred $9.1 million to the Virginia Democratic party because Senator Charles Robb was facing a major challenge from former Republican governor George Allen, while the Republican senatorial committee sent $5.4 to the state's GOP; and several key House races in California and Florida resulted in the Democratic congressional committee's sending $7.8 million to the California Democrats and the Republican

Table 2.2   Strategic Targeting of Transfers from National Party
Committees to State Parties, 1999–2000 Election Cycle

Battleground States: State Parties Receiving in Excess of $3 Million

Hard and Soft Money Transferred to State Party

By RNC		By DNC	
Florida	$12,753,385	Michigan	$15,966,163
Pennsylvania	11,280,751	Pennsylvania	13,422,664
Michigan	11,098,933	Florida	9,073,616
Ohio	9,624,308	Ohio	8,506,657
California	9,043,243	Missouri	7,086,388
Missouri	8,733,054	Wisconsin	6,512,027
Washington	6,621,648	Washington	6,249,244
Wisconsin	5,294,030	Oregon	5,434,742
Illinois	4,603,717	Iowa	4,658,266
Oregon	4,580,561	California	4,589,434
Iowa	3,342,391	Illinois	4,377,179
New York	3,069,595	Louisiana	3,248,361

States with Low Priority in the Campaign:
State Parties Receiving the Least Money

Hard and Soft Money Transferred to State Party

By RNC		By DNC	
Vermont	$7,286	Rhode Island	$6,371
Rhode Island	15,000	Mississippi	21,573
Kansas	15,025	Wyoming	26,613
South Dakota	43,300	Hawaii	29,642
Mississippi	52,288	North Dakota	33,578
Indiana	53,500	Alaska	35,299
Alaska	55,000	Indiana	42,193
West Virginia	102,500	Nebraska	44,638
Massachusetts	143,000	Vermont	45,964
Colorado	207,000	Utah	47,763

Source: Federal Election Commission, "Party Fundraising Escalates"
(Federal Election Commission, Washington, D.C., January 12, 2001), pg. 8.

congressional committee's transferring $2.7 million to the GOP of Florida
(Federal Election Commission 2001).

The national parties not only transfer money to their state parties but
also channel private-sector contributions to state party organizations that
are considered important to the national campaign strategy. Major donors
are asked to send money to states in which the parties' candidates are in
highly competitive races.

Party Integration and Nationalization

As has been noted, the national party organizations have used their ample financial resources and legal authority to nationalize the parties' campaign efforts. Leon Epstein has characterized this process as analogous to categorical grant-in-aid programs that the federal government has used to enlist state and local governments in achieving national policy objectives. Like the federal government, which requires state and local governments to comply with federal guidelines in order to receive grants-in-aid, the RNC and DNC also attach conditions—albeit quite flexible conditions—to the assistance they give to state parties and candidates (Epstein 1986, 233). In the process, the national parties have achieved greatly increased influence with their state parties.

Through their programs of technical and financial assistance to state parties, the RNC and DNC have reversed the direction of resource flow since the 1970s. In the past, funds flowed from the state parties to the national committees, and with those funds went substantial state party influence over the activities of the national committees. As Alexander Heard (1960) accurately observed, concerning the direction of influence, "[A]ny changes that freed the national party committees of financial dependence on state organizations could importantly affect the loci of power" and enable the parties to develop a "more cohesive operational structure" (294).

The more cohesive operational structure that Heard envisioned has in fact been realized. Now that the national committees are able to raise unprecedented amounts of money and then allocate those funds to their state affiliates, the RNC and DNC have gained substantial autonomy from as well as leverage with the state parties. The national-state party relationship, however, is not hierarchical in nature. It is more in the nature of a partnership characterized by shared goals—such as electing both federal and state officials—but one in which national and state parties often also have some differing priorities and interests (Morehouse 2000, 11). The national party committees seek to work with and use the state parties to achieve national party goals, for example, in electing a president or winning control of the U.S. House and Senate, while the state parties place greater emphasis on winning state governorships and legislative seats. National-state party relations are not always smooth. For example, Texas and New York Democratic leaders have complained that they believe state parties have received an inadequate share of the take from the DNC's lucrative soft-money fund-raising events held within their states (Morehouse 2000, 10).

The heightened level of intraparty integration and party nationalization that has occurred since the 1970s constitutes a major change in the American party system. No serious observer can now assert, as did the author of the leading 1960s text on parties, that "no nationwide party organization exists. . . . Rather, each party consists of a working coalition of state and local parties" (Key 1964, 315). Thanks in part to the assistance provided by the national party committees, state parties have gone through a process of strengthening. In the process, they have also been more closely integrated into the national party structure and lost some of their traditional autonomy.

State Elections and National Politics

Although state parties are organizationally stronger on the whole than they were in the 1960s, their electoral fortunes are affected by national-level factors over which they have little control, such as economic conditions, presidential popularity, and public perceptions of the national parties. Partisan loyalties are normally forged in the fires of presidential campaigns, and it is extremely difficult for a state party to sustain a public image in state politics that is at odds with its national image. An example can be found in the Democratic parties of the South, which traditionally sought to project a policy posture to the right of the national party and its presidential nominees. This disparity between the national and state parties, along with the changing population and economy of the region, allowed the Republican presidential nominees Eisenhower, Nixon, and Goldwater to win key southern states in the 1950s and 1960s. These Republican inroads were followed by significant Republican victories in gubernatorial, senatorial, congressional, and even state legislative victories after the 1960s. As the electoral alignment of southern voters has become increasingly congruent with that of the rest of the nation, the Republicans have continued to make gains at all levels in southern elections.

Analysis of the relationship between presidential and state legislative election outcomes has shown that legislative elections are affected by the drawing power of the parties' presidential candidates (Campbell 1986). In an effort to insulate state elections from such national influences, almost three fourths of the states have scheduled elections for governor and state constitutional offices as well the state legislature in nonpresidential years. Despite the reformers' best intentions, though, national economic and political conditions continue to intrude and play a significant role even during these off-year elections (Chubb 1988, 113–154; Simon et al., 1991; Stein 1990). Thus, in 1994, continuing public concern about the economy, weak approval ratings for President Clinton, and a concerted effort by the Republicans to nationalize the issues of the campaign contributed to a GOP sweep that included gaining twelve governorships and eighteen state legislative chambers. In every off-year election since World War II, with the exception of 1986 and 1998, the president's party has lost governorships, and the president's party has lost control of legislative chambers in every postwar off-year election but 1998, just as it has normally lost seats in the House of Representatives. The vulnerability of governors in midterm elections reflects the competitive nature of statewide races and the high visibility of governors within their states. As the most visible figures on the midterm election ballots, they are likely to be held accountable for the state of their states and to be convenient targets of discontented voters.

State and Local Party Organizations as Networks of Issue-Oriented Activists

In the post–World War II era, party organizations in the United States changed from being essentially local associations that mobilized local electorates into national entities that directed resources, recruited candidates, and supplied expertise (J. Wilson 1995, xiii). State parties have become an integral part of these national entities and in the process have become organizationally stronger and capable of providing essential campaign services to candidates, in part because of their having been given national party money and expertise. To a significant extent, the national party organizations, especially the Republicans, rely on direct-mail solicitations for funds, which are most effective when the people thus approached have ideological views of politics or strong commitments on particular issues. With coaching from their national parties, the state parties have successfully made similar appeals for funds.

These fund-raising techniques reflect an emerging characteristic of party organizations. Increasingly, they are becoming networks of issue activists (Shafer 1996, Chapter 1). The influence of the Christian right within state and local Republican organizations is one manifestation of this pattern (Wilcox 2000, 74–79); pro-choice, environmentalism, and minority rights activism within the Democratic party is another. Activists associated with causes such as these play a major role in seeking to influence party nominations and in voter-mobilization efforts.

Evidence of the extent to which parties are becoming networks of issue activists can be seen in the extent to which national convention delegates deviate from the policy and ideological views of party rank-and-file voters. Republican delegates are substantially more conservative than GOP voters, while Democratic delegates lean more to the left than do Democratic voters (Green et al. 1999; see also Bruce et al. 1991).

The increasing involvement of individuals whose motivation to participate in party politics is based not on material rewards such as patronage jobs but instead on ideological and issue concerns is creating a somewhat schizophrenic party structure in some states: Elected officials need broad electoral appeal in order to win, but they must exist side by side with a growing body of party organizational activists concerned about ideology and principles. The conflicts inherent in this mix were apparent within the Texas GOP when Governor George W. Bush in 1997 found himself in open conflict with the state's right-wing GOP chairman over tax policy. To deal with this situation, Bush and his campaign chairman cut off funding to the state party by directing most large contributions to a separate fund controlled by Bush's personal organization (Morehouse 2000, 16). In Colorado's 1998 governor's race, the GOP state chairman, a social conservative, expressed doubts about supporting the party nominee, Bill Owens, because of ideological disagreements; and in Kansas, the state Republican chairman resigned his post so he could run in the 1998 primary against the party's incumbent governor, Bill Graves, whom the chairman considered insufficiently conservative.

The Democrats have also been afflicted with issue-oriented group influence that has at times made it difficult to maintain rank-and-file voters' support. An analysis of Democratic party–interest group relations concluded, "No one decided that the party would be the party of . . . liberal causes at the expense of middle-class voters. The Democrats became the party of these causes because it was effectively lobbied" (Berry and Schildkraut 1995, 29).

The trend toward parties as networks of issue-oriented partisans is creating conflicts between these activists and their parties' elected officials. To the extent that state party organizations become networks of issue activists, conflicts between elected officials and the party organization such as those in Texas, Colorado, and Kansas are likely to proliferate and intensify. In addition, issue activist–dominated party organizations are likely to widen the policy differences between the Republican and Democratic parties, thereby heightening the intensity of interparty conflict.

The Adaptable and Enduring State Party

State parties in the first decade of the new century are substantially changed and stronger than they were in the 1960s and 1970s. They have adapted to the challenges posed by candidate-centered campaigning and the emergence of PACs as a major campaign funding source. They have also become more closely integrated into the national parties' campaign structures. As a result of this party nationalization process, the state parties have lost some of their traditional autonomy. But at the same time, a series of judicial decisions has granted them relief from the most onerous of state regulations and FECA restrictions, thereby providing the state parties with greater flexibility in achieving their objectives.

Although the state parties' record of adaptability and durability since the 1960s is impressive, the American political environment is not conducive to strong European-style parties that are capable of controlling nominations and running political campaigns. From a cross-national perspective, therefore, American political parties appear as rather modest political organizations that supplement the personal campaign organizations of candidates.

One of the most significant questions concerning the future of state parties is the nature of their relationship to increasingly strong national party organizations. The national parties now give extensive assistance to and exert unprecedented influence over their state affiliates. The national parties' priorities, however, are not necessarily identical to those of the state organizations. And national influence may not be a constant. National party finances may not continue to grow as they have since the 1970s. Campaign finance reforms, for example, could cut into national party revenues and make it impossible to assist state parties at the level or with the regularity that they have come to expect. Such a development would slow the process of party integration and perhaps cause some weakening of the state parties.

The growing tendency of state and local party organizations to become networks of ideological and issue-oriented activists also threatens to create conflicts between these activists and party-affiliated elected officials and makes it more difficult for the parties to nominate candidates capable of making the broad-based popular appeals essential for winning general elections. However, given their demonstrated resiliency and adaptability, state parties will doubtless continue to be significant participants in America's politics.

3

National Party Organizations at the Dawn of the Twenty-First Century

PAUL S. HERRNSON

Once characterized as poor, unstable, and powerless, national party organizations in the United States entered the twenty-first century as financially secure, institutionally stable, and highly influential in election campaigns and in their relations with state and local party committees.* The national party organizations—the Democratic and Republican national, congressional, and senatorial campaign committees—have adapted to the candidate-centered, money-driven, "high-tech" style of modern campaign politics. This chapter examines the development of the national party organizations, their evolving relations with other party committees, and their role in contemporary elections.

Party Organizational Development

Origins of the National Parties

American political parties are principally electoral institutions. They focus more on elections and less on initiating policy change than do parties in other Western democracies (Epstein 1986). This is reflected in the birth and subsequent development of the national party organizations. National party development also has been influenced by forces impinging on the parties from the broader political environment and pressures emanating from within the parties themselves. The Democratic National Committee (DNC) was formed during the Democratic national convention of 1848 for the purpose of organizing and directing the presidential campaign, promulgating the call for the next convention, and tending to the details associated with setting up future conventions (Cotter and Hennessy 1964). The Republican National Committee (RNC) was created in 1856 at an ad hoc meeting of future Republicans for the purposes of

---

*I wish to thank Peter Francia and Atiya Stokes for their assistance in researching this chapter.

bringing the Republican party into existence and conducting election-related activities similar to those performed by its Democratic counterpart. The creation of the national committees was an important step in a process that transformed the parties' organizational apparatuses from loosely confederative structures to more centralized, federal organizations.

The congressional campaign committees were created in response to electoral insecurities that were heightened as a result of factional conflicts that developed within the two parties following the Civil War. The National Republican Congressional Committee (NRCC) was formed in 1866 by Radical Republican members of the House who were feuding with President Andrew Johnson. The House members believed they could not rely on the President or the RNC for assistance so they created their own campaign committee to assist with their elections and to distance themselves from the President. As is often the case in politics, organization begat counterorganization. Following the Republican example, pro-Johnson Democrats formed their own legislative election committee—the Democratic Congressional Campaign Committee (DCCC).

Senate leaders created the senatorial campaign committees in 1916 after the Seventeenth Amendment transformed the upper chamber into a popularly elected body. The Democratic Senatorial Campaign Committee (DSCC) and the National Republican Senatorial Committee (NRSC) were founded to assist incumbent senators with their reelection campaigns. Like their counterparts in the House, the Senate campaign committees were established during a period of political upheaval—resulting from the success of the Progressive movement—to assuage members' electoral insecurities during an era of exceptionally high partisan disunity and political instability.

During most of their existence the six national party organizations have not possessed abundant power. Flow charts of the party organizations are generally pyramid-like, with the national conventions at the apex, the national committees directly below them, the congressional and senatorial campaign committees (also known as the Hill committees, a reference to their having been located in congressional office space at one time) branching off the national conventions, and the state and local party apparatus placed below the national party apparatus (Frantzich 1989). However, power is not and has never been distributed hierarchically. Throughout most of the parties' history, and during the height of their strength (the late nineteenth and early twentieth centuries are considered the golden age of political parties), power was concentrated at the local level, usually in countywide political machines. Power mainly flowed up from county organizations to state party committees and conventions, and thence to the national convention. The national, congressional, and senatorial campaign committees had little if any power over state and local party leaders (Cotter and Hennessy 1964).

Local party organizations are reputed to have possessed tremendous influence during the golden age of political parties. Old-fashioned political machines had the ability to unify the legislative and executive branches of local and state governments. The machines also had a great deal of influence in national politics and with the courts. The machines' power was principally rooted in their virtual monopoly over the tools needed to run a successful campaign. Party bosses had the power to award the party nominations to potential candidates. Local party committees also possessed the resources needed to communicate with the electorate and mobilize voters (Sorauf 1980).

Nevertheless, party campaigning was a cooperative endeavor during the golden age, especially during presidential election years. Although individual branches of the party organization were primarily concerned with electing candidates within their immediate jurisdictions, party leaders at different levels of the organization had a number of reasons to work together (Ostrogorski 1964; Schattschneider 1942). They recognized that ballot structures and voter partisanship linked the electoral prospects of their candidates. Party leaders further understood that electing candidates to federal, state, and local governments would enable them to maximize the patronage and preferments they could exact for themselves and their supporters. Party leaders were also conscious of the different resources and capabilities possessed by different branches of the party organization. The national party organizations, and especially the national committees, had the financial, administrative, and communications resources needed to coordinate and set the tone of a nationwide campaign (Bruce 1927; Kent 1923). Local party committees had the proximity to voters needed to collect electoral information, conduct voter registration and get-out-the-vote drives, and perform other grassroots campaign activities (Merriam 1923). State party committees had relatively modest resources, but they occupied an important intermediate position between the other two strata of the party organization. State party leaders channeled electoral information up to the national party organizations and arranged for candidates and other prominent party leaders to speak at local rallies and events (Sait 1927). Relations between the national party organizations and other branches of the party apparatus were characterized by negotiations and compromise rather than command. Party organizations in Washington, D.C., did not dominate party politics during the golden age. They did, however, play an important role in what were essentially party-centered election campaigns.

Party Decline

The transition from a party-dominated system of campaign politics to a candidate-centered system was brought about by legal, demographic, and technological changes in American society and by reforms instituted by the parties themselves. The direct primary and civil service regulations instituted during the Progressive Era deprived party bosses of their ability to hand-pick nominees and reward party workers with government jobs and contracts (Key 1958; Roseboom 1970). The reforms weakened the bosses' hold over candidates and political activists and encouraged candidates to build their own campaign organizations.

Demographic and cultural changes reinforced this pattern. Increased education and social mobility, declining immigration, and a growing national identity contributed to the erosion of the close-knit, traditional ethnic neighborhoods that formed the core of the old-fashioned political machine's constituencies. Voters began to turn toward nationally focused mass media and away from local party committees for their political information (Ranney 1975; Kayden and Mahe 1985; McWilliams 1981). Growing preferences for movies, radio, and televised entertainment underscored this phenomenon by reducing the popularity of rallies, barbecues, and other types of interpersonal communication at which old-fashioned political machines excelled.[1] These changes combined to deprive the machines of their political bases and to render many of their communications and mobilization techniques obsolete.

The adaptation to the electoral arena of technological innovations developed in the public relations field further eroded candidates' dependence on party organizations. Advancements in survey research, computerized data processing, and mass media advertising provided candidates with new tools for gathering information about voters and communicating messages to them. The emergence of a new corps of campaigners, political consultants, enabled candidates to hire nonparty professionals to run their campaigns (Agranoff 1972; Sabato 1981). Direct-mail fund-raising techniques helped candidates raise the money needed to pay their campaign staffs and outside consultants. These developments helped to transform election campaigns from party-focused, party-conducted affairs to events that revolved around individual candidates and their campaign organizations.

Two recent developments that initially appeared to weaken party organizations and reinforce the candidate-centeredness of American elections were party reforms introduced by the Democrats' McGovern-Fraser Commission and the Federal Election Campaign Act of 1971 and its amendments (FECA). The McGovern-Fraser reforms, and reforms instituted by later Democratic reform commissions, were designed to make the presidential nominating process more open and more representative. Their side effects included making it more difficult for long-time party "regulars" to attend national party conventions or play a dominant role in other party activities. They also made it easier for issue and candidate activists who had little history of party service (frequently labeled "purists" or "amateurs") to play a larger role in party politics. The rise of the "purists" also led to tensions over fundamental issues such as whether winning elections or advancing particular policies should have priority (J. Wilson 1962; Polsby and Wildavsky 1984). Heightened tensions made coalition building among party activists and supporters more difficult. Intraparty conflicts between purists and professionals, and the purists' heavy focus on the agendas of specific candidates and special interests, also resulted in the neglect of the parties' organizational needs. The reforms were debilitating to both parties, but they were more harmful to the Democratic party that introduced them (Ranney 1975; Polsby and Wildavsky 1984).

The FECA also had some negative effects on the parties. The FECA's contribution and expenditure limits, disclosure provisions, and other regulatory requirements forced party committees to keep separate bank accounts for state and federal election activity. The reforms had the immediate effect of discouraging state and local party organizations from fully participating in federal elections (Price 1984; Kayden and Mahe 1985). The FECA also set the stage for the tremendous proliferation of political action committees (PACs) that began in the late 1970s. The Federal Election Commission's SunPAC Advisory, given in response to Sun Oil's query about whether it could legally form a PAC, in 1976 opened the gateway for PACs to become the major organized financiers of congressional elections (Alexander 1984).

The progressive reforms, demographic and cultural transformations, new campaign technology, recent party reforms, and campaign finance legislation combined to reduce the roles that party organizations played in elections and to foster the evolution of a candidate-centered election system. Under this system candidates typically assembled their own campaign organizations, initially to compete for their party's nomination and then to contest the general election. In the case of presidential elections, a candidate who succeeded in securing the party's nomination also won control of the national committee. The candidate's campaign organization directed most national committee election activity. In congressional elections, most campaign activities were carried out by the candidate's own organization both before and after the primary. The parties' seeming inability to adapt to the new "high-tech," money-driven style of campaign politics of the 1960s and 1970s resulted in their being pushed to the periphery of the elections process. These trends were accompanied by a general decline in the parties' ability to encourage voters to identify themselves with a party, to vote for that party's candidates (Carmines, Renten, and Stimson 1984; Beck 1984), to furnish symbolic referents and decision-making cues for voters (Burnham 1970; Ladd and Hadley 1975; Nie, Verba, and Petrocik 1979; Wattenberg 1984), and to foster party unity among elected officials (Deckard 1976; Keefe 1976; Clubb, Flanigan, and Zingale 1980).

National Party Reemergence

Although the party decline was a gradual process that took its greatest toll on party organizations at the local level, party renewal occurred over a relatively short period and was focused primarily in Washington, D.C. The dynamics of recent national party organizational development bear parallels to changes occurring during earlier periods. The content of recent national party organizational renewal was shaped by the changing needs of candidates. The new-style campaigning that become prevalent during the 1960s places a premium on campaign activities requiring technical expertise and in-depth research. Some candidates were able to run a viable campaign using their own funds or talent. Others turned to political consultants, PACs, and interest groups for help. However, many candidates found it difficult to assemble the money and expertise needed to compete in a modern election. The increased needs of candidates for greater access to technical expertise, political information, and money created an opportunity for national and some state party organizations to become the repositories of these electoral resources (Schlesinger 1985).

Nevertheless, national party organizations did not respond to changes in the political environment until electoral crises forced party leaders to recognize the institutional and electoral weaknesses of the national party organizations. As was the case during earlier eras of party transformation, crises that heightened officeholders' electoral anxieties furnished party leaders with the opportunities and incentives to augment the parties' organizational apparatuses. Entrepreneurial party leaders recognized that they might receive payoffs for restructuring the national party organizations so that they could better assist candidates and state and local party committees with their election efforts.[2]

The Watergate scandal and the trouncing Republican candidates experienced in the 1974 and 1976 elections provided a crisis of competition that was the catalyst for change at the Republican national party organizations. The Republicans lost 49 seats in the House in 1974, had an incumbent President defeated two years later, and controlled only 12 governorships and four state legislatures by 1977. Moreover, voter identification with the Republican party, which had previously been climbing, dropped precipitously, especially among voters under 35 (Malbin 1975).

The crisis of competition drew party leaders' attention to the weaknesses of the Republican national, congressional, and senatorial campaign committees. After a struggle that became entwined with the politics surrounding the race for the chairmanship of the RNC, William Brock, an advocate of party organizational development, was selected to head the RNC. Other party-building entrepreneurs were selected to chair the parties' other two national organizations: Representative Guy Vander Jagt of Michigan took the helm of the NRCC in 1974 and Senator Robert Packwood of Oregon was selected to chair the NRSC in 1976. The three party leaders initiated a variety of programs aimed at promoting the institutional development of their committees, increasing the committees' electoral presence, and providing candidates with campaign money and services. All three leaders played a major role in reshaping the missions of the national parties and in placing them on a path that would result in their organizational transformation.

The transformation of the Democratic national party organizations is more complicated than that of their Republican counterparts because DNC institutionalization occurred in two distinct phases. The first phase of DNC development, which is often referred to as party reform and frequently associated with party decline, was concerned with enhancing the representativeness and openness of the national committee and the presidential nominating convention. The second phase, which resembles the institutionalization of the Republican party organizations and is frequently referred to as party renewal, focused on the committee's institutional and electoral capabilities.

Democratic party reform followed the tumultuous 1968 Democratic National Convention. Protests on the floor of the convention and in the streets of Chicago constituted a factional crisis that underscored the deep rift between liberal reform–minded "purists" and party "regulars." The crisis and the party's defeat in November created an opportunity for major party organizational change. The McGovern-Fraser Commission, and later reform commissions, introduced rules that made the delegate selection process more participatory and led to the unexpected proliferation of presidential primaries; increased the size and demographic representativeness of the DNC and the national convention; instituted midterm issue conferences (which were discontinued by Paul Kirk after his selection as DNC Chair in 1984); and resulted in the party's adopting a written charter. Some of these changes are believed to have been a major cause of party decline (Crotty 1983).

Other changes may have been more positive. Upon adopting the decisions of the McGovern-Fraser Commission, the DNC took on a new set of responsibilities regarding state party compliance with national party rules governing participation in the delegate selection process. The expansion of DNC rule-making and enforcement authority has resulted in the committee's usurping the power to overrule state party activities connected with the process that are not in compliance with national party rules.[3] This represents a fundamental shift in the distribution of power between the national committee and the state party organizations. Democratic party reform transformed the DNC into an important agency of intraparty regulation and increased committee influence in both party and presidential politics.

The second phase of Democratic national party institutionalization followed the party's massive defeat in the 1980 election. The defeat of the incumbent, President Jimmy Carter, the loss of 34 House seats (half of the party's margin), and loss of control of the Senate constituted a crisis of competition that was the catalyst for change at the Democratic national party organizations. Unlike the previous phase of national party development, Democratic party renewal was preceded by widespread agreement among DNC members, Democrats in Congress, and party activists that the party should increase its competitiveness by imitating the GOP's party-building and campaign service programs (Cook 1981).

The issue of party renewal was an important factor in the selection of Charles Manatt as DNC chair and Representative Tony Coelho as DCCC chair in 1980. It also influenced Democratic senators' choice of Lloyd Bentsen of Texas to chair the DSCC in 1982. All three party leaders were committed to building the national party organizations' fund-raising capabilities, improving their professional staffs and organizational structures, and augmenting the Republican party-building model to suit the specific needs of Democratic candidates and state and local committees. Like their Republican counterparts, all three Democratic leaders played a critical role in promoting the institutionalization of the Democratic national party organizations. Later party chairs would augment the work of their predecessors to ensure that national party organizations continue to play a significant role in party and campaign politics.

Institutionalized National Parties

The institutionalization of the national party organizations refers to their becoming fiscally solvent, organizationally stable, and larger and more diversified in their staffing and to their adopting professional-bureaucratic decision-making procedures. These changes were necessary for the national parties to develop their election-related and party-building functions.

Finances

National party fund-raising improved greatly from the 1970s through 2000. During this period the national parties sent several fund-raising records, using a variety of approaches to raise money from a diverse group of contributors. The Republican committees raised more federally regulated "hard" money, which could be spent expressly to promote the elections of federal candidates, than their Democratic rivals throughout this period. However, during the early 1980s the Democrats began to narrow the gap in fund-raising. They managed to shrink the Republican national party organization's hard money fund-raising advantage from 6.7 to 1 in the 1982 election cycle to 1.7 to 1 in 2000.

Table 3.1 National Party Hard Money Receipts, 1976–2000 (in million $)

Party	1976	1978	1980	1982	1984	1986	1988	1990	1992	1994	1996	1998	2000
Democrats													
DNC	13.1	11.3	15.4	16.5	46.6	17.2	52.3	14.5	65.8	41.8	108.4	64.8	124.0
DCCC	.9	2.8	2.9	6.5	10.4	12.3	12.5	9.1	12.8	19.4	26.6	25.2	48.4
DSCC	1.0	.3	1.7	5.6	8.9	13.4	16.3	17.5	25.5	26.4	30.8	35.6	40.5
Total	15.0	14.4	20.0	28.6	65.9	42.9	81.1	41.1	104.1	87.6	165.8	125.6	212.9
Republicans													
RNC	29.1	34.2	77.8	84.1	105.9	83.8	91.0	68.7	85.4	87.4	193.0	104.0	212.8
NRCC	12.1	14.1	20.3	58.0	58.3	39.8	34.7	33.2	35.2	26.7	74.2	72.7	97.3
NRSC	1.8	10.9	22.3	48.9	81.7	86.1	65.9	65.1	73.8	65.3	64.5	53.4	51.5
Total	43.0	59.2	120.4	191.0	245.9	209.7	191.6	167.0	194.4	179.4	331.7	230.1	361.6

Source: Federal Election Commission press releases.

Note: All figures include funds raised from January 1 of the year preceding the election through December 31 of the election year.

The GOP's financial advantage reflects a number of factors. The Republican committees began developing their direct-mail solicitation programs earlier and adopted a more business-like approach to fund-raising. The demographics of their supporters also make it easier for the Republican committees to raise money. The GOP's supporters possess greater wealth and education, and are more likely to be business executives or owners. These individuals are accustomed to spending money to improve their material interests (Francia et al. 1999). For many of them, making a campaign contribution is not far removed from paying dues to a trade association. Finally, the Republicans' minority status in Congress provided them with a powerful fund-raising weapon prior to the GOP takeover following the 1994 elections, as did Bill Clinton's occupancy of the White House after 1992. The GOP used its minority-party status in Congress and out-party status vis-à-vis the White House to attack the Democrats. Negative appeals, featuring attacks on those in power, are generally more successful in fund-raising than are appeals advocating the maintenance of the status quo (Godwin 1988).

The competitiveness over control of the House and Senate following the Republican takeover of Congress in 1995 helped fill both parties' campaign coffers. All three of the Democrats' Washington party committees set fund-raising records over the course of the 2000 election cycle. Combined, they collected $212.9, a 70 percent increase over the sum they had collected during the 1998 midterm elections and a 28 percent improvement over the amount they had raised to contest the 1996 presidential election year contests. Despite the fact that the NRSC raised less hard money during the 2000 election cycle than in the previous eight elections, the Republicans also raised record funds. The GOP's combined $361.6 million war chest is 57 percent larger than it was during the 1998 midterm elections and 9 percent larger than it was during the 1996 presidential contest.[4] Although the Democrats have made strides in improving their hard-money fund-raising programs, whether they can catch up to the GOP committees remains in question owing to the differences in the parties' constituencies.

The national parties raise most of their hard-money contributions of under $100 using direct mail. Telemarketing solicitations also are effective at raising funds from individuals who contribute because they care about salient issues or believe they will benefit economically when their preferred party has more clout in Washington. Fund-raising dinners, receptions, and personal solicitations are important vehicles for collecting contributions of all sizes, and are essential to raising large donations. Events are particularly effective for raising contributions of all sizes from individuals who enjoy the social aspects of politics (Brown, Powell, and Wilcox 1996; Webster et al. 2001).

National-party soft money, which is raised and spent largely outside the FECA regulations, is collected primarily by means of personal solicitations that routinely involve the participation of presidents, congressional leaders, and national party chairmen.[5] Soft money traditionally has been used to purchase or rent the buildings that house party operations, buy equipment, strengthen state and local party organizations, help finance national conventions and voter registration and get-out-the-vote drives, and broadcast generic television and radio advertisements designed to benefit the entire party ticket. The parties began to spend substantial sums of soft money to broadcast so-called "issue-advocacy" advertisements on television and radio during the 1996 elections, after the Supreme Court ruled that such ads were permissible (Potter 1997). Issue-advocacy ads resemble candidate ads in many ways. They focus on individual candidates, emphasize the candidate's campaign themes, are frequently aired on prime-time TV and radio, and use compelling visuals, music, and scripts. They are distinct in their financing, in that they cannot expressly advocate the election or defeat of a federal candidate, and in that they tend to be more negative or comparative than are candidate ads (Herrnson and Dwyre 1999; Krasno and Goldstein, 2001).

Issue-advocacy ads have provided parties with a new vehicle to campaign for their candidates and have increased the pressures on the national parties to raise more soft money. As a result, the parties' soft-money receipts have escalated dramatically, especially when compared with their hard-money receipts. During the 2000 election cycle, the Democratic national party committees raised $245.2 million in soft money, and the Republicans collected $249.9 million. These figures represent increases of 162 percent over 1998 and 98 percent over 1996 for the Democrats, and 89 percent and 81 percent for the Republicans. Soft money accounted for 53 and 41 percent, respectively, of the national Democrats' and the national Republicans' receipts in 2000.

Soft-money donors include wealthy individuals, corporations, trade associations, unions, and other organizations. They possess many of the same motives as do individuals and groups that contribute hard money. The perks that donors who give large amounts of soft or hard money receive are considerable, including opportunities to attend events and briefings hosted by the President, cabinet officials, or congressional leaders. They generally ensure donors access to powerful members of the government.

Table 3.2   National Party Soft Money Receipts, 1992–2000 (in million $)

Party	1992	1994	1996	1998	2000
Democrats					
DNC	31.4	43.9	101.9	57.0	136.6
DCCC	4.4	5.1	12.3	16.9	56.7
DSCC	.6	.4	14.2	25.9	63.7
Total	36.3	49.1	123.9	92.8	245.2
Republicans					
RNC	35.9	44.9	113.1	74.8	166.2
NRCC	6.1	7.4	18.5	26.9	47.3
NRSC	9.1	5.6	29.4	37.9	44.7
Total	49.8	59.2	138.2	131.6	249.9

Source: Federal Election Commission, "FEC Reports Increase in Party Fundraising for 2000," press release, May 15, 2001.

Note: Totals do not include transfers among the committees.

The Democrats' top 10 soft-money donors in 2000 were seven labor unions, two commercial enterprises, and a so-called "joint fund-raising committee" or "victory committee" that was created to boost First Lady Hillary Rodham Clinton's successful bid to become senator from New York. The victory committee, New York Senate 2000, which was affiliated with the Democratic party, contributed almost $8.6 million to the DSCC. The Republicans' top donors were heavily weighted toward the corporate sector, including such industrial giants as AT&T, Philip Morris, and Bristol-Meyers Squibb. The National Rifle Association and the Republican Party of California also contributed large sums. The party's soft-money donor bases reflect their underlying constituencies: the Democrats rely heavily on organized labor and the entertainment industry; the Republicans call on the corporate sector and conservative groups for support. The contributions of New York Senate 2000 and the California GOP are part of a larger scheme of arrangements that enables the parties to raise more money, swap hard money for soft money, and deliver the appropriate mix of funds where they will have their greatest impact on elections.[6]

Infrastructure

Success in fund-raising has enabled the national parties to invest in the development of their organizational infrastructures. Prior to their institutionalization, the national party organizations had no permanent head-

Table 3.3   Top Soft Money Donors to the Political Parties

Democratic Donors	
New York Senate 2000	8,585,961
AFSCME	5,949,000
Service Employees International Union	4,257,696
Carpenters & Jointers Union	2,873,500
Communications Workers of America	2,405,000
United Food & Commercial Workers Union	2,146,450
International Brotherhood of Electrical Workers	1,730,000
American Federation of Teachers	1,657,000
Slim-Fast Foods/Thompson Medical	1,543,000
Saban Entertainment	1,496,000
Republican Donors	
AT&T	2,423,151
Philip Morris	2,086,812
Bristol-Myers Squib	1,527,701
National Rifle Association	1,489,222
Pfizer Inc.	1,398,817
Freddie Mac	1,373,250
Republican Party of California	1,325,000
Microsoft Corp.	1,313,384
Enron Corp.	1,138,990
Amway/Alticor Inc.	1,138,500

Source: Center for Responsive Politics, www.opensecrets.org/parties/asp/
softop.asp?/txrCycle=2000&Sort=amnt [June 4, 2001].

quarters. For a while, the four Hill committees were headquartered in small offices in congressional office buildings. Upon leaving congressional office space they became transient, following the national committees' example of moving at the end of each election cycle in search of inexpensive office facilities. The national parties' lack of permanent office space created security problems, made it difficult for the parties to conduct routine business, and did little to bolster their standing in Washington (Cotter and Hennessy 1964).

All six national party organizations are now housed in party-owned headquarters buildings located only a few blocks from the Capitol. The headquarters buildings furnish the committees with convenient locations for carrying out fund-raising events and holding meetings with candidates, PACs, journalists, and campaign consultants. They also provide a secure environment for the committees' computers, records, and radio and television studios (Herrnson 1988).

Staff

Each national party organization has a two-tiered structure consisting of members and professional staff. The members of the Republican and Democratic national committees are selected by state parties and the members of the Hill committees are selected by their colleagues in Congress. The national parties' staffs have grown tremendously in recent years. Republican committee staff development accelerated following the party's Watergate scandal, while the Democratic party experienced most of its staff growth after the 1980 election. In 2000, the DNC, DCCC, and DSCC employed 150, 75, and 40 full-time staff, while their Republican counterparts had 250, 63, and 75 full-time employees.[7] Committee staffs are divided along functional lines; different divisions are responsible for administration, fund-raising, research, communications, and campaign activities. The staffs have a great deal of autonomy in running the committees day-to-day operations and are extremely influential in formulating their campaign strategies (Herrnson 1989, 2000).

Relationships with Interest Groups and Political Consultants

Although it was first believed that the rise of the political consultants and the proliferation of PACs would hasten the decline of parties (Sabato 1981; Crotty 1984; Adamanay 1984), it is now recognized that many political consultants and PACs try to cooperate with the political parties (Herrnson 1988; Sabato 1988; Kolodny 2000). Few if any would seek to destroy the parties. National party organizations, consultants, PACs, and other interest groups frequently work together in pursuit of their common goals. Fund-raising is one area of party-PAC cooperation; the dissemination of information and the backing of particular candidates are others (Herrnson 2000). National party organizations handicap races for PACs and arrange "meet and greet" sessions for PACs and candidates. The national parties also mail, telephone, and "fax" large quantities of information to PACs in order to advise them of developments in competitive elections. Some PAC managers use party-supplied information when making contribution decisions.

Relations between the national party organizations and political consultants also have become more cooperative. During election years, the national parties facilitate contacts and agreements between their candidates and political consultants. The parties also hire outside consultants to assist with polling and advertising and to furnish candidates with campaign services. During nonelection years, the parties hire private consultants to assist with long-range planning. These arrangements enable the parties to draw upon the expertise of the industry's premier consulting firms and provide the consultants with steady employment, which is especially important between election cycles.

The symbiotic relationships that have developed between the national parties, political consultants, PACs, and other interest groups can be further appreciated by looking at the career paths of people working in electoral politics. Employment at one of the national party organizations can now serve as a stepping stone or a high point in the career of a political operative. A pattern that has become increasingly common is for consultants to begin their careers working in a low-level position for a small consulting firm, campaign, PAC, or other interest group, then to be hired by one of the national party organizations, and then to leave the party organization to form their own political consulting firm or to accept an executive position with a major consulting firm, PAC, or interest group. Finding employment outside the national parties rarely results in the severing of relations between consultants and the national party organizations. It is common for the parties to hire past employees and their firms to conduct research, give strategic or legal advice, or provide campaign services to candidates. The "revolving door" of national party employment provides political professionals with opportunities to gain experience, make connections, establish credentials that can help them move up the hierarchy of political operatives, and maintain profitable relationships with the national parties after they have gained employment elsewhere.

Party Building

The institutionalization of the national party organizations has provided them with the resources to develop a variety of party-building programs. The majority of these are conducted by the two national committees. Many current RNC party-building efforts were initiated in 1976 under the leadership of Chairman Brock. Brock's program for revitalizing state party committees consisted of (1) appointing regional political directors to assist state party leaders in strengthening their organizations and utilizing RNC services; (2) hiring organizational directors to help rebuild state party organizations; (3) appointing regional finance directors to assist state parties with developing fund-raising programs; (4) making computer services available to state parties for accounting, fund-raising, and analyzing survey data; and (5) organizing a task force to assist parties with developing realistic election goals and strategies. Brock also established a Local Elections Campaign Division to assist state parties with creating district profiles and recruiting candidates, to provide candidate training and campaign management seminars, and to furnish candidates for state or local office with on-site campaign assistance (Bibby 1981; Conway 1983).

Frank Fahrenkopf, RNC chair from 1981 to 1988, expanded many of Brock's party-building programs and introduced some new ones. The national committee continues to give Republican state parties financial assistance and help them with fund-raising, and the NRCC and NRSC began to do so in recent years. An RNC computerized information network created during the 1984 election cycle furnishes Republican state and local party organizations and candidates with issue and opposition research, newspaper clippings, and other sorts of electoral information. RNC publications such as *First Monday* and *County Line* provide Republican candidates, party leaders, and activists with survey results, issue research, and instructions on how to conduct campaign activities ranging from fund-raising to grassroots organizing.

DNC party-building activities lag slightly behind those of its Republican counterpart and did not become significant until the 1986 election. During that election Chairman Paul Kirk created a task force of 32 professional consultants who were sent to 16 states to assist Democratic state committees with fund-raising, computerizing voter lists, and other organizational activities. In later elections, task forces were sent to more states to help modernize and strengthen their Democratic party committees. The task forces are credited with improving Democratic state party fund-raising, computer capacities, and voter mobilization programs and with helping Democratic state and local committees reach the stage of organizational development achieved by their Republican rivals in earlier years.

National committee party-building programs have helped to strengthen, modernize, and professionalize many state and local party organizations. These programs have altered the balance of power within the parties' organizational apparatuses. The national parties' ability to distribute or withhold money, party-building assistance, and other help gives them influence over the operations of state and local party committees. The DNC's influence is enhanced by its rule-making and enforcement authority.[8] As a result of these developments, the traditional flow of power upward from state and local party organizations to the national committees has been complemented by a new flow of power downward from the national parties to state and local parties. The institutionalization of the national party organizations has enabled them to become more influential in party politics and has led to a greater federalization of the American party system (Wekkin 1985).

National Party Campaigning

The institutionalization of the national parties has provided them the wherewithal to play a larger role in elections, and national party campaign activity has increased tremendously since the 1970s. Still, the electoral activities of the national parties, and party organizations in general, remain constrained by electoral law, established custom, and the level of resources in the parties' possession.

Candidate Recruitment and Nominations

Most candidates for elective office in the United States are self-recruited and conduct their own nomination campaigns. The DNC and the RNC have a hand in establishing the basic guidelines under which presidential nominations are contested, but their role is defined by the national conventions and their recommendations are subject to convention approval. The rules governing Democratic presidential nominations are more extensive than those governing GOP contests, but state committees of both parties have substantial leeway in supplying the details of their delegate selection processes.

Neither the DNC nor the RNC expresses a preference for candidates for its party's presidential nomination. Such activity would be disastrous should a candidate who was backed by a national committee be defeated, because the successful unsupported candidate would become the head of the party's ticket and its titular leader. As a result, candidates for the nomination assemble their own campaign staffs and compete independent of the party apparatus in state-run primaries and caucuses. Successful candidates arrive at the national convention with seasoned campaign organizations comprising experienced political operatives.

The national party organizations may, however, get involved in selected nominating contests for House, Senate, and state-level offices. They actively recruit some candidates to enter primary contests and just as actively discourage others from doing so. Most candidate recruitment efforts are concentrated in competitive districts, where a party seeks to nominate the best-qualified candidate for the district. However, party officials also encourage candidates to enter primaries in districts that are safe for the opposing party so that the general election will not be uncontested. The GOP used this latter approach in the late 1970s, 1980s, and early 1990s to strengthen its party organizations and candidate pool in the South. The strategy ultimately paid off in 1994, when the increased number of southern members helped the party win control of Congress.

When participating in candidate recruitment, national party staff in Washington, D.C., and regional coordinators in the field meet with state and local party leaders to identify potential candidates and encourage them to enter primaries. Party leaders and staff use polls, the promise of party campaign money and services, and the persuasive talents of party leaders, members of Congress, and even presidents to influence the decisions of potential candidates. Once two or more candidates enter a primary, however, the national party organizations rarely take one candidate's side. Situations where a party member challenges an incumbent traditionally have been the major exception to the rule. The NRCC also occasionally has backed a nonincumbent candidate for a Democratic-occupied or open seat when the candidate's entire state delegation in the House and local party leaders have endorsed such a decision. Until the

2000 elections, the DCCC avoided involvement in contested primaries. However, during these elections the committee took the unprecedented step of endorsing four primary candidates and one candidate involved in a primary runoff. Three of these candidates—California assemblyman Mike Honda, Kentucky state representative Eleanor Jordan, and Arkansas state senator Mike Ross—won their nominations, and Honda and Ross were ultimately elected. Nevertheless, the DCCC's involvement in the other two contests put the committee in the awkward position of trying to convince campaign donors, voters, and the media that the candidates the party had originally opposed were worthy of support. The Democrats ultimately lost both races.

The Democrats' control over most state and local offices traditionally gave them an advantage in candidate recruitment. Prior to the 1990s the NRCC had only limited success in encouraging candidates to run for the House who had either held elective office or had significant unelective experience in politics. The Republicans' lack of a congressional "farm team," particularly the small numbers of Republican state legislators and municipal officials, was thought by many to be a major contributor to its persistence as the minority party in the House (Ehrenhalt 1991). However, by the 1994 elections the party-building and candidate recruitment and training efforts of the RNC, GOPAC (a leadership PAC sponsored by House Republicans), and Republican state and local party organizations had begun to pay off, significantly increasing the number of Republicans occupying state and local offices.

The NRCC also turned to other talent pools in search of House candidates in 1994. Although previous officeholding experience is thought by many to be the mark of a well-qualified Democratic House challenger, strong Republican candidates have traditionally come from more diverse backgrounds. Political aides, party officeholders, previously unsuccessful candidates, administration officials, and other "unelected politicians" have long been an important source of strong Republican, as well as Democratic, House candidates (Canon 1990; Herrnson 1994, 2000). Wealthy individuals have often been viewed by GOP and Democratic strategists as good candidates because of their ability to finance significant portions of their own campaigns.

The GOP's party-building and recruitment efforts resulted in its fielding record numbers of challenger and open-seat contestants in 1994, making it the first contest in recent history in which more Republicans than Democrats ran for the House and more Republican-held than Democratic-held House seats went uncontested. From that campaign through the 2000 elections the Republicans continued to field more candidates than the Democrats.

National party candidate recruitment and primary activities are not intended to do away with the dominant pattern of self-selected candidates assembling their own campaign organizations to compete for their party's nomination. Nor are these activities designed to restore the turn-of-the-century pattern of local party leaders' selecting the parties' nominees. Rather, most national party activity is geared toward encouraging or discouraging the candidacies of a small group of politicians who are considering running in competitive districts. Less focused recruitment efforts attempt to arouse the interests of a broader group of party activists by informing them of the campaign assistance available to candidates who make it to the general election (Herrnson 1988, 2000).

National Conventions

The national conventions are technically a part of the nomination process. After the 1968 reforms were instituted, however, the conventions lost control of their nominating function and became more of a public relations event than a decision-making one. Conventions still have platform-writing and rule-making responsibilities, but these are overshadowed by speeches and other events designed to attract the support of voters.

The public relations component of the national conventions reached new heights during the 1980s and 1990s. Contemporary conventions are known for technically sophisticated video presentations and choreographed pageantry. Convention activities are designed to be easily dissected into sound bites suited for television news programs. National committee staffs formulate strategies to ensure that television newscasters put a desirable "spin" on television news coverage. Any disputes that arise among convention delegates over party rules or platforms are resolved in meeting rooms where they attract relatively little media attention. Protestors are directed to special "protest sites" away from the convention halls so as to minimize coverage by the press.

Both parties' 2000 national conventions were public relations extravaganzas, featuring dynamic speakers and engaging video clips. The Democratic National Convention stressed education, health care, and social security. The party emphasized its youthfulness and diversity by featuring speakers such as Representatives Jesse Jackson, Jr., of Illinois and Harold E. Ford, Jr., of Tennessee, as well as the New York Senate candidate, Hillary Rodham Clinton. The Republican National Convention stressed similar issues, as well as tax cuts and defense policy. It showcased George P. Bush, the GOP nominee George W. Bush's nephew and a Latino, retired General Colin Powell, Condoleezza Rice, and Senator John McCain of Arizona in an effort to present a show of diversity and party unity.

Convention organizers have made special efforts to cultivate the media at recent conventions. Both parties have given television stations across the country the opportunity to use live satellite feed from their conventions in their nightly news shows. In 1996, the Republicans set a new precedent when they went so far as to televise their own convention coverage and broadcast it over the Family Channel, Pat Robertson's cable-TV station.

Not all members of the press are happy with the made-for-television aspects of modern conventions. Some have complained that the conventions have become extended campaign commercials that no longer generate any real news. In 1996, Ted Koppel, the host of the television news show *Nightline,* became so disenchanted with the packaged quality of the Republican convention that he departed early and stayed away from the Democratic convention entirely. The 2000 conventions received only limited media coverage.

The national parties also conduct less visible convention activities to help nonpresidential candidates with their bids for office. Congressional and senatorial candidates are given access to television and radio satellite up-links and taping facilities. The Hill committees also sponsor "meet-and-greet" sessions to introduce their most competitive challengers and open-seat candidates to PACs, individual big contributors, party leaders, and the press. The atrophy of the national conventions' nominating function has been partially offset by an increase in its general election–related activities.

The General Election

Presidential Elections.   Party activity in presidential elections is restricted by the public funding provisions of the FECA. Major-party candidates who accept public funding are prohibited from accepting contributions from any other sources, including the political parties. The amount that the national parties can spend directly on behalf of their presidential candidates is also limited. In 2000, the Republican nominee George W. Bush and Vice President Al Gore each received just under $67.6 million in general election subsidies for the 2000 election. The national committees were allowed to spend almost $13.7 million each on "coordinated expenditures" made on behalf of their presidential candidates. Most of these monies were spent on research, polling, media advertising, or other activities to expressly advocate the candidate's election. Both the party and the candidate have a measure of control over what is purchased with coordinated expenditures.

The legal environment reinforces the candidate-centered nature of presidential elections in other ways. Rules requiring candidates for the nomination to compete in primaries and caucuses guarantee that successful candidates will enter the general election with their own sources of technical expertise, in-depth research, and connections with journalists and other Washington elites. These reforms traditionally have combined with the provisions of the FECA to create a regulatory framework that limits national-party activity and influence in presidential elections.

Nevertheless, the national parties do play an important role in presidential elections. The national committees furnish presidential campaigns with legal and strategic advice and public relations assistance. National committee opposition research and archives serve as important sources of political information. The hard money that the national committees spend on coordinated expenditures can boost the total resources under the candidates' control by over 15 percent.

The national committees also assist their candidates' campaigns by distributing both hard and soft money to state parties that the latter use to finance voter mobilization drives, party-building activities, and issue-advocacy ads. During the 2000 elections, the DNC transferred $114.6 million to state and local parties and the RNC transferred $129.1 million, much of it to help their presidential candidates. The national committees transferred the money to state party committees rather than broadcast the ads themselves because under Federal Election Commission regulations state parties are allowed to spend more soft money for every dollar they spend in hard money than national parties. The rise of issue advocacy has enabled the national parties to become very involved in their candidates' campaigns. In fact, the 2000 election marks the first time the political parties spent more on television advertising than the presidential candidates did. The Democrats spent an estimated $35.2 million on issue ads to help the Gore-Lieberman ticket, and the Republicans spent an estimated $44.7 million to improve Bush and Cheney's prospects. The two presidential campaigns combined spent only $67.1 million. Numerous allied interest groups also spent roughly $16.1 million on issue ads to influence the presidential elections (Brennan Center for Justice 2000).[9]

Congressional Elections. The national party organizations also play a big role in congressional elections. They contribute money and campaign services directly to congressional candidates and provide transactional assistance that helps candidates obtain other resources from other politicians, political consultants, and PACs. They also broadcast issue-advocacy ads to win voter support for their candidates. Most national-party assistance is distributed by the Hill committees to candidates competing in close elections, especially to nonincumbents. This reflects the committees' goal of maximizing the number of congressional seats under their control (Jacobson 1985; Herrnson 1989, 2000).

As is the case with presidential elections, the FECA limits party activity in congressional races. National, congressional, and state party organizations are each allowed to contribute $5,000 to House candidates. The parties' national and senatorial campaign committees are allowed to give a combined total of $17,500 to Senate candidates; state party organizations can give $5,000. National party organizations and state party committees also are allowed to make coordinated expenditures on behalf of congressional candidates. Originally set at $10,000 per committee, the limits for coordinated expenditures on behalf of House candidates were adjusted for inflation and reached $33,780 in 2000.[10] The limits for coordinated expenditures in Senate elections vary by the size of a state's population and are also indexed to inflation. They ranged from $67,560 per committee in the smallest states to $1.64 million per committee in California during the 2000 elections. In addition to directly giving these contributions, the four Hill committees also encourage current and former members of Congress to contribute money from their leadership PACs and campaign accounts to congressional candidates. These "party-connected" contributions are subject to the FECA's $5,000 contribution limit for leadership PACs and a $1,000 limit for other political committees.[11]

Republican party organizations made almost twice as much in contributions and coordinated expenditures in 2000 as did their Democrat rivals, reflecting the GOP's longstanding advantage in raising hard money. Most party hard money, especially in Senate elections, is distributed as coordinated expenditures, reflecting the higher legal limits imposed by the FECA. Most of these funds originate at one of the Hill committees and are distributed in accordance with the spending strategies they formulate. The Hill committees routinely make arrangements with national and state party committees that allow them to increase their roles in the financing of congressional campaigns. In the past, when state party committees were short on hard dollars, the Hill committees used to make agency agreements allowing them to assume some of the state party committees' coordinated expenditures. More recently the Hill committees have swapped their soft money for the state parties' hard money, paying the state parties a 10 to 15 percent premium for the exchange. This has enabled the Hill committees to spend more hard dollars in competitive congressional races. The Hill committees make some of these expenditures directly as contributions or coordinated expenditures. They make others indirectly by transferring the funds to the party's national committee or to a state party organization with explicit instructions on how the funds are to be spent. By means of these complicated transactions the Hill committees maneuver within and around the law to concentrate their resources in close House and Senate races (Dwyre and Kolodny 2002).

"Party-connected" contributions are another set of financial transactions involving parties (Herrnson 2000). These are made by current or former members of Congress and the leadership and the PACs they sponsor rather

Table 3.4   Party Contributions and Coordinated Expenditures in the 2000 Congressional Elections ($).

	House		Senate	
	Contributions	Coordinated Expenditures	Contributions	Coordinated Expenditures
Democrats				
DNC	$10,215	$12,323	$0	$968,408
DCCC	573,925	2,593,614	840	0
DSCC	5,000	0	285,530	127,157
State and local	401,769	733,086	76,600	3,987,495
Total	990,909	3,339,023	362,970	5,083,060
Republicans				
RNC	$400,000	$1,149,350	$0	$9,002,290
NRCC	688,158	3,696,877	10,611	0
NRSC	10,000	0	372,334	172
State and local	657,451	393,811	144,597	1,838,099
Total	1,755,609	5,240,038	527,542	10,840,561

Source: Federal Election Commission, "FEC Reports Increase in Party Fundraising for 2000," press release, May 15, 2001.

than by formal party committees. Leadership PAC contributions, like PAC contributions generally, are limited to $5,000 in each stage of the campaign (primary, general election, and runoff). Contributions from the campaign account of one member of Congress (or from the account of a retired member or a member who is leaving office) to another candidate's campaign account are limited to $1,000 in each stage of the campaign. During the 2000 elections, party-connected contributions to House candidates exceeded $17.5 million, amounting to almost 55 percent more funds than the party committees distributed in contributions and coordinated expenditures. Senate candidates raised a total of $4.1 million in party-connected contributions, 277 percent less than they raised in party contributions and coordinated expenditures. The comparatively generous ceilings for party coordinated expenditures in Senate races and the small number of senators and senator-sponsored leadership PACs largely account for the differences between House and Senate elections.

Republican House candidates typically receive more financial assistance from party committees than their opponents. The same holds true for party-connected contributions they raise from members of Congress, congressional retirees, and leadership PACs. During the 2000 elections both the Democratic and Republican party organizations targeted open House seats for their largest contributions and coordinated expenditures because these races tend to be the most competitive. Candidates for those seats received more party contributions, coordinated expenditures, and party-connected contributions, on average, than did incumbents or challengers. They also spent more. These generalizations hold true for candidate expenditures and total spending, which includes party coordinated expenditures. The figures for the party share of total spending indicate that party money made up a larger share of the typical open-seat candidates' campaign resources than it did the typical incumbent's or challenger's resources.

There are some important partisan differences in the candidates' campaign receipts and in their contribution strategies for 2000. GOP incumbents collected substantially more party support than their Democratic counterparts because more Republican House members were involved in close races, and the NRCC had a strong commitment to protect them. Republican open-seat candidates also raised substantially more party-connected contributions than their Democratic counterparts, reflecting the GOP's greater wealth. Democratic challengers were the only group of House candidates who raised close to the same amount, on average, as their Republican counterparts. Last, Republican House candidates, particularly candidates for open seats, were more dependent on party support for their finances than Democratic candidates.

Party activity in the 2000 Senate elections shows both similarities with and differences from party efforts in House elections. Republican Senate candidates raised more party-connected contributions on average than their Democratic opponents. The disparities were greatest among challengers and open-seat contestants. Republican open-seat candidates were especially reliant on parties for support, raising on average nearly $1.1 million, or 12 percent of their resources, from party committees and other party-connected sources of support.

Of course, parties consider more than incumbency when distributing campaign resources. Most party money is targeted to competitive elections. During the 2000 elections, formal party committees, current and former members of Congress, and their leadership PACs contributed $150,000 or more in connection with each of 78 House candidacies and $1,000 or less in connection with 255 others.[12] Challengers who show little promise and incumbents in safe seats usually receive only token sums, whereas incumbents in jeopardy, competitive challengers, and contestants for open seats typically benefit from large party expenditures. Party money played a decisive role in at least a few House contests. In the open-seat race in West Virginia's 2nd Congressional District, for example, Republicans gave Shelley Moore

Table 3.5:   Average Party Contributions in the 2000 Congressional Elections ($)

	House			*Senate*		
	Incumbent	*Challenger*	*Open Seat*	*Incumbent*	*Challenger*	*Open Seat*
Democratic Party						
Party contributions	$1,792	$2,216	$6,103	$8,073	$11,890	$10,900
Party coordinated expenditures	4,945	6,972	34,004	249,168	23,794	382,870
Party-connected contributions	18,251	12,290	56,922	32,095	40,517	66,602
Candidate expenditures	810,295	358,327	1,035,729	3,665,803	3,276,504	23,311,843
Total spending	886,125	371,056	1,080,366	4,224,634	3,314,082	23,765,106
Party share of total spending	2.0%	4.0%	8.0%	6.0%	5.0%	3.0%
(N)	(170)	(166)	(34)	(11)	(17)	(5)
Republican Party						
Party contributions	$2,958	$3,322	$15,468	$17,451	$11,230	$19,385
Party coordinated expenditures	8,020	8,788	44,009	225,573	147,173	879,367
Party-connected contributions	26,741	13,535	95,618	85,067	26,449	176,293
Candidate expenditures	958,541	239,890	1,262,790	5,142,573	1,712,091	12,473,350
Total spending	1,039,313	249,781	1,327,580	5,161,844	1,903,024	12,906,438
Party share of total spending	3.0%	5.0%	11.0%	5.0%	6.0%	12.0%
(N)	(166)	(170)	(34)	(17)	911)	(5)

Source: Compiled from Federal Election commission data and Center for Responsive Politics data.

Notes: Includes general election candidates in major-party contested races only. Total spending equals candidate expenditures plus party coordinated expenditures. Party share of total spending denotes the percentage of all campaign money provided by a party committee or politician over which the candidate had some control (party contributions, party coordinated expenditures, party-connected contributions).

Capito $14,649 in contributions, $56,814 in coordinated expenditures, and $203,438 in party-connected money, accounting for 19 percent of the $1,367,504 that was under her control. These funds were instrumental in helping her defeat the Democrat, Gordon Humphreys, who

spent $6,969,933 on the race, including more than $6.1 million he contributed himself.[13]

The discrepancies in party spending in Senate elections were even
greater, in part reflecting party strategy, electoral competition, and the
FECA's contribution and spending limits. At one extreme, the Democratic
party committees, politicians, and their leadership PACs contributed $1.9
million in contributions and coordinated expenditures to help Hillary
Clinton. The Republicans spent almost $1.9 million in hard money to
help Clinton's opponent, Congressman Rick Lazio.[14] At the other extreme, in Minnesota the Democratic Senate challenger, Mark Dayton,
who defeated the one-term Republican incumbent, Rodney Grams, received no party contributions, coordinated expenditures, or party-connected contributions from his party. Dayton's millions—his ability to sink
$11.8 million of his own funds into his campaign treasury—encouraged
the Democrats to focus their resources in other elections.[15]

Even though individuals and PACs still furnish candidates with most
of their campaign funds, political parties currently are the largest single
source of campaign money for most candidates. Party money comes from
one, or at most a few, organizations that are primarily concerned with
one goal—the election of their candidates. Individual and PAC contributions, on the other hand, come from a multitude of sources that are motivated by a variety of concerns. In addition, it is important to recognize
that dollar-for-dollar, national party money has greater value than the
contributions of other groups. National party contributions and coordinated expenditures often take the form of in-kind campaign services that
are worth many times more than their reported value. Moreover, national
party money is often accompanied by fund-raising assistance that helps
candidates attract additional money from PACs. National party issue advocacy also draws donors' attention to close congressional races.

In addition, the national parties furnish many congressional candidates with a variety of campaign services. Most of these are distributed
to competitive contestants, especially those who are nonincumbents.
National party help is more likely to have an impact on the outcomes of
campaigns waged by competitive nonincumbents than those of incumbents holding safe seats or nonincumbents challenging them (Herrnson
1988, 2000).

The national parties hold training seminars for candidates and campaign managers, introduce candidates and political consultants to each
other, and frequently provide candidates with in-kind contributions or
coordinated expenditures consisting of campaign services. They help
congressional campaigns file reports with the Federal Election
Commission and perform other administrative, clerical, and legal tasks.
Most important, the national parties furnish candidates with strategic assistance. Hill committee field workers visit campaign headquarters to

help candidates develop campaign plans, develop and respond to attacks, and perform other crucial campaign activities.

The national party organizations assist congressional candidates with gauging public opinion in three ways. They distribute analyses of voter attitudes on issues and report the mood of the national electorate. The Hill committees also conduct district-level analyses of voting patterns exhibited in previous elections to help congressional candidates in competitive contest locate where their supporters reside. They also commission surveys for a small group of competitive candidates to help them ascertain their name recognition, electoral support, and the impact that their campaign communications are having on voters.

National party assistance in campaign communications takes many forms. All six national party organizations disseminate issue information on traditional party positions and the policy stances of incumbent presidents or presidential candidates. The Hill committees send to competitive candidates issue packets consisting of hundreds of pages detailing issues that are likely to attract media coverage and win the support of specific voting blocs. The packets also include suggestions for exploiting an opponent's weaknesses. Additional research is disseminated by party leaders in Congress (Herrnson, Patterson, and Pitney 1996).

The national party organizations also helped some candidates with mass media advertising in 2000. From the late 1970s through the late 1990s, the NRCC used its media studios and editing suites to help many of its competitive candidates produce TV and radio spots. The DCCC provided similar help to its candidates during the 1980s and 1990s. The development of inexpensive video cameras and desktop publishing software reduced the demand for these services, and the media studios' primary use changed from electioneering to incumbent communications prior to the 2000 campaign season. The congressional campaign committees gave fewer candidates hands-on communications assistance.

Instead of this direct communications assistance, the Hill committees aired millions of dollars' worth of televised ads during the past three elections. In 2000 the Democrats televised 28,930 television ads, with an estimated worth of $24 million in House races. Virtually all of them were broadcast in the 41 closest House races. The Republicans aired 23,917 ads, worth an estimated $18.8 million, all of which were aired in close contests, including the Capito-Humphreys race in West Virginia. Most of the ads the parties broadcast in House races were issue-advocacy ads tailored to the candidates' districts and campaign themes.[16] A large portion of the ads were either negative or comparative in tone. Party ads accounted for about 22 percent of the total broadcast in these contests; candidates were responsible for 61 percent and interest groups for the remaining 17 percent (Herrnson 2002).[17] Only a tiny fraction of them even mentioned the party name. The messages conveyed in the ads demonstrate the degree to which the parties continue to conform to the candidate-centered environment rather than impose a party-focused message on it.

Traditionally the DSCC and NRSC have not become as deeply involved in their candidates' campaign communications, offering advice, criticisms, and occasionally pretesting their candidates' television and radio advertisements. The senatorial campaign committees played only a limited role because Senate candidates typically have enough money and experience to hire premier consultants on their own. The committee's roles changed somewhat in 1996 in response to the Supreme Court's rulings loosening up restrictions on party spending, which opened the door for the parties to make issue advocacy ads and independent expenditures (Potter 1997). The Democrats aired 30,610 ads at an estimated cost of $21.7 million in connection with the 2000 Senate election, and the Republicans aired 22,412, worth an estimated $15.8 million.[18] All of these ads appeared in media operating in districts of the 12 most competitive contests. Party ads accounted for 23 percent of the advertising in Senate elections; candidates aired 72 percent of them and interest groups the remaining 5 percent (Herrnson 2002).[19] As was the case with party ads broadcast in conjunction with House elections, the party ads designed to influence Senate races were candidate-focused.

The national parties help their congressional candidates raise money from individuals and PACs both in Washington, D.C., and in their election districts. As noted earlier, many congressional party leaders contribute money from their campaign accounts and leadership PACs to junior members and nonincumbents involved in close contests. The leaders also help these members raise money from wealthy individuals and PACs. During the 2000 elections, House leaders carried out an unprecedented effort to redistribute the wealth to other candidates.

The Hill committees help congressional candidates organize fund-raising events and develop direct-mail lists. The Hill committees' PAC directors help design the PAC kits many candidates use to introduce themselves to the PAC community, mail campaign progress reports, fax messages, and spend countless hours on the telephone with PAC managers. The goal of this activity is to get PAC money flowing to the party's most competitive candidates. National party endorsements, communications, contributions, and coordinated expenditures serve as decision-making cues that help PACs decide where to invest their money. National party services and transactional assistance are especially important to nonincumbents running for the House because they typically do not possess fund-raising lists from previous campaigns, are less skilled at fund-raising than incumbents, have none of the clout with PACs that comes with incumbency, and begin the election cycle virtually unknown to members of the PAC community.

Independent expenditures, made without the knowledge or consent of the candidates they are meant to help or harm, provide another avenue for party campaign activity. In the midst of the 1996 elections, the Supreme Court declared such expenditures permissible. In connection with the 2000 congressional elections the parties spent approximately $3.6 million in independent expenditures on items such as phone banks and direct mail. The congressional and senatorial campaign committees directly accounted for roughly 80 percent of the parties' independent expenditures in congressional races. Hill committee financial transfers are spent by state committees to supplement congressional candidates' campaigns with issue ads and grassroots efforts. During the 2000 elections, the two Republican Hill committees distributed nearly $58.3 million to GOP state party organizations, and the two Democratic committees distributed $76.8 million to their Democratic counterparts.

State and Local Elections.   There are both similarities and differences between national party activity in local election programs and in congressional elections. Some of the similarities are that the DNC, the RNC, and affiliated organizations such as the Democratic Legislative Campaign Committee and GOPAC work with state party leaders to recruit candidates, formulate strategy, and distribute campaign money and services. The national committees hold workshops to help state and local candidates learn the ins and outs of modern campaigning. The committees also recommend professional consultants and disseminate strategic and technical information through party magazines and briefing papers.

Despite the availability of the same type of help from national parties for local and congressional elections, there are important differences between what national parties will do in state and local contests compared to congressional elections. First, the parties give less campaign money and services to state and local candidates, reflecting the smaller size of state legislative districts and the committees' focus on national politics. During the 2000 elections, the Democratic and Republican national party organizations contributed $12.8 million and $6.1 million, respectively, to state and local party candidates. Second, national party strategy for distributing campaign money and services to state and local candidates is influenced by considerations related to House, Senate, and presidential races. In 1999, for example, Democratic party organizations and members of Congress contributed well in excess of $500,000 to Democratic state legislative candidates in Virginia, and national Republicans contributed roughly $1.3 million to their opponents. The GOP's donations were instrumental in helping the Republicans gain control of the state house and win control of the redistricting process in the state prior to the 2002 elections (Mercurio and Von Dongen 1999).

Party-Focused Campaigning. In addition to the candidate-focused campaign programs discussed above, the national parties conduct generic, or party-focused, election activities designed to benefit all candidates on the party ticket such as voter registration, helping voters apply for absentee ballots, get-out-the-vote drives, and other grassroots efforts. Many are financed by the national, congressional, and senatorial campaign committees and are conducted in cooperation with the parties' federal, state, and local party committees and candidates. National party organizations often provide the money and targeting information needed to perform these activities effectively, while state and local organizations provide foot soldiers who help carry them out.

Conclusion

American national party organizations were created to perform electoral functions. They developed in response to changes in their environment and the changing needs of their candidates. Internal pressures and the efforts of party leaders also influenced the national parties' development.

National party organizational change occurs sporadically. Electoral instability and political unrest have occasionally given party leaders opportunities to restructure the national parties. The most recent waves of party organizational development followed the turbulent 1968 Democratic convention, the Republicans' post-Watergate landslide losses, and the Democrats' traumatic defeat in 1980. These crises provided opportunities and incentives for party entrepreneurs to restructure the roles and missions of the national, congressional, and senatorial campaign committees.

Other opportunities for party change were created as a result of technological advances and changes in the regulatory environment in which the parties operate. The development of direct-mail techniques created new opportunities for party fund-raising, the advent of satellite communications enabled the parties to enhance their communications, and these and other technological advancements gave the parties a greater role in their candidates' campaigns. Recent Supreme Court rulings on issue advocacy and independent expenditures have had a similar impact. The content of these communications, particularly their focus on candidates, demonstrates that parties continue to conform to the candidate-centered style of American election campaigns.

The result is that the national parties are now stronger, more stable, and more influential in their relations with state and local party committees and candidates than ever. National party programs have led to the modernization of many state and local party committees. National parties also play an important role in contemporary elections. They help presidential candidates by supplementing their campaign communications and voter-mobilization efforts with party-sponsored campaign activities. The national parties also give congressional candidates campaign contributions, make coordinated expenditures and campaign communications on their behalf, and provide services in aspects of campaigning requiring technical expertise, in-depth research, or connections with political consultants, PACs, or other organizations possessing the resources needed to conduct a modern campaign. The national party committees play a smaller and less visible role in the campaigns of state and local candidates. Although most national party activity is concentrated in competitive elections, party-sponsored television and radio ads and voter mobilization efforts help candidates of varying degrees of competitiveness. The 1980s witnessed the reemergence of national party organizations. These organizations have become very important players in party politics and elections at the dawn of the twenty-first century.

Notes

1. The development of radio and especially television were particularly influential in bringing about an increased focus on candidate-centered election activities. These media are extremely well suited to conveying information about tangible political phenomena, such as candidate images, and less useful in providing information about more abstract electoral actors like political parties (Ranney 1983; Graber 1984; Robinson 1981; Sorauf 1980).

2. For further information about the roles that political entrepreneurs played in restructuring the national party organizations during the 1970s and 1980s, see Herrnson and Menefee-Libey (1990).

3. This power has been upheld by a number of court decisions, including U.S. Supreme Court decisions in *Cousins v. Wigoda* and *Democratic Party of the U.S. v. La Follette*. The DNC, however, has retreated from strict enforcement of some party rules. For example, it decided to allow Wisconsin to return to the use of its open primary to select delegates to the national convention following the 1984 election (Epstein 1986).

4. The term "soft money" was coined by Elizabeth Drew (1983). See also Corrado (1997).

5. The FECA requires that national party organizations disclose their soft-money receipts and expenditures. The amount of soft money a national party committee can transfer to a state is determined by means of a formula that takes into consideration the number of federal, state, and local offices up for election. American citizens, foreigners who are permanent U.S. residents, domestic corporations, and U.S. subsidiaries of foreign corporations can legally contribute soft money.

6. See Note 5.

7. Estimates provided by party committee staffs.

8. As explained in Note 3, the DNC has not been inclined to fully exercise this power.

9. The figures for issue ads include only ads broadcast in the nation's 75 largest media markets. Ad frequencies refer to the total number of ads of any type broadcast, not the number of unique ads aired. The figures for party and interest group issue-advocacy spending include only media buys, not production costs. Party group and candidate ads are not strictly comparable because broadcasters charged candidates the lowest unit rate, as required by law, and the parties were charged premium rates, which were considerably higher during the last few weeks of the election.

10. Coordinated expenditure limits for states with only one House member were set at $67,560 per committee in 2000.

11. These limits apply separately to each stage in the election (primary, general election, and runoff).

12. These figures include candidacies in two-party contested races only.

13. The Democrats made $5,500 in contributions, $34,044 in coordinated expenditures, $25,000 in party-connected contributions, and approximately $137,000 worth of issue ads on Humphrey's behalf.

14. Figures include party-connected contributions.

15. Grams received $630,535 in hard money from Republicans, and the GOP spent $685,821 to air 652 issue-advocacy ads on his behalf.

16. The parties spent roughly $2.6 million in independent expenditures in the 2000 House elections.

17. When measured in dollars, party spending accounted for 21 percent of all funds spent on televised ads for House candidates.

18. The figure for Republicans includes the Conservative party's spending for Lazio.

19. When measured in dollars, party spending accounted for 22 percent of all funds spent on televised ads for Senate elections.

4

Party Identification
and the Electorate at the Start
of the Twenty-First Century

WARREN E. MILLER
(Updated by Kenneth Goldstein and Mark Jones)

In 1952, at the same time the University of Michigan's Survey Research Center was conducting its first major study of electoral behavior in an American presidential election, V. O. Key, Jr., was bringing out the third edition of his classic text, *Politics, Parties, and Pressure Groups* (1952). In the opening paragraphs of Chapter 20, "Electoral Behavior: Inertia and Reaction," Key drew two broad conclusions about the American electorate:

> In substantial degree the electorate remains persistent in its partisan attachments. The time of casting a ballot is not a time of decision for many voters; it is merely an occasion for the reaffirmation of a partisan faith of long standing. . . . A second main characteristic evident in electoral behavior is that under some conditions voters do alter their habitual partisan affiliations. To what condition is their shift in attitude a response?

Latter-day political scientists have spent the better part of four decades testing these two conclusions and trying to answer Key's single question. Under the impetus of the Michigan research, "party identification" replaced "habitual partisan affiliation," but the basic terms of the query into the nature of the citizens' enduring partisan attachments have remained very much as Key identified them.

The results of the first four major Michigan studies of the national electorate were entirely in line with Key's first assertion as well as with his preoccupation with persistence and inertia as attributes of mass electoral behavior. From 1952 to 1964, national survey data, bolstered by a study that plotted individual change over time, documented a great persistence in citizens' identifications with the Democratic and Republican parties. There was a brief upturn in Democratic support in 1964, but it disappeared

Table 4.1   Party Identifications 1952–2000 by Gender, Region, and Race (%)

| Year | National Electorate [a] | | | | White Males | | White Females | | Blacks |
	D	I	R	B	South	Non-South	South	Non-South	
1952	47	26	27	20	59	8	54	5	39
1956	44	27	28	14	55	5	39	−3	31
1960	45	25	29	16	40	3	39	2	27
1964	52	24	25	27	43	15	46	14	65
1968	45	31	24	21	29	4	36	8	83
1972	40	36	24	17	21	5	24	8	60
1976	40	37	23	16	25	6	22	3	66
1980	41	37	22	18	15	4	20	12	67
1984	37	36	27	10	13	4	16	0	60
1988	35	37	28	8	0	−6	18	5	56
1992	35	39	26	10	1	−6	11	8	60
1996	38	33	29	10	−10	−6	12	11	61
2000	35	41	24	11	−19	−3	3	9	65
1980–2000	−6	+4	+2	−7	−34	−7	−17	−3	−2

Source: Michigan Survey Research Center of the Center for Political Studies, National Election Studies series.
Note: Entries are proportions of Republican identifiers, strong and weak, subtracted from proportions of Democratic identifiers, strong and weak. Data are for the entire eligible electorate.
[a] D=Democrat I=Independent R=Republican B=Balance.

four years later, drawing perhaps too little attention to a condition under which partisan attitudes had shifted. Other than that temporary perturbation, Democrats enjoyed a consistent 15- to 18-point edge over Republicans. During the same period, the measures of the strength or intensity of partisan attachments seemed to confirm the thesis of partisan stability; in election after election, strong identifiers outnumbered nonpartisans by virtually identical margins of about 25 percentage points.

Without destroying the suspense or giving away the story line (as the latter is not without its complexities), it is appropriate to note that the period from 1952 to 1964 is now often referred to as the "steady-state" era (Converse 1966). A series of inquiries into this era established party identification as distinctly different from the partisan character of the single vote, both in concept and in operational measure. The role of party identification as a predisposition that powerfully influences citizens' perceptions and judgments was spelled out (Campbell et al. 1960). And in some reifications or glorifications of more sober analysis, party identification was sometimes referred to as the "unmoved mover" or the "first cause" of electoral behavior.

Certainly, the evidence was all that V. O. Key could have hoped for as documentation of his hypothesis that partisan attachments had great stability at the level of the individual as well as that of the aggregate.

At the same time, the theme of party realignment continued to attract attention among political analysts. This was particularly so among Republican enthusiasts who saw in the Eisenhower victories (and the initial Republican congressional successes that accompanied them) the possibility of a resurgence for the Republican party. The narrow Kennedy victory in 1960, in the face of a presumably daunting Democratic plurality in the eligible electorate, added fuel to the Republican fire and, at least in part, aided the Republican nomination of Barry Goldwater in 1964 on the premise that he would mobilize latent conservative Republican sympathies and bring an end to the Democratic hegemony (Converse, Clausen, and Miller 1965).

Although the Goldwater candidacy was something less than a triumph of Republican expectations, another four years later the Republican Nixon was elected, and for the first time since systematic modern measurement had dominated social scientific analysis of electoral behavior, the bedrock of party identification cracked. The partisan balance was not disturbed and the Democratic dominance was unchanged, but the strength and intensity of partisanship declined. First in 1968, then in 1972, and finally again in 1976, each successive reading taken at election time revealed fewer strong partisans and more citizens devoid of any partisan preference.

Party Alignment, 1952–1980

Fortunately for the stability of the country, it was largely political scientists and not national leaders who reacted to the decline in the fortunes of party in the electorate. Political scientists, however, made the most of it, and many made far too much of it (Burnham 1975). Even though persuasive evidence of a national party realignment was not to appear for another 20 years,[1] the literature on parties, elections, and electoral behavior from 1968 on was replete with analysis and discourse on party dealignment and realignment. When such analysis rested on a proper disaggregation of national totals and the examinations of subsets of citizens experiencing real change under local political conditions, the facts are not in dispute. Change was occurring in the South (Beck 1977). Hindsight makes it particularly clear that change in party identification had begun among white southerners as early as 1956. A massive realignment was simply accentuated and accelerated in the late 1960s under the combined impetus of Goldwater's "southern strategy" and Johnson's promotion of civil rights. Legislation such as the Voting Rights Acts of 1964 and 1965, the other Great Society programs, and the economic as well as the foreign policies of the

Democratic party leaders in the 1970s and 1980s did not enthrall southern Democrats and instead persuaded them to turn to the Republican party (Black and Black 1987).

The most vivid contrast between the changes occurring in the South and the virtually total absence of change outside the South is provided in the comparison of white males in Table 4.1. In 1952, the one-party nature of the post–Civil War South was reflected in the fact that self-declared Democrats outnumbered Republicans among southern white males by 70 to 11.[2] The McGovern candidacy in 1972 saw that margin reduced to 42 to 21; and 1988 witnessed a virtual dead heat, 29 to 30. Apparently the Democratic candidacies of Johnson and Carter had slowed the tides of change without completely stemming them. Outside the South, there is no evidence among men or women of a trend either away from the Democrats or toward the Republicans until 1984. The year of Johnson's election, 1964, saw a brief surge of Democratic sympathies that was immediately followed by a decline, or return to "normalcy," among white citizens. Even so, the two regional patterns stand in stark contrast to each other.

The changing distributions of the party identifications of black citizens is, of course, a story unto itself. The figures in Table 4.1 understate the spectacular changes in the contributions of blacks to recent political history because they do not reflect the changes in the politicization and mobilization of blacks during the 1950s and 1960s.

The aggregation of the various patterns created by differences in gender, race, and region appears in the first columns of Table 4.1. The net result, nationally, does reflect meaningful year-by-year differences, but it also supports the overall conclusion that prior to 1984, there was little manifestation of a realignment that would end Democratic dominance of popular partisan loyalties.

Despite occasional Election Day evidence of some resurgence of Republican affinities and despite reports of increased Republican organizational strength, the dominance of Democrats over Republicans in the eligible electorate across the nation did not waver throughout the 1960s or 1970s. Even despite the election and reelection of Richard Nixon in the 1968 and 1972 presidential elections, the data on the underlying partisan balance of party identification did not change. Not even in the 1980s— when Ronald Reagan's victories gave the Republicans five out of six wins for the presidency, with another Republican landslide making history with the defeat of an incumbent (Democratic) president—was there a suggestion of basic changes in partisan sentiments outside the South.

In order to reconcile all the evidence of stability and change in party identification and in the vote between 1952 and 1980, it is necessary to separate the analyses of the directional balance of partisanship between Democrats and Republicans from the study of changes in the strength of party identification (i.e., the ratio of strong partisans to nonpartisans).

Table 4.2   Strength of Partisanship, by Four-Year Age Cohorts, 1952–2000

Age in 1952	Year of First Vote for President	1952	1956	1960	1964	1968	1972	1976	1980	1984	1988	1992	1996	2000	Age in 2000
	2000													−11	18–21
	1996												16	0	22–25
	1992											−1	10	3	26–29
	1988										5	1	11	4	30–32
	1984									0	6	4	16	21	33–36
	1980								−5	6	16	3	22	21	37–40
	1976							−9	−8	10	14	18	21	14	41–44
	1972						−10	−3	0	11	14	22	22	21	45–48
	1972					−1	−8	2	9	17	11	14	30		45–48
	1968				−4	−4	−1	10	10	16	20	42	31		49–52
	1964			16	−3	0	0	4	10	32	18	21	37		53–56
	1960		14	20	17	1	0	18	23	18	27	38	33		57–60
	1956	15	23	23	19	3	6	23	25	31	35	20	34		61–64
21–24	1952	23	13	17	25	27	12	11	23	36	35	21	30	19	65–68
25–28	1948	24	23	28	29	11	20	25	18	23	28	27	35	51	69–72
29–32	1944	23	23	24*	24	12	20	21	20	31	31	38	29	21	73–76
33–36	1940	16	22	27	30	13	19	24	27	35	35	33	37	43	77–80
37–40	1936	30	24	29	27	27	28	20	25	31	41	37	49		81+
41–44	1932	26	31	32*	37	30	23	11	42	40	26	43			
45–48	1928	25	32	24	52	32	24	40	33	34	38				
49–52	1924	36	36*	38	37	36	34	25	40	40					
53–56	1920	38	35	40	30	34	37	36	30						
57–60	1916	44	40*	32	53	43	31	32							
61–64	1912	37	40*	23	50	43	37								
65–68	1908	36	38	53	42	35									
69–72	1904	45	51	54	20										
73–76	1900	32	47	53											
77–80	1896	38	56												
81+	1892	53													
National Totals		29	27	26	30	19	12	91	31	82	11	7			

Source: Michigan Survey Research Center for the Center for Political Studies, National Election series.

Note: Entries are differences between the proportion of strong party identifiers and the proportion of Independent-Independents.

*These cells have been "smoothed" by replacing those entries with the average of those in adjoining years and cohorts. The assigned values for these cells, reading by column, are as follows: 36 was 24, 40 was 30, 40 was 53, 24 was 11, and 32 was 19. This smoothing attempts to remove the most obvious instances of sampling error by substituting innocuous entries for those that are otherwise anomalous.

Changes in the Strength of Partisanship

The story of the apparent decay and rebirth of partisanship is fascinating and complex, and it rests on evidence surrounding the elections of the 1980s. The first national decline in the strength of party identification after 1952 occurred in 1968, coincident with a retreat among white citizens outside the South from the partisan Democratic high of 1964. The drop in strength of party identifications was apparent in national estimates and was widely interpreted as an indication that strong partisans were rejecting old loyalties and taking on the role of nonpartisans. A relatively simple analysis of changes in the relationship between the level of partisanship and the age of citizens might have forestalled—or at least modified—such interpretations. It is true that the decline in the strength of partisanship was reflected in a temporary diminution of partisan intensity among older citizens, but the portent for the future, as well as the reason for the apparent decline in Democratic party fortunes, was contained in the contrast between the partisanship of the youngest and the oldest cohorts.

In keeping with established regularities that had found strength or intensity of party identification very much a function of increasing age, by 1968 the oldest cohorts, who were literally dying off, were (like those who had preceded them and like those who were to follow) the strongest carriers of partisan attachment. Their "replacements," the young cohorts newly eligible to vote, not only followed the pattern of having the weakest of partisan attachments but also in 1968 far exceeded their counterparts from previous years in the extent to which they were nonpartisans, and were not strong partisans when they had partisan inclinations at all.

Throughout the 1950s and early 1960s, the youngest members of the eligible electorate had been less partisan than their elders, but, as Table 4.2 indicates, they had always counted many more strong partisans than nonpartisans among their ranks, usually by a margin of 10 to 20 percentage points (compared to margins of 45 to 55 points among the oldest cohorts). In 1968, however, the entering cohort of those eligible to vote for president for the first time actually contained more nonpartisans than strong party identifiers.

To the extent that 1968 ushered in an antiparty era of weak party control and weak party loyalties, the consequence was immediately and massively evident among the young, but it was scarcely reflected at all in the partisanship of the middle-aged and older cadres (Jennings and Markus 1984). Indeed, by 1972 the strength of party sentiments among citizens over 60 years old had pretty much returned to the levels of 1960–1964. Among the very large number of citizens in their late teens and twenties, however, nonpartisans clearly outnumbered strong partisans. By 1972, these youngest cohorts made up a full 33 percent of the total electorate. The contribution of the young to national estimates of the strength of partisan sentiments was the primary source of the apparent nationwide decline in strength of party identification that continued until sometime after the election of 1976 (Miller and Shanks 1982).

In examining the full set of four-year cohort data, following each new entering class across the 48 years and 13 presidential elections covered by the Michigan data and presented in Table 4.2, we may reasonably conclude that the traumas of the late 1960s and early 1970s—failed presidencies, international frustrations, domestic turmoil, and the disruptive effects of civil rights protests, anti–Vietnam War demonstrations, and counterculture happenings—did create a period effect felt throughout the electorate. The strength of partisan sentiments among the older cohorts rebounded in 1972 and 1976, but since 1992 these sentiments have not continued to advance to the high mark set by the oldest cohorts almost half century earlier. At the same time, the larger impact of the antipolitics decade seems to have been a generational effect: The young reacted to the events of the period more sharply and possibly even more permanently than did the older cohorts. It was the refusal and delay of the young in accepting partisan ties, not the lasting rejection of loyalties once held by their elders, that produced the indicators of dealignment in the mid–1970s.

It now seems clear that too many of the scholarly discussions of dealignment and realignment—given the aggregate figures, which showed fewer strong partisans and more nonpartisans—inaccurately attributed the cause of this change. They simply assumed that dealignment had occurred because old partisans actively rejected former party loyalties in favor of dealignment, professing no support for either party in preparation for switching party loyalties. The absence of party loyalty among the large numbers of young people, with no implications of rejection, conveys a quite different sense. This is an important distinction because the post–1976 evidence points to an increase in the incidence of party attachments among the young and the strengthening of their partisan sentiments.

Indeed, particularly where the strength of partisan sentiments is concerned, a pervasive upturn since the 1970s has been led by the same young cohorts whose original entry into the electorate was dominated by nonpartisans. Each of the younger cohorts who contributed so much to the apparent national dealignment has experienced a dramatic increase in both the incidence and the intensity of partisan sentiments in each of the elections of the 1980s and 1990s as the political climate normalized. Their level of attachment in 2000 remained slightly below the norm that we associate with their generational counterparts in the 1950s, but this is primarily because they started from such an abnormally low point when they first entered the electorate. They have in fact made a large contribution to the national indications of renewed partisanship.

In 2000, the ratio of strong partisans to nonpartisans in the younger cohorts had shifted by 10 to 20 points from a quarter century earlier. And

by 2000, the post–1976 cohorts numbered more than 43 percent of the total electorate. Between 1976 and 2000, the four youngest cohorts from
1976 increased their strength of partisanship by an average of 29 points;
the remaining four oldest cohorts in 1992 had risen only 7 points in the
same 12 years. At the same time, the composition of the electorate does
continue to change over time inasmuch as old cohorts, whose normally
quite intense feeling of party loyalty strengthened as they aged, continue
to leave the electorate. Their departure has slowed the overall rate of recovery in national strength of partisanship, which otherwise would have
reflected more clearly the increase in partisanship being contributed by
the younger cohorts since 1976.

In sum, many arguments that took indicators of the declining strength
of party identification in 1972 or 1976 as indicators of impending party
realignment erred in the interpretation of these indicators. The actual reduction of intensity of individual partisan commitments was real, but it
was very limited in magnitude and constituted a very brief episode for
older members of the electorate. For the younger members, the turmoil
of the late 1960s and early 1970s delayed but did not forestall their development of party loyalties. The magnitude of the delaying effect on
them was so great, and they have been such a large and growing part of
the electorate, that their simple lack of partisanship has been the largely
unrecognized primary source of the indications of what was called
dealignment but what was, in reality, nonalignment. To be sure, a nonalignment of the young may be followed by a first-time alignment that
will differ from that of the old, and that might ultimately reshape the
party alignment of the entire electorate. But the dynamics of partisan
change that follow from such a beginning will probably be quite different from those anticipated or imagined when it was thought that an experienced electorate was rejecting its old loyalties in preparation for a realignment involving switching parties by the individual citizen.

Some Implications of New Alignments

Before considering further the topic of the realignment of national partisan sympathies, we may find it useful to reflect on some of the implications of the period effects and generational differences that have just been
suggested. The very introduction of the idea of cohort analysis emphasizes the consequences of compositional change of the electorate during
a period of political turbulence. Notwithstanding the rapid but ultimately
incomplete rejuvenation of partisanship among older voters between
1972 and 1976, the concern with the changing composition of the electorate leads directly to the question of Key's basic interest in individual-
level stability and change in partisanship.

In approaching that question, we should first note that the observed generational differences that appeared rather suddenly in 1968 suggest that we modify some of the traditional as well as revisionist notions of the origins of party identification. Historically, party identification was thought to have been shaped by national traumas and watershed events such as the Civil War of the nineteenth century or the Great Depression of the 1930s. The lasting effects of such realigning epochs were thought to be carried by the influence of parents on the social and political attitudes of the successor generations. Early evidence for this view was provided by the recall of parental predisposition and was supplemented by insightful arguments that described a waning transmission of the original reasons for party identification through successive generations that are more and more remote from the shaping cataclysms (Beck 1977). This latter theme was intended to account for the diminution of partisanship—the dealignment that might logically precede realignment.

The evidence of cohort differences in partisanship that we have reviewed would be consonant with the thesis that new disruptions of the party system simply accentuate the decay of family traditions and familial transmission of party loyalties. But the situation is more complex than this. The very abruptness of the cohort differences that appeared in 1968 suggests an active intrusion of new events into the process whereby partisanship is acquired among the young. This disruption of familial lines of inheritance may or may not have lasting effects that produce real discontinuities in the partisanship of the electorate. But it certainly produces short-term change, which was not anticipated in the early theories of political socialization. And the rapid recovery of partisanship among the older cohorts, with a much slower rate of development and growth in the younger (filial) generations, creates a generational gap that belies a pervasive influence of the older over the younger (Jennings and Niemi 1981). In short, whatever the role of the family in shaping and preserving party traditions, the events of the late 1960s and early 1970s had an impact of their own on the partisan predispositions of the younger cohorts entering the electorate. Those most affected were not realigned, and not even dealigned. They simply entered the electorate more often unaligned, with no partisan preference.

Moreover, the immediacy of that impact of events in young people did not allow for the habituation to behavioral patterns that has become a choice explanation of the origins of party identification (Fiorina 1981). The notion that acts of crossing partisanship—Democrats voting for Eisenhower in 1952 and 1956, for Nixon in 1968 and 1972, or for Reagan and Bush in 1980, 1984, and 1988—have an impact on one's sense of party identification is not at issue (Converse and Markus 1979). Rather, as with generational differences and family tradition, the sharp break with the partisanship of entering cohorts prior to 1968 makes the absence of partisanship in the new cohorts of 1968 more of a comment on the immediate impact of historical context than an extension of either family influence or rational-choice theory as the explanation for new partisan identities.

The amassing of new data that capture variations in historical context has enriched our understanding of the origins of party identification and partisanship. As an aside, we should note that the growing evidence of a multiplicity of origins may upset some old orthodoxies, but it does not necessarily address the question of whether the significance, meaning, and consequence of party identification are similarly enriched or altered. The meaning of "I generally think of myself as a strong Democrat/ Republican" may vary with the origin of the sentiment, but that possibility must be the subject of much future research. In the meantime, we simply note the proliferation of evidence that party identification, in its origins, is a fascinating and many-splendored thing.

Political Engagement and Partisan Stability

The extent to which the incidence, strength, and direction of party identification vary with the context experienced by the identifiers is further illuminated if we define context in terms of the political depth of the partisan engagement of the individual citizen. We have already noted some of the correlates of the political context at one's time of coming of political age.

We have also noted how aging, or experience, inoculates one against change in later years of life. An even more dramatic insight into the durability of partisanship is provided when we subdivide citizens into voters and nonvoters.

Let us turn first to national assessments of the strength of partisanship. In the "steady-state" elections of 1952–1964, strong partisans among voters outnumbered those with no partisan preference by a ratio of 39 to 7; among nonvoters, the comparable averages were 26 (strong partisans) and 8 (no partisan preference). At the height of the excitement about dealignment (1968–1976), the ratio of strong partisans to nonpartisans was still 30 to 10 among voters; however, it had reversed to 16 (strong) to 19 (no preference) among nonvoters. In the elections of the 1980s, the ratio for voters was back to 35 (strong preference) to 8 (no preference); for nonvoters, it was still 18 to 17. Thus, there was some weakening of the aggregate indicators of the strength of partisanship among voters; indeed, the role of the young nonpartisan cohorts in changing the partisan composition of the entire electorate has already been noted. However, the dramatic change in the intensity of partisan sentiments that began in 1968 and persisted through the 1980s occurred primarily among nonvoters—that is, nonparticipants in the presidential elections of the period. The high point of contrast occurred in 1976, when strong partisans still

Table 4.3   Party Identification of Voters, 1952–1988

Year	Democrat	Independent	Republican	Partisan Balance
1952	46	24	31	+15
1956	44	24	32	+12
1960	45	22	33	+12
1964	52	20	28	+24
1968	45	28	27	+18
1972	40	31	28	+12
1976	39	34	27	+12
1980	41	32	27	+14
1984	38	31	30	+8
1988	36	30	33	+3
1992	37	35	28	+9
1996	39	28	33	+6
2000	36	35	29	+7

Source: All of the data are based on the Michigan Survey Research Center of the Center for Political Studies, National Election Studies series.

Note: In 1980, 1984, and 1988 the distinction between voters and nonvoters was validated by the National Elections Studies staff. For all other years the distinction relies on the self-reports of individuals.

outnumbered nonpartisans among voters by a ratio of 28 to 11; among nonvoters, however, the ratio was reversed, 12 to 22. Of course, the contrast was occasioned in part by the disproportionate incidence of young people among the nonvoters, as occurs in every election year.

In other words, the cry of alarm that the partisan sky was falling, with all of the strong implications for the future of the electoral process, was occasioned by indicators emanating primarily from the nonparticipants in presidential politics. A "dealignment" of these apathetic nonparticipants might also have deserved comment and even some analytic thought, but unfortunately it was the mistaken belief that future elections would no longer be shaped by a continuation of the party identifications of the past that commanded the attention of most analysts and commentators. Both the diagnosis (alienation of the voters) and the prognosis (realignment of partisanship at the polls) were flawed because it was largely the nonvoters who constituted the source of the alarming (or promising) indicators of impending change.

Now that we have separated voters and nonvoters in order to reexamine the aggregate indicators of partisan dealignment, it is a natural extension to turn directly to the theme of party realignment. Here we find still more evidence of the persistence of party identification, even as we introduce the first description of a significant shift in the numerical balance of the two parties. Table 4.3 indicates that prior to 1984 there was little hint in the national party identification distributions among voters of an impending realignment that would see the Republican party in the ascendancy. Indeed, the only visible departure from a 30-year span of Democratic pluralities of some 14 percentage points occurred during and after the election of 1964. In that year, still an underanalyzed episode, party loyalties shifted and enhanced the "steady-state" Democratic margin by a full 10 points. Despite the chaos of the Democratic nominating convention in Chicago in 1968, and perhaps as a partial explanation of Hubert Humphrey's near victory in the fall election with strong black support, the preelection Democratic plurality of party identifications in that year remained visibly above the norms of the 1950s and 1970s. By 1972, however, and again despite the limited national appeal of the Democratic candidate, George McGovern, a kind of normalcy had returned to the two-party competition for party loyalties. The proportion of voters with no party identification had increased by one third over that of the late 1950s, but those numbers drew almost equally from Democrats and Republicans. The Democratic margin of party loyalties in 1972 and 1976 was virtually identical to that in 1956 and 1960. And that margin persisted through Reagan's first candidacy and his defeat of Jimmy Carter in 1980.

Between 1980 and 1988, however, at least a limited version of the long-heralded partisan realignment took place. After eight elections, a span of 28 years during which Democrats outnumbered Republicans by almost identical margins among those voting for president, the Democratic edge virtually disappeared in the election of 1988. The Democratic plurality dropped from a "normal" 14 points in 1980 to no more than 3 points in 1988. A tentative explanation—or at least a description—of that change will be offered shortly. In the meantime, it is worth noting that the 11-point decline among voters was accompanied by a bare 4-point shift among nonvoters. The disparity stemmed in part from the fact that the Democratic edge among nonvoters actually appeared to increase between 1984 and 1988 (from 14 to 17 points), whereas it continued to erode among voters. This difference and others between the politically engaged portion of the eligible electorate and those less involved provide direction to our next effort to account for the equalizing realignment in the 1980s.

Just as the disaggregation of the eligible electorate into voters and nonvoters casts a very different light on the historical ebb and flow of partisan sentiments, so a deeper probing into differences in the level of political engagement among voters amplifies our understanding of those sentiments. In general there is clear, if not dramatic, evidence that those voters who are the least engaged by or sophisticated about politics are

the most volatile in their political attitudes, including their political identities. A simplified version of the measure of "levels of conceptualiza-
tion" introduced in *The American Voter* (Campbell et al. 1960) can be used
to sort voters into two groups: the more politicized (at the higher two
levels) and the less politicized (at the lower two levels). Doing so is a step
toward further refining our sense of the conditions under which party
identification is persistent and stable and of the circumstances under
which voters alter their habitual party affiliations.

On average, interelection shifts in the partisan balance of party identification among the voters classified as reflecting the higher levels of con-
ceptualization amounted to changes of only 2 or 3 percentage points between 1952 and 1988. Among the remaining less politicized voters, the
same average shift across the nine pairs of elections approximated 5 or 6
points. On average, the changes are not great in either case, hence they
reflect the relative stability of party identification among voters, if not always among nonvoters.

However, closer examination reveals that the apparent greater volatility among the less sophisticated, or less engaged, voters is almost entirely the product of two election eras: 1960 to 1964 and 1980 to 1984.
Between 1960 and the 1964 Johnson landslide, there was an astronomical
35-point shift in party identification favoring the Democrats within the
ranks of the less sophisticated voters. This shift erased a 13-point
Republican margin in 1960 and produced a 22-point Democratic lead
four years later, in 1964. The proportion of Democratic identifiers increased by 19 percentage points (from 37 to 56, with 406 and 450 cases in
1960 and 1974, respectively), whereas the proportion of Republicans
dropped 36 points (from 50 to 34). It should be noted that this massive
exchange took place among voters during such a brief period that
turnover in the composition of the electorate cannot be held responsible.
There is nothing in the literature on party identification that provides a
theoretical basis for anticipating such a high incidence of change.

Moreover, while the less engaged 40 percent of the voters in 1964 were
moving precipitously toward the Democrats and away from the
Republicans, the more engaged 60 percent were moving in the opposite
direction. Although the net figures for changes in party identification
among the more sophisticated voters (6 points between 1960 and 1964)
did not depart from their average change of 5 points across nine pairs of
elections, the direction of change favored Barry Goldwater and the
Republicans rather than Lyndon Johnson, the Great Society, and the
Democrats.

There was clearly something about the period from 1960 to 1964 that
evoked very different responses from the more politicized and less
politicized voters. This anomaly clearly merits greater attention than it

has received because the election of Lyndon Johnson in 1964 marked the one and only significant net shift in the balance of party loyalties among voters between the first Eisenhower election of 1952 and the second Reagan election 32 years later, in 1984. It is true that the overall Democratic gain of 11 points among voters in 1964 was not a lasting gain; by 1974, things were back to the three-decade norm. Nevertheless, the 1964 Democratic landslide was both a political event of significance and an occasion to learn more about the conditions under which party identifications change.

A similar pair of changes took place, though to a lesser degree and somewhat different in kind, between 1980 and 1984. Among the more sophisticated voters, the proportion of self-declared Democrats dropped 2 points as the proportion of Republicans went up 3 points between the two Reagan elections. Among the less sophisticated voters, the Democratic loss was 6 and the Republican gain was 7. An even greater contrast occurred on Election Day. Despite the pro-Republican shift in party identification, the more sophisticated voters increased their 1984 Democratic vote over their 1980 record, from 53 percent Republican and 47 percent Democrat to 48 percent Republican and 52 percent Democrat (a majority voted for Walter Mondale). In contrast, the less sophisticated voters turned their 1980 vote, which favored Reagan by a margin of 63 percent Republican to 37 percent Democrat, into an 80 to 20 percent rout on his behalf in 1984. By these calculations, Reagan was reelected by the less sophisticated voters.

It is, however, of at least equal interest to the student of political change to note that once again the more politicized and less politicized voters moved in opposite directions in response to changing events in the world of national politics. Nevertheless, the contrasts in these responses should not be overdrawn. Apart from the two election periods just discussed, the parallelism between the two sets of voters has been notable in election after election over a period of 30 years.

The Realignment of 1980–1988

The 1980–1988 realignment among voters apparently took place in two phases, each phase affecting one of the two somewhat different groups of voters we have just noted. Between 1980 and 1984, at least some changes in party loyalties took place pretty much across the board, but the shifting loyalties were concentrated in two familiar sectors. First, young voters shifted more to the Republican side than did the old, again suggesting greater malleability or susceptibility to the winds of change among the less experienced voters. At the same time, among young and old alike, the voters with fewer resources for coping with complex matters of politics swung more heavily to the Republicans. Thus, it was the less-educated young people who changed the most: A Democratic margin of 23 points dwindled to 9 points, resulting in a 14-point shift between 1980 and 1984. Among the better-educated older voters, a small 3-point plurality of Republicans grew to an 8-point margin, a shift of only 5 points.

During the second phase of the realignment, there was a further shift to the Republicans in only one sector of the voting population. Table 4.3 showed that across the entire voting population, the Republicans gained only 5 points between 1984 and 1988. Apparently, all of that gain was concentrated in the ranks of the older, better-educated voters. These voters—precisely the group that had been most resistant to the national move into the Republican camp between 1980 and 1984—went from a modest 40–to–32 Republican margin in 1984 to a solid 46–to–28 plurality in 1988. If the first phase of the realignment was a tribute to the charismatic attraction that Ronald Reagan held for the less involved, less political of the voters, the second phase seems to have engaged the more ideologically predisposed voters who had come to appreciate that Reagan really was a conservative Republican president (N. Miller 1986).

Of course it is possible that the realignment of the Reagan years may vanish as swiftly as did the increment that Lyndon Johnson's election gave to the Democrats in 1964. Certainly every national leader is well aware of the speed with which short-run disaster can overtake long-term expectations. Prior to the election of 1992, it seemed more likely that the realignment of the late 1980s was a relatively durable part of the Reagan legacy to American politics. The rationale for such a forecast derives from a basic perspective on the nature of democratic political processes. That perspective in turn brings this chapter full circle as we move on to another insight expressed by V. O. Key, Jr.: that the electoral process is an echo chamber in which voters echo the message of political leaders. The more nuanced version of this view is presented as the conclusion to his *Public Opinion and American Democracy* (1961). Key posited political leadership as the wellspring of mass politics and argued that it is members of the political elite, activists who form the political subculture, who articulate the alternatives that shape public opinion.

The political elite, including political leaders such as presidents, also gives definition to the political party. There are many reasons for the half-century dominance of American politics by the Democratic party, but not the least of these is the sense of habitual party affiliation that came to many citizens from voting four times for Franklin Delano Roosevelt as the leader of the Democratic party, three times to reaffirm a preference for having him continue as President. It is difficult to reconstruct the public opinion of 50 years ago, but the incomparable longevity of Roosevelt's presidential leadership must have contributed much to the contemporary meaning of being a "New Deal Democrat."

As we search for the roots of party identification, we may easily forget that following Truman, who had been Roosevelt's vice president before he succeeded to the presidency and then won his own election, Eisenhower's hallmark in the public presentation of self was his emphasis on bipartisanship. And although his signal contribution to postwar domestic politics may well have been his conversion of the Republican Party from the party of isolationism and America First to the party of internationalism and the United Nations, his legacy was not the redress of the partisan balance in the electorate. It was Eisenhower, not Stevenson, who warned in 1960 of the future dangers of the military-industrial complex. And only rare commentators foresaw a party realignment at the end of Eisenhower's term.

We have already commented on the Kennedy-Johnson era, but it is worth noting again that in the aftermath of New Frontier, Camelot, and Great Society euphoria, there were the hot summers and burning riot-torn cities of the late 1960s, Woodstock and the counterculture, and protests against Vietnam and for civil rights. As an antidote to the repressions of the 1950s, American foreign policy, and the heritage of racial discrimination, the decade of protest was undoubtedly overdue; but it was not calculated to endear the Democratic establishment to Main Street America any more than to the hearts of the protesters. In hindsight, it is remarkable that the Democratic party did not suffer more as a consequence of the rejection of its leadership in 1968 and 1972, but in fact there was little subsequent evidence of realignment.

The Nixon era, like the Eisenhower years, was another opportunity to realign the electorate that the Republican party missed despite eight years of presidential leadership. Nixon's personal triumph was almost unequaled in his reelection in 1972, but that outcome, Watergate, and the scandals surrounding the Committee to Reelect the President (CREEP) were all well separated from the Republican party and thus possibly prevented a "failed presidency" from actually disadvantaging Nixon's party.

Carter presided over yet another failed presidency, in large part because he was not the Democratic party's leader. He campaigned as an outsider from Plains, Georgia, and he presided as an outsider. Like Johnson, he benefited from his regional identification, and he momentarily slowed the southern white flight from his party with his 1976 campaign when he ran against the Washington establishment. Like Nixon, he did not appear to hurt his party—at least not at the grassroots level, where party identification flourishes—but he scarcely took honors as the revitalizing leader of the party in the electorate.

Ronald Reagan was the only president of the postwar era who took office as an avowed partisan and an unvarnished ideologue; held office for eight years, during which he championed his conservatism and his Republicanism; and retired at the end of two full terms with a legacy of goodwill sufficient to elect his successor. The textbooks say that the president is the titular head and leader of the party. Reagan may not have satisfied all the factions within the Republican party, but not because he was not an articulate Republican spokesman and an active campaigner openly partisan on the election trail as well as in Washington. And despite trials and tribulations that would have ended some careers, he remained popular to the end and retired from office with the country relatively at peace with itself and others.

In a more detailed account of the changes in party identification between 1980 and 1984, I attribute much of the 1980–1984 change to Reagan's personal popularity among the less experienced and less sophisticated sectors of the electorate (N. R. Miller 1986). That analysis explicitly examined and rejected the hypothesis that it was the Reagan administration's conservatism rather than its Republicanism that provided the foundation for changing partisanship. Four years later, in 1988, it appeared that his sustained personal popularity as President prevented any visible backsliding on the part of the recent converts to Republicanism.

Another relatively elaborate analysis of the 1988 election (Shanks and Miller 1989) provides two sets of evidence that conform to our interpretation of the two-stage sequence of realignment. In the first place, there is pervasive and powerful evidence of Reagan's contribution to the Bush victory. The election was in some ways a retrospective triumph for Reagan— a triumph of popular satisfaction with his policies, with the general state of the world and of the nation as he left office, and with his performance (Shanks and Miller 1989). In the absence of evidence to the contrary, there seems no reason not to attribute the carryover of the 1984 increases in Republican party identification to Reagan's carryover popularity.

The second pertinent finding from this election analysis is of a different order. Across the three elections preceding 1988, the distribution of ideological predispositions among voters had not changed from the 13-point margin of self-designated conservatives over self-designated liberals. In 1988, that margin increased by 8 points. In disaggregating voters by age and education, which has been done to locate those who changed their party identification, it appears that the older, better-educated voters who had a 15-point increase in their Republican margin (from a slim 34 to 31 in 1980 to a solid 46 to 28 in 1988) between 1980 and 1988 experienced a very substantial 17-point increase in their conservatism during the same interval. Among the better-educated young voters, a comparable increase in conservatism was associated with a full 7-point increase in Republicanism. By contrast, among the less-educated voters, whose pro-Republican shift occurred entirely between 1980 and 1984 (in response to Reagan's popularity), there was no 1980–1988 increase in conservative predispositions at all. In 1988, the less-educated voters were more Republican than they had been in 1980, but they were not more conservative; the better-educated voters were both more Republican and more conservative.

This analysis of the 1988 elections thus supports the thesis that a significant first phase of the 1980–1988 realignment occurred between 1980 and 1984 among the less experienced and less sophisticated voters who responded to Reagan's personal leadership with an increase in Republicanism. A smaller but perhaps more meaningful second phase then occurred between 1984 and 1988, particularly among the older and better-educated voters, who ultimately responded favorably to the Reagan administration's emphasis on conservatism. Thus, ideology and personality, articulated and presented by the same presidential party leader, may have reshaped the sense of party loyalty among different sections of the voting public. The same two-pronged explanation of the 1980–1988 realignment is persuasive because it seems to fit a relatively broad view of the origins of party identification and yet makes explicit the importance of presidential leadership for party as well as for country.

In this chapter, Warren E. Miller undertakes a broad overview of the distribution and strength of party identification during the latter half of the twentieth century. Using data from the American National Election Studies (ANES), which he did so much to create, Miller documents two basic trends: a decrease in the Democratic party's advantage in the electorate and a decrease in the strength of citizens' partisan attachments. Consistent with more extensive arguments that he made elsewhere (Miller and Shanks 1996; Miller 1992), Miller discusses how these changes can be explained by differences in generational cohorts. He makes his most forceful claim in regard to strength of partisanship, arguing that generations with stronger levels of partisanship are being replaced in the electorate by generations with weaker levels of partisanship. Although the strength of partisanship does increase as citizens age, younger cohorts are entering the electorate with lower rates than that of preceding generations.

We have updated the evidence in this chapter to incorporate ANES data from the 1996 and 2000 elections. Data from those two presidential election years, along with data from 1992, suggest a solidification of the trends that Miller identified. Although there was a slight increase in the number of Republicans and a slight decrease in the number of independents in 1996, the general picture that emerges from an examination of these three presidential elections years is one of stability. Among the overall population (voters and nonvoters), independents are the single largest voting block and Democrats have about a 10 percent advantage over the GOP in party identification. The story is slightly different among voters with fewer self-identified independents and a Democratic advantage in the 6- to 7-point range for those who reported casting ballots in the particular years.

In terms of partisan balance, at the aggregate level, these numbers are also similar to the distributions that ANES researchers found in 1984 and 1988. The years between 1980 and 1984 were when the major change in the partisan landscape among the mass public occurred. During this time the Democratic advantage moved from the 15–20 percent range to the 8–10 percent range that we typically see in today's data. This move away from the Democratic party lagged by three elections an increase in the number of independents and a decrease in partisan intensity.

We end with Miller's original concluding paragraph, which remains poignantly accurate today.

> This rendering of the recent history of the persistence of partisan attachments and this examination of the conditions under which voters alter their habitual partisan affiliations are somewhat incomplete. Except for limited speculation about recent presidencies, government as a participant in the shaping of mass partisan sentiments has been ignored. And the disaggregations of the mass have not reached up to either the political activists or the nongovernmental elites that are so much a part of our political processes. Nonetheless, accumulated data resources have permitted explorations and reconstructions that were not available to earlier generations of scholars. The old question "What is a political party?" is answered as before: It is people, the people's leaders, and the symbols they present for public approval. The old question "What causes stability and change in the people's attachment to party?" is now, more than ever, an important question with a very complex set of possible answers rooted in the successes and failures of political leadership.

Notes

1. At least since the time of Key's seminal article "A Theory of Critical Elections" (Key 1955, 3–38), analysts have used the concept of political alignment to describe the composition of the competing sides in electoral competition. Realignment occurs when changes take place in the competitive balance between the parties. Realignment may also be geographic, as regional alignments change; group-based, as social or economic groups shift their party support; or simply

numerical, as one party grows in size relative to the other. The idea of individuals or groups not taking sides is inherent in the concept of nonalignment, just as moving from support for one side to a middle ground between the parties is described as dealignment. For a good summary discussion, see Sorauf and Beck (1988).

2. In 1952, 80 percent of southern white males identified with one or the other of the two major parties: 68 percent Democratic and 12 percent Republican, for a Democratic advantage, as shown in Table 4.1, of 56 percent.

5

Competing for Attention and Votes: The Role of State Parties in Setting Presidential Nomination Rules

BRUCE E. CAIN AND MEGAN MULLIN

A curious aspect of American politics is that while general election rules for Congress and the presidency are fixed and uniform, nominating rules are not. General elections are always held on the first Tuesday after the first Monday in November, and the winners must obtain either a district plurality (for Congress) or an Electoral College majority (for the presidency). There is no significant effort to change these rules from election to election to suit the needs of particular candidates or parties.

The same cannot be said of candidate-nomination processes. In many states, nomination rules vary across parties and across elected offices. Constant change is a given, and political actors—candidates, political parties, and the states—strategically calculate the impact that proposed rule changes will have on their fortunes. By far the most fluid electoral arena is the presidential nomination process, which is characterized by quadrennial shifts in the timing of state nomination contests, variations in whether states use caucuses or primaries, and important differences in the criteria governing participation in primary elections. Two important factors have contributed to the diversity of the presidential nomination rules over time and across states: the relatively high autonomy that the courts have accorded political parties in determining their candidates, and the deference that national party organizations have generally shown to state parties in these matters.

Unlike the process of electing a president, neither the Constitution nor federal law dictates how a party must conduct its nomination. Aside from the Supreme Court-imposed constraint that the major parties cannot prohibit members of a given race from participating in their nomination contests, the parties are otherwise free to set their own rules and processes for choosing a presidential candidate. Though the national parties have the formal right to impose their rules upon the state parties, both the Democrats and Republicans have de facto allowed nomination rules to be set at the state level. This flexibility has resulted in a complicated system of caucuses, conventions, and primary elections, some run and financed by state governments and others by state parties. Beginning in the 1970s, the Democratic national party took a more active role in setting requirements for state nomination rules, resulting in a power shift away from state party officials and toward the voting party member. Although the Republican national party did not impose its own set of requirements, Republican nominating practices changed in many states when Democrat-dominated legislatures altered the rules for state-sponsored nominating events.

There is a wide consensus that changes in the presidential nomination process have altered candidate strategies and party organization, sometimes in unintended ways (Polsby 1983). However, few have paid attention to the continuing instability of state nomination rules 12 years after the last change in national party requirements. The general trend in both parties is toward opening up participation in their nominating events. During the 1990s, Republicans in particular seemed dedicated to the idea of opening up their nomination rules. But this trend obscures the many diverse and nonlinear paths that individual states have taken. In this chapter we examine the motivations and tactics of state political actors in setting presidential nomination rules in an attempt to explain both the overall trend toward openness in the nomination process and the many exceptions to it.

Party Definition

It may seem surprising that the federal government and national parties play such a limited role in setting rules for presidential nominations. But this hands-off approach is consistent with the Supreme Court's doctrine that political parties are at least to some degree private associations of like-minded individuals. If a party is a private organization like a labor union or the Boy Scouts, then party members ought to have the right to determine their own process for selecting their leadership. Interfering with a party's decisions about membership and participation would infringe upon the party's constitutional right of association. On the other hand, the Supreme Court has sometimes thought of political parties as similar to regulated utilities. Because there is a natural duopoly created by the state-imposed electoral system and because most primary elections are publicly funded, the Court has asserted the right to intervene when the parties have engaged in unconstitutional discriminatory behavior. On the whole, however, the Court has come down more on the side of party autonomy than strict party regulation in matters of party governance and rule-making.

States have somewhat more leverage than the federal government over the party nomination process by virtue of their role in funding and administering nomination events. When states opt to hold a primary election, the state legislature can choose to set rules for the timing and management of the event. This opportunity is available in the majority of states, since most states now use a primary nomination system and almost all primaries are publicly funded—in 2000, only one Democratic and three Republican primaries were party-run. However, even in state-run primaries, parties maintain the right to set their own rules for participation. The Supreme Court affirmed this right in *Tashjian v. Republican Party of Connecticut* (1986), ruling that the Democrat-dominated Connecticut legislature could not prohibit the state Republican party from allowing independents to participate in its primary election. However, it is still possible for a legislature dominated by one party to pass a law changing the date or procedures for a state-sponsored event against the will of the opposing party. In such a case, the minority party would need to sponsor its own event or else abide by the rules of the state-sponsored election.

The Court has also determined that nomination rules cannot be imposed by citizen-sponsored initiative over the opposition of the parties. In *California Democratic Party v. Jones* (2000), the Court relied on the concept of parties as predominantly private associations in deciding that the California blanket primary system imposed by voters on the parties through a ballot proposition violated the parties' rights of association. The blanket primary would have allowed all voters, no matter what their party affiliation, to vote for any candidate in each race on the primary ballot. By allowing voters to cross over and vote in other parties' nomination contests on a race-by-race basis, the blanket primary system opened up the possibility that non–party members might strategically cast their ballots in order to corrupt the outcome of a party's nomination. Since this nomination system was implemented against the will of the parties, the Court ruled that it forced the party to associate with non–party affiliates for no compelling reason, and was therefore unconstitutional.

The key exception to the autonomy principle is the prohibition on racial discrimination in the nomination process. In a series of decisions called the "white primary cases," the Court ruled that African Americans could not be excluded on the basis of their race from participating in the nomination process of the Texas Democratic party, even when the nominating event in question was a caucus and not a primary election. The federal government also plays an active role in ensuring that primary elections are not discriminatory through its enforcement of the Voting Rights Act of 1965. Section 5 of this law mandates that any change in election law or procedure in jurisdictions with a history of disenfranchisement on racial grounds must be precleared by the Department of Justice. As a consequence, any change in nomination rules in the nine states covered by Section 5 must be reviewed and approved before the change can take effect, placing a constraint on state political actors attempting to achieve their goals through nomination rule changes.[1]

Party Federalism

Granting that parties and not state governments have principal sovereignty in nomination rules, the parties themselves are not always unified in their positions with respect to how delegates should be allocated. Frequently, conflict develops between national and state party organizations over the most desirable nomination goals and strategies. The national Democratic party first got involved in disputes with state parties over nomination procedures when it sought to force southern Democratic parties to support the national ticket, and then to guarantee that state parties did not discriminate in their own nomination contests. In the 1970s, the national party implemented a broad set of state delegate selection and allocation standards. Some states resisted the assertion of national party authority, but in 1975 the Supreme Court upheld the national party's right to set delegate selection rules in the *Cousins v. Wigoda* decision. The Court ruled that the national party's interest in protecting its right of association outweighed the purported state interest. Since that decision, the Court has continued to side with national parties when their rules have been challenged by state organizations. The Republican party's hesitance to interfere in state party activities has resulted in fewer intraparty federalist conflicts than in the Democratic party, but ironically, as we will discuss shortly, greater conflict among the state Republican parties.

Currently the two areas of greatest contention among the national and state organizations for both major parties are the timing of nominating events and the openness to participation by non–party members in those events. Both of these issues highlight the conflicting incentives for the national and state parties: on the one hand, the state parties' desire to compete for attention with other states, and on the other, the national parties' dual interests in promoting participation among party members and protecting the nomination process from interference by outsiders. Although the national parties' right to set rules for their state affiliates is legally recognized, the national organizations also understand the political importance of allowing state parties to abide by local custom and to compete with rival parties on the state level. Consequently, the national parties do not always exert the control that they might. In *Democratic Party of the U.S. v. Ex rel. La Follette*, 450 U.S. 107 (1981), the Supreme Court affirmed the right of the national Democratic party to prohibit Wisconsin's open primary rules, which allowed voters to select any party ballot they wanted to in the privacy of the voting booth. After nearly a decade of battling with the Wisconsin party, however, the national organization decided to allow the state party to continue conducting its nominating event according to its open rule. Maintaining harmony between the party organizations became a more important goal than preventing participation by non–party members.

Opportunity Costs and Rule Changes

Even though the national Democratic party ultimately allowed Wisconsin to continue with its open primary system, the amount of money and energy it expended in challenging Wisconsin's rules indicates that the party regarded those rules as potentially threatening. The national party suspected that the rules shaped nomination strategies and outcomes in critical ways. Under the Wisconsin open primary system, the participation of nonaffiliated voters—independents, Republicans, and members of minor parties—would help some candidates and hurt others. Experience also teaches that the weaker the obstacles to non–party members, the greater the likelihood that they will cross over party lines to participate in a nominating event.

Nomination rules lie on a continuum with respect to the ease by which crossover voting can occur. Systems vary in the opportunity costs they impose, meaning the value of what a voter gives up by participating in the nomination process. Opportunity costs exist on two dimensions: whether or not a voter needs to declare partisan affiliation, and whether or not the voter loses the opportunity to participate in other races. At the most open end of the continuum, nomination rules do not require voters to affiliate with a party in order to participate in its nominating event. In the Wisconsin system, voters selected a party ballot in the privacy of the voting booth. In the California blanket primary system, voters were allowed to select candidates on a race-by-race basis, potentially voting in different party primaries in different races. Neither system requires voters to declare a party affiliation publicly. The blanket primary offers the greatest choice since it allows voters to choose their favorite candidate in each race without sacrificing the opportunity to choose another party's candidate in another race.

Next on the continuum are open primaries that require voters to publicly select one party's ballot before entering the voting booth. Party registration does not constrain voters' opportunity to participate in either party's primary, but their ballot choice is public information that becomes available to the parties after the election. States that do not register voters by party most often use this system. Parties tend to be somewhat more receptive to this type of primary than to the Wisconsin system, because under these rules a voter must choose to affiliate with a single party, even if just for a day. Many voters would prefer the more open system which allows party selection in the voting booth, as voters may not want their selection to become part of the public record.

Somewhat more restrictive are semi-open primaries, in which only party members and independents are allowed to participate. Because this system excludes other party affiliates from participating, there generally is less vulnerability to a "hijacking" of a party's nomination by strategic voters. The semi-open system allows parties to reach out to unaffiliated voters without the problems associated with allowing potentially hostile loyalists of other parties to participate.

The primary system with the highest participation barriers is the closed primary, in which only preregistered party members are allowed to vote. If a non–party member wants to participate in a nominating event in order to support a particular candidate, he or she would have to change party registration before the state's deadline prior to the election. This poses a substantial barrier to outsiders who want to participate in a party's nomination. By their nature, caucus and convention systems tend to be even more restrictive because they require voters to spend several hours during an evening or weekend participating in discussions and many sequences of votes. Like primary systems, caucus rules for participation vary across states, but the time investment required even for an open caucus creates greater opportunity costs than for a closed primary.

It is hard to argue against openness and freedom of voter choice in the abstract, but state parties have not always been happy with their experiments in greater openness. The Democratic reforms of the 1970s caused states to shift from restrictive caucuses to more open primary systems, but several election cycles after the most recent national party reforms states continue to tinker with their nomination rules. In the aggregate, primaries continue to gain popularity, and more voters are allowed to participate in party nominations than ever before. But national reforms have not caused state rules to become more settled. Some states have reverted to more closed nomination forms after experimenting with more open rules. Why?

The Trend Toward "Openness"

Throughout the 1990s, when state parties or state legislatures changed the rules for participation in the presidential nominating process, the predominant trend was toward primary elections and away from caucuses and toward open rather than closed primaries. Using the 1988 nomination rules as a baseline and counting each party separately, over the next three elections there were 37 changes to presidential nomination procedures across the 50 states. Two thirds of these changes opened the process for more voters to participate in the nomination process, and just 12 created a more closed nominating system. These net figures are useful for identifying the overall trend toward openness, but they conceal a fluid process of change that is shaped by political competition. In the 1992 and 1996 elections, 10 state parties implemented temporary rule changes as experiments—for example, holding a primary instead of a caucus—but then returned to their previous nomination rules in a subsequent election. These trials account for 20 of the 37 rule changes and, curiously, for all but 2 of the 12 more restrictive changes. By extending the analysis further back in time, one of the remaining reversions to a more closed system is also explained by an abandoned temporary experiment: In 1992 the Virginia Democratic party returned to a caucus system after trying a presidential primary for the 1988 election.

It would be a mistake to ignore the back-and-forth movement between closed and open participation rules caused by states that experiment with and then retreat from alternative nomination systems. The short duration of these trials suggests that some rule changes are better explained by strategic behavior on the part of political actors than by some abstract commitment to openness. The 10 experiments in the 1992 and 1996 nomination races took place in eight states. Sometimes they involved both parties, but mostly they did not. Both parties in Kansas and Missouri experimented with an alternative nomination system and then returned to their previous method. In the other six states, only one state party acted to alter its nominating rules. Some of these trials were intended to last for only a single election, while others were unsuccessful attempts at permanent change. All of the short-term changes involved shifts between primary and caucus systems—in most cases, from a caucus system to a primary election. The one exception is the Louisiana Republican party's 1996 experiment with a caucus before returning to its traditional primary. Missouri's short-term change in the 1990s also fits this pattern, but the state, which traditionally used a caucus system, has changed its rules three times in recent elections, experimenting with a primary in 1988, returning to a caucus in 1992, then opening up its nomination rules again with a primary in the 2000 election. If rule changes could be explained solely by an increasing commitment to openness on the part of state parties, one would expect to see unidirectional, permanent shifts toward expanding opportunity for participation. Clearly, the picture at the state level is not so clear.

During the 1990s nomination rules were more likely to fluctuate between primary and caucus systems than between different standards for participation within either of these systems. All of the temporary trials involved shifts between primary and caucus systems, and only 2 of the 16 nontrial changes involved opening participation within a primary system to allow independents to participate in primaries that previously had been open only to party members. Thirteen rule changes created primary systems where the nomination had traditionally been decided through caucuses, and the North Dakota Republican party canceled its primary in favor of a caucus. When state parties switched from caucus to primary after 1988, they frequently adopted rules that allowed some non–party members to participate in the party primary. Of the 13 nonexperimental shifts to a primary, 4 resulted in semi-open primaries that allowed independents to participate, and 7 in primaries that were open to all registered voters. Only two state parties that traditionally nominated through a caucus system adopted a closed primary in the 1990s. Even the primaries that did not last beyond a single election tended to be open to unaffiliated voters—of the eight short-term experiments with a primary system, two were semi-open and five wholly open to all voters.

As a consequence of these shifts from a caucus nomination to a semi-open or open primary, the 2000 nomination processes across all 50 states were much more open than they had been in 1988. In 1988, 36 state parties used a caucus system to allocate their delegates to the national conventions; by 2000, that total had dropped by nearly a third to 25. During that time period, the number of semi-open primaries increased from 9 to 14, and the number of open primaries increased from 28 to 35. The number of closed primaries remained the same. As can be seen in Table 5.1, the strategic incentives driving the trend toward more open nominating rules appeared to be operating for both major parties.

Just what incentives exist for political actors—either state parties or state legislatures—to open up their nomination processes? In order to answer that question, we need to consider these actors' goals and how changing nomination rules might affect their ability to achieve their goals. Politicians who move to promote expanded participation in the presidential nomination process will surely attribute their own actions to lofty democratic ideals. While these ideals may indeed be firmly held, the politicians will also recognize the likely outcome of the rule change for the balance of political power. The rules of the game do much to determine political outcomes, and politicians understand the importance of rules. Politicians may err in their forecasts of the likely effects of a rule change (and in the recent history of presidential nomination rules that has often been the case), but generally they will support a change if it is expected to strengthen their position relative to that of other political actors. Examining the rule changes that served to open the nomination process in many states during the 1990s, the proponents of greater open-

Table 5.1   Types of Nominating Events

| | Caucus | | Closed Primary | | Semi-Open Primaries | | Open Primaries | |
	Dem	Rep	Dem	Rep	Dem	Rep	Dem	Rep
1988	20	16	14	14	4	5	13	15
1992	17	12	15	13	6	8	13	17
1996	17	12	13	15	7	8	14	17
2000	15	10	14	14	6	8	16	19

Note: In all four elections, Texas Democrats used both a caucus and an open primary. In 1996 and 2000, Washington Republicans used both a caucus and an open primary. In 1996, Louisiana Republicans used both a caucus and a closed primary.

ness sought to strengthen their position relative to three other sets of actors: other states, opposing parties within their state, or a rival coalition within their own state party.

Competition Among States

The presidential nomination season provides one of the few opportunities for state parties and state officeholders to attract national attention. Especially in small states that lack major media markets, ambitious politicians may have only one chance every four years (or even less frequently, if a nomination is uncontested) to establish a national reputation. The political incentives for doing so are numerous. The politician might be seeking a political appointment in the presidential administration, support and a fundraising base for his or her own run for higher office, influence over a national policy issue, or simply an opportunity to draw attention to the issues that concern his or her state. Given these incentives, it is not surprising that states compete to attract the attention of candidates and the press during the nomination season. From our analysis of press accounts of nomination rules changes, it appears that more than half of the 23 shifts from a caucus to a primary between 1988 and 2000 can be attributed wholly or in part to an effort by states to strengthen their position relative to other states.

Competing with other states for national attention is an incentive particularly for small states, whose share of national convention delegates will rarely make a difference in deciding the winning candidate. The two main strategies that small states have used to overcome this disadvantage are regional primaries and frontloading—moving nominating events earlier in the political calendar so as to have a greater influence on national politics. Regional primaries have long been promoted as a solution to the contest among states for a favorable position in the nominating season. These efforts were revived when 13 southern states joined together in 1988 and agreed to hold their primaries on the same day, dubbed Super Tuesday—even though in that case the megaprimary was driven more by ideological considerations than by pure competition for attention. Since the mid–1980s, a string of western governors has encouraged Rocky Mountain states to schedule primaries on the same day in order to increase the regional clout of the West and force candidates to address western issues such as water policy and management of public lands. In 1992, Colorado introduced its first presidential primary as part of an effort to promote a regional strategy to presidential nomination politics, but the effort failed to take off that year. For the 2000 election Governor Mike Leavitt of Utah made another attempt to put together a regional primary; it would involve nine states and allocate 10 percent of the delegates needed to win the Republican nomination and 6 percent of those needed on the Democratic side. Leavitt won bipartisan support for the plan in his home state, and Utah adopted its first presidential primary as a boost for the regional effort. Again the regional effort ultimately failed to take off owing to concerns in many western states about the cost and timing of a regional primary, but Utah and Colorado did hold their primaries the same day.

The New England states met with more success in their effort to establish a regional primary. In early 1995 the secretaries of state from Connecticut, Maine, Massachusetts, Rhode Island, and Vermont met and agreed to try to put together a regional primary. According to the Massachusetts secretary of state, the existing schedule of primaries and caucuses "basically diminishes New England's influence because of the disarray of dates spread throughout March" (Phillips and Lehigh 1995). With its primary positioned as first in the nation, New Hampshire did not participate in the negotiations, but the remaining New England states—all of them small- and medium-sized—agreed that a regional primary would enhance their influence in presidential politics. The regional primary required Maine and Vermont to change their caucus systems. The Maine Democratic party had already voted to adopt a primary in 1996 before negotiations for the New England primary began (Jackson 1995), but the Republicans voted in 1995 to adopt a primary in order to participate in the regional effort (Jackson 1995). The incentive of increased influence and national media attention also attracted the state parties in Vermont, which decided on a return to the presidential primaries they had held in the 1970s in order to participate in the regional primary.

The other way that state parties have tried to enhance their national stature is to move their nomination events up earlier in the nomination season in order to have a better chance of influencing the outcome. Early nominating events play a critical role in paring down the field of candidates and building momentum for a front-runner. Hence, candidates and the national media focus heavily on these early events. The small states of Iowa and New Hampshire receive a disproportionate amount of attention every four years relative to their share of the national electorate owing to their protected status of hosting the first caucus and first primary in the nation, respectively. Several states have attempted to challenge this protected status in order to position their own nominating events early enough in the season to make a difference in the outcome of the race. In some cases, states have altered their nomination rules as part of this frontloading strategy.

Frontloading of presidential nominating events poses a collective action problem for the political parties. Each state acting on its own has an incentive to move its caucus or primary earlier in an effort to influence the outcome of the nomination. However, most observers agree that the collective outcome of frontloading the nomination process is negative, because candidates that start out with less funding and less national recognition do not have the opportunity to build support and momentum over the nominating season. Frontloading forces potential contenders out of the nomination race before any votes are cast, and gives an advantage to states with the earliest events. Without a national strategy to control frontloading, each state has a strong incentive to schedule its event early enough that it might make a difference in deciding the nomination, collectively worsening the problem.

The national parties have taken different approaches to the problem of frontloading, creating different constraints on state party actions. The Democratic National Committee (DNC) has formally protected the status of Iowa and New Hampshire with a 1984 rule prohibiting any other state from hosting a primary or caucus before the first Tuesday in March. The party allows Iowa to host its caucus 15 days before that date and New Hampshire to host its primary eight days later. This rule is consistent with the two states' own laws—New Hampshire law requires that its primary be first in the nation by at least seven days, and Iowa has passed legislation requiring that its caucus be scheduled eight days before the New Hampshire primary. Under national party rules, all other states must hold their nominating events between the first Tuesday in March and the second Tuesday in June. The DNC's involvement in setting guidelines for the timing of nominating events follows the national party's practice of using the presidential nomination process to promote such values as representation and inclusion. Despite these guidelines, the DNC gets involved almost every election cycle in brokering disputes between states over the timing of nominating events.

Unlike the Democratic national party organization, the Republican National Committee (RNC) traditionally has not interfered with the state parties' delegate selection and allocation processes. It is up to the states to negotiate the nomination calendar. This hands-off approach by the national party occasionally leads to showdowns as states attempt to challenge the privileged position of Iowa and New Hampshire. In order to protect their placement on the Republican nominating calendar, Iowa and New Hampshire have an incentive to schedule their events earlier in the year, sharpening the frontloading trend and creating a conflict with the national Democratic party rules. In 1996, delegates to the Republican National Convention voted to take on the frontloading issue with an incentive program that would reward states with bonus delegates for scheduling their nominating events late in the season. Few states took advantage of the inducement, however, and in 2000 the frontloading trend continued. At the 2000 convention, the RNC voted 92–57 to break with its tradition of noninterference and adopt a reform plan that would have spread out the Republican nominating calendar. The "Delaware plan" would have set up a four-month calendar of nominating events, with the smallest states allocating their delegates in February and states of increasing size holding their events in March, April, and May. The proposal appeared to be headed for a vote on the convention floor, but at the last minute the Bush campaign stepped in to oppose the plan, leading to its defeat in a vote of the Republican national convention rules committee. The Bush campaign had insisted that Bush was neutral on the plan, but he feared that a floor fight over the proposal between large and small states would interfere with the picture of party harmony that he hoped to project (Broder 2000). As a result, the Republican national party will continue to allow states to negotiate the primary calendar themselves in the 2004 election.

States' efforts to compete for national attention by scheduling an early nominating event accounted for several rule changes in the 1990s, and the differences between the national parties in their response to these efforts form a complex picture of strategic negotiation by political actors. Delaware offers a prime example. The state passed a law in 1992 establishing a primary and setting the date for four days following New Hampshire's primary; this created a direct conflict with New Hampshire's state law that requires its primary to take place seven days ahead of all others. Delaware's interest in challenging New Hampshire's week-long window led to standoffs between the two states in 1996 and 2000. Because DNC rules would not allow Democratic participation in such an early primary, in 1996 the Delaware Democratic party chose to continue allocating delegates to the national convention on the basis of its March caucuses, and President Clinton opted not to place his name on the state-run primary ballot.

New Hampshire Republicans did not have national party rules to protect their window of influence, so they attempted to put pressure on Delaware in other ways. New Hampshire convinced all the Republican candidates other than Steve Forbes and Phil Gramm to boycott Delaware's primary. The Delaware legislature passed a law placing all the candidates (including Clinton) on the ballot even without their consent, but the state's effort to use an early primary to attract candidate and press attention clearly had failed. Four years later, Delaware again set an early primary date in order to challenge New Hampshire, but when New Hampshire convinced the Republican candidates to boycott the Delaware vote for a second time, the Delaware Republican party opted to hold its own primary three days after the state-sponsored event in order to give New Hampshire a full week's lead. The Democratic candidates appeared on the state-sponsored primary ballot, but the party treated the results as a nonbinding "beauty contest" and allocated delegates through its caucus process. As a result, the state sponsored a primary election that neither party used for candidate selection. The frustration of Delaware Republicans in their attempts to attract attention with an early primary led them to sponsor the "Delaware plan" that was rejected at the 2000 national convention.

As can be seen in the Delaware case, the Republican national party's unwillingness to dictate rules for a nomination schedule sometimes leaves candidates to resolve differences between states. The candidates then must weigh the costs and benefits of siding with one state over another. Long-shot candidates might see an opportunity by participating in a nominating event that more established candidates are boycotting, but they risk jeopardizing their relationships with the important early states and angering potential supporters. Steve Forbes's gamble paid off when he won the 1996 Delaware primary, which all other candidates except Phil Gramm of Texas had boycotted.

Gramm not only failed in Delaware, but his involvement in a Louisiana challenge that same year drew criticism from party insiders and failed to benefit his candidacy as expected. In 1996 Louisiana Republicans switched from their traditional primary to a predominantly caucus system as they moved up the date of their nominating event in order to challenge Iowa's position at the top of the calendar.[2] Gramm was accused of engineering the early caucus in order to get a jump in a neighboring state where he had strong support, but he insisted that he had argued for Louisiana to remain a part of the Super Tuesday primary (Germond and Witcover 1996). For its part, the Republican party in

Louisiana maintained that the move to an early nominating event was intended to boost the profile of the South in nomination politics. Carrie Fatger, the Louisiana state party chief of staff, argued, "There is no fix for Gramm. . . . The South is now becoming the base of the Republican Party, and it can serve as a weather vane, just like Iowa. Louisiana is a good state to show how the conservative Southern states fit in, and it will give a balanced perspective" (Wilkie 1995).

Iowa fought to maintain its leadoff position, and failing to convince Louisiana Republicans to move their caucus date forward, Iowa had all the Republican candidates except Phil Gramm, Pat Buchanan, and Alan Keyes sign a pledge to boycott the Louisiana event. Through his involvement in the Louisiana effort Gramm jeopardized his relationship with Republican officials and Iowa voters, and the risky strategy seemed particularly foolish when he lost the Louisiana caucus vote to Buchanan. The state party also failed to convince the leading Republican candidates to participate in the event. Nonetheless, the Louisiana caucus did attract national press attention because of the unexpected victory of the conservative commentator Pat Buchanan. In 2000 the major Republican candidates again refused to participate in Louisiana's challenge to Iowa, and consequently the state party returned to a closed-primary nomination system.

Competition Within States

In addition to providing a rare opportunity for state politicians to build a national profile for themselves or their states, the presidential nomination process is an occasion for the two major parties in any single state to compete for attention and votes. Each state party hopes that its nominating event is more exciting and consequential than the opposing party's; while much of that is dictated by the dynamics of the national race, a strategic rule change within a state can serve to boost or dull interest in a party's nominating event. Changing nomination rules might affect a party's fortune in November. To the extent that voting in one party's primary predicts supporting that party's nominee in the general election, each party has an incentive to attract as many voters as it can to participate in its contest. Moreover, politicians frequently seek to attract attention and voters to their party's nominating event in order to affect the outcome of down-ballot races. In all, newspaper accounts of rules changes suggest that competition between parties played a role in more than a third of the states that implemented a rule change in at least one of their nominating events between 1988 and 2000.

Parties in several states have adapted their rules in order to try to win over the growing number of voters who choose not to affiliate with either political party. Competition for the votes of independents in the general election has driven some state parties to open their nominating events to unaffiliated voters, under the assumption that many voters will choose to stick with the same party through both elections. During the 1990s the North Carolina Democratic party and the Maryland Republican party both opened their existing primaries to unaffiliated voters in order to build an affinity for their party among independents. The decision to allow independents to participate in nominating events is controversial, as many party loyalists believe that a party's nominee ought to be selected only by those who are willing to identify themselves as party members. An opponent to the decision by Maryland Republicans argued, "I don't mind them coming into the church if they're inclined to. . . . I just don't want them selecting the minister." Another opponent was less generous in his attitude toward independents: "They are political cowards who do not deserve our time of day" (Dresser 1999).

Many party members who support opening a nominating event to unaffiliated voters feel that this move is necessary in order to stay competitive in the state. In the 10 years leading up to the North Carolina Democratic party's decision to expand participation in its primary, Democratic registration in the state had fallen by 7 percent while registration of Republicans had risen 42 percent and unaffiliated voters were up 120 percent (Lineberry 1995). The state Democratic chair felt that the party had no choice but to open up its primary to independents: "I grew up just a hard-core Democrat. My inclinations are, under the best of all worlds, only registered Democrats would participate in our primary. I think we just have to take the hand we are dealt" (Lineberry 1995). Ironically, when Republicans in North Carolina opened up their primary to independents for the first time in the 1988 election, it was done to attract support in a traditionally Democratic-dominated state (Cochran 1996).

Competition for independents' votes is also a consideration for new primary states. After Utah established its first presidential primary in 2000, both parties voted to allow the 85 percent of registered voters who were unaffiliated to participate. A Republican state committee member commented, "The Republican Party kept the big tent open. We want to encourage the unaffiliated to join our party" (Harrie 1999). Instead of using a closed primary as an incentive to recruit new registered voters, the parties opted to allow independents to maintain their unaffiliated status and choose a party at each presidential primary election.

State parties also have adjusted the timing of their nominating events in order to avoid allowing the opposing party to dominate the political debate during an important stage of the election. Key Democratic officials in Michigan unsuccessfully sought a waiver from national party rules in 2000 in order to move their caucus back to three days before the early Republican primary in that state, arguing that waiting for their scheduled March caucus date would allow the Republicans to dominate the political debate through February (Hoffman 1999). South Carolina's move from a caucus to a primary in 1992 seems to have been motivated at least in part by the Republicans' success in using the primary as an organizational tool. After the 1988 nominating season, in which the Republicans drew more than four times the number of voters to their pre–Super Tuesday primary than Democrats attracted in post–Super Tuesday caucuses, the Democratic party decided to schedule its own early primary to increase participation and enhance its organizational strength. According the *Greenville Times*, "[T]he contrast between the 1988 caucuses and the GOP primary may have been a political watershed of sorts for South Carolina Democrats and their once standoffish attitudes towards presidential politics" (Hoover 1989). After 1992, Democrats returned to using a caucus system.

Occasionally a state Republican party has taken advantage of the differences between the national parties' nomination rules in order to gain a political lead over the Democrats in their state. The most extreme case of this behavior took place in Arizona in 1996. In 1992 the Republican-dominated state legislature passed a law setting Arizona's first primary for 1996 on the same day as New Hampshire's event. Governor Fife Symington, a Republican, sought to challenge New Hampshire's lead-off position. Symington ultimately backed down in his contest with New Hampshire, but the legislature then set the primary date for a week following New Hampshire's event, still too early to comply with national Democratic rules. The state Democratic party made it clear that the national rules would prohibit its participation in the primary, but the Republicans disregarded the Democrats' concerns. Democrats perceived the move as intentional; according to the chair of the state party, "It means less participation by Democrats, and the Republicans want that" (Mayes 1999). The chair of the Republican state party argued that it was the Democrats' own rules that prevented their inclusion: "We're not opposed to them participating at all, but they never woke up and changed their bylaws" (Mayes 1999). Rather than continuing to use a caucus system as both parties had done previous to 1996, Democrats chose to compete with the Republicans by hosting their own primary election in March. Whereas the Republican primary was funded by the state at a cost of $2 million, the Democratic event was self-financed with $10,000. Furthermore, the Democrats allowed same-day registration for their primary, effectively opening it up to all interested voters. In 2000 the situation in Arizona had not changed, but the Democrats adapted by allowing Internet voting in addition to voting at polling places.

Competition Within a State Party

We have seen that state parties and state legislatures make changes to nominating rules in order to compete with other states for national attention and to compete within their own state for political advantage over the opposing party. Both of these processes suggest that state party members agree on political goals and strategies for achieving those goals. However, as indicated in our discussion of decisions to open primaries to participation by independents, sometimes disagreement exists within the state party itself about goals and strategies. Political actors change nomination rules in order to favor their preferred candidate over a primary opponent or just to gain political power over their rivals within the party. Competition within a state party can result in opening or closing the nomination system, depending on the objectives of those who are able to change the rules.

Many of the shifts from a caucus to a primary in the 1990s can be attributed to intraparty competition. Because of the high opportunity costs associated with a caucus system, only the most avid party loyalists tend to participate. Collectively, these loyalists have more extreme ideological views than the larger population of primary voters. Furthermore, candidates with limited funding and name recognition are better able to organize their supporters to make a strong showing in a caucus system than to broadly appeal to a primary electorate. As a result, a caucus system tends to favor more liberal Democratic candidates and more conservative Republican candidates, putting moderates at a disadvantage. State politicians understand this, and they frequently will work to implement a nominating system that favors candidates who share their own ideological view. During the period that our analysis covers, competition between moderate and extreme factions was particularly common among state Republican parties.

After the Louisiana Republican party shifted from a primary to a caucus in 1996 to challenge Iowa's leadoff position—a move that some argued was intended partly to assist Phil Gramm's candidacy—the party again scheduled an early caucus in the 2000 election. Iowa convinced the leading candidates to boycott the event, leaving only the conservative candidates Gary Bauer, Alan Keyes, and Senator Orrin Hatch in the race. The popular Republican governor, Mike Foster, urged the state Republican chair to drop his caucus plans, arguing that the caucus would stifle voter participation, divide the state's delegation, and create a national embarrassment (Wardlaw 1999). The conservative party chair, Mike Francis, refused, arguing, "Our honor is at stake" (Anderson 1999a).

In fact, most observers agreed that the quarrel was not over participation and process questions, but rather over candidates and control of the state party. As a Bush supporter, Foster sought nomination rules that would allow his candidate to participate without antagonizing Iowa. Francis backed Gary Bauer, a former Reagan policy adviser who was likely to win over Keyes and Hatch in a caucus vote but would have little chance against Bush in a primary. Foster and Francis had battled over control of the state party for four years, the governor allied with moderate Republicans and Francis representing the socially conservative right wing of the party (Anderson 1999b). In a state party meeting described as "confusing and sometimes disorderly" (Anderson 1999b), Foster's allies ultimately were able to cancel the 2000 caucuses. Bush won the March primary with 83 percent of the vote, and in that election Foster's slate of party central committee candidates took over the party from Francis's socially conservative faction.

Intraparty competition is not always as dramatic as was the case in Louisiana. In some cases, politicians pursued rule changes in order to benefit home-state candidates. Missouri adopted a primary in 1988 in order to assist the candidacy of Representative Dick Gephardt, a Democrat, and then returned to the caucus system in 1992. Republicans in the state wanted to continue holding primaries, fearing special interest domination over their caucuses, but the Democratic party opposed continuing the primary because of its cost and organizational demands. The Republican party sought a primary even more strongly after conservative Buchanan supporters won a majority of the state's delegates in the 1996 caucus, but not until the home-state candidates Congressman Gephardt and Senator John Ashcroft, a Republican, expressed interest in the presidency did legislation pass to reintroduce a primary election (Mannies 1998). In 1996, the Kansas legislature debated whether or not to continue its 1992 experiment with a primary election. Governor Bill Graves, a Republican, had called the primary a needless expense in his 1994 campaign, but as the election approached he began to advocate for a primary in order to ensure a victory for the Republican frontrunner, Senator Bob Dole, in his home state. Conservative party members attempted to corner Graves on the issue, as the head of the House Appropriations Committee said he would approve the funds for a primary only if Graves formally requested it (Dvorak 1995). Graves finally secured funding for the primary, but then canceled the election in February 1996 when it became clear that Dole would have an easy victory under any nomination system (Petterson 1996).

State parties are not always loyal to their local candidates, however. In Utah, the Republican party took its decision to include unaffiliated voters in the new primary over the objections of supporters of Senator Orrin Hatch. Governor Mike Leavitt worked behind the scenes to make sure that the party committee voted to include independents. Leavitt said he supported both Bush and Hatch, but conservatives perceived him as working on behalf of Bush's interests. According to one conservative, Leavitt's efforts paid off for his preferred candidate: "The governor is a George Bush man. The governor got his people out" (Harrie 1999). Even when parties are acting on behalf of their home candidates, the results might not be what they expect. In 1988, the Virginia Democratic party adopted a Super Tuesday primary first as an effort to support the candidacy of Governor Chuck Robb and then, once he opted not to run, as a way to support a southern moderate candidate (Baker 1992). Jesse Jackson's victory in the primary was an unwelcome surprise to many who had supported the change in nomination rules. The state legislation authorizing the 1988 primary was good for only one year, and four years later no one recommended holding a primary again.

Closing the Nomination Process

Throughout the 1990s, most of the nomination rule changes that took place in states served to open up the process to nonaffiliated voters. In all but one case, rule changes that closed a nomination event were part of a short-term trial, either closing the nomination for a single election or reintroducing more restrictive rules after a brief experiment with opening the nomination. When nomination rules did become more closed, the shift could be explained by at least one of three factors: the failure of an experiment to achieve the intended effect, the interference of the national parties, and cost.

We have seen that political actors can be strategic in crafting rules that will help them achieve their political goals. Occasionally these efforts backfire, however, and the rule change they have sought fails to produce the intended outcome. When that occurs, the state party may return to its previous system for the next election. In the case of Virginia, Robb did not anticipate the low turnout in 1988 that allowed Jackson to win the primary. Four years later, the Democratic party returned to the caucus system it used previously. The 1988 primary in Missouri delivered the intended victory for Gephardt, but his loss in his hometown of St. Louis to Jesse Jackson caused some embarrassment for the state party and may have contributed to its decision not to maintain the primary in 1992 (Cook 1991). Not all rule changes that do not achieve their intended outcome are dismissed, however. Even though Colorado failed in its attempt to establish a regional primary, the state continues to allocate delegates through a semi-open primary, not through its pre-rule.

The constraints posed by national parties also can cause a state party to close its nomination rules. We have seen that national party rules prohibit Democratic state parties from participating in early nominating events. In addition, the national parties have interfered with shifts toward openness. Michigan held primaries throughout the 1970s, and then national Democratic party rules prohibiting open primaries forced the state to shift to caucuses in the 1980s. Low participation and intraparty competition led to the primary's return in 1992. In that open election, voters were required to name a party preference before entering the voting booth. In 1995, Governor John Engler, a Republican, signed legislation returning Michigan to primary rules that allowed voters to choose their party ballot in the voting booth. National party rules would not allow Democrats to participate in a primary that did not require voters to publicly affiliate with the party for that day; therefore, to comply with party rules, Democrats returned to a caucus nomination system in 1996 and 2000. In Washington State, the Democratic party refused to allocate delegates on the basis of the 1992 state-run primary because the secretary of state did not require voters to affiliate with a party for the day. The Democratic state chair argued that the party was not asking for a serious commitment: "We were willing to say that asking for a ballot application was a statement of party affiliation. We were willing to wink. We just wanted that fig leaf" (Connelly and Boren 1992). Although the national Democratic party has become much more accommodating of non–party members since the decision in *Democratic Party of the U.S. v. Ex rel. La Follette*, 450 U.S. 107 (1981), the party still asks for nomination participants to affiliate with the party at least for one day.

The most common reason that some states moved to more restrictive nominating procedures was to save costs. In many cases, state legislatures or state parties do not want to take on the high cost of a primary election, especially if the event is not likely to involve a spirited contest or to make a difference in determining the final nominee. During the 1990s, primaries were canceled in Kansas, Minnesota, Missouri, and North Dakota at least in part because of the cost of conducting the election. States facing fiscal shortfalls frequently see a primary as an unnecessary expenditure, and few state parties can take on the expense of conducting their own primaries. As a consequence, participation in the nomination process becomes limited to those voters who are willing to dedicate an evening to attending a caucus.

Conclusion

What are the virtues and drawbacks of having such a decentralized, fluid, and complex nomination process? The problems are pretty clear. First, as we have seen, there is a lot of room for strategic manipulation with the aim of advancing the interests of specific candidates and states over others.

The advantage of fixed and uniform rules is that they eventually achieve some legitimacy, because people become accustomed to them and/or they know that the rules are not merely in place to help a specific candidate or state politician. Endless tinkering has the opposite effect, and lays the groundwork for ill feelings that can carry over into the November election. Strategic manipulation can undermine the perception of that an election has been won legitimately.

Another problem is instability itself. The underlying logic of frontloading sets in motion an unseemly competition to move to the front of the line. This generates bitterness between the states and puts candidates in an awkward position when they have to choose whether or not to participate in a given state's event. Eventually, the competition may get out of hand and the sequential primary system abandoned, because no state will be content to have its event anywhere except at the beginning for fear of being irrelevant to the final choice. In the meantime, the national parties struggle to find a balance between upholding the autonomy of state parties and treating all states fairly, while attempting to maintain a competitive advantage over the other party for the general election.

Finally, there is the problem of equity. Why should voters in small, unrepresentative states like Iowa and New Hampshire have influence over the final outcome out of proportion to their actual share of the U.S. electorate? Voters in small states already enjoy unequal influence over the presidential choice in the general election, given that in the Electoral College each state gets two votes for its senators regardless of its size. It seems gratuitous to give them a greater say in the nomination process as well.

But against all these negative considerations, there are reasons to value the fluidity and variation of the current system. To begin with, the variety of different rules and types of state contests provides a fertile ground for many types of candidacies. The Iowa caucuses advantage the well-organized but less well financed campaigns of candidates like Gary Bauer and Pat Buchanan. Open primaries in the 2000 election season allowed John McCain to attain some important early victories against George Bush that he almost certainly would not have achieved if they had competed only in closed primaries. Frontrunners like George Bush and Al Gore, who enjoyed the support of the parties' mainstream voters, did better in closed-primary states. A national primary with uniform process might encourage a trend toward fewer types of candidacies, and winnow the field to well-financed establishment candidates even before the first primary vote.

Second, the sequence of different contest types allows the voters to see candidates perform in different types of settings. The privileged position of Iowa and New Hampshire forces candidates from large-media-market states like California into face-to-face contact (called retail campaigning), allowing voters the personal contact necessary to assess them as individuals. Pete Wilson, who was governor of California for two terms, did not need to engage in personal grassroots politics in order to win in his home state. But to win the presidency he had to come across well in the more intimate settings of Iowa and New Hampshire. Governor Bill Clinton could do it. Governor Pete Wilson could not.

So there are some virtues in the chaos of the current system. The principles of party autonomy and federalism are the reasons we have the current system, but the unintended effects are not altogether bad in an era in which money and establishment support often conspire to decide elections before the campaigning begins.

Notes

1. Section 5 also applies to specific counties and townships in seven additional states, but coverage of these jurisdictions does not affect changes to state nomination rules.

2. A portion of the party's delegates were still chosen through the state primary.

6

The Party Role
in Congressional Competition

L. SANDY MAISEL, CHERIE MAESTAS,
AND WALTER J. STONE

Perhaps the most fundamental role that parties play in the political process involves guaranteeing that offices are contested so that citizens can make a choice.[1] Frequent competition for office is fundamental to citizen control in a democracy. In the American two-party form of democracy, the recruitment and support of candidates for public office is a function of the major parties. To the extent they perform it, citizens are provided the choice they need to maintain control over government.

Parties' Historical Party Role in Contesting Offices

In the nineteenth century, the importance of the party in contesting offices was clearly understood. The two political parties, through mechanisms of their own choosing often far removed from public view, designated candidates for office. We know, for instance, that the congressional caucus was used to nominate presidential candidates in the early years of that century. We know that party conventions replaced the caucus at mid-century, though we know little about how convention delegates were chosen. We know that legislative caucuses formally chose United States senators throughout the nineteenth century, but we know little about how those to be chosen by the legislatures were themselves selected.

Beyond that, much of our knowledge of "party nominations" is impressionistic. Party bosses and party machines dominated in some areas, particularly one-party areas. In these "machine" areas, party workers wound their way through the ranks and were rewarded with political offices, in which they served at the bidding of the boss. A different sort of organization existed in non-machine areas; ballot positions and offices were filled, but we know little of how.

The democratizing reforms of the Progressive Era took dead aim at the power of the political machines. State legislatures (and thus party leaders) lost the power to choose United States senators. And parties lost what many consider to have been their most important power—control over the ballot. The direct primary election was seen as a means to take power from the party leaders and give it directly to the people, where it belonged. As a result, the party role in recruiting candidates and in guaranteeing the contest for office was restricted. How could parties be expected to recruit candidates, to find the best candidates for office, if they could not even guarantee nominations to those candidates?

The actual means through which candidates were selected for party nominations throughout the twentieth century varied from time to time, from region to region, from office to office, and, perhaps of most significance, from political context to political context. If one thinks about the United States House of Representatives, for instance, the stereotypical view of the contest for office during, say, the mid-twentieth century would be candidate-centered campaigns in which the candidates essentially self-recruit, in which nomination contests are fought among candidate camps with little party intervention, and in which the successful candidates owe little to their political parties. Once elected, these candidates continue in office on the basis of the strength of their personal organizations and their ability to do effective constituency service (Maisel 2002, Chapters 7 and 8).

To the extent that that view is accurate, it reflects the situation in the majority party in one-party districts or perhaps in competitive districts when the seat is open. In other political contexts, however, very different scenarios could be painted. In the few areas still dominated by political machines, such as Cook County, Illinois, the machine would designate a candidate. He (never "she" in the era of the Daley machine) would be nominated and elected without opposition, unless antimachine elements chose to take him on in a primary. In many other areas, skeletal party organizations attempted to find a candidate to fill the slot of the ballot. Often they were not successful.

If that picture is accurate for the U.S. House, it is even more the case for lower offices. Rarely are these offices so valued that more than one candidate in either party is interested in the nomination. Party leaders try to recruit candidates, but they have few incentives they can offer. Their support, in a era of weakened organization and weakened allegiance to party, was worth little. Party organizations were weakening; thus party leaders were severely handicapped in their efforts to guarantee that the offices on the ballot in their jurisdictions were contested.

Again, consider elections to the House of Representatives over much of the last half of the twentieth century. The South was dominated by the

Democratic party; few Republicans ran, much less could be elected, throughout much of the region.[2] The Farm Belt was dominated by the GOP to almost the same degree; so too were some areas of New England. Political scientists began to worry about declining marginal seats (Mayhew 1974) and both decried and sought explanations for the lack of competition in House races. On the national scene, the Democrats controlled the House for an unprecedented 40-year period, from 1954 to 1994.

Recent Changes in the Party Role in Contesting Elections

The end of the last century saw two important changes in the picture just painted. First, the parties sought and found new roles in the electoral process (see Chapters 2 and 3 in this book; Bibby 1990, 1994, 1998; Herrnson 1990, 1994, 1998). At both the state and national levels, these roles were political and financial. The parties have sought relevance in the electoral arena, after a period in which many observers wrote them off as meaningless residue from an earlier era (Broder 1971). In the case of congressional elections, this new role has been performed by the two parties' Capitol Hill committees, the National Republican Congressional Committee (NRCC) and the Democratic Congressional Campaign Committee (DCCC).

Second, since the Republicans regained majority status in 1994, competition for control of the House has become intense. The Democrats have made major efforts to recapture the House in each of the last three election cycles; the Republicans have fought just as hard to retain control. The situation in the once-solid Democratic South has changed drastically. Regionally, one could say the South has become two-party competitive, with Republicans elected in 72 of the 125 seats in the former states of the Confederacy in the 2000 election. Similarly, the political situation has changed in areas once dominated by Republicans. As examples, Democrats now hold seats such as Kansas's 3rd congressional district or Utah's 2nd, once thought to be solidly Republican areas and well beyond their reach.

Despite these changes in regional patterns, there remains a marked lack of competition in most congressional races. In only seven of the southern seats, three won by Democrats and four by Republicans, did the victor win by less than 55 percent. In 38 of the seats one party or the other failed to field any candidate. Reversing the previous Democratic trend in the South, Republicans won 23 seats without Democratic competition, whereas only 15 Democratic candidates got free rides (Cook 2001).

The recent experience in the South points to a significant difference between the competition for control of the national and state legislatures (and the roles political parties play in those efforts). Party competition

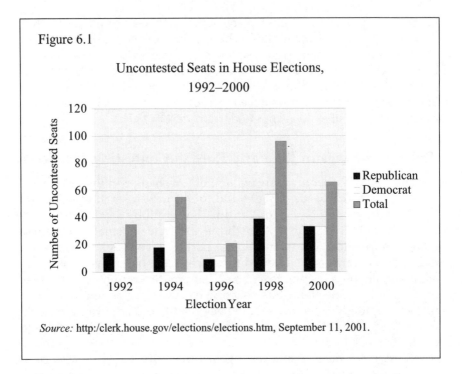

Figure 6.1

Uncontested Seats in House Elections,
1992–2000

Source: http:/clerk.house.gov/elections/elections.htm, September 11, 2001.

today is intense and focused on the relatively few marginal seats that are thought to control the partisan balance of power in the relevant legislature. In the House of Representatives in the last decade that has typically meant heated competition for approximately 50 to 75 seats.

Party leaders play crucial roles in this era of national competition. Party strategists figure out which specific seats are likely to be "in play."[3] They actively recruit candidates to contest these seats. They pledge party support to these candidates, though often that support is contingent on the chosen candidate's winning the party nomination. Though nominations are still won or lost in direct primary elections, party leaders try to ease the path to party activist approval for their preferred candidates—sometimes with success and sometimes not.

Competition in House Elections Today

This party role in "guaranteeing" competition is drastically different from the more general role of guaranteeing the contest for office. For while party leaders act strategically and concentrate their resources in the seats they are most likely to win, they all but ignore other seats. Figure 6.1 shows the number of seats, in each election in the last decade, in which one major party or the other did not field a candidate for the House of Representatives. Though some variation is apparent, in the average election one party or the other has not fielded a candidate in approximately one fifth of all House races. That means that in one fifth of the districts across the country citizens cannot "throw the scoundrel out" because no one is running against the "scoundrel."

The mere presence of a name on the ballot is not sufficient to guarantee that the citizenry has an effective choice. In order to contest an election effectively, a candidate must be able to get his or her message out. Quality candidates are those who can communicate their views on the issues of the day to the electorate in a way that is heard. Challengers to incumbents must be able to present and criticize the incumbent's record, to point out shortcomings, to stress where they would have acted differently. Effective candidates must be able to engage the electorate in a discussion of the public issues of the day, to state their views, to solicit public feedback, and to draw out the views of their opponents, so that the citizenry can make an informed decision.

The quality of a candidacy can be measured in various ways. After the fact, two ways are evident. First and most obviously, one can measure how many votes a candidate received. Tables 6.1 and 6.2 show the percentage of votes received by challengers in recent elections and the percentage of votes received by the losing candidate in open-seat races. It is clear from the tables that open seats are more closely contested than are those in which incumbents seek reelection. No surprise here. It is also clear that most challengers to incumbents do not fare very well.

Table 6.1   Percentage of Votes Received by Challengers Against Incumbents

	Challengers in 1998 (N=402)	Challengers in 2000 (N=403)
More than 50	1.6	1.2
40–49.9	20.4	17.1
30–39.9	31.6	35.2
20–20.9	16.9	23.6
10–19.9	8.2	6.0
Less than 10	0.7	1.5
No Challenger	20.6	15.4

Table 6.2   Percentage of Votes Received by Losers in Open-Seat Races

	Losers in 1998 (N=33)	Losers in 2000 (N=32)
40–49.9	67.9	50.0
30–39.9	14.7	22.5
20–20.9	11.8	12.5
10–19.9	5.9	6.3
Less than 10	0.0	0.0
No Challenger	0.0	3.0

But the win/lose results do not necessarily reflect on the quality of the campaign run by the losing candidate. We know that some districts are drawn to favor candidates of one party or the other. Even the best Republican candidate running a superb campaign in New York's 15th district would not draw many votes against Charles Rangel. The district is too heavily Democratic. A Rangel landslide might reflect a poor challenger, a poor campaign by that challenger, or the fact that the citizens had the chance to contrast two candidates and their stands on the issues and overwhelmingly selected Rangel.

Second, one can use campaign spending as a surrogate for an effective campaign. In an age of media campaigning, in which most congressional districts contain over 600,000 citizens, congressional campaigns are expensive. Just *how* expensive they are varies from district to district as well as in terms of the costs entailed in different settings. Media costs are much higher in metropolitan areas than they are in rural areas; in some metropolitan areas they are so high as to be prohibitive and other means of reaching the electorate must be found. But travel costs are often higher in rural districts than in urban districts. It is thus difficult to set an amount of money that is needed to run an effective campaign.[4] Tables 6.3 and 6.4 present campaign finance data for the 1998 and 2000 elections. The specific numbers are not so important as the pattern.

In the last two election cycles, no challenger who spent less than 60 percent of the money spent by an incumbent won a seat. In fact, all but four of the winning challengers spent at least 90 percent of the money spent by the incumbent, with six spending the same amount or more than the incumbent. All of the challenger winners spent over $800,000; nine spent over $1 million.

The real point, though, is that the challenger candidates who had low budgets were not able to communicate their messages nearly so effectively as the incumbent winners. In each of the last two election cycles

Table 6.3　Challenger Spending as a Percentage of Incumbent Spending

	1998 Election (N=402)	2000 Election (N=403)
No Challenger	20.6	14.9
Less than 10	40.0	45.2
10–24.9	10.7	12.4
25–49.9	12.2	12.2
50–74.9	7.5	7.2
75–99.9	6.5	3.7
100 or more	2.2	4.2

less than 20 percent of the incumbents seeking reelection faced candidates who spent even half as much money as they did. More than half of the incumbents who faced any competition at all faced challengers who spent less than 10 percent of the money spent by the incumbents. The citizens did not really have a chance to hear about the incumbents' records nor to express their views on the issues of the day.

The link between these less-than-stellar campaigns and the efforts of party leaders is clear. Party leaders have limited resources to expend—their time, staff time, and most of all campaign money. They concentrate their efforts on seats in which the candidates of their party have the highest likelihood for success (see Tables 6.5 and 6.6.) That is sound strategy. They use their limited resources effectively to maximize their chances for achieving success, defined as controlling as many seats as possible. Parties are more likely to give large sums of money to their candidates in "marginal" districts, whether they are challengers or incumbents. From

Table 6.4　Open-Seat Loser Spending as a Percentage of Open-Seat Winner Spending

	1998 Election (N=33)	2000 Election (N=32)
Less than 10	27.3	31.3
10–24.9	18.2	9.3
25–49.9	18.1	9.4
50–74.9	18.2	18.8
75–99.9	12.1	25.0
100 or more	6.1	6.2

Table 6.5a   Party Contributions to Challenger, by Competitiveness of District, 1998 (%)

	Marginal District (Incumbent won by 60% or less in 1996) (N=112)	Nonmarginal District (Incumbent won by more than 60% in 1996) (N=145)
Under $10,000	78	95
Over $10,000	22	5

Source: Federal Election Commission Data

Table 6.5b   Party Contributions to Incumbent, by Competitiveness of District, 1998 (%)

	Marginal District (Incumbent won by 60% or less in 1996) (N=116)	Non-Marginal District (Incumbent won by more than 60% in 1996) (N=213)
Under $10,000	78	99
Over $10,000	22	1

Source: Federal Election Commission Data

the party perspective, this makes perfect sense because incumbents in marginal districts are at risk of losing the seat, thus need shoring up by the party, while challengers in marginal districts have the best chance of gaining new seats for the party.

One consequence of the decisions made by party leaders, however, is that competition and participation in the remaining districts is virtually guaranteed to be low. Citizens lose their ability to participate effectively in campaigns if one candidate does not have the resources to get his or her message across. Fewer citizens turn out to vote in less competitive districts. This decrease in participation is particularly acute in districts where one of the parties fails to field a candidate. In the 2000 general election, the average turnout in districts with contested elections was approximately 231,000; if one party failed to field a candidate, turnout decreased by 20 percent, to 185,000 (Cook 2001). Since 10 of those uncontested seats were in Florida in 2000, we are left to speculate on how increased turnout might have affected the outcome of the presidential campaign.

Quality Candidates in Noncompetitive Districts

To understand fully the role of the party in encouraging competition, we must also understand how potentially strong candidates make decisions to run for office. For the last two election cycles the authors have studied potential candidates for the House of Representatives within the framework of the Candidate Emergence Study, which examines decision-making processes by potential candidates (PCs) in a randomly selected sample of 200 congressional districts. We identified our pool of PCs by first surveying a sample of politically knowledgeable informants in each of our sample districts. We asked these informants to tell us about the district and the incumbent and to provide us with names of and information about a group of PCs in their district. In a second stage of our study, we surveyed the PCs identified by our informants. Our concern throughout this study has been that little competition exists in many districts and that one cause of this lack of competition is that many potential candidates decide not to run. We want to understand the many factors that create this democratic dilemma, including the role that parties and party leaders play.

We think of candidate quality as having two dimensions: *strategic* resources that bear directly on an individual's ability to mount a successful campaign, and *personal* characteristics that are important both in the campaign and as an officeholder.

> [T]he best candidate is one who has both desirable leadership qualities *and* the ability to run an effective campaign. So recognizing that personal qualities are important does not mean that they are enough. But neither is the sheer ability to get elected. (Maisel et al. 2000)

Our informants were able to identify a group of high-quality PCs for the U.S. Congress in district after district throughout the country, and in both political parties, regardless of the political context of the district (Maisel et al. 2000). Therefore, the lack of competition that exists in many districts where incumbents are challenged only weakly or not at all is not the result of a lack of high-quality potential candidates in these districts. Rather it is partially the result of decisions by these candidates not to seek seats in the House of Representatives. In districts where the most recent election was dominated by the incumbent (those in which the incumbent ran unopposed or those in which the election was not hotly contested), our informants were able to identify PCs in both political parties. Further, the PCs whom they did identify scored high on our strategic-quality index and extremely high on the personal-quality index.

Party Leaders as Recruiters: How Active Are They? Where Are They Active?

We also know from our study that party officials are in fact active in contacting potential candidates for office (Maisel 2000). Approximately two out of every five of the potential candidates we were able to identify were contacted by someone at some level of party organization. Many were contacted by more than one such party official (see Table 6.6). But PCs were more likely to be contacted in some types of districts than others. Those in open seats were the most likely of all PCs to be contacted by party officials. Those in districts in which an incumbent was secure were less likely to be contacted than those in competitive districts. Table 6.7 shows that a similar pattern is observed in party contact by all levels of party organization. Local organizations are more likely to contact PCs than state organizations, and state organizations are more likely to do so than the national parties. Interestingly, the national parties, though least likely to contact PCs, have the most to offer to those PCs whom they do contact. These results clearly demonstrate that the political parties invest more effort recruiting candidates in districts that are expected to be competitive than they do in districts they regard as unwinnable.

Table 6.6   Percentage of PCs Contacted by Any Party Organization, by District Type

	N	% Contacted
All Seats	449	41
Secure seats (incumbent's margin was greater than 20% in previous election)	282	34
Marginal seats (incumbent's margin was less than 20% margin in previous election)	143	52
Open seat in 1998	24	54

Source: Candidate Emergence Survey Data.

Table 6.7   Percentage of PCs Contacted by Each Level of Party
Organization, by District Type

District Type	District Party	State Party	National Party	N
All Seats	35	22	17	449
Secure seats (incumbent's margin was greater than 20% in previous election)	27	18	11	282
Marginal seats (incumbent's margin was less than 20% in previous election)	46	28	28	143
Open seat in 1998	54	38	33	24

Source: Candidate Emergence Survey Data.

Beyond district structure, parties also make strategic decisions concerning *whom* they contact. Parties are in the business of winning, so they contact those they view as most likely to win. This effect is most apparent at the national level, because the national party must make tough choices about how to deploy its limited resources. Thus, they seek candidates who are best able to translate scarce resources into a win for the party. Table 6.8 shows how different factors influence the chances that a potential candidate will be contacted about running by his or her national party organization. The data for this analysis come from survey responses from potential candidates and political informants who participated in the Candidate Emergence Study, as well as archival data on the competitiveness of congressional races. The dependent variable in this model comes from a survey question asking whether or not the potential candidate was contacted by the national party, and is scored either 0 for no contact or 1 for contact. The independent variables thought to influence contact include district characteristics such as whether the seat was open or whether the seat was won by a close margin in the previous election, and potential candidate characteristics such as age, political skill, and income. The entries in the right-hand column indicate how much each factor, independent of all other factors, increases or decreases the chances that a potential candidate would be contacted.[5] So, for example, the chances that a PC will be contacted by the party increases by

.16 when he or she is in an open-seat district, and increases by .17 in a marginal district. Both of these findings are quite consistent with the previous tables showing the percentage of PC's contacted in competitive districts.

The most interesting finding in this table, however, is that PCs with certain characteristics are much more likely than others to be contacted by their national party. It should come as no surprise that we find parties are more likely to contact candidates that are likely to have a high chance of winning.[6] In this case, the PCs' chances of winning are derived from survey questions answered by the *informants* who recommended them. We use the informant judgments of the PC's quality rather than PCs' own judgments because PCs who are contacted may believe their chances of winning are better *because they have been contacted.* Indeed, in the next section we provide evidence of this. The informants, however, have made their assessments prior to contacting the PC. Similarly, PCs who already hold a state legislative office are more likely to be contacted. From the party's perspective, state legislators are attractive candidates because they have already demonstrated their ability to wage a winning campaign. Finally, PCs with higher income levels are more likely to be contacted by a national party. Although it is not clear whether this stems from the fact that wealthy individuals might be better known in the community or from the fact that wealthy individuals might be in a better position to muster additional resources, it is clear that money helps.

While these strategic factors, candidate strength, experience, and income increase the chances of contact, other factors—age and party of the PC—decrease the chances of contact. Parties seem to seek candidates who are younger rather than older, perhaps because younger PCs are more ambitious or have a longer potential "shelf life" once in office. More significant, parties are much less likely to contact PCs in the same party as the incumbent. This reflects the fact that the parties do not stand to gain anything by recruiting a candidate to compete against one of their own. Only in the rarest of circumstances would a party seek a candidate to challenge a sitting incumbent of their party.

The conclusion to be drawn from Table 6.8 is that party leaders are not very creative in determining what kinds of PCs they will encourage. They go after the obvious candidates and leave some of the less obvious ones alone. We know that this strategy has not always been successful. The obvious candidates have not always done well. Many of those who have defeated incumbents, like the Democrat Rush Holt in New Jersey in 1998, came into races without the support of party leaders. Any conclusion made on the basis of these data must be speculative, but one is led to ask whether party leaders could play a more active role in the recruitment

Table 6.8   OLS Model of National Party Contact (standard errors) (N=312)

Independent Variables:	Dependent Variable:
	PC Contacted about running by national party in 1998
Chances the potential candidate would win the seat (informant assessments)	.22** (.09)
Potential candidate is a state legislator	.11* (.05)
Potential candidate age	−.07** (.02)
Potential candidate income	.03* (.01)
Potential candidate is a Democrat	.03 (.05)
Potential candidate is in same party as incumbent	−.19** (.05)
Incumbent won with less than 60% of vote in 1996	.17** (.04)
Seat is open in 1998	.16* (.17)
Constant	.23
Adjusted R squared	.14
Number of Cases	312

Source: Candidate Emergence Study
Note: *p<.05   **p<.01, one-tailed tests

process and perhaps whether they might be more effective if they based their decisions on whom to contact on a wider set of criteria.

Party Contact as a "Message" to Potential Candidates

The likelihood that PCs will run for office is improved by a statistically significant amount if they are contacted by party officials. This stems in part from the fact that parties are most active in contacting PCs when there are better opportunities to win, as shown in the earlier tables; but it

Table 6.9a   The Effect of Party Contact on PCs' Chances of Running

	Chances of Running in 1998		Chances of Running in 2000	
	Contacted	Not Contacted	Contacted	Not Contacted
Local party committee	.19	.09	.17	.09
(N)	(141)	(266)	(66)	(156)
State party committee	.20	.10	.17	.10
(N)	(91)	(316)	(43)	(179)
National congressional campaign committee	.23	.10	.24	.10
(N)	(68)	(339)	(24)	(198)
National party committees	.29[a]	.11	.30	.10
(N)	(35)	(372)	(16)	(206)

Source: Candidate Emergence Study.

[a]Chances of running are based on potential candidates' views of how likely he/she is to run, and are converted to a scale that ranges from near 0 (no chance of running) to near 1.0 (sure to run).

also stems from the fact that PCs recognize the benefits of having the support of their party. This dual message is important because it tells a PC the seat is winnable and the party will help the candidate win. The increased chance of winning in turn increases the chances the PC will run.

Tables 6.9a and 6.9b show the overall effect of party contact on the chances a strong PC will run. The data for this table come from survey questions asking strong PCs how likely (or unlikely) they were to run for office in 1998 and 2000. Since they have also provided information about which level of their political party, if any, has contacted them about running, we can compare PCs' average chances of running according to what level of party organization contacted them. It should come as no surprise that the chances of running are highest among PCs contacted by the national political party committee, followed closely by those contacted by their national congressional campaign committee. National-level organizations typically have more resources to offer candidates to help them win than lower-level organizations. Further, since the national party organizations take a very strategic approach in their allocation of resources to competitive races, they are most likely to contact PCs in competitive districts or open-seat districts. The dual effects of the party support and district conditions create powerful incentives for strong PCs interested in seeking a House seat. However, even contact by the party organization at the state and district level lead to a greater chance a PC will run, as compared to those who were not contacted. Notably, table 6.9b suggests that multiple party contacts can have a cumulative effect. PCs who were contacted by more than one party committee about running are far more likely to run than those contacted by only one.

To summarize what the data from the Candidate Emergence Study tell us, we know that party organizations are active in recruiting quality candidates; we know that their activity increases in districts thought likely to be competitive; we know that party encouragement increases the chances a strong PC will run; and we know that strong PCs exist even in districts in which one party or the other is not likely to be competitive. Yet these data tell only a portion of the story of the role that party officials are playing in candidate recruitment. We know anecdotally that the strategy national party leaders follow is to concentrate resources on districts most likely to be winnable. One must surely accept this strategy as most likely to result in success, if success is defined as winning more

Table 6.9b   Cumulative Effect of Party Contact on PCs' Chances of Running

Level of Contact	Chances of Running in 1998	Chances of Running in 2000
No party contact	.09 [a]	.08
(N)	(241)	(140)
Contacted by 1 party level	.13	.16
(N)	(69)	(40)
Contacted by 2 party levels	.15	.11
(N)	(49)	(26)
Contacted by 3 party levels	.21	.15
(N)	(24)	(7)
Contacted by all 4 party levels	.32	.39
(N)	(24)	(9)

Source: Candidate Emergence Study.
[a] Chances of running are based on potential candidates' views of how likely he/she is to run, and are converted to a scale that ranges from near 0 (no chance of running) to near 1.0 (sure to run).

seats—a perfectly reasonable definition for party leaders to explore. We are left to question, however, whether the democratic process in districts not thought to be competitive in advance of an election suffers as a result of this strategy. Perhaps that is not and should not be a concern of party leaders as they determine how to allocate scarce resources, but it is a concern of those interested in stimulating citizen participation in their democracy in a meaningful way.

Conclusions

Party officials, particularly national party officials, have played an increasingly important role in candidate recruitment in recent election cycles. They see their role, quite rightly, as striving to help their party either to maintain or to achieve majority status in the Congress.[7] They have pursued this goal by concentrating on marginal districts, open seats, and districts with vulnerable incumbents. Again, this strategy makes perfect sense given their desired end.

However, one consequence of the strategy is that competition in the remaining districts is all but nonexistent. Citizens in those districts vote in smaller numbers; they do not have access to electoral choice as a mechanism for evaluating the performance of the incumbent; they are not involved in ongoing policy debates through a competitive electoral process. As a result, citizen engagement in the political process dwindles.

Strong PCs do exist in noncompetitive as well as in competitive districts. However, party officials, particularly national party officials, largely ignore these candidates. They do not encourage them to run. They do not offer much support to those who do run. We conclude that party efforts might well make a difference in attracting some of these quality candidates into the electoral arena. Party officials think strategically in considering where to place their resources; they think traditionally in terms of what qualities are possessed by candidates they contact.

We believe that better candidates run better races. They are better able to articulate the issues. They are more likely to communicate effectively to citizens. They are more likely to be able to discuss an incumbent's record in detail. If citizen engagement is a civic virtue to be pursued, quality candidates in races as visible as congressional elections should add to that involvement.

That is not to say, however, that these higher-quality candidates are likely to change the outcomes of races in districts that are currently noncompetitive. That issue can be argued two ways. Some would claim that many districts are drawn to favor one candidate or the other and that the quality of the candidates is unlikely to change the outcome, though it might change the nature of the debate. Others claim that political context over the long run can be changed by the quality of the candidates running, that some districts that are not now competitive might well become so if better candidates were running better campaigns and raising important questions. The resolution of that debate remains for another day.

Notes

1. We are grateful for support from the National Science Foundation for the surveys on which this paper is based (SBR–9515350). We would like to thank our home institutions, Colby College, the University of California–Davis, and Texas Tech University, for assistance on the project. We would also like to thank the research assistants who have worked on the Candidate Emergency Study, especially Brooke McNally and Marla Southerland, who contributed to the analysis in this chapter.

2. If there was little two-party competition for House seats in the South in this era, there was even less for seats in state legislatures. The Republican party contested for the presidency and, increasingly as time went on, for statewide office, but Republican party nominations were forfeited for most offices in most regions of the South during this period.

3. In this effort they are aided by national political analysts who handicap House, Senate, and gubernatorial races for subscribers to their services. The *Cook Political Report* and the *Rothenberg Political Report* comment early and often on which races are likely to be competitive and which are safe for one party or the other. These political analysts rely on the actions of party leaders to reach their conclusions; the party leaders look to the perceptions of the political analysts to reinforce their judgments.

4. Many practical politicians feel these differences impede any effective public financing reform for House campaigns. Agreement cannot be reached on how much is needed to run an effective campaign, because that amount various tremendously from district to district, sometimes even within the same state.

5. The model presented is an ordinary least-squares model. Since the dependent variable is a dummy variable, the model can be interpreted as a linear probability model where the coefficients represent the marginal change in probability of contact, holding all else constant. Of course, there are a number of problems with linear probability models such as out-of-sample predictions and heteroskedasticity, which can be solved by using a logit model. However, we present the more easily interpretable OLS coefficients. The substantive results do not change if we use logit rather than OLS.

6. The informants' ratings are based on survey questions about the potential candidates' chances of winning the nomination and the general election, which

are recoded to a "pseudo" probability scale, where 0 is no chance of winning and 1 is certain to win.

7. We believe but do not know for certain that parallel actions to identify PCs are being taken by state and local officials, particularly to locate candidates for seats in state legislatures whose partisan control is in doubt.

7

Following the (Soft) Money: Party Advertisements in American Elections

MICHAEL FRANZ AND KENNETH GOLDSTEIN

In 1992, the Democratic party raised over $36 million dollars in soft money. In 2000, the party raised over $245 million. Similarly, the Republican party raised almost $50 million in 1992, and almost $250 million in 2000.[1] Joe Andrews, the former Democratic National Committee chairman, noted that Democratic party fund-raisers pulled in over $21 million dollars in soft money in the full year before the 2000 presidential election contest.[2] Such a permanent campaign mentality fueled the party's electoral campaigns across the country during the most contentious and balanced election cycle in recent memory. For many, such figures stand as conclusive evidence of what party scholars have been arguing for over a decade—political parties are back.

Less is known, though, about how parties are spending this new influx of capital and to what effect. The Federal Election Commission requires the detailed reporting of party contributions to candidates and of coordinated expenditures with candidates, but the disclosure of how soft money is spent is not required.[3] Opponents of campaign finance reform assert that soft money is being used in ways that build a party character within the electorate, as well as to establish an organizational infrastructure. Others counter that soft money is being used to win elections with the goal of gaining political power; they argue that party building is more an illusion than a reality. This chapter makes use of a unique source of data about television commercials to examine the role of party ads in the 1998 and 2000 elections. Campaign advertising has become one of the most important means of transmitting political messages, and parties are using their resurgent organizational agility to fund their advertising efforts. These data allow us to explore from a new perspective the murky question of what parties are doing with soft money.

Party Money: The Role of Soft Money

Parties can use money to aid candidates in three ways: direct contributions to a candidate's campaign, coordinated expenditures with candidates, and independent efforts known as soft money (or nonfederal money). Direct contributions are subject to the limits established in the 1974 Federal Election Campaign Act (FECA). Limits on coordinated expenditures, also established in FECA, were recently upheld in the 2001 Supreme Court decision *FEC v. Colorado Republican Federal Campaign Committee*, 533 U.S. 431 (2001)—the case is known as Colorado Republican II; Colorado Republican I is *Colorado Republican Party v. FEC*, 518 U.S. 604 (1996).

Since the mid–1990s, though, when the courts upheld the unlimited use of independent expenditures in Colorado Republican I, soft money has become the weapon of choice for the Democratic and Republican parties. So long as parties avoid "express advocacy" of candidates (the definition of which was established in a footnote to the Supreme Court's 1976 decision in *Buckley v. Valeo*, 421 U.S. 1 (1976), parties are free to spend unlimited funds. Such expenditures are intended for activities that "build the party."

Table 7.1 shows the soft-money receipts by each party's national, congressional, and senatorial campaign committee since 1992, the first year the Federal Election Commission required full reporting of soft money donations (disclosure of how the money is spent is not required). The sharp increases in soft-money receipts are apparent, most prominently among the congressional and senatorial committees. For example, in 1992 the Democratic Senatorial Campaign Committee (DSCC) raised just over $500,000; in 2000, the DSCC raised over $63,000,000. In recent years the two parties have established a division of labor between national and legislative campaign committees whereby the national committee handles presidential contests and transfers of funds to state parties and the legislative committees handle House and Senate contests.

The recent debate over campaign finance reform, and the McCain-Feingold legislation, which seeks to ban the use of soft money, has spawned discussion of the role of soft money in contemporary elections.[4] There is little doubt that soft money is being used to directly support candidates. There is little doubt that parties are using soft money to gain political power. In this sense, soft money is proof of the parties' adaptation to a political environment that once threatened their legitimacy.

There is a question, however, as to how much parties use soft money to convey a party agenda and establish a stronger party-in-the-electorate. The FEC does not require full disclosure of soft-money outlays, and consequently there are limitations as to what scholars can find out and the confidence with which they can make broad claims about the ways soft

Table 7.1 Soft-Money Receipts

	2000	1998	1996	1994	1992
Democrats					
National committee	$136,563,419	$56,966,353	$101,905,186	$43,923,516	$31,356,076
Senatorial campaign comm.	$63,717,982	$25,880,538	$14,176,392	$372,448	$566,111
Congressional campaign comm.	$56,702,023	$16,865,410	$12,340,824	$5,113,343	$4,368,980
Total	$245,202,519	$92,811,927	$123,877,924	$49,143,460	$36,256,667
Republicans					
National committee	$166,207,843	$74,805,286	$113,127,010	$44,870,758	$35,936,945
Senatorial campaign comm.	$44,652,709	$37,866,845	$29,395,329	$5,582,013	$9,064,167
Congressional campaign comm.	$47,295,736	$26,914,05	$18,530,773	$7,371,097	$6,076,321
Total	$249,861,645	$131,615,116	$138,199,706	$ 52,522,763	$49,787,433

Source: Federal Election Commission.

money is used. Soft money's most ardent supporters tout its role in re-building political parties and infusing excitement about politics within the electorate. For example, Senator Mitch McConnell (R-Ky.) has emerged as one of the strongest defenders of soft money. He argues that soft money is vital in helping political parties perform a crucial task in American politics: "smoothing ideological edges and promoting citizen participation. The two major parties are the big tents where multitudes of individuals and groups with narrow agendas converge to promote candidates and broad philosophies about the role of government in our society" (*New York Times*, April 1, 2001, p. 17).

McConnell's assertions imply that parties are designed to foster a party identity within the electorate; that parties have some higher motive than gaining political power. More specifically, McConnell's defense of soft money is premised on the claim that soft money performs a function in elections that candidate money does not—that soft money spurs participation; makes elections more competitive; allows the party to convey a unified party message; and provides a forum for new and often-ignored ideas. Fortunately, such claims are empirical questions. What exactly do parties do in contemporary elections? Is there evidence that parties are in fact using soft money in the manner that opponents of reform claim?

Or are the reformers right? Are parties in fact simply focusing their energies and their soft money solely on helping candidates win elections? That is, is party soft money simply *more* of the same money, as opposed to *different* money? In the end, if the evidence indicates that parties care less about establishing a strong base than about simply putting candidates in office, we will acknowledge that the parties' chief goal has always been winning elections; the use of soft money and party advertisements is simply the modern-day means by which parties gain power.

Because both major parties mostly use soft money for campaign advertisements, the spending of soft money is particularly difficult to track. In the past, analysis of campaign advertisements has been somewhat problematic. Some scholars have gathered data through the purchasing of advertising records from candidates (Shaw 1999). Such data, however, do not contain information concerning the content of the advertisements, nor do the records report airings of party and interest group ads. Others have obtained advertising information by visiting television stations directly and asking them for their records (Magleby 2001). But the number of stations across the country makes this style of data collection impractical for comprehensively examining an election cycle's advertising content.

Now, a new source of data on campaign advertising is opening the door to a more systematic analysis of party influence in American elections. By examining the type of party ads and their distribution across elections and election contexts, scholars can begin to understand the full impact of the party's most recent adaptation to the political environment.

The Advertising Data

The data on campaign advertisements for the 1998 and 2000 election cycles include two types of information: frequency data and content data. Frequency data are a record of when ads aired and in which markets. A commercial firm, Campaign Media Analysis Group (CMAG), collected this set of frequency data.[5] CMAG has "Ad Detectors" in each of the top 75 media markets, and these detectors track advertisements on the four major broadcast networks and 25 national cable networks.[6]

It is interesting to note that the United States Navy originally developed this technology with the intention of tracking Soviet navy vessels by measuring and recording the unique sound patterns of Soviet submarines. CMAG now uses the technology to track campaign advertising by listening for unique sound patterns in television advertisements. The system's software recognizes the electronic seams between programming and advertising and identifies the "digital fingerprints" of specific advertisements. When the system does not recognize the fingerprints of a particular commercial spot, the advertisement is captured and downloaded. Thereafter, the system automatically recognizes and logs that particular commercial wherever and whenever it airs.

The frequency data are extremely accurate. To ascertain the accuracy of the data, project staff at the University of Wisconsin–Madison traveled to a number of television stations and viewed their advertising logs. In every case, when the CMAG data indicate that an ad aired, the television logs confirm the airing to the minute. On the other hand, estimates of the cost of an ad should be regarded with caution, for they surely *underestimate* the amount of money spent by the sponsor. CMAG estimates the cost of an ad buy on the basis of the market and the cost of a regular advertisement in a particular time slot. In the heat of an election, however, television stations tend to overcharge parties and candidates. To confirm this, we compared the logs for the television stations we visited with the CMAG estimate of the cost of the spot. In almost every case, the CMAG data understated how much the sponsor spent for the ad.

The data set also contains a content code for each unique advertisement. CMAG provided a storyboard for each ad, and students at Arizona State University and the University of Wisconsin coded each storyboard.[7] The storyboard contains transcripts of all audio and a still of every fourth second of video. Coders were asked to determine the advertisement's tone, purpose, sponsorship, and even commonly used adjectives, among a number of other things. Some of the criteria were clearly very objective

(Did the ad mention the candidate? Did the ad urge voters to contact someone?), whereas other criteria were more subjective (Is the ad positive, negative, or contrasting in tone? "Contrasting" refers to an ad that mentions both the favored and opposing candidates and compares their policy and political stands).[8]

To create the data set, these coded data were merged to the larger data set of when each ad aired. Thus, the completed data set for each election cycle contains information on when each ad aired, as well as the focus and message of the ad. Consequently, every time an ad aired during the campaign, it was entered into the data set. If an ad aired 4,000 times, it has 4,000 entries. In the final data set, every entry stands for one airing of one ad, containing information on the date, time, and location of the ad (meaning the media market in which it was aired), as well as the list of codes concerning the content of the ad.

Party Advertising in the 1998 and 2000 Elections

Overview

The years 1998 and 2000 represent very different electoral environments. The presidential election in 2000 guaranteed that the airwaves would be packed with hundreds of thousands more campaign advertisements. In addition, the two-year gap between 1998 and 2000 allowed political operatives more time to master the still-developing and ever-growing game of soft-money fund-raising. Because the use of soft money became most prevalent in the late 1990s following Colorado I, the court case that upheld unlimited expenditures by parties, parties have had only a few years to understand the electoral implications of this legal blank check. In 1998, there were 302,344 political advertisements—a combination of candidate ads, party ads, candidate and party coordinated expenditures, and interest group–sponsored advertisements. By 2000 this had jumped to 970,410. Of the almost 1 million ads aired in 2000, 93 percent had an electoral objective; thus, only 7 percent of all ads aired in 2000 (about 62,000) were focused *only* on issue advocacy. In 1998, a little more than 3 percent (about 9,500 ads) were solely devoted to issue advocacy.

Table 7.2 shows the amount of money spent on candidate, party, and interest-group advertisements in the presidential, Senate, and House general election contests for 2000. As the numbers demonstrate, the parties clearly played a dominant role in these elections. The Democrats spent over $81,000,000, and the Republicans over $80,000,000 in 2000; looking beyond the parity in these aggregate numbers, we see that the Republican party spent more in the presidential contest, but the Democrats took the lead in the Senate and House races. These numbers should be regarded with caution, however; they surely *underestimate* the amount of money spent, as noted before.

Table 7.2   Expenditures for Advertising in 2000 General Election

	Presidential Race	*Senate Races*	*House Races*
Democratic candidates	$23,986,251[a]	$66,577,515	$43,429,993
Republican candidates	$16,186,159[b]	$63,178,384	$36,016,296
Democratic party	$35,697,348	$21,720,947	$24,026,562
Republican party	$45,847,137	$15,787,645	$18,687,788
Pro-Democratic IGs[c]	$12,412,894	$4,222,031	$10,685,012
Pro-Republican IGs[c]	$2,583,292	$6,097,535	$14,034,181

Source: Federal Election Commission.

[a] Al Gore; these numbers are for general election candidates only.

[b] George Bush; these numbers are for general election candidates only.

[c] IGs = interest groups.

In both 1998 and 2000, political parties aired solely electoral ads, meaning there were no party-sponsored spots that were solely aired with the intention of relating party-based issues. Party ads accounted for 34 percent of all campaign spots in federal contests in 2000 (about 230,000 ads) and 15 percent in 1998 (about 45,000 ads). Clearly, political parties quickly learned to take advantage of the new advertising environment; they aired more than five times the number of advertisements in 2000 than in 1998—no doubt owing to the high stakes of the 2000 election, where each party saw the possibility of gaining unified control of the House, Senate, and executive branch.

For the most part, however, parties played the same essential role in both election cycles. More specifically, political parties have mastered the ability to play the bad guy: In 1998, 62 percent of party ads were negative, compared to only 20 percent of candidate ads. In 2000, 45 percent of party ads were negative, compared to only 16 percent of candidate ads. At the same time, 55 percent of candidate ads were positive in 1998 and in 2000. One could argue that candidates and parties have developed a fairly sophisticated game of good cop/bad cop.

Nonetheless, this distinction remains somewhat curious—in that party ads and candidate ads are nearly indistinguishable in content. A voter would be hard-pressed to distinguish between a party ad and a candidate ad beyond the often indecipherable tag line at the end of the advertisement. Furthermore, a vast majority of all campaign advertisements chose to avoid mentioning the party label. For example, in 1998, 88 percent of candidate ads did not mention either the candidate's party or his opponent's. Eighty-three percent of party ads failed to mention a party label. The percentages are even more striking from the 2000 cycle, where 95 percent of candidate ads avoided mention of a political party and 92 percent of party ads eschewed an overt party identification.

Consider the text from the following two advertisements:

AD 1

Gore: George Bush and I actually agree on accountability in education.
Announcer: The Gore Plan begins with accountability.
Gore: We need smaller classes and better-trained teachers.
Announcer: One hundred thousand more teachers to lower class
   size. Increase discipline in learning.
Gore: We need help for middle-class families to help pay college tu-
   ition by making it tax-deductible.
Announcer: A ten thousand-dollar deduction every year for college
   tuition.
Gore: We are making education the number one priority.

AD 2

Gore: Strengthening education begins with us, not the government.
   Parents simply have to get involved and take responsibility to
   make sure their children study and learn. But government has to
   take responsibility for what it can do. Fix failing schools, reduce
   the class size, set higher standards for students and for teachers.
   We're in an information age. We have a responsibility to make
   sure our schools are the very best in the entire world.

One would be hard-pressed to correctly identify ad number 1 as an ad
paid for by the Democratic party and ad number 2 as an ad paid for by
the Gore campaign.

Table 7.3   Tone of 1998 House and Senate Advertisements (No. of Ads)

	House			Senate		
Tone	Candidate Ads	Party Ads	Interest- Groups Ads	Candidate Ads	Party Ads	Interest- Groups Ads
Positive	62,509	6,530	1,582	63,912	5,379	77
(%)	(64)	(36)	(18)	(51)	(22)	(11)
Negative	16,263	9,618	6,142	29,913	17,671	233
(%)	(16)	(54)	(70)	(24)	(71)	(32)
Contrast	21,383	1,805	1,084	32,017	1,923	416
(%)	(20)	(10)	(12)	(25)	(7)	(57)

Table 7.4   Tone of 2000 House and Senate Advertisements (No. of Ads)

Tone	House			Senate		
	Candidate Ads	Party Ads	Interest-Groups Ads	Candidate Ads	Party Ads	Interest-Groups Ads
Positive	64,897	7,336	12,465	77,919	6,001	4,981
(%)	(52)	(14)	(31)	(57)	(11)	(38)
Negative	23,204	35,991	25,900	21,457	8,075	7,028
(%)	(19)	(68)	(65)	(16)	(53)	(53)
Contrast	35,685	9,317	1,439	7,622	18,946	1,170
(%)	(29)	(18)	(4)	(27)	(36)	(9)

What does this imply? First of all, one could argue that the difference in message tone across candidate and party advertisements is evidence that parties are increasingly acting as money-laundering organizations whose major purpose is to allow candidates to avoid being labeled "negative campaigners." Second, the absence of a party label on most party ads (whose lawful justification is, after all, to "build the party") stands as interesting evidence for the new role of parties in elections. If parties are powerful players in politics by virtue of their use of soft money, why are parties avoiding the party label? Indeed, the organizational strength of parties is clearly not going to waste; more than likely the intention is not to establish strong partisans, but to win elections and gain power.

In the next two subsections, we analyze party, candidate, and interest-group advertising activity in the 1998 and 2000 House and Senate elections, and then give an overview of the distribution of advertising in the most recent presidential election.

House and Senate Elections

In 2000, 479,079 ads were aired for primary and general election candidates for House and Senate seats. The effect of the presidential election and the stakes of the particular 2000 election cycle account for the substantial increase from the 302,377 ads aired for House and Senate elections in 1998, prompting in particular a substantial increase in the airing of party and interest-group advertisements. Tables 7.3 and 7.4 show 1998 and 2000 candidate, party, and interest-group ads for Senate and the House elections in terms of tone taken by the ads.

As can be seen, candidates clearly took the high road in the majority of their own ads (meaning the majority of candidate ads were positive in tone), whereas party ads were mostly negative. Note, however, the sheer increase in the volume of party ads in 2000. While the number of candidate ads remained fairly similar in both election cycles, parties aired four times as many negative ads in House elections in 2000, and party negative ads in Senate elections increased by nearly 60 percent. This is indicative of a substantial increase in fund-raising and organization in the two years from 1998 to 2000.

Note also the increased role of interest groups. Groups also aired mostly negative ads in both cycles (except in Senate elections in 1998, where over half of the group-sponsored ads were coded as contrast ads), but the main story is in the increase in the *number* of ads. In 1998, groups aired 8,808 ads in House elections and practically ignored Senate races, airing a total of 726 ads. In 2000, however, interest groups aired 39,804 ads in House elections and 13,179 ads in Senate elections.

The overall pattern of party ads eschewing the party label holds for the House and Senate elections in 1998 and 2000. Tables 7.5 and 7.6 highlight the number and percentage of candidate, party, and interest-group advertisements that mentioned a party label (of either the favored or opposing candidate). The overwhelming majority of all ads did not mention the party in any fashion.

Clearly, political parties desire to win elections. However, if party money were being used mostly to lay a foundation for a stronger partisan electorate, or if money were being spent to convey a unified party message, one might expect more party ads in noncompetitive races. We do not see that here. With 435 House elections and over 30 Senate elections every two years, even the most well funded parties and interest groups must spend money where they are likely to receive the greatest return. And because the Republicans in both 1998 and 2000 did not have secure majorities in either branch of Congress, it is no surprise that the competitive elections received the most attention from parties and groups. Table 7.7 highlights the difference in candidate, party, and group ads in competitive and noncompetitive House and Senate elections in 2000.[9] It is no surprise that candidates air more advertisements in competitive elections (given the heightened political environment), but the numbers show that parties and groups virtually ignored non-competitive races.

At the same time, Table 7.8 shows the tone of ads used in House and Senate competitive and noncompetitive races. Interestingly, candidates in both competitive and noncompetitive races steered clear of negative advertisements; nonetheless, there was a difference in the tone of ads. More specifically, candidates in competitive races shifted the tone of advertisements from positive to contrast—as noted, contrast ads mention both the favored and opposing candidates and compare the policy and political

Table 7.5 Number of 1998 House and Senate Advertisements and Mentions of Party

	House			Senate		
Tone	*Candidate*	*Party*	*Interest-Groups*	*Candidate*	*Party*	*Interest-Groups*
Party not mentioned	88,319	12,447	5,528	114,642	24,231	1,027
(%)	(87)	(70)	(63)	(90)	(95)	(100)
Party mentioned	13,606	5,336	3,208	13,132	1,148	0
(%)	(13)	(30)	(37)	(10)	(5)	(0)

Table 7.6 Number of 2000 House and Senate Advertisements and Mentions of Party

	House			Senate		
Tone	*Candidate*	*Party*	*Interest-Groups*	*Candidate*	*Party*	*Interest-Groups*
Party not mentioned	115,252	49,306	39,563	135,835	49,238	12,919
(%)	(93)	(94)	(99)	(99)	(93)	(98)
Party mentioned	8,872	3,338	322	1,184	3,750	260
(%)	(7)	(6)	(1)	(1)	(7)	(2)

stands of the candidates. A fairly uncontroversial hypothesis would be that contrast ads tend to be negative in tone, in that they are designed to make the opposing candidate look bad when compared to the favored candidate; nonetheless, they are clearly not *as* negative as the pure negative spot because at least the appearance of a genuine issue comparison between candidates is maintained. Thus, it appears that candidates who aired contrasting ads were clearly trying to avoid the stigma of a being negative campaigners, and even when the stakes were high (as they are in competitive elections), candidates avoided a purely negative attack on the opposition.

As Table 7.8 makes clear, candidates enabled parties to go on the offensive. For example, although parties did not air many ads in noncompetitive House races in 2000, the distribution of ads across tone was not as apparent as in competitive House elections, where party ads were overwhelmingly negative. Although ads were mostly negative in both competitive and noncompetitive Senate races, there was a higher percentage of positive party ads in noncompetitive races than in competitive contests.

It is clear that parties and interest groups favored competitive contests, but what of the dynamics across elections? When a competitive race in one year becomes noncompetitive in the next contest, do parties and groups now ignore the race? A story of party building might expect parties to continue airing ads in races no longer featuring a competitive contest—so as to build on the foundation built during the competitive contest. Indeed, to understand the intention behind party expenditures it is important to examine them over time. One could argue that parties do not spend money in noncompetitive races because either the loyalty of the base to one's own party is already established or it is already firmly entrenched with the opposition. A competitive contest, however, indicates that a district is in play and that the base is not firmly behind one party. If parties desire to establish themselves, they would undoubtedly have to continue cultivating the base after the election.

David Magleby (2001) and his associates have extensively documented the activity of groups and parties in competitive contests in 1998 and 2000. We briefly examined four races that were listed as highly competitive in 1998 but noncompetitive in 2000 and that were featured in Magleby's analysis. For each race we examined the candidate, party, and group ads aired in the major media market(s). Magleby's analysis is more comprehensive in that it examines a number of electoral activities (television, radio, print media, etc.), and it also contains some information on advertisements in smaller markets not covered by the CMAG data. The brief analysis offered here, however, will allow us to see what parties do when the race is no longer competitive.

In 1998, Iowa's 3rd district featured a highly competitive contest between Leonard Boswell, an incumbent Democrat, and the Republican Larry McKibben. Boswell received support from his party in the form of 309 ad airings in the Des Moines media market, in addition to 129 spots by organized interests. Republican party officials aired almost 500 spots for McKibben, more than the candidate aired for his own campaign. In 2000 the contest was not competitive. The parties aired zero ads in the Des Moines market. Boswell won again.

The 1998 competitive race for New Mexico's 3rd district was between an incumbent Republican, Bill Redmond, and the Democrat Tom Udall.

Table 7.7   Number of Advertisements in 2000 House and Senate Elections by Competitiveness

	House		Senate	
	Noncompetitive	*Competitive*	*Noncompetitive*	*Competitive*
Candidate ads	48,347	75,303	42,358	93,048
Party ads	1,147	51,497	7,362	45,660
Interest-groups ads	5,289	34,696	2,053	11,126

Table 7.8   Number of Advertisements in 2000 House and Senate Elections by Competitiveness and Tone

		House		Senate	
		Non-competitive	*Competitive*	*Non-competitive*	*Competitive*
Candidate ads	Positive	30,377 (63%)	34,436 (46%)	32,406 (77%)	44,657 (48%)
	Negative	8,403 (17%)	14,524 (19%)	5,085 (12%)	6,179 (17%)
	Contrast	9,324 (20%)	26,117 (35%)	4,846 (11%)	32,212 (35%)
Party ads	Positive	571 (50%)	6,765 (13%)	2,284 (31%)	3,717 (8%)
	Negative	319 (28%)	35,672 (69%)	3,993 (54%)	24,082 (53%)
	Contrast	257 (22%)	9,060 (18%)	1,085 (15%)	17,861 (39%)
Interest-groups ads	Positive	2,275 (44%)	10,190 (29%)	964 (47%)	4,017 (36%)
	Negative	2,833 (55%)	23,067 (66%)	1,089 (53%)	5,939 (53%)
	Contrast	0 (0%)	1,439 (5%)	0 (0%)	1,170 (11%)

Note: When the number of positive, negative, and contrast ads in each of the above categories (i.e., House, noncompetitive, candidate ads) are added up, there may be slight differences between the total and the number in the previous table. This is because the numbers in the table above exclude the handful of ads that coders could not identify as having a tone.

Table 7.9   1998: Top Issues in Candidate and Party Ads, House and Senate Races (No. of Mentions)

	Democratic		Republican	
	Candidate Ads	Party Ads	Candidate Ads	Party Ads
	House Races	**House Races**	**House Races**	**House Races**
	Education (8,539)	Social Security (751)	Taxes (8,164)	Taxes (4,559)
	Political record (4,974)	Education (595)	Social Security (5,420)	Honesty (1,973)
	Social Security (4,326)	Crime (498)	Background (4,285)	Education (1,855)
	Health care (4,138)	Minimum wage (367)	Education (4,008)	Clinton (1,397)
	Background (3,135)	Child care (225)	Honesty (3,298)	Crime (944)
	Senate Races	**Senate Races**	**Senate Races**	**Senate Races**
	Education (9,854)	Health care (1,898)	Taxes (11,270)	Social Security (2,644)
	Health care (6,756)	Education (1,597)	Education (8,418)	Taxes (2,239)
	Honesty (4,822)	Medicare (1,593)	Political record (4,002)	Medicare (905)
	Taxes (3,841)	Minimum wage (1,238)	Attendance record (3,839)	Political record (725)
	Social Security (3,517)	Political record (974)	Honesty (3,833)	Trade (565)

Source: Federal Election Commission.

The Udall campaign aired 800 ads, almost twice as many ads as the Redmond campaign, in the Albuquerque media market. The Democratic party basically stayed out of the race—owing to money issues and the sense that Udall was ahead (Magleby 2001). The Republican party, on the other hand, aired almost 700 ads for Redmond, enough to make up Udall's advantage in candidate ads. Nonetheless, with the Democratic party sitting out the ad race, pro-Udall interest groups aired almost 800 ads, giving him an upper hand that helped him to win the race. In 2000 the race was considered noncompetitive, and both parties and interest groups stayed out of the race, airing zero ads.

In 1998, Ohio's 6th district was listed as a competitive contest between the incumbent Democrat, Ted Strickland, and the Republican Nancy Hollister. Ads were tracked by CMAG in the Cincinnati, Charleston, and Columbus media markets. The candidates showed near parity in the airing of candidate ads, but there was a huge presence of Republican party ads, 1,319, motivated by the belief that Strickland was vulnerable. Though pro-Strickland interest groups attempted to make up for the meager Democratic party presence, they were dwarfed by the Republican party presence. Nonetheless, Strickland prevailed. In 2000 the race listed as noncompetitive, and neither party aired any ads in the district.

In 1998, the race for Wisconsin's open 1st district was between an incumbent Democrat, Lydia Spottswood, and the Republican Paul Ryan. Ryan had almost twice as many candidate ads as Spottswood, and there was rough parity in party ads—250 airings for Spottswood and 256 airings for Ryan in the Milwaukee media market. Pro-Democratic interest groups made up some of the difference for Spottswood, airing over 200 spots, but the Ryan campaign, helped by a strong Republican presence, took the seat. In 2000 the race was noncompetitive, and both the Democratic and Republican parties ignored it.

Clearly, parties are highly pragmatic in soft money expenditures. There is little indication thus far that parties use money to cultivate a party following. Their goal is to win elections, pure and simple.

Finally, Tables 7.9 and 7.10 compare the top issue mentions in candidate and party ads for Democrats and Republicans in the 1998 and 2000 House and Senate elections. If a party were attempting to use its advertisements to convey a unified political message, we may expect to see similar issues in House and Senate party ads. For the 2000 elections, the Democrats appear to be unified in their message, having the same top five issues for House and Senate elections, but the Republicans in 1998 and in 2000, and the Democrats in 1998 appear to have no consistent message across House and Senate elections. Thus, one might argue that parties are using soft money to air ads that are race-specific; that is, parties are using their advertisements to help candidates in specific contests, not to project generalized messages about themselves.

Table 7.10   2000: Top Issues in Candidate and Party Ads, House and Senate Races (No. of Mentions)

Democratic		Republican	
Candidate Ads	Party Ads	Candidate Ads	Party Ads
House Races	**House Races**	**House Races**	**House Races**
Health care (11,789)	Health Care (5,515)	Background (10,580)	Taxes (4,603)
Background (6,593)	Education (3,268)	Taxes (6,916)	Honesty (3,208)
Education (5,861)	Social Security (2,784)	Education (6,690)	Education (2,525)
Medicare (4,439)	Medicare (2,733)	Social Security (4,792)	Background (1,889)
Social Security (4,235)	Political Record (1,911)	Health Care (4,761)	Gov't Spending (1,536)
Senate Races	**Senate Races**	**Senate Races**	**Senate Races**
Health care (10,143)	Health Care (6,223)	Political Record (9,965)	Political Record (4,550)
Education (9,760)	Political Record (3,813)	Education (8,304)	Taxes (3,729)
Political record (7,181)	Social Security (3,755)	Social Security (5,565)	Social Security (2,739)
Background (5,677)	Education (3,026)	Taxes (5,518)	Education (1,681)
Budget/surplus (3,240)	Medicare (1,977)	Health Care (5,517)	Health Care (1,548)

Source: Federal Election Commission.

Tables 7.9 and 7.10 do not provide much support for that thesis because they show data from so many races. To see if candidate and party ads have the same themes within specific contests, we examined candidate and party ads in competitive Senate races in 2000. For the most part, there is consistency within contests, with less consistency for party ads across contests, although as noted above, the Democrats were fairly unified in their messages for the 2000 election cycle. Consider the Republicans in the Michigan Senate race. The topics Senator Abraham's campaign aired the most ads about were health care (1,838 ads), taxes (1,080), and education (820). The Republican party aired 3,733 ads, about half as many as the Abraham campaign, and its favored topics were social security (827 ads), drugs (734), candidates' political record (643), crime (441), honesty (438), education (334), and taxes (316). In the other contests, the Republican party aired a significant number of ads about special interests (Minnesota), the deficit (Minnesota), abortion (Virginia), Medicare (Missouri, Nevada), and gun control (Virginia). Although such an analysis is far from conclusive, the evidence points to contest-specific decisions about what issues to mention. There is no clear party program that party operatives are using advertisements to convey.

The 2000 Presidential Election

Of the 970,410 political advertisements in 2000, presidential spots accounted for 302,450, a figure that includes party, candidate, and pro-candidate interest-group advertisements in both primaries and the general election. Thus, in 2000 there actually were 106 more *presidential* ads than all political ads combined (302,344) in 1998.

The vast majority of presidential ads, 247,224, were aired by Gore and Bush and their allies after June 1, when their nominations had long since been assured. This number far exceeds the 162,160 presidential election ads aired by Clinton and Dole in 1996. Figure 7.1, "2000: Presidential Ads," highlights the distribution of ad sponsorship for each campaign. Interest groups, parties, and coordinated expenditures accounted for an overwhelming majority of pro-Bush and pro-Gore ads. Indeed, Gore hard money accounted for only one fifth of all Gore advertisements and Bush hard money accounted for just less than a third.

These numbers illuminate the role of party advertisements specifically and soft money more generally in the 2000 campaign. To be sure, the Republican National Committee's ad barrage was 3 percent greater than the Democratic National Committee's, but the principal overall message is that party advertisements greatly outweighed candidate advertisements in both campaigns. Note also the presence of coordinated expenditures

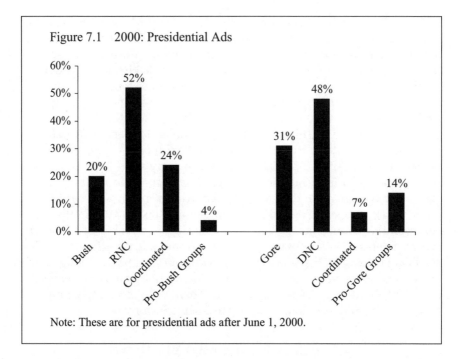

Figure 7.1   2000: Presidential Ads

Note: These are for presidential ads after June 1, 2000.

and pro-candidate issue advertisements. Nearly a quarter of Bush's advertisements were coordinated expenditures between the Republican party and the Bush campaign. Only 4 percent of pro-Bush ads were sponsored by interest groups. Gore, on the other hand, relied to a greater extent on interest-group advertisements and to a much lesser extent on coordinated expenditures. Pro-Gore interest groups aired a substantial number of ads in a few key markets, most specifically St. Louis (1,684 ads), Philadelphia (1,630), Detroit (1,417), Portland, Oregon (1,104), and Milwaukee (966). Bush received no comparable interest-group support in any of the 75 top media markets.

Tables 7.11 and 7.12 break down the distribution of candidate and party advertisements by highlighting the top media markets in which pro-Gore and pro-Bush ads aired. When we compare candidate and party ads in the top markets, we find that the Gore campaign and the Democratic party were fairly consistent. For example, Pittsburgh was the only market in the Democratic party's top 10 that was not also a top Gore market. Nonetheless, even within similar top markets, we can witness how the party ads dominated. In no markets did the Gore campaign air more ads than the Democratic party, and in only one market (Albuquerque–Santa Fe) was there rough parity. This contrasts slightly

Table 7.11   Number of Candidate and Party Ads in Top 10 Gore Markets

Candidate Ads	*Party Ads*
Albuquerque–Santa Fe—2,332	Seattle–Tacoma—2,530
Green Bay—1,948	Green Bay—2,506
Portland, Ore.—1,908	Albuquerque – Santa Fe—2,495
Grand Rapids—1,799	Detroit—2,341
Milwaukee—1,651	Portland, Ore.—2,317
Flint—1,636	Milwaukee—2,290
Detroit—1,634	Grand Rapids—2,248
Philadelphia—1,581	Philadelphia—2,153
Des Moines—1,553	Flint—2,112
Seattle–Tacoma—1,506	**Pittsburgh**—2,021 (1,368 candidate ads)

Note: Boldface entries indicate top markets for party ads but not for candidate ads.

Table 7.12   Number of Candidate and Party Ads in Top 10 Bush Markets

Candidate Ads	*Party Ads*
Miami–Ft. Lauderdale—2,427	**San Diego**—2,175 (361 candidate ads)
Albuquerque–Santa Fe—2,219	Seattle–Tacoma—2,170
Seattle–Tacoma (2,180	Tampa–St. Petersburg—2,124
Portland, Ore.—1,887	Grand Rapids—2,074
Grand Rapids—1,802	Miami-Ft. Lauderdale—2,034
Tampa–St. Petersburg—1,758	Portland, Ore.—2,001
Spokane—1,753	**Orlando–Daytona Beach**—1,964 (1,654 candidate ads)
Philadelphia—1,719	**Cleveland**—1,914 (1,346 candidate ads)
Detroit—1,716	**Sacramento**—1,892 (234 candidate ads)
Green Bay—1,703	**Kansas City**—1,831 (1,671 candidate ads)

Note: Boldface entries indicate top markets for party ads but not for candidate ads.

with the Bush campaign. As Table 7.12 makes clear, party ads dominated in a few markets such as San Diego and Sacramento, markets that the Bush campaign essentially ignored, but Bush campaign ads did outnumber Republican party ads in other key markets, such as Miami–Ft. Lauderdale. There is little reason to believe, however, that national party officials are acting independent of the two major presidential candidates. Undoubtedly there are high levels of coordination between campaign and party officials in the spending of money. The disparity in ad buys between Bush and the RNC in California markets is likely due to Bush operatives simply choosing to spend RNC money in those areas.

Finally, Figures 7.2 and 7.3 highlight the distribution of advertisements by week for the Bush and Gore campaigns after June 1. As can be seen, the Gore campaign aired zero advertisements in the summer months prior to the party national conventions. The Democratic party aired all pro-Gore advertisements during this time. The Bush campaign aired some advertisements during this time, and there is less of a clear division between the airing of pro-Bush candidate and party advertisements. Recall, however, that Gore, during his primary campaigns against Bill Bradley, had chosen to abide by spending limits. His campaign was somewhat strapped for cash in the summer months as it awaited federal money for the general election. The Democratic party simply picked up the slack during the slow summer months. Note also the airing of inter-est-group ads. Throughout the fall campaign, pro-Gore interest groups aired a number of advertisements. By contrast, pro-Bush groups aired al-most zero advertisements until the final week of the campaign.

Future Directions

The CMAG data represent a truly innovative avenue into the investiga-tion of modern political parties, and open the door for a comprehensive analysis of the role of parties in contemporary elections. There are at least two lines of research that are deserving of further examination here, if only to outline what will hopefully become a productive research agenda.

First, the CMAG data may be used to examine how increased party strength in one form affects party strength in another form. The study of political parties has long been split into three separate research agendas: party organizations, party cohesion in government, and party strength among the electorate. In recent years, however, scholars have noted the benefits of theorizing across these programs and hypothesizing the rela-tionships between them (Baer and Bositis 1988; Coleman 1996). The CMAG data allow a step in this direction. For example, do incumbents who toe the party line in Congress receive more party advertisement support? This question raises the empirically testable proposition that party strength in government has implications on the use of party orga-nizations.

Even more interesting is the possibility of assessing the effects of indi-vidual-level measures of exposure to party advertisements. Goldstein and Freedman (1999, 2000) match survey responses with the advertising data and estimate an individual-level measure of advertising exposure, which they use as independent variable to predict turnout and vote choice. With the use of CMAG data in this way, scholars may explore whether exposure to party advertising messages affects the level of party identification within the electorate. If it does not, such evidence would indicate that party

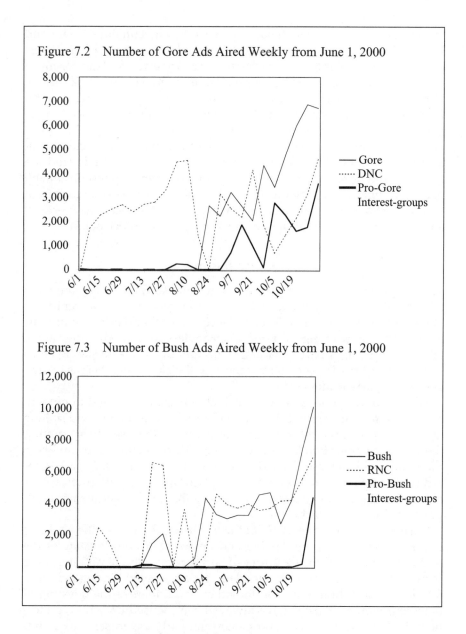

Figure 7.2   Number of Gore Ads Aired Weekly from June 1, 2000

Figure 7.3   Number of Bush Ads Aired Weekly from June 1, 2000

expenditures are doing little to build the party base. This would support the claim that parties have little interest in doing this in the first place.

Second, the data may also be used to theorize anew the relationship between parties and interest groups. Democratic theory has long assumed that interest-group politics and party politics stand in opposition to each other. The classic debate, between Schattschneider (1942) and Dahl (1956), for example, indicates that the relationship between interest groups and parties is best characterized as an inverse one. And for much of American history, such a description may have been accurate. However, in the postreform political environment of the early twenty-first century, there is evidence that parties and groups now see it as in their mutual best interest to cooperate.

Such cooperation, however, may not be the same in all electoral contests and in all campaign environments. For example, one might envision a vertical and horizontal theory of cooperation, where interest group and party coordination becomes increasingly sophisticated as you move from House elections to Senate elections and presidential elections (vertical) and across noncompetitive and competitive contests (horizontal).

Conclusion

This chapter takes advantage of a unique analysis of data on campaign advertisements to explore in detail how parties are using a significant portion of their soft money. The evidence shows that parties are primarily interested in winning elections. They are less concerned (if they are at all) with infusing a party character throughout the electorate. Even as people lament the lack of a strong party in the electorate, there is no evidence that party leaders care.

The literature espouses a party revival in organization and in government. It is clear that party cohesion in Congress is on the rise and so long as campaign finance reform does not preclude the use of soft money, there is every indication that the party's ability to spend money and help candidates will increase. There is even growing evidence that parties coordinate campaign activities with interest groups, a curious empirical reality given the claims of democratic theory that posits their being in opposition (Herrnson, forthcoming).

What is one to make of this? On the one hand, if there is little evidence that party ads are having lasting and broad effects on the state of the party as a whole, then the influx of soft money may be nothing more than a candidate-inspired money-laundering scheme hidden behind a façade of "party building." On the other hand, there is the question of party motivation. Parties have always been focused on winning elections; in that case, the use of soft money and party advertisements is simply the modern-day means by which parties gain power.

Finally, there is also the question of what we want parties to do and whether it matters if winning elections is the goal. It matters if we make policy on the assumption that parties seek to cultivate a base grounded in the kind of public enthusiasm for parties that existed 150 years ago. Opponents of campaign finance reform want to grant parties the means by which to build that base through the continued use of soft money. And over 50 years ago, the American Political Science Association report on parties recommended that programmatic parties were good for democracy. Intellectuals may believe this; some politicians may believe this. Has anyone asked whether party leaders are listening to them?

Notes

1. Figures from the Federal Election Commission.

2. From National Journal Online (www.NationalJournal.com), October 1, 2001.

3. See Sorauf (1998) for an analysis of how parties in recent years have contributed to candidates and coordinated expenditures with them.

4. See information posted October 1, 2001, by the Brennan Center for Justice (www.BrennanCenter.org) on the recent debate over campaign finance.

5. The purchase of data from CMAG was made possible by a grant from the Pew Charitable Trusts to the Brennan Center for Justice at New York University.

6. Starting with the 2001 election cycle, CMAG will track and record campaign advertisements in the top 100 markets. The top 75 media markets are as follows: Albany-Schenectady-Troy, Albuquerque–Santa Fe, Atlanta, Austin, Baltimore, Birmingham, Boston, Buffalo, Charleston-Huntington, Charlotte, Chicago, Cincinnati, Cleveland, Columbus Ohio, Dallas–Ft. Worth, Dayton, Denver, Des Moines–Ames, Detroit, Grand Rapids–Kalamazoo–Battle Creek, Fresno-Visalia, Green Bay–Appleton, Greensboro–High Point–Winston-Salem, Greenville-Spartanburg-Asheville, Harrisburg-Lancaster-Lebanon-York, Hartford–New Haven, Houston, Indianapolis, Jacksonville-Brunswick, Kansas City, Knoxville, Las Vegas, Lexington, Little Rock–Pine Bluff, Los Angeles, Louisville, Memphis, Miami–Ft. Lauderdale, Milwaukee, Minneapolis–St. Paul, Mobile-Pensacola, Nashville, New Orleans, New York, Oklahoma City, Omaha, Orlando-Daytona, Philadelphia, Phoenix, Pittsburgh, Portland-Auburn (Me.), Portland (Ore.), Providence–New Bedford, Raleigh-Durham, Roanoke-Lynchburg, Rochester (N.Y.), Sacramento-Stockton, Salt Lake City, San Antonio, San Diego, San Francisco–Oakland, Seattle-Tacoma, Spokane, St. Louis, Syracuse, Tampa–St. Petersburg, Toledo, Tulsa, Washington, D.C., West Palm Beach–Ft. Pierce, Wichita-Hutchinson, Wilkes Barre–Scranton.

7. Michael Franz, as a graduate student at the University of Wisconsin–Madison, was directly involved in coding the 2000 advertising data.

8. Goldstein and Krasno (2000) discuss tests of coder reliability in determining advertisement tone. Agreement among coders for the 1998 and 2000 data was extremely high.

9. For House races, we used Charles Cook's classification of the 46 most competitive elections in 2000; for Senate races, we classified the races in Michigan, Washington, Missouri, New York, Minnesota, Delaware, Florida, Nevada, Montana, and Virginia as competitive.

8

Political Parties in the Era of Soft Money

RAY LA RAJA

The debates in the 107th Congress over campaign finance reform demonstrate just how much parties changed in the 1990s. At the top of the reform agenda was a ban on party soft money, the funds parties raise that exceed the "hard" limits established by federal regulation. The virtual silence about the role of political action committees (PACs), which were the focus of concern in the 1980s, indicated that parties replaced them as the demons of the campaign finance system. How did parties change so quickly? In what ways did they take advantage of soft money to strengthen their position in American campaigns?

To understand party transformation it is necessary to review briefly the history of campaign finance reform and the effect of reform measures on different political actors. Parties emerged as central players under a new set of laws created in the 1970s that were intended to do away with the worst abuses highlighted by the Watergate scandals. The recent controversy over soft-money contributions and party-sponsored "issue ads" is a classic story about the unintended consequences of political reform.

But it is also a classic story about party adaptation. At mid-century, it appeared that party organizations were increasingly obsolete, but beginning in the 1970s parties found a new and influential role in campaigns. By adapting themselves to the cash economy of modern political campaigns, American parties assumed an important role in financing and organizing them. Through their strategic use of soft money, the national parties became critical patrons to candidates and to lower levels of the party.

The Emergence and Growth of Party Soft Money

Little did reformers realize in the 1970s that their well-intentioned efforts to tighten up the process of raising and spending political money would lead to a surge in noncandidate campaign activity in the 1980s and 1990s. The drafters of the Federal Election Campaign Act (FECA) in 1971 worked on the assumption that candidates rather than parties would raise campaign money, and they focused heavily on preventing potential abuses of candidate committees.[1] In contrast, the FECA regulations on the party were complex but rather vague. Parties exploited ambiguities keenly, constantly testing the limits of the regulations so they could gather and spend money that candidates could not. Ironically, the FECA that enshrined candidate committees at the center of the campaign finance regulatory system ended up opening an opportunity for party expansion.

At the time, the FECA was the most comprehensive campaign finance legislation in the nation's history. Its major provisions included limits on contributions to candidates and a public funding program for presidential candidates. To dampen the money chase, Congress initially included limits on campaign spending. But the Supreme Court struck down the statutes on spending limits in *Buckley v. Valeo*, 424 U.S. 1, 39–59 (1976), claiming that they "impose direct and substantial restraints on the quantity of political speech."[2] The Court acknowledged that the government could impose restraints on contributions to thwart the classic *quid pro quo* of favors from politicians in return for donations, but political *spending* was seen to be much less vulnerable to corruption. An expenditure, which is controlled and spent directly by the spender, conveys political expression, which is at the core of First Amendment freedoms. The Court's distinction between contributions and expenditures critically affected the campaign strategies pursued by candidates and outside groups, including the parties, and led to what many see as new abuses in the campaign finance system.

Without expenditure limits, candidates lack an incentive to hold back campaign spending, particularly if they face a tight election.[3] Under federal laws, the one important restraint on their spending is their willingness and ability to raise money in relatively small increments: $1,000 or less from individuals, and $5,000 or less from PACs per election. For the fortunate few candidates with personal wealth, they can also contribute unlimited amounts to their own campaigns and increasingly they do so.[4] Thus, the never-ending "money chase" is a fact of life for many politicians. Incumbents attend weekly fund-raisers to refill their campaign treasuries in anticipation of their next contest, or simply as a tactic to scare off potential rivals.

As electoral costs mounted during the post-FECA era, candidates turned to parties for help. Campaigns had become extraordinarily drawn-out affairs, occupying the full-time attention of incumbents and affordable only for an exclusive set of challengers with personal wealth (Steen 2000). Through the late 1970s and early 1980s, parties developed the capacity to help candidates raise money and provide in-kind support in the form of polls, mailing lists, and other campaign services (Herrnson 1988). Given the incentive for party leaders to pursue or defend legislative majorities, party organizations developed into rather effective mechanisms for redistributing resources to close races where money could have the biggest impact on the electoral outcome (Kolodny 1998; Malbin and Gais 1998; Thompson, Cassie, and Jewell 1994).

Political parties, however, bump up against contribution limits—notably in federal elections—when trying to help candidates in the toughest races. Parties cannot contribute more than $10,000 to House candidates and $17,500 to Senate candidates in an election cycle. Parties are permitted to help their congressional candidates in more substantial ways through "coordinated" (or "on behalf of") expenditures. Unlike contributions, coordinated expenditures have been adjusted for inflation since the passage of the FECA in 1974. In 2000, the parties could spend $33,800 for House candidates and a much larger amount for Senate candidates, ranging from $67,000 in the smallest states to $1.6 million in California (the amount depends on the number of voting-age residents in each state). Although these party limits are more generous than for PACs and individuals, the caps frustrate the party's goal of concentrating resources efficiently in the most competitive races. Once the party reaches its contribution and spending limits for competitive contests, it can only redistribute its remaining funds among candidates who face little or no competitive threat.

Taking advantage of the Supreme Court's distinction between political contributions and expenditures, the national parties have tried to circumvent contribution limits through so-called "independent" and "soft money" expenditures. In 1986, the Republicans began spending money independently of their Senate candidate in Colorado, attacking the Democratic candidate, Tim Wirth, with radio ads prior to the selection of a Republican nominee. In spite of efforts by the Federal Election Commission (FEC) to count this spending as party contributions, which are subject to limits, the courts ruled otherwise. Drawing on its 1971 decision in *Buckley v. Valeo,* the Supreme Court declared in *Colorado Republican Federal Campaign Committee v. Federal Election Commission,* 518 U.S. 604 (1996) that parties had as much right to spend as other groups.[5] If parties engaged in campaigns without coordinating with the candidate, then their spending was "independent." The FEC had no right to infringe on the free speech of the organization. Strangely, the path of reform—reconfigured by a series of judicial decisions—had pushed the political system to an unusual situation in which political parties had to declare their independence from their own candidates in order to support them.

While parties exploited independent expenditures to help candidates, they simultaneously pushed the boundaries for spending soft money. Unlike the case with hard money, there are no restrictions on raising soft money. Parties can solicit money from individuals, corporations, labor unions, and other organizations without adhering to the limits contained in federal law pertaining to candidates. Contrary to popular belief, however, soft money *is* regulated on the spending side. Parties may use funds solely for party-building activities rather than candidate support. Moreover, parties must comply with state laws when raising and spending these funds in a particular state.

After using soft money to develop their permanent party headquarters, which was permitted by the original law, the parties spent it increasingly for less tangible activities by exploiting ambiguities in the FECA and taking advantage of muddy decisions by the FEC, which administered the federal campaign finance laws. For instance, facing little resistance from the FEC the parties interpreted "party building" broadly, claiming that administrative and fund-raising expenses, as much as bricks and mortar, reflected party-building expenses. State and local party leaders also pushed Congress to amend the FECA to allow their organizations to spend unlimited sums on mobilization and basic grassroots activities in presidential elections.[6] In a decision that many came to regret, the FEC had also agreed that some portion of party-building funds could be raised under state laws, since party leaders argued that their organizations served both federal *and* state candidates. The ability of parties to raise and spend money according to state laws that did not prohibit unlimited corporate or union contributions was the loophole that permitted soft, i.e., nonfederal, money in federal elections.

In the early 1980s, Tony Coelho, leader of the Democratic Congressional Campaign Committee (DCCC), was among the first to seize on soft money as a valuable campaign resource for the national parties and he wasted no time encouraging corporations and unions to contribute funds to the party, in addition to the hard money they gave to candidates through their PACs. Coelho recognized astutely that soft money could help the Democrats catch up with the Republican war chest of hard money.[7] Taking advantage of the muddy decisions by the FEC, Coelho moved soft money into congressional districts to mobilize Democratic partisans in congressional races that were expected to be tight (Jackson 1988).

The aggressiveness of Coelho and other party leaders to exploit loopholes in campaign finance law might be explained given the electoral context. They were responding to problems candidates faced trying to mount effective campaigns in an environment of escalating costs and intensified partisan competition. As Figure 8.1 shows, the average cost of a

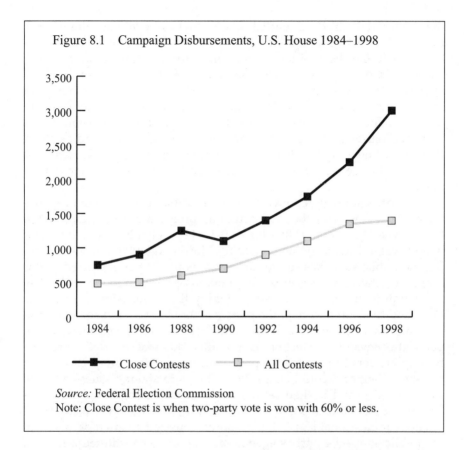

Figure 8.1   Campaign Disbursements, U.S. House 1984–1998

Source: Federal Election Commission
Note: Close Contest is when two-party vote is won with 60% or less.

House race tripled between 1984 and 1998. In the most competitive contests, costs almost quadrupled during this same period. Some of these additional outlays were no doubt due to the increased use of expensive television advertising (Gans 1996). Advanced campaign technology, such as targeted direct mail and intensive polling, also contributed to costs. As the sophistication of campaign technology began to outstrip the capacity of candidate committees to pay for it, the parties assumed a larger role in brokering campaign services (see Kolodny 1998; Aldrich 1995; Herrnson 1988). For instance, parties purchase campaign services in bulk and parcel them to candidates at cheaper rates than they could buy in the open market. They also provide training seminars for candidates and campaign staff, and "lend" them research, polling data, and lists of potential contributors.

The party maneuver that catapulted soft-money fundraising to the fore was the use of issue ads to support the presidential candidates. In the spring of 1995, President Clinton's chief political consultant, Dick Morris, designed a media strategy to boost the president's poll numbers and frame the political debate more than a year before the 1996 elections. Morris urged the Clinton-Gore reelection team to run ads in important swing states, denouncing the Dole-Gingrich Congress and trumpeting themes such as Medicare, education, and the environment that put Clinton in a favorable light.[8] In earlier elections Republicans had used party-sponsored ads sporadically to highlight broad electoral themes, but never before had a party aired so many advertisements designed and targeted to buttress the electoral prospects of the incumbent president.[9]

The Morris strategy required more money than the $37 million spending ceiling allowed by the public funding program during the presidential primary.[10] His plan called for a 10–to–12-week advertising blitz that would cost at least $1 million a week.[11] Morris urged the president to reject the public subsidies so the campaign would not be restricted to this limit, but other top advisers were united in opposition to that approach. The Clinton strategists decided to deploy the advertising through the DNC and took advantage of the party's ability to raise and spend unlimited soft money for party-building activities. In careful consultation with party attorneys, the reelection team crafted ads that avoided words exhorting viewers to vote for the president. By avoiding an electioneering message, the party could claim these ads were about "issues" and not campaigns.[12] The FEC had set the stage for this media loophole by allowing the Republican party to claim that their media advertising to influence congressional legislative proposals reflected an attempt to inform the public about the party's agenda and therefore constituted a form of party building that was allowable under the FECA.[13]

The Dole-Kemp campaign responded to the Morris plan with its own party-based media strategy. After an expensive primary squaring off against the self-financed millionaire Steve Forbes, the Dole team lacked leftover funds from the primary to pay for ads. They would not collect the $62 million lump sum in federal funds for the general election until after the August convention, and yet the battle for the presidency was being waged in early spring.

Once the media strategies were in place, the fund-raising began in earnest. With apparently little consideration for how the public would perceive their actions, the candidates' pursuit of soft money led to excesses such as inviting major donors to White House "coffees" with the president, overnight stays in the Lincoln Bedroom, and meetings at plush resorts and sporting events to mingle with party leaders. Both parties were also embarrassed when it was discovered that they had accepted foreign contributions, which are illegal under the FECA, though it was

Table 8.1   Party Fund-Raising, 1992–2000 ($ Millions)

	1992	1994	1996	1998	2000
Democrats					
Federal [a]	178	139	222	160	275
Nonfederal [b]	36	49	124	93	245
(percentage nonfederal)	(17)	(26)	(36)	(37)	(47)
Republicans					
Federal	267	246	417	285	466
Nonfederal	50	53	138	132	250
(percentage nonfederal)	(16)	(18)	(25)	(32)	(35)
Total Party Receipts	531	486	900	669	1,236

Source: Federal Elections Commission.
[a] Includes national, state and local federal receipts.
[b] Includes national receipts only.

unclear at the time whether this prohibition applied to the donation of soft money.[14]

The scandals, however, did not deter parties and candidates from raising soft money in subsequent elections. After tripling their soft-money receipts between 1992 and 1996 (from $86 million to $262 million), the parties almost doubled their take in the 2000 elections with $495 million (see Table 8.1). Because the law required the parties to match a portion of soft dollars with hard dollars for every activity, parties raised more hard money as well. But to the alarm of many, party soft money has come to make up an increasing portion of total party receipts. In 1992, soft money accounted for 17 percent of Democratic and 16 percent of Republican receipts. By the 2000 elections, these percentages had risen to 47 percent and 35 percent, respectively.[15] What worries reform advocates is that the surge in soft money challenges the basic principles of the FECA. Party soft money, which lacks contribution limits, undermines the goal of preventing corporations and other cash-rich institutions or individuals from using their wealth to unduly influence politics. Corporations and unions now routinely contribute political money in federal elections, where once this was off-limits. The expenditures made by parties and interest groups to air issue ads appear to short-circuit the goal of limiting political contributions, since these expenditures can be as helpful to the candidate as writing a check to his or her campaign committee.

The story of soft money demonstrates how reforms can have several unintended consequences. The mismatch between high campaign costs and low contribution limits puts pressure on candidates to find alternative means of campaign support. The contribution caps for congressional candidates and the public subsidy program for presidential contenders have been inadequate in a campaign environment requiring huge outlays to broadcast political messages. In this instance, political money that could not be given to candidates was redirected through the parties, which were already emerging as important service organizations for candidates. Parties were in the best position to exploit campaign finance laws and they had strong incentives to push the laws to their limits. Consequently, parties now control substantial campaign resources as compared to those of candidate committees and PACs. The arrangement has had important effects on both party activity and elections.

New Party Role in Campaigns

The controversy over fund-raising and party-sponsored issue ads obscures a longer trend among parties. While much soft money raised by the national parties now goes toward airing issue ads to support federal candidates, the infusion of party money—both hard and soft—enables the parties to play a vastly different role in campaigns from the one they played just 30 years ago, when the FECA was written. Parties are no longer marginal players in candidate-centered campaigns; they are central actors in key races. The campaigns are still not as party-centered as they were in the nineteenth century, since election activity continues to focus on the individual candidate. But party-based decision makers have gained more influence in choosing the content and strategies of campaigns since the golden age of parties over a century ago.[16] Moreover, the financial power of the national committees has altered the party hierarchy. State and local parties, which used to be the traditional power centers, now occupy the unfamiliar role of branch organizations in the party infrastructure. Increasingly, campaign decisions are centralized at the national level, with local organizations carrying out the strategic decisions of party professionals in Washington.

The transition of party operatives from marginal players to central actors is difficult to demonstrate concretely, given the nature of the financial data collected by the FEC. Traditional forms of party support in candidate campaigns understate the party presence. For example, candidates get little more than 10 percent of their support from parties, and this has not changed much in two decades, even though party hard money receipts have risen rapidly (Ornstein, Mann, and Malbin 1998). In fact, as Table 8.2 demonstrates, direct contributions to candidates in real dollars declined during the 20-year period between 1980 and 2000, from $13.0 million to $6.7 million. In spite of this, however, parties increased

Table 8.2 Party Support of Candidates, 1980–2000* ($ Millions)

Type of Support	1980	1982	1984	1986	1988	1990	1992	1994	1996	1998	2000
Direct party contributions	13.0	13.0	12.4	8.0	7.4	5.8	6.0	5.8	6.5	4.0	6.7
Coordinated expenditures	36.2	31.4	48.2	36.6	59.1	25.6	75.9	48.2	58.8	36.2	51.3
Independent expenditures	0.0	0.0	0.0	0.0	0.0	0.0	0.0	0.0	12.6	1.9	3.9
Total	49.2	44.4	60.6	44.6	66.5	31.4	81.9	54.0	77.9	42.1	61.9
Party budget (hard money)	432.0	453.8	657.0	502.8	569.4	383.4	546.2	447.0	700.34	70.1	465.8
Support of candidates as % of party budget	11%	10%	9%	9%	12%	8%	15%	12%	11%	9%	13%

Source: Federal Election Commission
*Adjusted for inflation; in 2000 dollars.

their coordinated spending and experimented with independent spending in the 1990s. Though there are no limits on how much the parties may spend independent of candidates, they must still raise this money according to federal standards that limit annual individual contributions to the party to $20,000 and PAC contributions to $15,000. An important drawback of independent spending is that parties cannot coordinate campaign activities with their candidates. This means that candidates have little control over the timing and content of party-sponsored ads.

In recent elections, parties have provided most of their candidate support through soft money by targeting issue ads and voter mobilization activities to closely contested federal races. There are two distinct benefits of using soft money. First, the parties can raise these funds in large increments. Although most soft money contributions are relatively small—the average per source is less than $10,000—the parties solicit large amounts from corporations, unions, and wealthy individuals. According to the Center for Responsive Politics, two thirds of soft money in the 2000 elections came from just 800 donors, each of whom gave more than $120,000.

The other important advantage of soft money is that the parties can concentrate these funds in key races. By exploiting soft-money rules, the parties effectively sidestep the federal ceilings that prevent them from allocating resources efficiently in the closest contests. To navigate around the federal restrictions on soft money the parties have developed close ties with their state parties because these affiliates receive special exemptions for contributions for party-building activity. The national parties take advantage of these special exemptions by transferring funds to state parties, which then purchase the television ads and organize telephone banks and canvassing. This arrangement also allows the national committees to benefit from local expertise when placing ads and contacting voters.

One indication that the party wants to support a particular race is to observe which state parties receive the bulk of transfers from the national committees.[17] Table 8.3 demonstrates that in 1998, states with close Senate contests received the most national party money. The Republicans transferred an average of $2.2 million per state to states where the election was won by a margin of 10 percentage points or less. Similarly, the Democrats transferred an average of $2.9 million per competitive state. In contrast, states with less competitive contests or no contest at all received approximately $600,000 from each party.[18] The fact that there is little difference between transfers to states with no Senate election and states with a noncompetitive election suggests that the parties efficiently

Table 8.3   Effect of a U.S. Senate Contest on State Party Activity, 1998 ($ Thousands)

	Competitive Contest*	Noncompetitive Contest	No Contest
Average Transfers** from National Committees Committees**			
Republicans	2,171	604	668
Democrats	2,974	599	597
Average Media Spending Republicans	1,068	117	127
Democrats	1,982	157	178
Average Mobilization Spending Republicans	748	114	183
Democrats	711	216	247
N	20	48	32

Source: Federal Elections Commission.
*Competitive Contest is when the winning candidate won by 10 percentage points or less.
**Includes hard and soft dollars.

allocate funds to the tightest races. Senate candidates in noncompetitive races appear to get no additional help from the party through soft money.

Table 8.3 also shows how state parties spend soft money differently, depending on the electoral context. When there is a close Senate race, the parties spend a lot more on media. For instance, Republican parties spent an average of $1 million on media in competitive states, while the Democrats spent almost $2 million per state. In contrast, in noncompetitive states under $200,000 was spent. The additional media spending in competitive states undoubtedly reflects expenditures on issue ads that help the Senate candidate. The Democrats rely more heavily than Republicans on the state party issue-ad strategy, probably because they have less hard money than the Republicans. In competitive states, both parties also allocated about $700,000, on average, for mobilization activities such as voter registration and get-out-the-vote drives, which was roughly $500,000 more than in states with little competition or no Senate contest.

To put these soft money investments in perspective, consider that each party provided an average of $250,000 in hard money (direct contributions and coordinated expenditures) to their candidate running for an open Senate seat. Party investments are at least 10 times higher if we assume that the soft money transferred to states was spent mostly on media and mobilization that directly benefited the candidate. With these sums, party resources now account for a major share of the total money spent in key congressional races.

The strategic allocation of party resources into states suggests that campaigns are not nearly so candidate-centered as they have been in the past. Staff and consultants working for party organizations appear to be making decisions independent from the candidates. In contrast, studies of party contributions during the 1980s demonstrated a classic collective action dilemma, with party personnel finding it difficult to allocate money rationally because they were not insulated from the rival claims of influential incumbents who wanted money for their own campaigns (see Jacobson 1985; Herrnson 1989). Incumbents pressured the party to contribute to their committees, even when the campaign risk was slight, to maximize their prospects for reelection.

Soft money apparently resolves this collective-action problem. Under the soft-money regime, party leaders in the Senate and House appear to have more control over committee money than in the past and they can concentrate it in the tightest races. The leverage of party leaders comes from their ability to raise most of the soft money, given their leadership rank. Although it is common practice for a candidate to encourage donors to give to the party when they have "maxed" their federal contributions to his or her committee, there is no guarantee that the party leadership will direct the money back into the candidate's race. While the party sometimes serves as a soft-money conduit for candidates, the flow of money appears to be driven more by poll numbers showing a closely contested race than by other factors. Thus, party staff and their consultants control substantial resources, choosing whom to support with targeted party-building activities and issue ads.[19] Of course, it is possible that criteria other than the tightness of a race enter the decision-making process: whether the candidate has been loyal to the party leadership, or whether the candidate was in fact responsible for raising party money.

The Arms War

One indication that the parties have been successful in their soft-money strategy is that campaign money is increasingly concentrated in the most competitive races. The gap in spending between candidates in competitive and noncompetitive House contests appears to be growing, as is shown in Figure 8.1. Using soft money, parties and allied groups pour money into the 40 to 50 key House and Senate races that are up for grabs. For this reason, candidates in close contests are most vulnerable to issue ads and independent expenditures run by outsider groups. The uncertainty about how much money will be spent against them compels them to amass as much hard money as possible in self-defense.

Since candidates have no way of knowing how much will be spent in their races, they prepare for the worst. In some instances, the only way a candidate can fight back against campaigning by outside groups is to rely on the party as its protector and will respond with counter ads to offset opposition spending. But parties do not simply defend their candidates. They mount "first-strike" attacks on the opposition, which triggers counterspending by other groups. According to a study by the Brennan Center for Justice at the New York School of Law, in the 1998 congressional elections more than half the party ads were so-called attack ads. In contrast, only one in five ads sponsored by candidate committees were attack ads.[20]

The rise in noncandidate spending carries important consequences. On the one hand, the ability of parties and other groups to invest significant resources in targeted areas means that no incumbent in a potentially competitive seat can rest easy. That might be good news for competition, though it certainly makes candidates feel like they are losing control of the campaign process to organized interests. One loser in the 2000 elections, a three-term incumbent battered by outside campaigning, complained that his race "was a poster child for why we need campaign spending limits. If there had been limits, there wouldn't even have been a campaign."[21] Inadvertently he expressed the pro-incumbent bias of campaign finance regimes that do not provide sufficient money to challengers. During the 1980s, incumbents prospered through lopsided PAC contributions to their reelection committees. Today, their war chests do not make them invulnerable, since interest groups and parties can inflict damage on any candidate through soft-money spending in targeted campaigns.

On the other hand, the presence of outsider groups can make the campaigns messy and confusing to voters. Who are these groups sponsoring ads against the local candidate? What do they stand for? Many of these groups conceal their identities through high-minded names like the "Foundation for Government," which was actually a campaign sponsored by the trucking industry (Magleby 1998). These tactics reduce accountability in elections and complicate the sending and receiving of political messages in campaigns. Candidates no longer stand squarely against their rivals; they must also turn every which way to parry with the parties and assorted interest groups. So while the content of American campaigns remains firmly candidate-centered, control over campaigns and financing has moved away from candidates and toward organized interests.

So far, most of the discussion has been about the actions of congressional party committees (NRSC, DSCC, NRCC, DCCC) in Senate and House campaigns, but the same pattern of behavior may be observed on the part of the national committees (RNC, DNC) in presidential campaigns. The presidential candidates face cost pressures and fund-raising constraints as severe as congressional candidates, even though the FECA provides public funds for the presidential contest. In the most recent presidential election, George W. Bush declined public subsidies to avoid the spending limits imposed on candidates who receive them. He ended up raising a record $194 million for the primary and general elections. Gore, who participated in the public funding program, received about $87 million in subsidies, on top of the $45 million he raised from individuals during the primary.[22]

One glaring problem with the current system is that the candidates do not receive public funds for the general election until after the convention. In the frontloaded primary system, however, the party nominee usually emerges much earlier than the convention. As the media war between the Clinton and Dole campaigns demonstrates, the battle to set the campaign agenda begins well before the convention, when a winner emerges from the early primaries. The de facto selection of the party nominee in the early spring gives presidential candidates a strong incentive to begin waging a media campaign against the presumed nominee of the opposing party. To do otherwise risks letting the opponent define the terms of the debate, a fundamental mistake of political campaigning. The candidate also needs to consider the strength of his field operations to mobilize voters in key swing states. His task is complicated if he went through a bruising primary in which he spent most of his funds on television advertising or created ill will among party activists in a state favoring another candidate.

Party leaders like Ron Brown of the DNC recognized that field operations needed to be in place before the party nominee was selected (Herrnson 1994). The party took on this role with the benefit of soft money. Although parties have always been active campaigning for the presidential ticket, the national committees played a minimal role until the last two decades. Prior to this, party campaign activity on behalf of the presidential nominee was left to the discretion of state and local party officials, who might help the candidate if they liked him, or if it helped the rest of the ticket. In the 1980s, the national committees sent soft money to state parties to supplement local party-building efforts. Some of it was used to distribute grassroots campaign materials such as placards and lawn signs but increasingly it was used for direct voter mobilization in key swing states through telephone banks, precinct canvassing, and direct mail. With the use of issue ads in 1996, parties moved beyond their field operations to play a significant role in media campaigns. In presidential campaigns, party issue ads make a charade of spending limits imposed by the FECA, but party behavior might easily be recognized as a rational response to a political finance system that failed to address the realities of campaigning in the 1990s.

Nationalization of Parties

The incentives that pushed the parties into the cash economy of modern campaigns had an important affect on intraparty relations. The ability of national parties to raise lots of money, particularly soft money, enhances their power relative to state and local organizations like never before. When Alexander Heard completed his seminal study of campaign finance in 1960, he observed that the national committees relied considerably on the goodwill of tightfisted state organizations to send them money to pay for basic expenses. He found, for instance, that in 1956 the RNC received more than a third of its total receipts from state organizations.[23] Heard believed the reversal of the flow of money would augment the authority of the national party and lead to greater coordination among levels of a party. To a considerable extent his prediction has been on the mark. National party money now flows to state organizations and comes with strings attached. Many state parties are formidable fund-raisers on their own (Morehouse 2000), but the national committees have been able to influence campaign strategy of lower-level organizations through financial transfers.

For the first time in the history of American parties, national organizations control much of the campaign activity in federal elections down through the party hierarchy. In the first half of the century, the RNC and DNC were rarely more than forums for organizing the presidential nominating conventions. Today, campaign strategies for federal offices are designed and implemented largely by national party operatives with national party money. To avoid shirking by state organizations that receive national party money, the national parties usually request detailed "coordinated campaign" plans that conform to guidelines created by national party personnel. With the Democrats, at least, national party money is not released until these plans meet the approval of staff in Washington.[24] In this way, the national parties have used their emerging financial power to influence the activities of state organizations (Bibby 1998).

As Heard also predicted, central control of resources creates greater intraparty coordination. In a recent survey of 70 state organizations, more than 63 ran campaigns with the joint participation of the national committees and candidates.[25] The so-called coordinated campaign, which was inaugurated by the Democrats in the 1980s, pools the resources of the parties, candidates, and outside groups to mobilize key voters that support candidates up and down the ticket. In some instances, the national parties put their own staff in the state to ensure the success of these operations. These committees then become the primary conduits for investing soft money in campaigns. In the 2000 elections, the national parties sent $280 million in soft money—more than 50 percent of their total—to state and local organizations for campaign operations and activity.[26] For this reason, a good way to understand the parties' new role in elections is to observe how state parties spend soft money.

Party Activity in the States

State parties have been investing increasing amounts of money directly into campaigns by pursuing two basic strategies simultaneously. In the first strategy, parties target campaign commercials at swing voters, a tactic that tends to benefit candidates at the top of the ticket. The other strategy, which is more difficult to track, is a "ground" campaign to generate turnout among the party faithful in support of the full party ticket. Though the media campaign generates controversy because it seems like an obvious maneuver around federal campaign finance laws, party stalwarts cite their mobilization efforts as evidence that parties are once again getting citizens to the polls.

But however much the parties may argue that soft money is good for party building and voter mobilization, it is plain that the most radical change has been the surge in media spending since 1996, a fact that is attributable to the national party strategy of transferring soft money to state parties to pay for issue ads. Whereas the state parties spent just 3 percent of their budgets on media activities during the 1992 presidential election year, this activity absorbed 44 percent of their party budgets in the 2000 elections. The shift is more striking in absolute terms: Media spending jumped from only $2 million to $149 million in just two presidential campaigns. As discussed earlier, the states with the most competitive races are targeted by the parties with their advertising. Spending on media during nonpresidential election years is not nearly so high, suggesting that the media strategies of presidential campaigns drive much of party soft-money spending, even though congressional campaigns too rely increasingly on such strategies.[27]

Complicating matters for those who want to ban party soft money, however, it appears that parties use some of the money for virtuous civic activities that Congress wanted to encourage when it amended the FECA in 1979 to allow unlimited spending on party building and get-out-the-vote (GOTV) activities. In the 2000 elections, state parties spent $42 million on voter mobilization and just over $11 million on basic grassroots activities that included distributing lawn signs, bumper stickers, and sample ballots. In every election cycle since 1992, spending for this basic party work has increased steadily and has not been crowded out by media spending. This is good news for local candidates facing tough elections who benefit from state party efforts to generate turnout.

It may also be good news for those concerned about the decline in voting. If there is merit to V. O. Key's theory that partisan competition spurs the parties to seek more voters, then self-interested parties should spend additional increments of money trying to mobilize previously marginal voters. Whether party efforts actually increase turnout is the subject of considerable debate (see Wielhouwer and Lockerbie 1994; Rosenstein and Hansen 1993). Members of the Congressional Black Caucus have been reluctant to support the Shays-Meehan reform bill, which bans soft money, because they claim that soft money is used effectively to mobilize African Americans.[28] Certainly, the Democratic party, which has the overwhelming support of African Americans, appears to use soft money for turnout more than Republicans, spending 24 cents per voter on mobilization against the Republican average of 14 cents per voter (La Raja and Jarvis-Shean, 2001).

It is also uncertain whether a ban on soft money will hurt the parties in other ways. Without soft money, will parties retain the administrative capacity to run effective campaign operations and perform various party work? It is clear, for instance, that soft money defrays costs at party headquarters. Parties spend a significant share on rather prosaic administrative costs such as salaries, rent, computers, and other office-related matters. In 1992, state parties spent $42 million on such overhead, and by 2000, this total had more than doubled to almost $100 million. These expenditures reflect mostly campaign work in the final four months before the election, but rising party operating budgets during the off-election year suggest that the parties are not simply tent operations that fold after the close of the campaign. Republican party operating budgets almost doubled in the 1990s, growing from $544,000 in 1991 to $986,000 in 1999 (see Table 8.4). Democrats started further behind and did not grow so rapidly, going from $395,000 to $556,000 during the same period. These findings are consistent with the organizational cultures of the two parties, the Republicans continuing a tradition of strengthening the party structure, which was fostered by the RNC chairman Ray Bliss in the 1960s (see Green 1994). The Democrats rely more on outside organizations, especially labor unions, to support party candidates, a practice that may retard their development. Another explanation is that the relatively cash-poor Democrats have less money left over from campaigns to support party infrastructure.

Conclusion: Does Soft Money Make Parties Stronger?

In 1950, a group of eminent political scientists issued a report on the health of the party system and included a recommendation for policymakers to craft campaign finance laws that encouraged funds to flow through parties as one way to strengthen them.[29] Today, through access to soft money, parties appear to be stronger electoral organizations than they were, although reliance on financial wealth alone may not give them the kind of influence over other aspects of the party system, such as party-in-the-electorate or party-in-government, that these political scientists hoped for. Thus, party scholars will continue to speculate whether the infusion of soft money in the last two decades really strengthens the party or simply buttresses the candidate-centered nature of campaigns.

What is beyond dispute is that the political parties adapted themselves to a changing electoral environment by exploiting campaign finance laws that constrained candidates. The mounting campaign costs and a modern-era dependency on television ads gave the parties an incentive to use soft money to expand campaign operations and seek ways of investing this money in critical electoral contests. The national parties fastened on soft money as a way to help their candidates, even though this money is supposed to be used for strengthening the party generally.

And yet, to say that parties are merely financial conduits for candidates to use soft money misses important changes occurring within the parties. The enormous growth in party treasuries helped strengthen party organizations significantly, especially at the national level. Soft money augments their administrative capacity, allowing them to professionalize operations and develop programs that serve candidates up and down the ticket. Soft money also gave the national committees unprecedented influence in federal campaigns, as well as an active role in party operations in the states. By centralizing resources nationally through coordinated campaigns, the parties overcame a collective-action problem that permitted them to maximize opportunities to control the White House, Congress, and state houses. Conceptually, then, parties moved from being marginal "service-vendor" organizations (Herrnson 1988) in the 1980s to influential patrons of candidates in the 1990s.

Table 8.4   Party Operating Budgets, 1991 and 1999 ($ Thousands)

	Mean	*Median*	*Minimum*	*Maximum*	*N*
Republicans					
1991	544	364	12	2,298	45
1999	986	554	73	5,229	45
Democrats					
1991	395	199	19	3,295	45
1999	556	369	26	2,568	45

Source: Federal Elections Commission.
Note: Data obtained from federal reports filed with the FEC, so they do not include sums related to party activity solely for state and local elections. Also, five states were not included because they have major state elections during odd years (Louisiana, Maine, New Jersey, Texas, Virginia). Figures not adjusted for inflation.

There is little doubt that candidates rely on parties more in the era of soft money than they did during the period just after the FECA legislation. The ability of parties or interest groups, such as the National Rifle Association and Sierra Club, to run targeted ads or mobilize partisans on short notice makes the election prospects of candidates increasingly uncertain. As powerful organized interests step into the campaign field, candidates need the party the way a feudal lord might have needed the king's army, on occasion, to ward off aggressive rivals. However, the increasing participation of parties in campaigns comes at a price. Candidates lose some control of their campaigns, and election costs escalate, since the provision of resources on one side usually leads to countermobilization. Moreover, the ability of outside groups, including the party, to concentrate so many resources in targeted races undoubtedly increases the cost of elections in these areas.

Although national parties experienced the most significant changes, state parties also appear to be as strong as ever. In a survey of 70 Democratic and Republican organizations, all but one had a permanent party headquarters, in contrast to the 1960s, when few state parties had such offices (Cotter et al. 1984). Even though the party chair is traditionally a volunteer position, one quarter of parties now pay the chair a full-time salary.[30] Parties also appear to provide more electoral services than in the past. About 90 percent of the state organizations recruit candidates and provide training for the candidate's team of consultants and volunteers; three quarters of them design and run polls. These figures are well above the percentages recorded by the Cotter team (1984) in their study of parties in the 1980s, suggesting that state-level organizations have continued to get stronger in the 1990s.

Certainly it is difficult to determine whether soft money raised by the national parties has been the engine of this transformation, but it seems plausible that soft money enabled the national party to invest in professional development and training for its state affiliates. This in turn helped state parties improve their own fundraising operations. The coordinated campaigns provided an opportunity for a transfer of skills, knowledge, and election data that pushed the state parties further in the direction of a professional campaign organizations.

And yet there are darker aspects to the rise of party soft money that must be fully acknowledged. For although political scientists usually like to see strong parties, an unavoidable question is: What kind of strong parties is it worth having? Frank Sorauf, a leading party and campaign finance scholar, is concerned that soft money elevates the influence of the legislative wing of the party at the expense of the executive wing. In his view, strong legislative parties, like those in Congress, sap potential for bridging the separation of powers etched in the Constitution. A legislative party that raises its own funds and runs its own campaigns has fewer incentives to work closely with its party counterpart in the executive branch. Even worse, he argues, the legislative party with a healthy appetite for campaign funds stands at the nexus of money and legislation, creating the greatest potential for corruption (Sorauf 2000).

Other scholars believe party reliance on soft money has encouraged them to forego the kind of grassroots activity that promotes partisan loyalty and civic participation (Burns 2000). Rather than invest money in local party building and volunteer networks, the national parties behave simply like mega-consultants when they use the money for television ads and direct-mail campaigns to promote candidates. Scholars who embrace the principles of strong parties articulated in the report by the APSA Committee on Political Parties hoped that soft money might be used to strengthen the party as a civic organization rather than as a campaign operation. From their perspective, the parties missed an opportunity to truly strengthen the party-in-the electorate because they failed to use soft money to develop a grassroots arena for citizen debate and voluntary activity.

While it is true that parties have not invested heavily in grassroots operations, they can hardly be blamed for responding to an electoral environment that puts a premium on expensive technology to reach voters. Party wealth enables candidates to locate and contact voters in an era when it seems increasingly difficult to reach them amid the clutter of junk mail and the proliferation of cable channels. In some parts of the nation, party money pays for intensive grassroots efforts that involve canvassing neighborhoods for voters and getting them to the polls with the help of volunteers. Although some believe greater reliance on volunteers would minimize campaign costs, there is no way to avoid significant outlays for telephones, campaign literature, and computers to manage voter files. In these areas, the parties have led the way.

Implications of a Ban on Party Soft Money

If soft money is banned, there is little doubt that parties will adapt. They have done extraordinarily well raising hard money in recent years, and they will focus more intensively on this supply of money. The McCain-Feingold bill also allows parties to raise more hard money by increasing the limit on individual contributions to national parties from $20,000 to $25,000, and to state parties from $5,000 to $10,000. In the short term, however, the parties will have less money, a fact that will reduce their presence in campaigns. Nevertheless, the parties will survive and possibly thrive. During the era of soft money, parties ratcheted up their role in elections, and it is unlikely, given the ongoing costly battles for control of Congress and the White House, that these organizations will withdraw from the field.

At the state level, new rules that limit soft money fund-raising will not present a problem for parties already constrained by similar limits under state law. But in states where campaigns are expensive and where parties rely on major donors, these federal laws will hamper party activity and create some confusion. To avoid problems, state parties might severely reduce their presence in federal campaigns, as they did in the 1976 presidential campaign before new rules gave them exemptions for certain generic party activities. Aggressive state parties might continue to run targeted party activities using nonfederal money solicited from large donors, claiming that they seek only to help state and local candidates—even though these activities benefit federal candidates too. Although state parties will adapt, the middling and weaker state parties might suffer the most because national party soft money often helped incorporate them into national campaign strategies, a process that probably advances professionalism at the state level. National party–coordinated campaigns frequently covered the debts of state organizations, and helped state parties maintain up-to-date voter files that benefit local candidates in subsequent elections.

In reviewing reform it is also important to consider the different effect of a ban on either of the major parties. The Democrats may be hurt more in the short term because they use soft money more intensively in the campaigns for issue ads and GOTV campaigns. Republicans, in contrast, have a significant hard-money advantage that will make the transition to the new campaign finance system easier for it. Most assuredly, the parties will take advantage of the court's decision that allows them to spend unlimited sums of money independent of their candidates. In all likelihood, if parties cannot use any soft money to air issue ads 120 days before a federal election (as the current bill requires), they will frontload issue ads during the summer and then spend hard money on independent ads up until the election.

Aside from the direct consequences of a soft-money ban on parties, it is also important to consider its effect on electoral outcomes. For instance, a ban could reduce political competition somewhat, since parties are instrumental in channeling resources to potentially competitive races. Or it might reduce turnout among different groups of voters if parties reduce mobilization efforts (see Ansolabehere and Snyder 2000; Rosenstone and Hansen 1993). Much depends on whether party strategists choose to pursue "air-war" strategies, which draw support from swing voters versus "ground-war" strategies, which mobilize partisans.

In trying to predict any scenario of unintended consequences, one must consider the possibility of new kinds of committees sprouting up. For instance, it is possible that campaign professionals will establish quasi-party committees that are legally separate from the party organizations to perform some of the functions associated with parties. These organizations, funded by partisan loyalists, would run issue ads and mobilization programs in targeted areas using soft money that the parties cannot use.

Parties might also coordinate their activities more effectively with allied interest groups. The parties could augment their election "briefings" on key campaigns for allied organizations, which could use this information to funnel resources to key races. Parties, however, would have less control over content and strategy. Ironically, without soft money, parties may become more beholden to those interest groups that have the capacity to run high-quality campaigns. No doubt, parties will suffer relative to other groups, especially if the courts declare unconstitutional any reforms designed to restrain interest-group activity. If the parties are removed as a critical venue for marshaling campaign resources, candidates will simply seek help from interest groups and wealthy individuals. One thing we can be sure of is that parties will figure out the ground rules and they will find an important role for themselves within the new campaign finance regime.

Notes

1. This section about the drafting of the FECA relies heavily on Sorauf's analysis (Sorauf 2000). As he argues, when the FECA was written in the 1970s, its struc-

ture reflected the electoral politics of the time. Parties had largely lost control of election campaigning to candidates, especially in national elections. The scandals involving political money were attributed mostly to candidate-related committees, such as the Committee to Reelect the President (famously called CREEP), which was a committee run by President Nixon and his staff.

2. *Buckley v. Valeo*, 424 U.S. 1, 39–59 (1976).

3. Even with expenditure limits, it remains questionable whether campaign spending in a particular race could be restrained. In the years since the passage of the FECA, outside groups have been making independent expenditures in races to support a favored candidate.

4. According to the logic of the decision in *Buckley v. Valeo*, candidates could not corrupt themselves by giving money to their campaign. Therefore, the government has no right to limit the amount of money candidates contribute to their own campaign committees.

5. The FEC lost its suit against the Republican party in district court. See *Federal Election Commission v. Colorado Republican Fed. Campaign Comm.*, 839 F. Supp. 1448, 1455 (D. Colo. 1993). After several appeals the Supreme Court finally ruled in 1996 that the party had not coordinated with the candidate, and therefore the advertisements were truly done independently from the candidate and the party was entitled to full protections under the First Amendment, i.e., the party could spend as much as it wanted so long as it spent hard money. See *Colorado Republican Fed. Campaign Comm. v. Federal Election Comm'n*, 518 U.S. 604, 613 (1996). The case appeared once again before the Supreme Court in 2001 to address another question raised by the case: Were limits on party-coordinated expenditures constitutional? In a close decision, the court decided that unlimited coordinated spending could corrupt the governmental process because the party could be used as a conduit to circumvent contribution limits to candidates.

6. An unintended consequence of the 1974 version of the FECA was that it "federalized" electoral activity in the states, making local political actors conform to federal laws even though they were engaged in nonfederal campaigns. State and local party leaders complained that federal laws limiting party support of presidential candidates prevented them from performing their traditional party hoopla—distributing lawn signs, bumper stickers and other campaign paraphernalia—that widely benefited federal, state, and local candidates. It was significant that Congress did not address the issue of whether state and local committees could use nonfederal, i.e., soft, money, to pay for these activities (see Corrado 1997). Later on, the FEC ruled that the parties could pay a share of these costs with nonfederal money. This effectively created the "soft money" loophole that permitted parties to pay for much of their federal activity with money raised under nonfederal rules.

7. Republicans have outpaced the Democrats in hard money since the 1970s, when they started an innovative direct-mail strategy to locate small donors. Democrats were at least a decade behind in pursuing this strategy, which is quite

costly and takes a long time to develop. Another possible reason for the Republican advantage is that their base includes more partisans who can afford to make political contributions.

8. Bob Woodward and Ruth Marcus, "Papers Show Use of DNC Ads to Help Clinton," *Washington Post,* September 18, 1997, A1.

9. The Clinton reelection team was the first to exploit fully the issue ad strategy although they copied the Republicans, who occasionally used party-sponsored advertising as early as 1980. In that year, the RNC aired party-oriented advertising around the theme "Vote Republican. For a Change" (see Menefee-Libey 2000, p. 95).

10. The FECA inaugurated a voluntary public subsidies program for presidential candidates in exchange for their agreement to limit campaign spending. In the primaries, candidates receive a dollar subsidy for every private dollar they raise in increments of $250 or less. They must also agree to strict spending limits for each state primary. In the general election, the party nominee receives a lump-sum subsidy after the convention if he agrees not to accept private contributions. In the 2000 elections this subsidy was $68 million.

11. Ruth Marcus and Charles Babcock, "The System Cracks Under the Weight of Cash," *Washington Post,* February 9, 1997, p. A1.

12. In *Buckley v. Valeo,* the justices had tried to distinguish between constitutionally protected free speech and electioneering messages that benefited a particular candidate. The ruling demonstrated that the courts would narrowly define "electioneering" to include messages that clearly exhorted citizens to vote for or against specific candidates. Parties could safely use soft money for issue ads that helped candidates so long as they avoided language that constituted "express advocacy" for a candidate. Such language includes use of the words "vote for," "oppose," "support," and the like.

13. Federal Election Commission, Advisory Opinion 1995–25, "Costs of Advertising to Influence Congressional Legislation Allocated to Both Federal and Nonfederal Funds."

14. On October 8, 1999, the D.C. Circuit reversed a lower court's ruling that the campaign finance rules did not apply to soft money. The appeals court held that laws prohibiting conduit contributions and foreign contributions to federal campaigns applied to soft money. See *U.S. v. Kanchanalak,* 192 F.3d 1037 (D.C. Cir. 1999).

15. These figures do not reflect the soft money that is raised by the state parties, which would raise these percentages.

16. Kolodny and Dwyre (1998) have aptly described parties as "orchestrators" of campaign activities, since the party operates at the center of the exchange of goods and services among candidates, consultants, contributors, and voters.

17. The national parties also have an incentive to spend soft money through state parties because of the configuration of FEC administrative rules that lets state parties spend more soft money relative to hard money.

18. No doubt some of these transfers went toward competitive House contests.

19. A good example of the party role is illustrated by the 2000 U.S. Senate contest in Nevada for an open seat. The Democratic candidate, Ed Bernstein, lagged far behind in the polls during the summer prior to the election. The Bernstein campaign spent all its funds in a bid to pull closer to the Republican, John Ensign, and get the attention of the party. The strategy worked and the DSCC sent $275,000 to the Nevada Democratic party to run issue ads supporting him. With party help Bernstein pulled neck and neck, until the NRSC weighed in with $1.3 million worth of issue ads. The Republicans wanted to send a strong signal to the Democrats that the Nevada seat would not be won cheaply. Would the Democrats call their bluff? To the chagrin of the Democratic candidate, party leaders did not, instead deciding to move resources to Senate races in Montana, Washington, and Michigan, where the odds looked better. The Democratic candidate ended up losing by 14 points.

20. Jonathan Krasno and Daniel E. Seltz, *Buying Time: Television Advertising in the 1998 Congressional Elections* (New York: Brennan Center for Justice 2000).

21. These are the comments of Congressman Brian Bilbray (R-Calif.), who spent $1.5 million and lost a bitterly fought race in which labor unions spent millions of dollars on issue ads. See Jean Merl and Laura Wides, "Democrats Strengthen Dominance in House Delegation," *Los Angeles Times,* November 9, 2000, Home Edition, Section A.

22. Federal Election Commission, Web site, June 21, 2001, posting (http://herndon1.sdrdc.com/cgi-bin/cancomsrs/?_00+CAN+00).

23. In 1956 the RNC received $1 million from 44 state-level committees. Heard also found that another $250,000 came from local Republican organizations in 24 states. The Republican Senate and House campaign committees were even more dependent on state and local parties, receiving upwards of two thirds of their resources from them. The Democrats' receipts have always been smaller but the national committees received as much as two fifths of their resources from sub-national party committees (Heard 1960, 287).

24. Jill Alper, Director of Coordinated Campaign in 1995–96 and DNC Political Director in 1997–98, telephone interview with author on December 17, 1999.

25. Author's own survey. In some instances, the national parties work very little with the state organization, simply installing their own campaign staff in the field and not working closely with the state leaders. But 60 percent of the state parties in the survey reported that their own staff managed the coordinated campaign.

26. The Democrats sent $149.8 million in soft money to state and local parties, and the Republicans sent $129.7 million. The parties also transferred hard money for matching purposes: The Democrats sent $115.9 million and the Republicans sent $57.4 million. Data source is the FEC: www.fec.gov/press/051501party fund/051501partyfund.html.

27. For more on congressional elections, see two reports funded by the Pew Charitable Trusts: Magleby (2000) and Krasno and Seltz (2000).

28. There may also be other reasons that members of the Congressional Black Caucus (CBC) fear a ban on soft money. They raise soft money to support the CBC PAC, which makes contributions to African American candidates and runs its own GOTV campaigns. Soft money is also raised for think tanks that analyze redistricting that might affect African American incumbents. See George Lardner, "For Black Caucus, Big Stake in Soft Money: PAC's Fundraisers, Creation of Think Tank Bring Questions About Disclosure," *Washington Post,* July 21, 2001, A04.

29. Committee on Political Parties 1950.

30. Since the sample includes 70 of 100 state parties, it may be biased toward the stronger parties that have the capacity to respond to surveys.

9

Political Parties in the Media: Where Elephants and Donkeys Are Pigs

MATTHEW ROBERT KERBEL

Imagine a time when political conventions were heralded with an out-pouring of public emotion, when torchlight parades illuminated the night and the faithful endorsed national tickets with the passion sports fans feel for playoff teams. There was such a time, during the middle decades of the nineteenth century, a time when politics was regarded as a partic-ipant sport in its own right. "When the national conventions chose the presidential candidates," Michael McGerr has written, "local party members 'ratified' the ticket with speeches, parades, bell-ringing, and cannon-fire" (McGerr 1986, 26).

Compare this with the situation today, when national conventions have been reduced to bad four-day television movies in which, David Broder of the *Washington Post* wrote, "[P]olicy and politics—the heart of conventions past—have given way to sentiment and sympathy" (Broder 1996a). Over the course of the twentieth century, the grand events of preindustrial America evolved into stage shows that register rather than make nomina-tion decisions (Ranney 1983; Polsby and Wildavsky 1996; Wayne 1996). Initially captivating television cameras with their spectacle and pomp, con-ventions were eventually stripped of their luster by planners who recog-nized the political advantage of presenting a tightly controlled message on live broadcasts. By 1992, continuous coverage of the conventions was rele-gated to all-news networks as the audience share for convention broad-casts plummeted. Citing the complete absence of newsworthy activity, *Nightline*'s Ted Koppel left the 1996 Republican National Convention after one day and did not bother showing up at the Democratic counterpart two weeks later. Tom Wicker, writing in the *New York Times*, called the major-party conventions "a national bore" (Wicker 1996).

Nonetheless, despite whining by journalists and an apparent lack of in-terest on the part of large segments of the public, two things remain plain: Most Americans, for better or worse, experience the political party con-ventions through mass media coverage rather than direct participation,

189

and no other event highlights the political parties as national institutions like the quadrennial conventions. Coverage of the conventions is therefore a natural place to turn to determine how mainstream media portray party structures and functions and to assess the content of messages communicated about political parties to interested spectators.

Ted Koppel may have had little regard for the conventions, but reporters as a group had a lot to say. During the four weeks from August 5 to August 30, 1996, a period spanning the Republican, Democratic, Reform, and Green party conventions, 231 stories about political parties appeared in five major outlets: the *New York Times*, the *Washington Post*, the *Los Angeles Times*, CNN, and *ABC World News Tonight*.[1] During a comparable period in 2000, however, coverage was off by more than half, with these media reporting a combined 104 stories. These convention stories, a subset of stories depicting the presidential campaign,[2] may be regarded as a national media tableau of political parties in 1996 and 2000, depicting how they are organized, what they do, how effectively they function—and how closely they mirror the institution described in academic literature.

This last point is somewhat problematic because despite great interest in the subject by scholars, the vast literature on parties is hamstrung by disagreement on definitions. The political scientist Ross K. Baker, writing in the *Los Angeles Times* in 1966, commented that "only two groups of Americans really care much about the parties: journalists and political scientists," and of the two, journalists paint a sharper and more consistent picture. Frank Sorauf succinctly stated the dilemma for academics: "As there are many roads to Rome and many ways to skin a cat, there are also many ways to look at a political party" (Sorauf 1964, 1). He proceeded to invoke an image of parties as home to such things as militant behavior and charismatic leadership, which hardly seems to capture prototypical party activity in the United States.

To the extent that an understanding exists about what a party *is*, it is expressed in the broad language of what a party *does*. Austin Ranney reviewed the literature and found common ground among five general functions: campaigning, fund-raising, providing a cognitive map for voters, interest aggregation, and unifying a fragmented system (Ranney 1983). Still, there is no consensus about the combination of functions that best captures the essence of a party. Some scholars define parties primarily in terms of their role in electoral competition (Downs 1957); others, in the context of their efforts to wield political influence (Sorauf 1964); still others, in terms of their educational and ideological functions (Duverger 1964). Some students of American parties are concerned with the ramifications of their decentralized structure; others make the procedural point that parties in the electorate are only loosely affiliated with parties in government (Key 1966; Burnam 1982). Thus, aside from the five areas noted above, it cannot be said that academics agree on a definition of party.

The mediated portrait of parties is more clear: They are highly personalized, nonideological organizations engaged in blurring rather than sharpening distinctions in an effort to present a compelling political image on television. In other words, reporters write about the people they see at conventions—mostly candidates, elected officials, and delegates—in terms of the political motives easily ascribed to those whose every gesture appears to invoke spin doctoring. The net effect is both surprisingly consistent with the academic picture of parties and disturbingly at odds with it. Electoral functions, particularly promoting candidates and raising money, are portrayed in textbook fashion. But the singular focus on political motivation leads reporters to where the heat is greatest, causing them to emphasize intraparty divisions that suggest parties are unable to successfully negotiate differences among elites or clear a path for voters through a decentralized political system. Attentive news consumers could decipher differences in the groups that support the major parties and the interests that offer them financial backing, but the stronger thematic message is that Democrats, Republicans, and even the Reform party play the same self-interested political games. Those seeking meaningful cognitive guidelines for political participation or even a reason to vote are told the parties will not respond.

People in Combat

The image of parties as television gladiators appears with ubiquity in the mainstream press. In his editorial postmortem on the 1996 conventions, Baker referred to party leaders as "franchisers, bankers and caterers," and summed up the festivities in terms of the big money–big television nexus: "What has been conspicuously on display in recent weeks has been the newest functions performed by the parties: catering national conventions and bankrolling campaign activities" (Baker 1996). Despite the assertion by a CNN reporter that "common interests and shared ideologies fuel today's party system" (CNN, August 26, 1996), far more commonplace were observations about the plastic, rootless quality of partisan debate necessary to contemporary political competition:

> Now that Mr. Gore is here, this Democratic convention will spend less time focused on the past, as it has with the Kennedys and Clintons in day one and two, and begin to focus on the team of Gore and Lieberman. They will

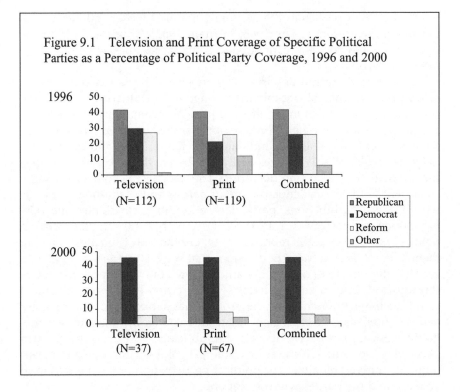

Figure 9.1   Television and Print Coverage of Specific Political
Parties as a Percentage of Political Party Coverage, 1996 and 2000

concentrate on the future. There has been ample praise, as you would expect, for Mr. Gore's leadership. But now the Democrats get into the final
phase of trying to make the message stick and acceptable enough to win.
(*ABC World News Tonight,* August 16, 2000)

The Republican party is a moving target. Less than two years ago, the party
appeared firmly under the guidance of a coterie of conservatives whose ar-
dor burned hotter than even that of Ronald Reagan. . . . But the backlash
that greeted the Republican-led Congress has clouded that vision. And now,
as the party heads into the general election campaign, its course is much less
clear. "We're redefining on the fly," said a senior aide to presidential nominee Bob Dole. (Gerstenzang 1996)

The share of attention accorded specific parties during their summer
conventions was largely proportional to the amount of shifting and redefining they had to do in order to position themselves for the fall. In
1996, Republicans had the greater task of healing primary-season wounds
and pacifying supply-siders, populists, and social conservatives; accord-

ingly, as Figure 9.1 shows, they received the greatest share of coverage as television and print reports conveyed these differences in terms of the electoral dilemma they posed. Because the Reform party offered something resembling a nomination fight between the quixotic Richard Lamm and the tenacious billionaire Ross Perot, the press (particularly CNN) devoted enough stories to the attendant infighting to rival the amount of attention accorded the relatively pacific Democrats.

The same rationale for covering the parties held in 2000, although different political dynamics altered the particulars of coverage. An open seat produced new nominees in both major parties, each emerging after a hotly contested primary campaign. Consequently, reporters paid roughly equal attention to the Democratic and Republican parties. And, as the 2000 figures in Table 9.1 indicate, the two major parties dominated party coverage. In a dramatic departure from four years earlier, the Reform party convention was barely a footnote, generating about as much notice as Ralph Nader's nomination as the Green party's standard-bearer. As the party of Perot suffered a decline in fortunes, it contributed little of note to the electoral drama, and reporters responded by not taking much notice of what it was doing.

The appetite for portraying parties as campaign vehicles helps explain why reporters personalize parties in their stories. Most party references invoked individuals rather than groups, organizations, or institutions, because people run for and hold office and staff campaigns—and interact with reporters as they do. Some references went so far as to reduce parties to people ("For a brief shining moment, [Newt] Gingrich was the

Table 9.1   Ten Most Frequently Mentioned Individuals in Television and Print Coverage of Political Parties, 1996 (N=300)

	Number of mentions	Percentage of all mentions
1. Ross Perot	45	15
2. Richard Lamm	35	12
3. Bob Dole	27	9
4. Jack Kemp	20	7
5. Bill Clinton	14	5
6. Pat Buchanan	10	3
7. Newt Gingrich	8	3
8. Hillary Clinton	6	2
9. Christopher Dodd	6	2
10. Russell Verney	6	2

Republican party" (R. Goodwin 1996)). Most simply discussed parties in terms of individuals, usually those involved in some aspect of electoral politics.

In 1996, six of the ten most frequently mentioned individuals were candidates.[3] The top two—Ross Perot and Richard Lamm—were the only ones engaged in a contested intra-party fight. Even though opinion poll results, the holy grail of political coverage, indicated the victor would be a non-starter in the fall campaign, Table 9.1 shows that better than one in four personalized party references were to the Reform Party tandem. The Republican ticket of Dole and Kemp took third and fourth place, respectively, in part because of the interesting political dynamics (read: differences) between them, and between Dole and primary nemesis Pat Buchanan, who ranked sixth. In contrast, the politically unchallenged incumbent president appeared in only 5 percent of stories about individuals.

Accordingly, reporters cast individuals in the role of candidate far more than any other.[4] In 56 percent of stories about individuals involved in the 1996 conventions, reporters portrayed their subjects as political contestants, even when it was possible to cast them in a different light (e.g., incumbent president, former Senate leader, multibillionaire). As Table 9.2 demonstrates, no other role came close to the attention afforded the person as candidate for office. This figure dropped slightly in 2000—to 45 percent—but candidate remained the most frequently invoked role.

No doubt, the tendency to personalize political parties is partly attributed to the visual requirements of television, which heavily influence the content and presentation of the story. Because cameras are hardly suited to photographing abstract institutions or groups, it is not surprising to find that 78 percent of television stories in 1996 defined parties in terms of specific actors—candidates and a few elected officials—who could serve as "talking head" party symbols.

But so did 66 percent of print stories, which were not confined by the restrictions of visual imagery and, consequently, were better equipped to present the structural components of the political party that account for its institutional diversity and sophistication, to say nothing of its texture and depth. This is the realm of candidate recruitment and mass-elite linkages, of organization-building and formalizing decision-making authority (Bibby 1981, 1997; Miller and Jennings 1986), none of which is easily personified but all of which is on display at the conventions and suited to coverage by print reporters, for whom personification is unnecessary. But print reporters largely pass by institutional interpretations of parties, choosing instead to echo the heavily personalized accounts appearing on television, equating parties with their candidates for high office and visible public figures.

Table 9.2   Ten Most Frequently Mentioned Individual Roles in
Television and Print Coverage of Political Parties, 1996 (N=300)

	Number of mentions	*Percentage of all mentions*
1. Candidate	170	56
2. Elected official	28	9
3. Delegate	23	8
4. Party elite	21	7
5. Speaker	13	4
6. Other/undefined	13	4
7. Lobbyist	11	4
8. Campaign adviser	9	3
9. Party supporter	7	2
10. First lady	5	2

Consider what this 1996 *Washington Post* account of Republican keynote speaker Susan Molinari says about what parties are and what they do:

> And now, the preferred face of the Republican Party, 1996: A gum-snapping feminist with a run in her stockings and new-mother shadows under her eyes, a pro-choice New Yorker who keeps a crib in her office and squeaky dog toys under her desk, a runner who chugs Diet Pepsi from 20-ounce bottles while dissecting tax reform. She is Susan Molinari, 38, congresswoman from Staten Island. "The perfect face for the '90s," says Christina Martin, deputy press secretary for the Dole Campaign. Or so they hope. And so they hype. (Blumenfeld 1996)

Barely hidden beneath the colorful adjectives is a tripartite message: that parties may be reduced in form to the individuals appearing on the screen; in function to making manipulative appeals to viewers' emotions for political purposes ("And so they hype"); and in essence to fronts for campaign operations (*they* are the Dole campaign). Notwithstanding the elements of truth contained in this account,[5] the *Post* hardly does justice to political parties in this piece, portraying them in the most unflattering single dimension possible.

Four years later little had changed. The Republican party was still being described as a manipulative operation that used individuals to front for a message with political value. In a piece headlined "The Props Talk Back"—a reference to the women and minorities paraded around

Philadelphia to hype (to use the word from 1996) the party message about diversity—the *New York Times* described Representative Mary Bono's organization for Republican women, Right Now, in personal terms as "hipper than the Republican Women's Federation" (Kuczynski and Purdy 2000). By appealing to "rock-n-roll Republicans," the group, we are told, plays directly to the message the Bush campaign hoped to convey about the inclusive reach of the Republican party as it tightly controlled the imagery of its convention in an effort to win the votes of young people, moderates, and women.

Where differentiated party structures do not exist, the effect is even more pronounced. Virtually all the coverage afforded the 1996 Green party and Reform party conventions centered on personality, as Figure 9.2 demonstrates. The celebrity power of Green Party nominee Ralph Nader was sufficient to reward this otherwise overlooked group with five print references to the fact that the party had met to nominate the consumer activist. The press's approach to the Reform party—which outdid its established competitors by holding *two* conventions on two successive weekends—was expressed by a CNN reporter, who said, "When you say the words 'third party' or 'Reform Party,' Ross Perot's name is usually the first thing that comes to mind" (CNN, August 12, 1996).

As far as correspondents were concerned, Perot was the only thing that came to mind. Coverage of the Reform party was coverage of the party as ego. There was no discussion of fund-raising, because Perot was the party's one financial supporter. There was no discussion of delegates because there were no delegates, only self-selected nonvoting representatives. There was no evidence of structural stability or inclusive membership (Sorauf 1964). The only party elite mentioned, other than the candidates, was the national coordinator, Russell Verney.

Otherwise, it was all Perot, or Perot versus Lamm in a peculiar race to see who would capture the nomination of a group Perot had founded and funded. When CNN announced, "After a long wait, and to very little surprise, the Reform party picked its founder and financial backer to be its presidential standard-bearer" (CNN, August 18, 1996), it proclaimed the predictable outcome of a contest that defined coverage of an entity that was regarded as a party institution by the press despite obvious indications to the contrary.

But if reporters overlooked things that might challenge the classification of the Reform movement as a "party," they readily discarded Perot's claim that his effort was about something more than seeking partisan advantage. On this score, coverage of the Reform party assumed the salient political characteristics found in stories about the major parties, only more so, because little beside the nomination fight was happening in the

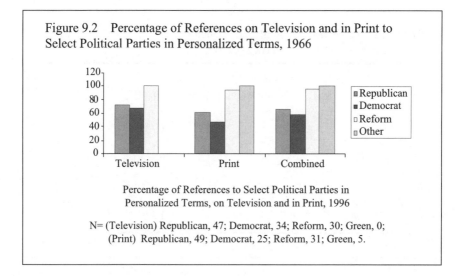

Figure 9.2   Percentage of References on Television and in Print to Select Political Parties in Personalized Terms, 1966

Percentage of References to Select Political Parties in Personalized Terms, on Television and in Print, 1996

N= (Television) Republican, 47; Democrat, 34; Reform, 30; Green, 0;
(Print) Republican, 49; Democrat, 25; Reform, 31; Green, 5.

Reform party to interest reporters. "For a party that promises politics not as usual," the *New York Times* wrote, "Ross Perot's Reform Party—on the eve of its first national presidential nominating convention—seems to be deeply mired in, well, politics as usual. As 2,000 of the Reform Party faithful headed to Long Beach, California this weekend for the opening session of a two-part convention, there was still another vituperative yes-you-did, I-did-not exchange of statements by Mr. Perot and former Gov. Richard D. Lamm of Colorado, the two contenders for the party's nomination" (Ayres 1996).

For the bulk of the convention period, readers and viewers were offered little more than an ongoing account of this sniping. In the personal, political contest between its two candidates, the press had stripped the Reform party to its essentials while forgoing the opportunity to assess what it takes to build the very thing its chief backer claimed the Reform party was: a viable new political organization.

Group Politics: Money, Not Ideology

Among the established parties, reporters made reference not only to a broader variety of individual actors but to an array of groups that were almost entirely missing from accounts of the Perot movement.[6] These groups—which, as Table 9.3 indicates, cover a wide range of interests and issues—offer a more detailed picture of how parties appear in the press. Although two and a half individual references were made for every

Table 9.3   Ten Most Frequently Mentioned Groups in Television and
Print Coverage of Political Parties, 1996 (N=122)

	Number of mentions	*Percentage of all mentions*
1. Demographic	40	33
2. Political	30	25
3. Business	27	22
4. Personal rights	11	9
5. Voters	8	7
6. Unions	3	2
7. Other/undefined	2	2
8. Social action	1	1

group reference, the assortment of groups in media coverage reveals the breadth of party affiliation as it suggests the selfish ways of identifiers. Group members appearing in print and on television are generally more concerned with giving money and gaining influence than debating issues and promoting ideas—unless in the process of advancing an agenda, they produce discord in the party.

In the press, the major parties are broad-based organizations, drawing a wide variety of identifiers even if they are not integrated into a cogent unit. In 1996, the most frequently cited type of group is demographic, accounting for one in three group references and comprising a wide range of individuals sheltered by the party umbrella. Groups were classified by their ideological predisposition (a total of 18 references encompassing conservatives, moderates, and liberals) and by gender (8 references), race (5), class distinctions (4), age (3), and region (2). The pattern of coverage for the 2000 election was similar.[7]

These classifications tended to be descriptive rather than functional. The press was adept at pointing out the diversity of party identifiers but rarely asserted group membership for the purpose of demonstrating an ideological connection to the demographics. Even references to "liberals" and "conservatives" were more likely to be political than ideological (for instance, the presence of conservatives at the 1996 Republican convention as an indication that the party would have trouble attracting moderates), with few references to groups that were attempting to advance a specific agenda. Mentions of gender, race, class, and age were similarly lacking in ideological purpose. As Table 9.4 attests, groups were rarely covered in an idea-generating context.

Consistent with the tendency to downplay ideological discussion, in the news groups organized around a personal rights agenda ("Log Cabin" Republicans, abortion activists) and social action (the Sierra Club) were a slender presence compared with two utilitarian groups: political organizers (convention planners and others engaged in producing the convention) and businesses (including corporations and lawyers).

Business groups are the more interesting of the two, as reporters invariably portrayed them in terms of contributing money, which in turn is one of the three group activities reporters most frequently cite.[8] Reporters left no doubt that raising money is "an obsession" among party leaders (Drew 1983), emphasizing where it comes from and what is expected in return. On matters of finance, the two major parties were treated equally during both election cycles, particularly in terms of the massive amounts of "soft money" they stockpiled:

The national fund-raising committees of the Democratic Party raised more than $65 million in "soft money" donations from wealthy individuals, corporations and labor unions in the 18-month period between January 1, 1995, and June 30. This is five times the $13 million the party raised in soft money in the same period four years earlier, when it didn't control the White House. (Babcock 1996a)

With a record $137.4-million in large contributions already collected, the Republican Party is flush with soft money, the unrestricted party checks. But

Table 9.4   Ten Most Frequently Mentioned Group Roles in Television and Print Coverage of Political Parties, 1996 (N=122)

	Number of mentions	*Percentage of all mentions*
1. Identifying with party	36	30
2. Differing with party	25	20
3. Money-related	23	19
4. Convention-related	12	10
5. Idea-related	7	6
6. Power-related	5	4
7. Socializing	5	4
8. Campaigning	4	3
9. Alienated/disinterested	3	2
10. Other	2	2

one of the central purposes of the [2000 Republican National Convention] is to motivate the party's most generous supporters to raise and give still more. (Border and Van Natta 2000)

Typically, reporters made the connection between money and influence. *ABC World News Tonight* underscored the bipartisan nature of corporate influence by stating, on July 31, 2000, that AT&T, General Motors, and other large entities were underwriting the Democratic and Republican conventions because they "value the relationship they have with the men and women that make the laws that affect their interests." The *Washington Post* reported a "lavish" contribution of soft money by trial lawyers to both major parties, mentioning that the organization had "bitterly fought a bill to limit lawsuits over defective products" and intoning that the donations were hardly the fruits of political efficacy. ABC News was particularly fond of emphasizing these connections. On *ABC World News Tonight* between August 9 and August 27, 1996, references to parties and money were made in nine separate stories which generally questioned the propriety of corporate lobbyists schmoozing with party elites, or linked their financial ties to the parties with matters pending before Congress and the administration.

Collectively, the ABC reports connected Democrats with no less than seven unions (including one that "may have ties with the Mafia"), the tobacco industry (two separate references to Philip Morris), two manufacturers of alcoholic beverages, three media conglomerates, two investment houses, a cosmetics company, two telecommunications giants, an oil company, and trial lawyers. For their part, Republicans were portrayed as the beneficiaries of big money from the same tobacco and alcohol producers as the Democrats, a different set of media conglomerates (including the one that owns ABC), the nuclear power industry, a large railroad, and the casino and gaming industry.

If distinctions between who supports whom (lawyers and unions backing only Democrats, for instance) were clouded by multiple references to those benevolent groups that spent money in bipartisan fashion, it was hard to miss the broader point that both parties peddle influence in exchange for money. Although the extent of the influence received by donors remains unclear, the cash-and-carry connection between monied interests and political attention emerges repeatedly from press reports.

Even reports about so trivial a matter as how convention delegates socialized were not immune from the suggestion that there is no rest for the influential. The *Washington Post* may have lightheartedly quipped that Republican delegates enjoyed an array of parties because "elephants are social creatures" (Roberts 1996), but it was all business when it reported on the "free packs of Marlboros and Merits" available to "top Republicans" who "mingled with a variety of lobbyists" on a Philip Morris yacht (Marcus 1996).

It may not be clear from press coverage what the parties and their leaders stand for, but it is fairly obvious whom they represent. And it is equally apparent that there are no differences between the parties when it comes to price.

Internal Divisions

The major parties share another distinction: Reporters cover them as if they are on the verge of falling apart. Variations on the theme of disharmony were pervasive. Typical commentary noted that Democrats were facing divisions over policy and their direction as a party, and Republicans house irreconcilable political and social groups. Both parties were trying to put on a unified front, but neither was as solid as its television image suggested. Reporters reacted to the prime-time "love-fest" offered to the home audience by reminding everyone who would listen not to believe what they were seeing.

Although Table 9.4 indicates that groups are most frequently mentioned in terms of their support for or identification with a party, reporters' skepticism abounds. The news of groups portrayed as supporting the party was often called into question by journalists who took their allegiance to be superficial. For instance, a *Washington Post* article acknowledged several demographic groups as Republican partisans, but only in the context of what it called "a televised montage of multiethnic images: a little black girl who has AIDS expressing hope for the future; a black former welfare recipient who has turned her life around; a Native American reciting the Pledge of Allegiance; a Hispanic singer who inspired convention delegates to dance in the aisles." Furthermore, it continues, "seeing is not necessarily believing. 'There's no revolution,' said Ben Andrews, a black alternate delegate from Connecticut. 'There's a lot of resistance in the party. Everybody wants to believe there's inclusion. They speak of it. But right now it's only a symbol moving toward reality'" (Merida 1996).

The theme of papering over differences for the cameras applied to Democrats as well:

> Given President Clinton's political rebound and his party's newfound confidence since the dark days after the Republican congressional victory in 1994, the Democrats could not have picked a more appropriately named arena— the United Center—for their national convention this summer. But behind

the Democrats' concerted message of unity looms a debate over the direction of the party, one that will begin quietly here this week and burst into
public view immediately after the November election, no matter who wins
the presidency. (Edsall and Balz 1996)

Reporters who found fissures in the two parties were no doubt reacting
to the controlling grip of convention organizers who knew the electoral
advantages of unity and were determined to paint a happy face over their
differences. The stifling news environment begged reporters to dig for
trouble, lest they be left with only the party line to report. Eagerly they
served up the premise that "a convention is a time for party members to
show their solidarity," only to swat it down by recounting "divisions in
the ranks" (CNN, August 26, 1996). They asserted that Republicans hoped
to demonstrate that everyone in the hall was "firmly and loyally in lock-
step behind George W. Bush," only to undermine this assertion by looking to the placement of the McCain-heavy New Hampshire delegation in
the back of the hall as an example of how "some scars haven't entirely
healed yet" (CNN, July 30, 2000). Variations on this theme were abundant
because it was an easy story to write. Every political reporter knows that
differences of opinion abound in organizations as broad as the major parties, and rifts from the primaries often resist a paper coating.

The dilemma this poses for parties is that differences are invariably
portrayed as problematic and troublesome rather than healthy and inevitable, projecting the misleading impression that parties are unable to
respond to the challenges of diversity. To be sure, party leaders interested
in electoral success do see differences as vexing (hence the effort to control the party image on television), but their considerations, like those of
the journalists who cover them, are short-term and political. Viewed
through a wider lens, the presence of internal debate is a sign that the
parties offer political shelter to a spectrum of interests whose inevitable
disagreements antecede moderation and compromise. Interests are aggregated through shouting and shrugging; these are signs the party is
functioning effectively.

But this is not the picture conveyed by the press. Indeed, Table 9.4
shows that one in five group references by TV and print journalists mentioned opposition to another group or to a party position, a theme repeated in countless individual references to delegates and even party
elites. The most pervasive differences surrounded social issues: for
Democrats, welfare reform; for Republicans, abortion and gay rights.
Most of these were differences over policy, although some stories about
the Republicans' problems raised doubts about the long-term viability of
pro-choice and gay partisans' positions.

Groups like urban Democrats might be expected to be energetic party
loyalists, but in 1996 the *New York Times* raised the welfare issue, and

suggested otherwise: "They say they enthusiastically support the President. They say they will work like crazy to bring out his vote come November. But when urban Democrats at the national convention here try to explain why President Clinton signed the Republican-sponsored Federal welfare bill, they fidget uncomfortably and lower their voices" (Dao 1996). Similarly, the *Times* found divisions over welfare among prominent individuals, even Democratic National Committee Chair Christopher Dodd, who was regarded as a metaphor for the divisions the paper found simmering below the surface of a carefully orchestrated convention. Mr. Dodd, the paper argued, "has internalized [the Democrats'] most obvious tensions, vocally opposing Mr. Clinton on the welfare bill" (Henneberger 1996). The *Washington Post* underscored the point by relating what it saw behind the scenes in Chicago: "Backstage . . . there is bad blood between Clinton and the congressional leadership, who have split over welfare, budget balance, NAFTA and other key issues" (Kuttner 1996).

Comparable stories originated from San Diego, where Republicans were portrayed as alternately resolute, angry, and distraught. Abortion was one cause for this. Some groups appeared unwilling to bend even in the wake of success: "On the [Right to Life] side of the party's deep divide over abortion, there was little indication of a desire to soften a victory won Monday, when platform writers discarded a 'tolerance clause' on abortion that Dole had asked for" (Shogan 1996b). The same determination to highlight disunity extended to individual delegates. Despite a call for moderation from Dole and Kemp, "A Buchanan delegate tells CNN he will vote for Buchanan 'Because I'm a committed delegate. I was voted by around 2,000 people, that's who I represent and that's who I'm going to vote for'" (CNN, August 14, 1996).

Such unyielding determination left others in despair:

> Republicans may have called a cease-fire in the ideological warfare over abortion and other social issues at this week's national convention, but some Republicans like Laurie Letourneau are wondering how long the truce will last now that the delegates are going home. Letourneau, a convention delegate from Massachusetts, says that disputes over abortion and squabbles between moderates and conservatives in her state have been so bitter that she is thinking of leaving the Republican Party. (Hook 1996)

> In a stained-carpet hotel north of downtown, far from the yacht-lined bay front where the Republican National Convention is convening this week, Republican activist Frank Ricchiazzi wonders how much further apart he and his party can possibly be. . . . Ricchiazzi, a Laguna Beach [California] resident, is a gay Republican, an uncommon commodity at a national convention dominated by social conservatives. (Martinez 1996)

The difficulties facing a minority voice in any party are, of course, understandable, as are the eternal struggles among factions for everything
from broader acceptance to agenda control. Certainly, they are part of the
story of party life. But, as the above passages illustrate, journalists were
quick to portray differences as irreconcilable when in fact Republicans
and Democrats have imperfectly managed their problems for generations, and did so again in 1996 and 2000. In the abortion piece, the *Los
Angeles Times* speculated about hypothetical future problems ("some
Republicans . . . are wondering how long the truce will last") even as—or
perhaps precisely because—the convention offered few fireworks. The
piece about gay Republicans is equally speculative ("Ricchiazzi wonders
how much further apart he and his party can possibly be"), overlooking
the obvious but important point that Ricchiazzi may have felt and been
treated like a second-class citizen, but he still elected to attend a convention where some may have been unwelcoming. Despite serious difficulties, strong doubts, and legitimate concerns, both delegates remained active members of their chosen party, a point lost in coverage that
emphasizes despair.

A Dime's Worth of Difference

It is just as easy to emphasize how parties manage to provide shelter for
a wide array of members as it is to underscore how deep divisions
threaten to pull them apart. It would be accurate to say that significant
and lasting battles over issues and interests are indicators of the flexibility of two enormous organizations that reflect the sometimes tumultuous
currents of American political discourse. But it would be hard for journalists to defend this seemingly soft approach to editors who share their
view that party leaders will do anything to use the media for their political benefit. And, it wouldn't make for an interesting story. So parties are
defined in terms of the problems they have yet to solve, and doubts are
cast on their ability to succeed. They appear to be another piece of a broken political system rather than a place for expressing differences and
gradually working out solutions.

Add to this the scent of tainted money used for electoral gain and it is
easy to understand why so many hold the parties in low regard. Between
their apparent inability to manage internal differences and their unresponsive posture to all but big contributors, there appears to be little accountability in the party system. Choosing not to explore the possibility
that parties also may provide a forum for the expression of principled
ideas, and that activist groups may not *only* be rigid and power-hungry,
reporters cast parties in the role of principal cooks in the sausage-making

enterprise that running for office is. They assert that parties should be as peaceful and harmonious in conference rooms as they try to be on television screens, deliberately overlooking the fact that such behavior would be as impossible as it would be undesirable.

Party divisions demarcate the fissures of democratic debate. Reporters no doubt believe that they advance this debate, or at least make it more visible, by pointing out the problematic nature of differences party leaders see as politically disadvantageous, and that they metaphorically hold the feet of Haley Barbour and Christopher Dodd to the fire of public scrutiny by detailing the hypocrisy of wearing a smiling face while hiding important off-camera arguments. What reporters apparently do not realize is that by doing this they insist that parties be understood exclusively in terms of their electoral function and, despite their best intentions, become unwitting allies with big contributors and political handlers in undermining support for the political process.

It is no wonder, then, that people lack confidence in the parties, given long-term shifts in the nature of participation that have rendered politics a living-room event for many. In the 1990s, large numbers wistfully longed for a third party, a fill-in-the-blanks fantasy that somehow would improve on what we have. But even among those who wished for something new, there was no consensus on what that party would stand for, or how it would differ substantively from Republicans and Democrats. Rather, the call for a third party was largely a call to do something about how the major parties behave—a call predicated on the belief that the major parties are unresponsive to the needs of ordinary Americans and unable to navigate a complex maze of public interests. As the recession of 1992 gave way to boom times, the call became faint, and the Reform party—once the hope of millions—disintegrated into factional warfare and political irrelevance.

There never was a reason to believe that a new party would more successfully respond to political demands than the existing two. By necessity broad-based, a new party would simply inherit the crosscutting interests that have long been housed within existing party structures. Inevitably, reporters would compare the new organization to its predecessors and find it subject to the same pressures and problems, no doubt asking whether any party can function responsively in our political system, overlooking the fact that parties already do. Notwithstanding the need for dramatic reform in the conduct and financing of *campaigns*—a matter involving but distinct from party structures—the nineteenth-century institutions we call upon to make sense of a complex political landscape quite effectively capture the ripples and cross-currents of public opinion.

It is also no wonder why people see no differences between the parties, given that they appear to stand united by greed and self-promotion rather than separated by ideas or ideology. It is hard to understand how handing one's vote to a party controlled by large corporations is any different than handing it to a party controlled by trial lawyers. Parties appear similar because they are covered the same way, in personal and nonideological terms suited to how the press covers the larger campaign process (Kerbel 1994). This is hardly surprising because they are covered mostly in terms of their campaign role, making parties just one factor in a larger battle between candidate and reporter for control of the news message, rather than making the campaign function performed by parties just one factor in a story about the larger purpose they play in the political system.

Reporters could defend themselves against spin-doctoring party leaders *and* perform a valuable service by offering a different take on political parties: one that emphasized the policy agendas underlying the fierce rhetoric as something intrinsically meaningful, not just labels for identifying the political players; one that treated party division as a healthy reflection of different perspectives rather than as a sign of institutional weakness; one that saw in the ongoing process of negotiating interests a manifestation of democratic problem-solving rather than a scorecard for who is temporarily in vogue in some short-term political sweepstakes. Something far more important than political soap opera is at stake when journalists cover parties, but for parties to appear responsive, reporters must act responsibly.

The balloons and the hype, the infighting and the noise will of course remain newsworthy, if not new; parties, after all, were about theater and politics long before television replaced torchlight parade routes and fair grounds as the center of pomp. But if vast majorities know parties only from what they read and see in their homes, it is especially important that reporters communicate what else parties are about. They could be for a broader audience the centers of debate and agenda setting that make politics meaningful and possible, even as reporters wrest the terms of coverage from the manipulative machinations of politicians and handlers. That would be newsworthy indeed.

Notes

1. These media were selected for analysis because of their status as major national outlets. The *New York Times* is widely regarded as the American newspaper of record, rivaled perhaps in the national political realm by the *Washington Post*.

The *Los Angeles Times* has a highly regarded political unit, and offers a perspective from California, where the 1996 Republican, Reform, and Green party conventions were held. CNN is the premiere all-news television service; *ABC World News Tonight* regularly draws the largest audience for network evening news.

2. An on-line database search was conducted to identify stories for this analysis. Stories were included if the headline or sub-headline (for newspapers), title "slug" (for CNN), or text (for ABC) made reference to a specific party or to political parties in general. The analysis includes general news and editorial items.

3. Individuals were recorded in the order in which they were mentioned in the story. Up to three individuals were recorded for each story.

4. Each time an individual was mentioned, a record was made of the role that person played in the story. Accordingly, the same individual could be portrayed in a variety of roles in different stories.

5. The truth of this account does not extend to equating the Republican party with the Dole campaign, each of which had a different set of interests. Although Dole managed to use the convention as a vehicle for launching his presidential campaign, he was only able to do so after negotiating a complex set of factional interests that led him, among other things, to abandon a compromise he had brokered with conservative groups on the wording of platform language on abortion. Some previous presidential candidates, most recently George Bush in 1992, were largely unable to wrest control of the convention from factional interests and therefore could not use the convention as a political showcase.

6. Groups were recorded in the order in which they were mentioned in the story. Few stories contained more than one group mention, although up to two groups were recorded for each story.

7. The overall figures for 2000 displayed a similar pattern to the 1996 data, inasmuch as the three most frequently mentioned groups were the same as in 1996: demographic (26 percent), political (48 percent) and business (14 percent). As in 1996, there was a steep dropoff in group references after these three, with little or no attention given to voters, unions, and personal-rights groups.

8. As with individuals, each time a group was mentioned, a record was made of the role they played in the story. Accordingly, the same group could be portrayed in a variety of roles in different stories.

10

Congressional Parties and the Policy Process

BARBARA SINCLAIR

The first national elections of the twenty-first century produced unified Republican government, if only barely, and both hopes and fears that, with the presidency, House, and Senate all controlled by one party, significant policy change would ensue. Those who instead feared—or hoped for—gridlock focused more on the narrow Republican margins in the two chambers of Congress than on potential problems with maintaining high Republican unity. Yet not so long ago most observers of American politics argued that fragmentation and lack of discipline are the cardinal characteristics of American political parties and make them incapable of carrying out the policy functions that proponents of responsible parties demand of them.

According to the theory of party government, the winning party is expected to organize the government, set the policy agenda, and enact that agenda into law. By doing so, the political party solves several key problems that beset democracies. Lawmaking is a complex enterprise that requires time, effort, and organization. If the majority party performs these tasks, the costs of assembling majorities will be minimized, since that task will not have to be begun from scratch on each new issue. With the same like-minded group of members formulating legislation across a range of issues, policy will display coherence. And, critical for democratic theory, the majority party will be responsible for what the legislature has done and thus can be held accountable by the voters at the next election.

This essay examines the congressional parties. What roles do the parties, especially the majority party, play in the contemporary Congress? How does the congressional party go about carrying out its functions? To what extent can the contemporary congressional parties, at least when working with a president who is a fellow partisan, perform the policy functions? How has this changed over time and why?

The Congressional Party's Historical Roles:
Stability and Variation

Since early in their history, the House of Representatives and the Senate have relied on both parties and committees to provide the structure that enables them to get their work done. Parties organize the chambers and provide coordination; committees do most of the substantive work on legislation.

After the biennial elections, each party in each chamber meets to organize. In the House, each party nominates a candidate for Speaker, the presiding officer of the House, and elects its floor leaders and chief whips. When the House itself meets for the first time in the new Congress, the candidate of the majority party is elected Speaker, almost always on a straight party-line vote. The Senate parties elect their floor leaders and whips. Unlike in the House, the Senate's top leader, the majority leader, is not the presiding officer nor an official of the Senate at all.

Members of Congress receive their committee assignments through their party. Each party in each chamber has a committee on committees, whose job it is to assign new members to committee posts and consider senior members' requests for transfers. The majority party has a majority of members on every committee except the ethics committees of the House and Senate and majority-party members chair all committees and subcommittees.

Party leaders are the only central leaders in the two chambers of Congress; the membership of the committees, where the substantive legislative work is done, is determined by the parties. These factors might lead one to expect congressional parties to be powerful as shapers of legislative outcomes. In fact, the strength of the congressional parties and the power and autonomy of congressional committees has varied over time (Cooper and Brady 1981; Matthews 1960; Sinclair 1989, 1995). From about 1890 to 1910, powerful party leaders dominated both chambers; high-ranking majority-party leaders chaired the most important committees and, especially in the House, the Speaker's great powers over committee assignments and over floor scheduling and procedure allowed the majority party to control legislative outcomes. These regimes were followed by a long period of committee government during which committees developed considerable independence of the party. No longer did the Speaker make committee assignments; committee chairmanships automatically went to the most senior majority-party member on the committee, depriving the party of any real control. The congressional party played little role as agenda setter or policy shaper.

If the congressional party sometimes plays a significant policy role and at other times merely carries out some basic organizational and coordination tasks, what makes the difference? The strength of parties within

Congress should depend on how members at a particular time weigh the benefits—what a strong party can do for them—against the costs—what a strong party can do to them. Those costs and benefits should depend to a significant extent though by no means solely on the homogeneity of the members' legislative preferences. Members of Congress do not owe and never have owed their elections to strong centralized parties; thus individual members are not bound to either work with or vote with their party colleagues. Yet the tasks a party can perform may be valuable to members as individuals; if, for example, the party facilitates the process of putting together majorities for legislation the member favors, the member has an incentive to work within the party and even to increase his party's capabilities (Sinclair 1995; Cox and McCubbins 1993). If the members of a party agree on the legislation they want to see passed, they have a powerful incentive to strengthen their party's legislative capabilities, allow their party leadership to use its powers aggressively, and even delegate more power to their party leadership.

Party Cohesion and Party Composition in the House of Representatives

In the House, members have voted along party lines much more frequently since the early 1980s than they did in the preceding decades.[1] From the mid–1950s through the mid–1960s (1955–1966) about 49 percent of the recorded votes saw a majority of Democrats voting against a majority of Republicans. The frequency of such party votes slumped in the late 1960s and early 1970s and then began to rise again, averaging 36 percent for the 1967–1982 period. After the 1982 elections, it jumped to over half the votes and continued to rise in the late 1980s. In the decade of the 1990s, it averaged 58 percent. Party unity scores which measure the frequency with which the average member voted with his or her party on party votes trace roughly the same pattern. In the 1990s, Republicans averaged 88 percent party unity; Democrats 86 percent.

It appears, then, that over the course of the last several decades the political parties in the House have become markedly more ideologically homogeneous internally and have moved further from each other in policy preferences.[2] If that is, in fact, the case one would expect it to be the result of change in the electoral constituencies of the members of the two parties, which—though by no means the only source of member's legislative preferences—is certainly an important one. And in fact both parties have changed.

From the late 1930s onward, the Democratic party was split into a conservative southern faction and a liberal northern faction. Since the late

1960s, however, the constituencies of southern Democrats have become more like those of their northern colleagues (Rohde 1991). In part, the convergence is the result of processes such as the urbanization of the South. More important, with the passage of the Voting Rights Act and growing Republican strength in the South, African Americans have become a critical element of many southern Democrats' election support. As a result, the policy views of the electoral coalitions supporting many southern Democrats are not drastically different from those of the average northern Democrat.

The House Republican party also changed in composition. As Republicans made inroads in the South, southerners became an increasingly significant component of the House Republican party. The percentage of southern House seats won by Republicans went from 26 in 1969 to 36 in 1984 to 59 in 2000. In 1969 southerners made up a meager 16 percent of the House Republican membership; in 2001 that figure stood at 37 percent. Southern Republicans have consistently been the most conservative segment of their party and, as southerners made up an increasing proportion of the Republican House membership, the party moved to the right.

The changing regional composition of the party by no means accounts completely for the House Republicans' growing conservatism (Connelly and Pitney 1994). Ronald Reagan's presidential victory in 1980 was both an indicator of increasing conservative strength and a boost to it. Reflecting the new strength of conservatives in the Republican party, the House Republican membership had begun to change in the mid- and late 1970s and continued to do so throughout the 1980s. Not only were fewer moderates being elected, more hard-edged, ideological conservatives were entering the chamber, from the South but from other regions as well. The huge Republican freshman class—73 strong—elected in 1994 consisted largely of aggressive conservatives, deeply committed to cutting the size and scope of government. Together with the sophomores, who were very similar in outlook, they made up over half of the Republican House membership in the 104th Congress, the first in which Republicans held a majority.

Political Parties and Party Leadership in the House

During the party government era of approximately 1920 to 1970, the congressional parties and their leaders played a relatively restricted role.[3] The party organized the chamber but exercised little control over the committees and their leaders. The party leaders played an important coordination role, especially by scheduling floor business. They mobilized floor votes for the passage of major legislation. However, neither the House majority party membership as an entity nor its leadership involved itself in agenda setting or in policy formulation. The committees performed these functions largely independent of internal party direction. The president, if of the same party, often set the agenda and took a strong hand in the shaping of legislation; but the committees were not bound to be responsive to his wishes.

By the late 1980s, the political party had become much more central to the policy process in the House (Sinclair 1995; Rohde 1991). The majority-party leadership had gained significant resources and involved itself actively in all phases of the legislative process. In response to the desires of the majority-party membership, the party and its leadership took an active part in setting the agenda and in shaping policy.

The decline in the ideological heterogeneity of the Democratic membership discussed earlier contributed significantly to this change. When the legislative preferences of a party's members are relatively similar, those members will perceive the party as a more useful—and a less threatening—instrument and will be more willing to have their party leaders exert strong leadership. Also crucial were changes in the political and institutional context in the 1970s and 1980s that altered the cost and benefits of a stronger party to members. The 1970s reforms decreased the power of committees and their chairmen, opened more of the legislative process to public scrutiny, and increased members' opportunities, resources, and incentives to participate, especially by offering amendments on the floor. The impact of the reforms combined with the constraints of the 1980s political environment (a conservative confrontational president and big deficits) to greatly increase the difficulty of enacting legislation, especially legislation Democrats favored. Within that context, Democrats needed a stronger party and a more active leadership to accomplish their policy goals.

The 1970s reformers, most of them liberal Democrats, had been motivated by concerns about both policy and participation. The changes they instituted would, they believed, produce better policy *and* provide greater opportunities for the rank and file to participate in the legislative process. The reforms did expand members' opportunities to participate, but by the late 1970s many Democrats had concluded that unrestrained participation, particularly on the House floor, hindered rather than facilitated the production of good public policy. And in the more hostile political climate of the 1980s, the policy costs of unrestrained and uncoordinated legislative activism rose further.

Included in the 1970s reforms were provisions augmenting the party leadership's resources. Leaders were given a greater role in making committee assignments and the Speaker was given the power to appoint all majority-party members of the Rules Committee. In the mid–1970s, the party's ideological heterogeneity and members' desire to fully exploit their new participation opportunities limited the leaders' use of their new tools. In the late 1970s and 1980s, in contrast, as legislating became increasing difficult, members not only allowed but began to demand that their leaders aggressively employ the tools at their command to facilitate passing the legislation members wanted.

The increased ideological polarization of the House parties combined with the more activist role of the majority party and its leadership during the 1980s meant that increasingly, the major legislative decisions were being made within the majority party. On the most important issues of the day, minority Republicans felt that they were excluded from the action and became increasingly frustrated. House Republicans adopted a strategy of confrontation and harassment of the majority party; Democrats responded by sometimes using their procedural powers in a heavy-handed fashion, and partisan rancor pervaded the legislative process.

When Republicans unexpectedly won control of the House in the 1994 elections, the new House majority was strongly and homogeneously conservative and perceived itself as having received an electoral mandate for major policy change. Newt Gingrich, the House Republicans' new leader, emerged from the elections with enormous prestige. In the eyes of most Republicans and the media, he was the miracle maker; he was seen as responsible for the startling Republican victory. These circumstances combined to give Gingrich and his leadership team enormous latitude to use party leadership powers and resources aggressively. In 1994 and 1995, the House Republican party acted remarkably like the cohesive, responsible party of party government theory (Ranney 1975). It proposed and ran on a policy agenda; it organized the chamber and empowered its leaders so as to facilitate the expeditious translation of the agenda into law; with the members maintaining high cohesion, the party delivered on its promises.

The leadership's and the party's extraordinary dominance of the House legislative process did not survive 1995; the budget debacle of late 1995 and early 1996 destroyed the extraordinary consensus on strategy as well as substance among House Republicans that had made the dominance possible. Yet, both parties remain quite ideologically cohesive; members require party and leadership help to attain their goals, so the party and the party leadership continue to play important roles, including policy roles, in the contemporary House.

Organizing the Chamber

Because they have major policy implications, assigning members to committees and choosing committee chairs are important functions. Both House parties delegate those tasks, though not the final okay, to broadly representative party committees. The Republican Steering Committee is composed of nine party leaders ranging from the Speaker to the secretary of the Republican Conference, the chairs of the three most important committees, 11 members who represent regional groupings of Republicans, and one representative from each of the three most junior classes. Top party leaders have considerable influence over the committee assignment process and House members have come to expect that party loyalty will be one criterion in determining who gets the best assignments. In fact, Republicans now give their two top leaders multiple votes; the Speaker has five votes and the majority leader has two. These two leaders as well as six of the other seven leaders on the committee are elected by the full Republican membership and are thus agents of that membership; in making committee assignment decisions, leaders must be sensitive to what members want in order to fulfill their policy goals and what they need for reelection.

These party committees also nominate committee chairs or, if the party is in the minority, ranking minority members. Only a formality before the 1970s reforms when seniority served as the sole determinant, the choice has increasingly become a real one. Democrats, when in the majority, several times passed over the most senior member. In the aftermath of the 1994 elections, Gingrich preempted the regular Republican process to make the selections himself, bypassing seniority in several instances. He assumed correctly that his stature would prevent anyone from challenging his choices. Subsequently, Republicans have returned to the normal process, but Speakers have continued to exercise a great deal of influence.

A change in House rules that Republicans instituted when they became the majority has further enhanced the influence of the party and its leadership over committee chairs. Republicans limited members to serving a maximum of six years as chair of a specific committee. As a result, 13 chairmanships became vacant in 2001. The Republican Steering Committee interviewed all 29 Republicans who sought chairmanships, asking them to lay out their plans for the committee in the 107th Congress.

In 10 of the 13 cases, more than one candidate sought a specific chairmanship and the campaigns were hard fought.

The decisions of the party committee on committees must be approved by the party membership collectively; this is done in the Republican Conference and the Democratic Caucus, as the organizations of all party members in the House are called. Both parties now vote on chair—or ranking member—nominations individually and by secret ballot; since committee leaders can be deprived of their positions by the party membership, they know that they must be responsive to their party membership.

The Conference and the Caucus meet at least once a week and serve as an important mechanism for communication within the party. Leaders use the forum to keep their members informed about substance and strategy; they also, of course, employ it to try to persuade their members to support the party position. As a Republican leadership staffer explained, "With our margin you need to have everyone invested every time you go to the floor, and the conference is used to get people on board." Rank-and-file members can use the conference as a forum to express their ideas, concerns, and complaints directly to their party and committee leaders. That too is helpful to leaders. "It's like the army," a leadership aide said wryly. "The troops are only happy when they're complaining. We worry when they're not saying anything."

Both parties have large and elaborate whip systems. In the 107th Congress (2001–2002), the Republican whip system had 67 members; the Democratic whip system, 113 members. In both cases, most of the whips are leadership appointees.

The contemporary House parties are much more elaborately organized and more active than their prereform predecessors. In addition to the conference/caucus and the whip systems, there are active policy committees, campaign committees, and task forces of various sorts.

These organizational entities serve several purposes. Most facilitate communication within the party and especially between leaders and the rank and file, both through meetings and through the myriad printed and e-mail messages they disseminate. The weekly meeting of the large Democratic whip system, for example, is a key mechanism for the exchange of information between leaders and members. For leaders, the meetings provided information on the wishes and moods of their members and an opportunity to explain their decisions to a cross-section of the membership. The meetings give members a regular opportunity to convey their concerns to their leaders on the whole spectrum of issues and a shot at influencing their leaders and shaping party strategy. Both whip systems distribute information on the legislative schedule to their members. With sizable professional staffs, various party organizations also produce a broad array of information as a service to their members. Thus, the House Republican Conference's publications include *FloorPrep*, which summarizes legislation and amendments scheduled for floor consideration each day, and *Legislative Digest*, which provides in-depth analysis of legislation scheduled for floor consideration each week, including bill highlights, background information, cost estimates, arguments for and against controversial measures, and other relevant information.

Many of these party organs also give party members an opportunity to participate in party efforts, including legislative efforts. By and large, House members are activists; successful party leaders accommodate rather than thwart their members' desires for participation. Continuous communication between members and leaders is essential for members to perceive themselves as "part of the action," but by itself is not sufficient. When they were the majority party, the Democrats found ways of channeling members' desires for participation into activities that served the party effort; the large whip system, House Democratic Caucus policy task forces, and ad hoc task forces to mobilize votes on specific legislation all served that function and continue to be used (Sinclair 1995). Gingrich, as a back-bencher determined to change the Republicans' minority status and then as a leader of the minority, had also employed inclusive strategies (Sinclair 1998). The process of formulating the Contract with America was predicated on broad inclusion and on the "buy-in" strategy, which is posited on the belief that participation gives participants a stake in the product (see below). The Republican leadership has continued to make sure members, especially junior members, have available a variety of ways of participating in the process through the party. House members can now pursue both their policy and their participation goals, often most effectively, through the party and with the help of its leadership; as a result, the congressional party has become more central to members' congressional lives.

Shaping Legislation and Mobilizing Votes

Majority-party members expect their party leaders and their committee leaders to facilitate the passage of legislation that furthers members' policy and reelection goals. When committee leaders are either unable or unwilling to do so, the majority-party membership expects the party leadership to fix the problem. The congressional reforms of the 1970s made committee leaders dependent on their parties for their positions and thus subject to influence from their party caucuses. The reforms, the difficult political environment of the 1980s and 1990s, and the very narrow margins of control of the latter 1990s and the 2000s all made passing legislation that majority-party members wanted difficult. Thus party leaders have often had to involve themselves early in the legislative process, well before the floor stage.

When committees are unable to put together major legislation that both can pass on the House floor and is satisfactory to most majority-party members, leaders often coordinate or even craft necessary compromises, either in committee or after legislation is reported out of committee but before it reaches the floor. When a committee is not sufficiently responsive to the party majority, it falls to the leaders to pressure committee members to become so. Conservative Republicans believe that the Republican members of the Appropriations Committee, which funds government programs, are big spenders, while Appropriations Committee Republicans believe conservative Republicans are politically unrealistic. The Speaker regularly mediates, making sure that Appropriations reports bills that satisfy most Republicans and can pass on the floor. Occasionally the leadership uses special task forces to draft legislative language on an issue considered too politically delicate for the committee of jurisdiction to handle. Managed-care reform is a difficult issue for Republicans; it is very popular with voters but strongly opposed by core business supporters of the Republican party and by many Republican members. In 1999 and again in 2001, the Speaker entrusted to a task force the job of coming up with a bill to counter the Democrats' version. Leaders can play such an assertive policy role because they do so as agents of a relatively homogeneous party membership. When the party leadership represents the membership, committee leaders know they must be responsive. The strong support of his membership made Speaker Gingrich's highly directive role vis-à-vis the committees in 1995 possible (Owens 1997; Aldrich and Rohde 1997).

As part of the reforms, party leaders gained the power to name their party's members of the Rules Committee, subject only to ratification by the Republican Conference or Democratic Caucus. As a result, the Rules Committee became an arm of the majority-party leadership. During the 1980s the Democratic leadership developed special rules from the Rules Committee into powerful and flexible tools for managing floor time, focusing debate, and sometimes advantaging the party's preferred outcome over others. Rules that limit the amendments that may be offered can be especially useful in holding together compromise packages worked out within the party at the prefloor stage; amendments that might split the majority party can be prohibited. The House majority party, whether Democratic or Republican, routinely brings major legislation to the floor under rules that restrict amendments. "[The Republicans] may make Democratic amendments in order, and even sometimes more Democratic than Republican amendments, but it will always be Democratic amendments that are either piddling or that have no chance of winning," a Democrat complained. During the period 1993–98, on average 61 percent of all rules and 79 percent of rules for major legislation were restrictive (Sinclair 2000b). A rule must be able to garner a majority vote on the House floor, thus majority leaders must be sensitive to their party members' wishes. By and large, restrictive rules now pass on party-line votes and the majority-party leadership seldom loses a rule vote.

The parties' large, well-staffed whip systems make possible vote-mobilization efforts on a nearly continuous basis. Given the number of whips, not all need be involved in every effort. The large size of the group thus allows flexibility and prevents burnout. Once the decision to "whip" a vote is made by the leadership, whips contact every member to determine his or her position; if a secure majority is not in hand, whips then attempt to persuade enough members to assure victory. If the whips are unsuccessful, top party leaders, including the Speaker, get involved in persuasion.

On both sides of the aisle, less senior members tend to be more active as whips. They have fewer other demands on their time and participation in whip efforts gives them a welcome opportunity to be in the thick of the action. They are backed up by experienced professional staffs as well as by the veteran top echelons of the whip system itself.

Both parties work with allied interest groups in their vote-mobilization efforts. Organized groups that are among a party's core supporters have always worked with their allies in Congress. Labor has been a mainstay of congressional Democrats' efforts for decades; it is organized, politically savvy, and, unlike most progressive groups, relatively affluent. As the congressional parties became more homogeneous and the party leaderships more active in the 1980s, coordination became routinized. Now, the top leaders all have staff members whose primary charge is working with groups. Meetings to plot and coordinate strategy are frequent. During the 104th and 105th Congresses (1995–98), the Thursday Group, a leadership-created entity consisting of lobbyists for both the ideological groups closely allied with the Republican party (the Christian Coalition and the National Rifle Association, among others) and for business groups with a major stake in the enactment of the Republican agenda met weekly with then Republican Conference Chair John Boehner. He and the Whip, Tom DeLay, worked to orchestrate these groups' lobbying efforts and to coordinate them with the internal whip campaign (Balz and Brownstein 1996, 198–199). Although they no longer meet every week, Whip DeLay and the current Conference chair, J. C. Watts, routinely meet and work with the same groups. During the effort to pass President Bush's budget and tax cut bill in 2001, the Republican leadership coordinated strategy closely with a broad coalition of major corporate and trade association lobbyists and conservative ideological groups. In opposition, Democrats worked with a coalition of over five hundred groups ranging from the AFL-CIO to church groups, from the Sierra Club to women's and African American groups (Edsall 2001).

The House parties are now much more active in policy formulation and the majority party has greater influence on policy outcomes than in the committee government era. On major legislation, committees more often make decisions by partisan processes and votes (Sinclair 2000a). The Bush tax cut, for example, emerged from the Ways and Means Committee on a straight party-line vote in the spring of 2001. When committees do not produce legislation satisfactory to most majority party members, the party leadership makes sure that the legislation is altered to make it satisfactory. The majority party's ideological homogeneity, which allows the leadership to take such an activist stance, combined with the tools—such as special rules and a big whip system—at the leaders' command produces a high floor win rate for the majority party even in this period of narrow margins.

Setting the Agenda and Framing Debate

By the middle of the twentieth century, Americans had come to expect that the president would set the public policy agenda. That expectation had developed during a period when unified government was the norm. Yet in the following years, Congress and the presidency were controlled by different parties with increasing frequency, and under those circumstances the congressional majority party was often dissatisfied with the president's agenda. With the election of the conservative Ronald Reagan as president in 1980 and the increasing ideological polarization of the parties, that dissatisfaction became more and more pronounced.

Reacting to their members' discontent, congressional leaders began to make attempts at putting together and promoting a party legislative agenda, and over time, setting the agenda and disseminating a party message became central functions of congressional parties and their leaders. House Democrats made forays at agenda setting in the 94th Congress, elected in the wake of Watergate, and in the 97th, the first congress of the Reagan presidency, but in neither attempt did they prove successful. Nevertheless, by the Reagan presidency, Democrats realized that they as individuals could not expect to get their issues on the agenda and that any real chance of success depended on collective party action. In 1987, at the beginning of the 100th Congress, House Speaker Jim Wright proposed an agenda consisting of issues such as clean water legislation, a highway bill, and aid to the homeless, which were broadly supported within the Democratic party. He relentlessly kept the spotlight on those items and used leadership resources aggressively to facilitate their passage. By the end of the Congress, all the items had become law and the Democratic Congress had gained considerable favorable publicity. Speaker Tom Foley, who succeeded Wright, also engaged in agenda-setting activities but was somewhat more cautious and, as a result, was often criticized by his members who had come to expect a clearly articulated party agenda. Democrats as a House minority continued to draft and promote a party agenda. During the Clinton presidency, the White House, Senate Democrats, and House Democrats coordinated their efforts and agreed upon a joint agenda.

When Republicans took control of Congress in 1995, they faced an op-position-party president hostile to their notions of good public policy. House Republicans had drafted and run on an agenda they called the "Contract with America," and that agenda guided Republican legislative action during the early months of 1995. House Republicans brought to the floor every item in the Contract during the first hundred days as they had promised they would, and, displaying near perfect voting cohesion, they passed every item except term limits, which as a constitutional amendment required a two-thirds vote.

The Contract with America was Newt Gingrich's idea and he oversaw its drafting, but the actual process of putting it together was a highly in-clusive enterprise in which broad participation was stressed (Koopman 1996, 142–147; Stid 1996, 6–8). In late 1993, Gingrich, then House minor-ity whip, had begun to talk about an agenda for the 1994 election cam-paign. At the House Republicans' annual retreat in February 1994, mem-bers held intensive discussions in small groups and took the first steps toward identifying the common principles and core beliefs that would guide the drafting of the Contract. Republican incumbents and chal-lengers were surveyed about what should be included. Leaders insisted that issues that seriously divided Republicans be excluded. Working groups of members and leadership staff then put together the actual bills. Any member who wanted to could participate, but younger activists were more likely to do so than senior committee leaders. Still, a large number of members did have a hand in putting together the Contract and so felt some pride of authorship. "By the time things got to the [Republican] conference, there was a great deal of buy-in already," Peter Hoekstra (R-Michigan), an activist member of the class of 1992, reported. "The members involved in the drafting had a great sense of empower-ment and that began to run through the conference" (Stid 1996, 7).

Although Republicans have not drafted and run on another such con-tract, they have regularly put together legislative agendas. In 2000, for example, Speaker Dennis Hastert's Web site touted "The Republican Common Sense Agenda," and stated that "Speaker J. Dennis Hastert has reserved the first ten House bill numbers for the top Republican legisla-tive priorities including improving education, saving Social Security, cut-ting taxes, and shoring up our national defense. Check back here to keep track of the progress of the Republican Common Sense Agenda." The 10 bills and their status were then listed. Other House Republican leader-ship sites also promoted the agenda.

On both sides of the aisle, the process of putting together the party agenda emphasizes broad participation; party retreats and working groups or task forces of members are common.

The congressional parties' agenda-setting efforts are only one part of a larger effort to participate in national discourse and frame the debate. During the 1980s, President Reagan taught Democrats that defining issues and party images to one's benefit was both possible and important and that competing as individuals with a media-savvy president was a losing strategy. How an issue is defined often determines the electoral risk inherent in a particular vote and, consequently, the opposing side's probability of legislative success. Moreover, specific legislative battles and broader controversies may leave residues on party images. Which party ultimately benefits and which loses in the court of public opinion, which gets the credit or which bears the blame, is largely determined by how the issue at controversy has been defined. Furthermore, partisan and ideological polarization and the suffusion of the political arena by news media with a negative bias and a voracious appetite for conflict lead to an increasingly conflictual politics that is played out increasingly on the public stage, often with audience reactions determining who wins and who loses. Within such an environment, political actors adept at using the media to push their issues to the center of the agenda and to frame the debate to favor their position are greatly advantaged; yielding the public forum to one's opponents is a recipe for policy and electoral defeat.

The parties have developed multifaceted and quite sophisticated means of promoting their agendas and disseminating their party message. They regularly stage press conferences, speeches, town hall meetings, and special events in Washington, D.C., and in members' districts. For example, on April 5, 2001, J. C. Watts, the chair of the Republican Conference, announced, "House Republicans are holding 128 events to promote tax relief and education during the April district work period. . . . As we near the close of the first 100 days of this Congress, House Republicans have a tremendous record to tell the Americans about" (www.GOP.gov). Because losing the White House deprived them of the president's bully pulpit, Democrats set up rapid response teams to reply to Bush initiatives quickly and thereby get their side of the story covered. When Bush unveiled his energy plan, for example, the energy team was ready with well-documented critiques of Bush's plan and with an alternative drafted by the House Democratic Caucus Energy Task Force. Both parties have become adept at manufacturing some sort of hook to entice the media to provide coverage. To make their point that the Bush tax cut was skewed to the rich, congressional Democrats displayed on the Capitol grounds a Lexus to represent what a rich person could buy with his tax cut and a muffler to show what a person of moderate income could purchase with his.

The parties' day-to-day message operations depend on well-staffed and equipped party entities under the auspices of the party leadership and on broad participation by the membership (Lapinski 1999). Both parties have institutionalized an important facet of their member-based message activities. House Democrats have a Message Group consisting of party leaders and particularly media-savvy members who meet daily to agree upon a message of the day; a larger group of members is charged with disseminating the message, especially through the one-minute speeches that begin the House's legislative day. The House Republican "Theme Team" performs a function similar to the larger Democratic group's; made up of 50 members, it is responsible for "communicating the majority party's legislative issues, plans and ideas . . . during speeches given on the House floor" (House Republican Conference Web site).

The parties hope to influence the small but interested C-SPAN audience and of course the media directly through these efforts. They also hope to encourage members "to sing from the same hymn book." Members agree that the party message is most likely to have an impact if they all are conveying the same message; yet leaders cannot actually prevent their members from sending conflicting messages and certainly cannot enforce uniformity. They can and do encourage and make it easy for members to stay "on message." The "message of the day" and the arguments most favorable to the party's position, often in the form of "talking points," are disseminated to members through a variety of means; the leaders hope that members will use these messages in their own contacts with the news media.

Parties and Party Leaders in the Senate

In the Senate, too, voting is now highly polarized by party. Between 1955 and 1990, on average 43 percent of recorded votes pitted a majority of Democrats against a majority of Republicans. Between 1990 and 2000, 57 percent of recorded Senate votes were such party votes. At the committee level as well, partisan decision making is more prevalent than it used to be (Sinclair 2000b). The greater intraparty ideological homogeneity and interparty polarization are at least in part traceable to changes in senators' electoral constituencies similar in broad outlines to those experienced by House members.

Partisan polarization has made participation through their parties more attractive to senators than it was when the parties were more heterogeneous and the ideological distance between them less. Partly in response to their members' demands, recent Senate party leaders have sought to provide more channels for members to participate in and through the party. On both sides of the aisle, the party organization and party processes have been much elaborated to provide services to members and to include members in all aspects of party functioning (Baumer 1992; Smith 1993). Each party holds a weekly senators-only lunch, which provides an opportunity for policy discussion and for communication between leaders and members. Democrats who traditionally concentrated the chairmanships of their various party organs in their majority or minority leader have devolved some of these positions, and more senators hold party leadership positions. The Senate Democratic Steering and Coordination Committee and the Technology and Communications Committee have both been spun off and have their own chairs. The Democratic and Republican whip systems have become more extensive and more active. The campaign committees have become highly professionalized. Like their House counterparts, the Senate parties sometimes designate ad hoc task forces of members to develop policy or to publicize party positions.

Both Senate parties now generate and publicize a party agenda each congress. They devote much time and resources to disseminating the party's message, in part through facilitating member media contact activities. The Democratic Technology and Communications Committee, for example, has television studios, extensive video-editing capabilities, and facilities for satellite hookups with local television stations that senators can use; the staff helps senators organize media events by doing everything from contacting reporters and selling them the story to reserving the room for the event (Sellers 1999). The Senate Republican leadership provides similar services for its members through the Republican Conference. "Our function really is a dual one: We promote the party's message, but we're also helping senators to promote their own messages," a Republican Conference staffer explained. "We send out talking points and that sort of thing. So, there is an effort to get individual senators to promote the party effort, but it has to be one of making it easier or providing information, not of coordinating senators who don't want to be coordinated."

The Senate majority leader lacks the control over the flow of legislation to and on the floor that the Speaker of the House possesses. The Senate majority leader is the leader of the majority party in the Senate but, unlike the Speaker, he is not the chamber's presiding officer. In any case, the presiding officer of the Senate has much less discretion than his House counterpart does. The only important resource the Senate gives the majority leader to aid him with his core tasks of scheduling legislation and floor leadership is the right to be recognized first when a number of senators are seeking recognition on the Senate floor to speak.

Unlike the case in the House, in the Senate greater ideological homogeneity did not induce members to give their leaders significant new powers. Differences in the two chambers lead senators to weigh the benefits and costs of strong leaders differently than do House members. Senate rules bestow great powers on senators as individuals. In most cases, any senator can offer an unlimited number of amendments to a piece of legislation on the Senate floor and those amendments need not even be germane. A senator can hold the Senate floor indefinitely unless cloture is invoked, which requires an extraordinary majority of 60 votes. As the political environment and the Washington political community changed radically in the 1960s and 1970s, an activist style based on a full exploitation of these prerogatives became attractive to more and more senators (Sinclair 1989). New issues and an enormous growth in the number of groups active in Washington resulted in senators being highly sought after as champions of groups' causes and made the role of outward-looking policy entrepreneur available to more senators. Successfully playing that role brought a senator a Washington reputation as a player, media attention, and possibly even a shot at the presidency. With this immense increase in the incentives to exploit fully the great powers Senate rules confer on the individual, senators began to offer many more amendments on the floor and to use extended debate much more often.

The Senate majority leader's and the majority party's control over the floor agenda are tenuous. A single senator can disrupt the work of the Senate by, for example, exercising his right of extended debate or objecting to the requests for unanimous consent through which the Senate does most of its work. The Senate majority leader conducts much of the Senate's business by asking for unanimous consent—to proceed to consider a specific bill, for example. If one senator objects, unanimous consent is denied. The majority leader could move to proceed to consider the bill, but that motion is subject to a filibuster. A partisan minority of any size can bring legislative activity to a standstill. The Senate of necessity operates in a more bipartisan fashion than does the House. As the majority leader makes decisions on the floor scheduling of legislation he confers on an almost continuous basis with the minority leader and, in fact, touches base with all interested senators.

In the 1990s, with the growth in partisan polarization, the minority party increasingly made use of Senate prerogatives to harass and stymie the majority, regularly extracting concessions on majority-supported legislation and sometimes killing such bills outright. In addition, exploiting Senate prerogatives to attempt to seize agenda control from the majority party became a key minority party strategy. If the majority leader refuses to bring a bill to the floor, its supporters can offer it as an amendment to most legislation the majority leader does bring to the floor. The majority leader can, of course, file a cloture petition and try to shut off debate, but he needs 60 votes to do so. In 1996 Senate Democrats used this strategy to enact a minimum wage increase, and in subsequent years they forced highly visible floor debate on tobacco regulation, campaign finance reform, gun control, and managed-care reform, all issues the majority party would have preferred to avoid. These procedural strategies have been accompanied by sophisticated public relations campaigns so as to garner as much favorable publicity as possible. It was the threat of such tactics that forced then Senate Majority Leader Trent Lott to schedule floor debate on campaign finance reform legislation in the spring of 2001 when he and most Republicans would much rather have focused on the Bush agenda.

This case also illustrates that, although senators are more willing to work with and through their parties than they used to be, individual senators exercise a great deal more discretion about when and under what conditions to participate on the party team than House members do; they have available attractive alternative channels for participation and they pay little price when they go off on their own. Republican John McCain was a central player in the campaign finance reform drive and refused to back off even when opposed by most of his party colleagues and a new president of his own party. Senator Zell Miller of Georgia, a junior Democrat, announced his support for President Bush's budget and tax plan in early 2001 without even informing the Democratic minority leader first. Democrat Max Baucus, then ranking minority member of the Senate Finance Committee, decided to cooperate with the Republican chairman, Charles Grassley, in writing and then quickly pushing to the floor a tax bill, even though most Senate Democrats opposed this.

Despite such examples, the Senate parties are more internally homogeneous ideologically and more polarized than at any other time in the previous half century. Even in the Senate, the majority party enjoys some advantages in rules and procedures. Legislation passed under the budget process—so-called reconciliation bills—are protected from filibusters and thus require only a simple majority to pass. Because floor scheduling is considered a prerogative of the majority party, it has an easier time getting its priorities to the floor. The change in the Senate's agenda when control shifted from Republicans to Democrats in June 2001 demonstrates the impact that a switch in control—without any change in membership—can have, especially when the parties are fairly ideologically homogeneous. Republicans had planned to spend June working on President Bush's energy program; when the Democrats took control after Senator Jim Jeffords of Vermont left the Republican party, Democrats put energy policy on the back burner and spent June on the patients' bill of rights, a party priority for a number of years. Although the Fourth of July recess was fast approaching, the majority leader kept the Senate in session until the bill passed.

The Congressional Parties and the President

Political parties in the House and in the Senate are now more cohesive, more active, and more involved in policy. Advocates of responsible parties argue that, in addition, parties can and should bridge the divide across the branches and chambers. Has the strengthening of the congressional parties led to more cooperation between the president and his party in Congress and to greater legislative productivity when one party controls both branches?

Although the president's constituency is national, he shares core supporters with the members of his party in Congress. When the legislators' electoral constituencies became more homogeneous, those of the president and of most members also became more alike. As a result, the president's agenda is likely to be reasonably satisfactory to most members of his party in Congress, at least when government is unified.[4] Certainly at the beginning of the Clinton and of the George W. Bush administrations, their congressional parties adopted the president's program as their own. To be sure, the president's and the congressional party's priorities were not necessarily identical; individual members had constituency-based objections to specific elements of the president's program (moderate, mostly eastern Republicans to Bush's environmental policies, for example); occasionally the difference in the scope of the president's constituency and that of members of the House led to direct conflicts (NAFTA is a preeminent example); and some members of the president's party wanted to go much further than the president proposed (with tax cuts in 2001, for example.) Yet by and large the members of the president's party in Congress could sign onto and support his agenda with considerable enthusiasm; much of it had in fact been incubated by them in previous congresses.

Members of Congress benefit from a president of their party's commanding the bully pulpit. Members are hyper-aware of the president's advantage in the struggle to focus attention and shape debate. They may complain that the president does not use his advantage skillfully enough and does not coordinate enough with the congressional party, but they nevertheless rely upon him to carry the party message. At the same time, however, they do not commit themselves to a vow of silence; the president cannot count on his congressional party members' consistently reinforcing his message. When they disagree with him, they often feel free to make their views public.

When the majority party in the House and Senate has a fellow partisan in the White House, party leaders receive invaluable help in building majorities. From the president's box seats at the Kennedy Center to district projects to a fund-raising appearance by a cabinet member or by the president himself to presidential support for a member's pet legislation, the administration commands enormous resources that can be used for persuasion. The president in turn benefits from the formidable clout his House party leaders now bring to the process and from the greater cohesion of his party's membership in both chambers.

More internally cohesive and polarized parties in Congress make it harder than it used to be for the president to persuade members of the other party to support his proposals (Fleisher and Bond 2000). When control is unified, this is especially a problem in the Senate. In the House a bare majority if it is cohesive can control the floor agenda and pass legislation. In the Senate, however, a majority may not be enough to pass legislation; on controversial legislation 60 votes are needed and seldom does one party have such a large majority. On the other hand, a Senate controlled by the opposition party is less of a problem for the president than a House so controlled.

While party polarization has made it more difficult for the president to draw support from the other party, greater intraparty ideological homogeneity has facilitated cooperation with his own congressional party. Still, the interests of the president, the House party, and the Senate party are not identical, and certainly those of individual party members and the president are not always the same. The structure of the U.S. government as set forth in the Constitution ensures that. To be reelected the president needs to appeal to a broader spectrum of voters than House members do. The president can help members of his party get reelected by raising money and campaigning for them, but he certainly cannot assure their reelection. A successful administration record will aid the reelection of members of the president's party, but only to the extent that the success penetrates into a member's district. Furthermore, all the House members and a number of the senators of the president's party will have to run for reelection two years before he does; understandably the president is most interested in election prospects in presidential years; many members of necessity have a shorter time horizon. To pass his program and establish a record for his reelection, the president may need to make compromises in the Senate that many members of his own party dislike. As a senior House Republican staffer said, "There's only one death you don't get over, and that's your own. So, for the president, well, yes, he wants to hold the Senate, but what's really important is being reelected in 2004. For us, well, you know, we want the president to be successful, but what really matters is that we maintain our majority."

The constitutionally specified structure of the U.S. government thwarts the full development of responsible party government. When the electoral constituencies of a party's elected officials are relatively homogeneous, parties can and do help to bridge the divide across the branches and chambers, but the electoral system ensures that our government is more accurately described as government by parties—presidential, House, and Senate—than as party government (Jones 2000).

Notes

1. The data in this section come from Congressional Quarterly Almanacs and Weekly Reports, various dates.

2. A change in these voting scores cannot, however, be taken as proof that party members' legislative preferences have changed. The issue agenda may have changed so that more votes are taken on issues that have always united the parties internally and divided them from each other.

3. This section is heavily based on Sinclair (1995 and 1999).

4. For the problems that divided government creates, see Sinclair (1999).

11

Governing by Coalition: Policymaking in the U.S. Congress

DAVID W. BRADY AND KARA Z. BUCKLEY

On June 28, 2001, the Republican-dominated U.S. House of Representatives dealt a blow to President George W. Bush's energy plan. In an attempt to alleviate rising gas prices, the Bush Administration proposed an increase in domestic drilling sites for oil and natural gas. As expected, many Democrats and environmental groups were up in arms. But, surprisingly, so were many conservative Republican members of the House. Seventy Republicans joined their Democratic colleagues to ban any new oil and gas drilling in the Great Lakes. One week earlier, the same 70 Republicans, with the support of the president's brother, Governor Jeb Bush of Florida, joined Democrats to bar drilling for oil off the coast of Florida. Was this coalition evidence of a "greening" of the Republican party? Not exactly.

Coalitions that come together for specific votes often divide for others. Moderate Republicans often vote with Democrats on environmental issues. In these two particular votes, conservative Republicans from Florida and the Midwest joined the "environmental coalition" to defeat drilling legislation in both regions. Although members of the alliance shared a similar goal, their reasons for casting antidrilling votes varied greatly. In an article titled "Local Environmental Issues Split Republicans," Congressman Ric Keller, a Florida Republican, explained his support: "We need oil rigs off the Florida beaches as much as we need crack houses next to our churches" (*New York Times*, June 23, 2001). Members of the coalition were as concerned about the impact of drilling on tourism and beach-front property values as they were about drinking-water quality and local species protection. The coalition reflected preferences that were pro-environment, pro-tourism, pro–states rights (anti–federal decision making), and even antiregulation of mining. What appeared on the surface as odd partners, liberal Democrats and conservative Republicans, made sense as a coalition of House members joining together to defeat a particular amendment to the Fiscal 2001 Energy and Water Appropriations Bill.

Understanding policy outcomes in the United States means understanding how and why members of Congress join together to form coalitions. The study of coalitions is complicated by the fact that their membership is fluid; for example, the environmental coalition's membership in
the House changes from vote to vote. Although environmental issues are
often championed by the Democratic party, party label or ideology may
not be the primary determinant of voting: 24 Democrats supported
drilling for oil off the coast of Florida. Constituent interests in Florida and
the Midwest (the Great Lakes border eight states) played a significant role
in solidifying a majority to defeat one element of Bush's energy plan. On
another element of the plan, however, the same constituent interests break
apart the very same coalition. Many of the Great Lake states are also home
to America's auto industry, and so in the subsequent vote to raise the
mileage standards for sports utility vehicles, many Midwestern members,
both Republicans and Democrats, positioned themselves against the coalition they just supported. Eighty-six House Democrats crossed party lines
to help the Republican president defeat the environmental coalition's push
for greater fuel efficiency.

In a political system with majority rule, relatively weak parties, and
strong ties to constituents, members of Congress must form coalitions to
pass or defeat legislation. In this chapter, coalitions are viewed as both
factions *within* the parties and as *cross-party* policy blocs. Sometimes coalitions form in such a way that the parties are united against each other, as
with the Roosevelt-Truman or New Deal coalition of northeastern and
southern Democrats that won five consecutive presidential elections between 1932 and 1948. At other times, factions within the parties cross
over to vote or work with members of the other party; for example, the
Conservative Coalition in Congress refers to Republicans and southern
Democrats who vote together against northern Democrats. Thus, the
study of coalitions in the U.S. Congress runs the gamut from responsible
parties to pure self-interested constituent voting, and from electoral coalitions to policy coalitions. Membership in coalitions is not always consistent; coalitions that form around elections may be driven apart by policy
positions. In the 2000 elections, Al Gore's most reliable support came
from the traditional Democratic alliance of unions and environmentalists. The 2001 Republican energy package in the House, however, split
the Democrat's electoral coalition. Yielding to pressure from the
Teamsters Union, 38 Democrats voted against environmentalists to open
the Arctic National Wildlife Refuge to oil drilling, a critical part of the
Bush energy plan, on the grounds that it would create jobs.

Such examples are not limited to the twentieth or twenty-first century.
In the first section, we explain that coalitions have been a critical part of
governance throughout American political history, necessitated by three

institutional constraints unique to the U.S. political system: the Constitution, the organization of Congress, and divided party control of the executive and legislative branches of government. These three constraints in particular have led to the development of coalitions within and across parties. First, specific features of the American Constitution, such as federalism, have promoted a fragmented party system in the electorate. Second, the decentralization of the House and Senate into committees has weakened party strength in the legislature. Finally, the American electoral system allows for divided government (the executive and legislative branches may be controlled by different parties). If we had a constitutional system that encouraged strong, responsible parties able to discipline members and to gain control of both executive and legislative branches simultaneously, then a study of coalitions in Congress would merely describe the factions *within* the two major parties. However, the American system with its institutional constraints does not encourage responsible parties; thus it is necessary to show how coalitions in the United States are both electoral and policy coalitions and how, consequently, coalitions form both within and across the parties.

In the second section, we trace the distinct stages in the historical development of American electoral and policy coalitions. We explain how the U.S. system of relatively homogeneous, strong congressional parties with few cross-party coalitions (1890–1910) transformed into a political system of heterogeneous, weak parties and stronger cross-party coalitions (1910–1964). With some Democrats to the right of Republicans and some Republicans to the left of Democrats, cross-party coalitions became critical and often deciding factors in policy outcomes. Since 1964, the growth of the personal vote—voters' support of individual candidates—and the prevalence of divided government gave rise to new cross-party coalitions.

In the third section, we model coalition building in Congress in terms of legislators' preferences. By locating members on a continuum from liberal to conservative according to their voting records, we can identify the critical voters on any given legislation; in a system of majority rule, these are members at or around the median position in the House and Senate. By introducing two supermajority institutions—the Senate filibuster and the presidential veto—to this simple median voter model, we demonstrate why gridlock (a lack of significant policy change) persists under both unified and divided control of the government. Any movement away from the status quo often requires cross-partisan coalition building.

In the fourth section, we apply our understanding of members' preferences, congressional parties, and majority and supermajority institutions to legislation proposed during Clinton's first term, a unique opportunity to compare unified and divided governments. In particular, we can assess the role of cross-party coalitions in passing and defeating legislation. Republicans and conservative Democrats joined to defeat President Clinton's health-care proposal in the 103rd Congress when the House, Senate, and presidency were all controlled by the Democratic party. The Democratic president and Democratic Congress could not pass health-care legislation too far to the left of median voters in Congress—members of *both* parties with similar policy preferences. Faced with a Republican House and Senate two years later, however, the Democratic president was able to move Congress's budget proposal to the left with the support of pivotal voters who could sustain a veto. Thus, regardless of unified or divided government, we show that coalitions within and across the parties are critical in determining the fate of legislation.

In the final section, we examine coalition building in a political environment where majority power is held by only slim margins. In the 107th Congress, where Democrats control the Senate by only one seat and Republicans maintain a mere six-seat lead in the House, *both* parties must build coalitions around moderate members to pass or defeat legislation. Coalition building among moderates is complicated by the fact that they are not one unified block, but individuals with varied preferences according to the issue at hand. Although moderate Republicans voted with their party and president to pass tax cuts in 2001, they formed a coalition with Democrats to pass campaign finance reform in the Republican-controlled Senate. Six months into the first session of the 107th Congress, Jim Jeffords of Vermont left the GOP, giving Democrats majority power in the Senate. Although party control of the government was once again divided, the senators at or around the median position essentially remained the same. The new Democratic majority in the Senate and the Republican leadership in the House could not pass their preferred version of the Patients' Bill of Rights without appealing to median voters. The White House and party leaders must position policy so as to convince these members to join winning coalitions; interparty as well as intraparty coalitions are essential for advancing policy goals, regardless of which party is in the majority.

Institutional Constraints
That Necessitate Coalition Building

The Constitution

The major features of the American Constitution that distinguish it from most other democratic countries' constitutions are federalism, separation of powers, and checks and balances. Federalism helped the founding generation ensure that the Congress and the president would reflect and recognize the social, economic, and religious differences among states and regions. Federalism institutionalized the differences inherent in a growing, widespread, diverse population (recall Madison's *The Federalist*, No. 51). The doctrines of separation of powers and checks and balances have resulted in an American system of government that is characterized by "separate powers sharing functions," which is in contradistinction to other Western democracies, in which power is centralized and functions are specific.

Although many aspects of the doctrines of federalism, separation of powers, and checks and balances have changed so as to make the system more democratic and centralized, the American system of government remains fragmented and cumbersome. Shortly after the Constitution took effect, difficulties inherent in governing within its framework presented themselves. Alexander Hamilton, Washington's secretary of the treasury, could not implement the policies he considered necessary without appropriate legislation. Thus, he commenced work on building organized support in Congress for Washington's policies; in effect, he became the leader of the pro-national faction in the Congress. Over time, factions with opposing views regarding the direction the national government should take developed into political parties. The goal of these nascent parties was to elect others to Congress who shared their views in order to form a majority for the policies they favored. Yet even though American parties were founded as a means to make governing less cumbersome, the same forces that produced them—federalism, separation of powers, checks and balances, and single-member districts with plurality winners—also worked to limit their strength. (See Cox and McCubbins 1993 for an interesting idea of party origins.)

The most basic effect of a federal form of government on the American party system is that instead of one national two-party system, we have 50 state party systems. Each state's party system has demographic, ideological, structural, and electoral peculiarities. For instance, the Democratic party in the electorate and as an organization in New York is distinct from the Democratic party in the electorate and as an organization in Georgia. The same fact applies to the components of the Republican party in these states. The heterogeneity of the state party systems is such that at the level of party in government, unlike-minded men and women bearing the same party label have come together in the U.S. Congress. Put another way, the federal system has brought to the Congress built-in differences among states and regions.

Although this arrangement may be useful in maintaining system equilibrium, it has more often formed an extremely poor basis on which to build coherent congressional parties; in effect, it has encouraged cross-party coalitions. The New Deal coalition of rural southern agricultural interests and urban northern industrial interests is a case in point. Long after this coalition had passed its major policy changes and the reasons for its formation no longer obtained, it continued to serve as the basis of the electoral coalition for the Democratic party. Even with a successful electoral coalition, however, the party was often divided on major policy issues.[1] In fact, on a number of major policy issues, such as civil rights and social welfare, the components of the New Deal coalition were poles apart. American political history abounds with examples of successful electoral coalitions that could not keep their members from forming cross-party legislative coalitions. Parties formed out of numerous and diverse state party systems tend to emphasize electoral success and to minimize policy cohesion.

The separation of powers and the system of checks and balances have also contributed to the fragmentary, disjointed status of American parties. When sectional, coalitional parties are given the opportunity to seek numerous offices both elective and appointive in the various branches, they become further factionalized. Thus, for example, one faction of the party may dominate presidential politics and another, congressional politics; and since both have powers over the courts, an equal division of court appointments may result. The Democratic party from 1876 to at least 1976 was characterized by just such an arrangement. The northern wing dominated presidential politics and elections, the southern wing dominated congressional leadership posts, and both wings influenced court appointments. Such a system may enhance representation of differences, but it does little to facilitate coherent party majorities capable of cohesive policymaking.

The constitutional arrangement of single-member-district plurality elections has also contributed to the fragmentation of the party system. House members elected on local issues by a localized party in the electorate generally build local party (or personal) organizations (Mann 1978; Fenno 1978; Mayhew 1974a; Fiorina 1989). Elected representatives, owing little loyalty to national party leaders, can behave in nonpartisan ways with few personal consequences. Indeed, throughout most of the Congress's history, party leaders have been able only to persuade, not to force, members to vote "correctly." Without even the threat of sanctions, party leadership is likely to be unsuccessful in building consistent partisan majorities. It is thus not surprising that the highest levels of voting along party lines in the history of the Congress occurred at a time, 1890–1910, when the Speaker of the House's sanctions over members were greatest and the Senate was run by a hierarchy that also could apply powerful sanctions. On the other hand, representatives elected by local majorities can work and vote on behalf of those interests regardless of the national party position; congressional leaders do not "persuade" from a position of power.

Local and state diversity is institutionalized in the American system of government in such a way as to allow that diversity to work its way up, almost unchanged, from the party in the electorate through party organizations to the congressional parties. Thus, at the top as at the bottom, the American party system reflects the cumbersome factionalism of the American system of government. It also facilitates cross-party coalitions. The fragmentation of the parties in the electorate and in government carries over into the organization of the legislature. In the following section the effect of this fragmentation on the organization of the House of Representatives is given as an example.

Organization of the House of Representatives

Like all such organizations, the House of Representatives has adapted to social change by creating internal structures designed both to meet the pressures or demands from its various constituencies and to perform its policymaking function.[2] The House has responded to the enormous range of interests in the United States and the concomitant pressures they generate with a division of labor. The result is a highly complicated committee system. When the country was in its infancy and government was limited, the House formed ad hoc committees; however, by the Jacksonian era, a standing committee system was in place. As the country grew more industrial and complicated, the House responded by expanding and enlarging the committee system. Early in this process, committees were established to deal with such policy domains as war, post offices, and roads, and the ways and means to raise revenues to support the government.

These committees—or "little legislatures," as George Goodwin (1970) described them—were organized around governmental policy functions; they were and still are decentralized decision-making structures. Both the making of Reconstruction policy after the Civil War and Woodrow Wilson's claim that "congressional government is committee government" attest to the power of committees in relatively early times (W. Wilson 1885; see also Bogue 1980 and Benedict 1974). Decentralizing power to committees was a necessary response to pressures for government action in certain policy areas; to the extent that the committees decided policy, however, party leaders were limited. The legislature has even further devolved with the proliferation of work groups (Cohen 1992) and task forces such as those created by the Republican House leadership to formulate policy in the 104th Congress, both of which have increased the fragmentation of the institution. As decentralized decision-making mechanisms, committees are dominated by members elected to represent local interests. This decentralized committee system of diverse local interests has become a powerful force that encourages members from different parties to cross party lines in order to achieve policy results. Throughout the 1950s, for example, a coalition of conservative Democrats and Republicans on the House Rules Committee was able to block or weaken civil rights legislation favored by northern Democrats.

What the division of labor pulls apart in organizations, integrative mechanisms must pull together. In the House, the major integrative mechanism is the majority congressional party. And as we have seen, congressional parties are limited by the governmental structure established by the Constitution as well as by the fact that members are elected by local parties or groups on the basis of local issues. Members responsible to and punishable only by local electorates tend to be responsive to constituents, not parties. Under such conditions, party strength tends to be low and coalitional strength high. Even when partisan voting was at its peak in the U.S. House of Representatives, it was low compared to that of other Western democracies. Even under ideal conditions, the congressional parties in the House have limited integrative capacity. Under normal conditions, policy decisions are thus likely to reflect localized committee interests, thereby limiting the national party leaders' attempts to build coherent congressional majorities. House voting patterns show that different coalitions are active on different policy issues (Clausen 1973; Sinclair 1982). Coalitions cut across regional party as well as social economic lines, making the party leaders' job a "ceaseless maneuvering to find coalitions capable of governing" in specific policy areas (Key 1952).[3]

Divided Government

A third institutional constraint that has promoted coalition building throughout American political history is the separate election of the president and Congress. Such an electoral system makes it possible to have divided government. The rules in many democracies make control of the executive and the legislature by different parties highly unlikely. In the United Kingdom and Japan, for example, the prime ministers are members of Parliament elected by their fellow legislators as chief executives. Divided control is possible in such cases only if enough Conservatives or Liberal Democrats vote with Labor or Liberals to elect the prime minister. In the United States, however, divided government is not only the norm today, but studies show it was frequent in the nineteenth century as well. From 1832 to 1900, during a period when it was difficult to split tickets—to vote for one party's candidate for president and another party's candidate for Congress—14 out of 34 elections resulted in divided government.[4] From 1900 to 1952, however, only four elections resulted in split party control of the government. Divided government returned to dominate the second half of the twentieth century: Since 1952, 16 elections have brought divided government to power, and only 8 have resulted in unified control (Fiorina 1996, 11).

The fact that divided government has become the norm in the United States since 1950 ensures a special role for coalitions in Congress. James Sundquist (1988, 1993) has decried this period dominated by divided party control as the "new era of coalition government," one lacking in party responsibility and effective policymaking. Split-party control of the government, he argues, puts parties head-to-head, inevitably resulting in policy impasses, legislative paralysis, and irresponsible parties. A political system that permits divided control is one that encourages "cross-partisanship," where one segment of a congressional party joins with the other to form a majority on a particular policy (Jones 1994). For example, President Reagan could not have passed such far-reaching tax and budget reforms in 1981 without the ideological support of conservative southern Democrats. President George W. Bush cannot pass any of his policy proposals—from his faith-based initiative to social security reform—without some support from Democratic members of Congress; and the Democrats in the 107th Congress cannot pass their policies—the Patients' Bill of Rights and campaign finance reform—over the president's veto without some Republican support. In short, divided government both implies and necessitates cross-party coalitions.

In sum, American institutional arrangements have fragmented parties in the electorate, constrained party responsibility in the legislature, and encouraged divided government. The combination of these features makes cross-party coalitions especially important in Congress. Without analyzing such coalitions, we cannot account for the direction of American public policy. But the institutional arrangements of the American system alone do not explain the importance of coalitions. One must also consider citizen preferences. If U.S. citizens wanted a strong party system, they could change the rules so as to strengthen parties; conversely, they could elect a Congress that would be of the same party as the president. But they have not changed the rules, nor have they often elected presidents and Congresses of the same party, so it must be the case that their preferences are consistent with weak parties and divided government. The next section emphasizes the role of constituent preferences and the weakening of parties in the historical development of congressional coalitions.

The Historical Development of Congressional Coalitions

The prevalence in the U.S. Congress of cross-party policy coalitions is largely attributable to the diverse electoral base of U.S. parties. The fact that liberals such as Senator Ted Kennedy (D-Mass.) and Representative

Henry Waxman (D-Calif.) share the same party label as conservatives like Senator John Breaux (D-La.) and Representative Charles Stenholm (D-Texas) helps to explain the existence of coalitions in which Democrats and Republicans vote alike. The intraparty heterogeneity of preferences leads directly to voting blocs that weaken party responsibility in the U.S. Congress. The coalitions are of two kinds: One is broadly ideological, and the other is issue- or policy-specific. The Conservative Coalition is an example of a broad ideological coalition that has formed across a wide range of issues. The policy-specific coalitions are more diverse and numerous; one example is the Urban-Rural Coalition composed of rural and urban representatives, regardless of their party affiliation, who combine forces to pass legislation that favors price supports for farmers and food stamps for the urban poor (Ferejohn 1986). Policy-specific coalitions can be based on members' constituent interests or, as in the case of the pro-Israel coalition, on members' preferences or ideology. There are three distinct stages in the historical development of these electoral and policy coalitions.

1890–1910: Homogeneous and Cohesive Parties

The development of congressional coalitions is obvious when we compare the current arrangement with the one that existed in the period 1890–1910, when parties were relatively cohesive and strong. During that earlier period, the number of cross-party coalitions was low. By tracing the rise of these coalitions we can determine the extent to which that rise was associated with electoral results.

Both the U.S. House of Representatives and the Senate at the end of the nineteenth century were partisan, centralized, and hierarchical. The congressional majority party for most of this period was the Republican party, and it was controlled by a small number of leaders who occupied both party and committee leadership positions. Thus power was centralized and it was hierarchical in that members took their voting cues from these party leaders (Brady 1973). Voting on the floor and in committees was highly partisan. For example, during the 55th and 56th Congresses (1897–1901), more than 90 percent of the roll-call votes were a majority of one party voting against a majority of the other party. In fact, more than half of all roll calls in these Congresses were extreme examples of this, in that 90 percent of one party voted against 90 percent of the other. Thus, it is fair to claim that at the turn of the century, congressional parties more closely resembled current European parties than they resembled current American parties.

How did we evolve from a system in which congressional parties were strong and cross-party coalitions were nonexistent or weak to one in

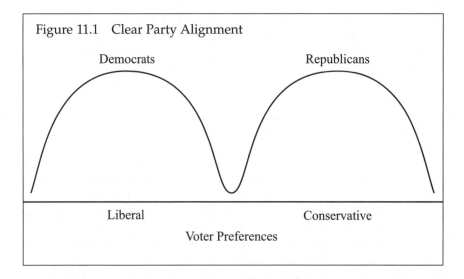

Figure 11.1   Clear Party Alignment

which cross-party coalitions are strong and parties are weak or unimportant (Broder 1971)? At the turn of the twentieth century, American parties were internally homogeneous and the two major parties had opposing views on governmental policy. The Republicans largely represented northern industrial districts, whereas the Democrats largely represented rural and southern districts. The Republicans supported policies that favored continued industrial development; they proposed tariffs to protect American industries, the gold standard (which favored Eastern moneyed interests and was the European standard), and the expansion of American interests abroad. The Democrats, who represented different constituencies, were opposed to the Republican ideas. They favored free trade, the coinage of silver at a 16:1 ratio with gold, and an isolationist foreign policy. Constituent preferences were in line with the policies supported by the parties (see Figure 11.1).

1910–1964: Heterogeneous Parties and Cross-Party Coalitions

As intraparty heterogeneity was introduced into the congressional parties, cross-party coalitions, both ideology- and policy-specific, resulted. In other words, as the distribution of preferences and the party alignment changed (shown in Figure 11.2), the probability of bipartisan coalitions increased. In contrast to the data in Figure 11.1, some Democrats were now closer to the Republicans than to the Democratic party median, and some Republicans were closer to the Democrats than to the Republican party median. If we were to include more than one policy dimension in the model, we would see even more cross-party similarity.

With the addition of a foreign policy factor, for instance, some Democrats might have shown up as economic liberals but foreign policy conservatives. In short, as the number of policy dimensions is expanded, the possibility of cross-party coalitions increases dramatically. The central point is clear: When intraparty heterogeneity exists, voting patterns and public policy change.

The rise of the Progressives in the early twentieth century introduced heterogeneity of preferences into the majority Republican party. Progressives such as Robert La Follette (R-Wis.), Albert Cummins (R-Iowa), and George Norris (R-Neb.) disagreed with Republican stalwarts such as Speaker Joseph Cannon of Illinois and Senator Nelson Aldrich of Rhode Island over issues such as income tax, government regulation of industry and banking, tariff schedules, and electoral reform. There were similar splits between southern and northern Democrats over immigration and civil rights policy. The combined result of this intraparty heterogeneity was a cross-party coalition of Democrats and Progressive Republicans that effectively changed the leadership in the House and Senate and permitted the passage of policies associated with President Woodrow Wilson (Holt 1967; Brady and Epstein 1997).

Under the alignment shown in Figure 11.1, the House and Senate were organized to accommodate a strong and unified majority party's policy agenda. In the House, for example, Boss Reed, the Speaker in 1889–1891 and 1895–1899, and Czar Cannon, the Speaker in 1901–1909, appointed committees, controlled the Rules Committee, and had the right to recognize anyone they chose to speak on the floor. In 1910–1911 a coalition of Progressive Republicans and Democrats stripped the Speaker of his appointive power, dropped him as chair of the Rules Committee, and restricted his floor powers. They did so largely because they believed that with centralized Speaker control they could not get their policies passed. In sum, after the Progressive reforms in the House and Senate, both bodies were organized to accommodate parties that had intraparty differences. This is not to say that party was irrelevant but simply that it was less important and had fewer sanctions over members' legislative careers.

In the 1920s, the major cross-party coalition was the so-called farm bloc, a coalition of Republicans and Democrats representing agricultural interests. After World War I the American economy developed rapidly, but throughout the decade of the twenties agriculture continued to be depressed because of overproduction and thus low prices. Representatives and senators from farm districts and states proposed price supports and parity payments, among other policies, to alleviate the effects of the depressed agriculture sector. The most hotly debated proposal was the McNary-Haugen bill. Introduced in 1924 by Charles McNary (R-Oreg.) and House Agriculture Chair Gilbert Haugen (R-

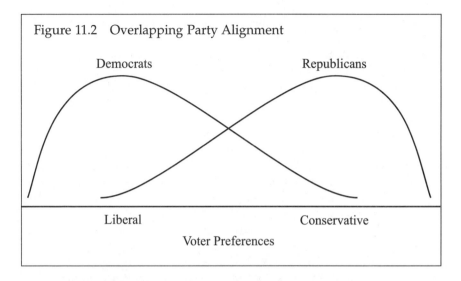

Figure 11.2   Overlapping Party Alignment

Iowa), the bill essentially set prices for staple crops, purchased farm sur-
pluses, and then sold them abroad, offsetting losses with an equalization
tax. At various times both the House and Senate passed versions of this
proposal, but the president vetoed it and it did not become public policy.
Nevertheless, the farm bloc was a powerful force in the U.S. Congress,
and it was bipartisan.

The Great Depression brought Franklin Roosevelt and the Democrats
to power, and from 1933 until 1938 they acted cohesively. Levels of party
unity and party voting increased during this era (Brady 1988). Roosevelt
and the Democrats achieved this unity and purpose by establishing what
Theodore Lowi (1979) called "interest group liberalism," which meant
that in each relevant policy area the affected parties were the relevant actors. The National Industrial Recovery Act tried to set quotas, prices, and
wages by allowing each industry to define its equilibrium point.
Agricultural policy was established by allowing those dealing in the different commodities (corn, tobacco, sugar, rice, and so on) to work out
their own arrangements regarding parity, price supports, and production
levels; and much the same held for labor and other affected interests.

This arrangement was restricted by the rise of the Conservative
Coalition in 1938. In 1937, Roosevelt had proposed the Fair Labor
Standards Act to the Congress, whose general goal was to standardize the
terms on which labor could be offered and hired. Among its features was
a set of provisions that would have reduced the ability of industries in the
South to attract investment with their lower wage rates than elsewhere in
the country. The act also encouraged union membership, which would
have equalized wages and stripped the South of its major economic

advantage—cheap labor. Southern Democrats were opposed to the Fair Labor Standards Act because it adversely affected powerful interests in their states and districts. Many Republicans were opposed as well, on the grounds of both constituent interests and philosophy. The Republicans and southern Democrats combined to block passage of the act and thus was born the Conservative Coalition. From 1938 to 1965, the Conservative Coalition was a dominant force in Congress. It was able to stop or seriously water down the passage of Medicare, civil rights, and fair housing legislation; increases in government management of the economy; welfare policies such as food stamps and Aid to Families with Dependent Children; and other legislation.

All of the cross-party coalitions from 1920 to 1965 were broadly ideological and sought to enact policies consistent with broad interests. Parties still mattered on some important issues (Mayhew 1966), and members of Congress were still elected primarily on the basis of their party affiliation. In the late 1950s and early 1960s, though, representatives and senators came to be elected less often according to party affiliation than on the basis of their personal vote. In the next section the development of the personal vote is traced, and its rise is shown to be concomitant with an infusion of cross-party coalitions that are policy specific in a narrow sense.

1964–Present: The Personal Vote and Divided Government

This section describes how members generated a "personal vote," further separating themselves from their parties and strengthening their ties with those who elected them. Members are "hired and fired" by their constituents, not the national party. With the rise of the personal vote, the hold of parties over their members was further diminished, and there was a concomitant rise in the number of general and special-interest coalitions. Another unique characteristic of the post–1964 period, the growing norm of divided party control of the government, necessitated cross-party coalition building within Congress.

The Personal Vote

As of the mid–1960s, members of Congress began winning reelection by larger margins, which reduced the number of competitive districts in congressional elections (Mayhew 1974a; Erikson 1972). Before 1964, incumbents held a mere 1–2 percent advantage over their challengers, but after 1964 they were winning by 5 percent, and by the mid–1970s the margins had increased to 8 to 9 percent. Today, incumbents have extended their advantage to as much as 96 to 98 percent over challengers (Fiorina 1996, 19). The extensive literature on the incumbency advantage identifies many reasons for such electoral success, from office perks (staffs, district offices, travel money, franked mail) to campaign finance. Morris Fiorina (1989) has even argued that members of Congress supported big government and bureaucracy so as to provide their constituents with goods and services for which they then took credit. The point is that after 1964, incumbents facing challengers in their reelection races held a distinct electoral advantage, an advantage based more on the benefits of their congressional seats and individual constituency service than on their party affiliation.[5]

To assert that individual members were able to separate themselves from their parties, we need to go one step further than noting a rising incumbency advantage to establish whether members enjoyed advantages because of partisan strength in their district or because of services they performed for constituents, name recognition, or other personal factors. Essentially we need to distinguish between partisan incumbent advantage, arising from the demographic or organizational strength of the incumbent's party in the district, and personal incumbency advantage, directly related to incumbency itself (Alford and Brady 1989). In other words, some districts are Republican or Democrat because they are populated by groups that are strongly Republican (e.g., whites with incomes over $75,000 per year) or strongly Democratic (e.g., minorities and liberal intellectuals). A rising incumbency advantage based on partisanship versus personal factors would have very different implications for coalitions after the mid–1960s. If an incumbent's margin of victory is primarily due to personal reputation and ties to the district, he or she would be encouraged to vote constituent preferences over party (when the two are in conflict), thus promoting cross-party coalitions.

The standard measures of the personal vote attributable to the incumbent are retirement slump and sophomore surge (combined as "slurge"). In each measure, the personal advantage of incumbency is taken to be the difference between a party's vote share in an open-seat contest and the vote margin of an incumbent of that party in an immediately adjacent election. For example, a Republican incumbent runs for reelection in 1948, wins 58 percent of the vote, and retires before the 1950 election, creating an open seat. In the 1950 election, the Republican candidate wins with 56 percent of the vote, runs for reelection in 1952, and captures 59 percent of the vote. The 1948 and 1950 elections produce a 1950 retirement slump estimate of -2 percentage points, the 1950 open-seat margin of 56 percent minus the 1948 pre-retirement margin of 58 percent. The 1950 and 1952 elections produce a 1952 sophomore surge estimate of +3 percentage

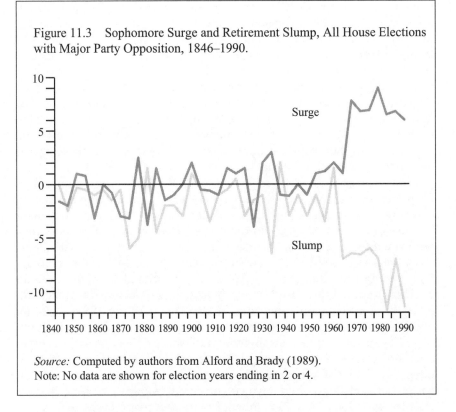

Figure 11.3   Sophomore Surge and Retirement Slump, All House Elections with Major Party Opposition, 1846–1990.

Source: Computed by authors from Alford and Brady (1989).
Note: No data are shown for election years ending in 2 or 4.

points, the 1952 first-incumbent reelection margin of 59 percent minus the 1950 open seat margin of 56 percent.[6]

Figure 11.3 presents the data for sophomore surge and retirement slump over the period 1846–1990. In each case the value for a given election year was derived by computing the mean slump or surge value for each party separately and then averaging together the two party surges or slumps irrespective of their individual *n*'s.

Any remaining doubt as to the historically unique nature of incumbency advantage in the post–World War II era should be put to rest by Figure 11.3. Prior to 1945, there was little evidence to indicate any even short-term personal advantage to incumbency. Had there been such an advantage, we would expect a sophomore surge for the period to be positive and retirement slump to be negative. But at that time, these trends occurred only 9 times out of 31 elections, or 28 percent of the total, compared to an expected 25 percent due purely to chance. After 1945 they occurred in 10 out of 12 elections. Moreover, slump and surge in the pre–1945 period never occurred in the expected direction for any adjacent pair of elections.[7] The record through 1990 is clear, but elections between 1992 and 2000 show a decline in the personal vote back to about half its average in the 1970s and 1980s.

The data presented thus far pertain to the House of Representatives. The data for the Senate are more difficult to interpret because there are only 33 or 34 elections per election year, compared to 435 House elections. But when the data on Senate elections are aggregated by decade, the number of elections rises to around 350. The results show that there is evidence for personal incumbency advantage in Senate elections:[8] The timing of the rise of the personal vote in the Senate is similar to that found in the House, albeit both retirement slump and sophomore surge are less marked. Thus, the same conclusions, though less strongly indicated, can be drawn for the Senate results as those drawn for the House, including the decline in slurge in the 1992–2000 elections (Jacobson 2000).

With the rise of the personal vote from the mid–1960s up to the most recent elections, the hold of party over member has further diminished. Members are nominated in primaries during which they must raise their own funds, organize and staff their own campaign machine, and distinguish themselves from opponents within their party. After winning the nomination, they must still rely on their personal organization and fundraising abilities. In the general election, presidential coattails no longer ensure the electoral success of legislators. For example, in the 1992 congressional elections, most Democratic candidates ran campaigns independent of the presidential race, and practically all received higher percentages of the vote than did President Clinton. In short, from the nomination through the election, members have come to rely on personal resources at the expense of political parties.[9]

Members of Congress elected on their own owe little to the party leaders on the Hill. At best, the leadership can coordinate the preferences of its party members; it has little or no ability to cajole or force members to vote with the party. As long as members can please their constituents, neither the national party nor the congressional party can affect members' electoral careers. Senator Phil Gramm (R-Texas) is a classic example. Gramm was initially elected to the U.S. House of Representatives as a Democrat from College Station, the home of Texas A&M University. His voting record was very conservative. In 1981–1982, he voted with President Reagan more than 95 percent of the time. In fact, he jointly proposed with Delbert Latta (R-Ohio) the now-famous budget-cutting resolution. The Democratic leadership sought to punish him in the next Congress by denying him a spot on the House Budget Committee. When the Democratic congressional caucus supported the leadership, Gramm resigned his seat, changed his affiliation to Republican, and won a special election held in his district to fill the seat he had vacated. In the 1984 election, he ran and won a Senate seat as a Republican. In sum, Gramm was not hurt by the Democrats' attempt to reprimand him for his voting record.

The point of this story is that, given weak parties and strong legislator-constituent relationships, cross-party coalitions are perfectly understandable. Post–1965, with the rise of the personal vote and the decline in the role of the parties in determining elections, there was a concomitant rise in the number of general and special-interest coalitions. Members can vote with members in the other party who share their ideology. The Conservative Coalition voting scores published yearly by the *Congressional Quarterly* attest to the pervasiveness of a major ideological coalition. In addition to cross-party ideological coalitions, there are cross-party coalitions based on district interest. During the energy crisis of the 1970s, a coalition of midwestern and eastern representatives formed to keep oil and energy prices low and to ensure that their constituents would not have to bear an undue share of the costs associated with the crisis. John Ferejohn (1986) has shown that an urban and rural coalition has formed around price supports and food stamps. That is, rural representatives vote for food stamps to aid urban poor, and in exchange urban representatives vote for farm price supports that aid rural communities.

Yet another type of coalition has formed around specific interests. Since the 1960s, the number of special-interest caucuses in Congress has risen, and these caucuses often bring together members of both the House and the Senate. Before 1970 there were 3 such caucuses, by 1980 there were 60, and in 1987 there were 120. The congressional Black Caucus, Women's Caucus, Hispanic Caucus, Irish Caucus, Steel Caucus, Pro-Life Caucus, Arts Caucus, Airport Noise Caucus, Blue Dogs Caucus, Diabetes Caucus, Urban Caucus, and Constitutional Caucus are but a few examples that demonstrate the range of interests represented. These caucuses meet on occasion, have staffs, present research papers, and in general try to influence relevant public policies. Although some of these caucuses' members all come from one party (e.g., the Blue Dogs), the fact that they exist outside the party system is a further indication of the importance of coalitions in the contemporary Congress.

Our listing of ideological, general, and special-interest coalitions is not meant to imply that representatives give precedence to these interests over their constituents' interests. Rather, our point is that representatives and senators can form coalitions with members of the other party if they can sell it to their constituents. As is evident in the rise of the personal vote, members' electoral fates are directly tied to their districts, not necessarily to the national party. In such a system, cross-party coalitions allow members to represent the interests of their constituents more effectively. Thus, in an important sense public policy in the United States is less party-oriented than it is in other democracies.[10]

Divided Government

Although the electoral connection between members and their party appears to have become weaker since 1964, the voting records of members have become more partisan since 1980. By any measure (Rohde 1988, 1991), Democrats and Republicans vote against each other more now than they did in the 1960s and early 1970s.[11] An additional piece of the puzzle is the claim made by many commentators and analysts since 1988 that the government cannot pass necessary legislation. Thus, we have weaker parties in the electorate, stronger parties in Congress (as measured by roll-call votes), and governmental gridlock. How is it possible to explain these phenomena? It cannot be done without discussing the phenomenon of divided government. In the post–World War II period, divided government has been the norm; in 17 sessions of Congress, the president's party did not control both houses, and in just 11 was there unified control. And this trend is stronger in the post–1970 period. In the 11 sessions of Congress between 1946 and 1970, 7 were unified. Since 1970, 12 have been divided and only 4 have been unified.

If we emphasize the differences between the parties, adopting a party-oriented interpretation of divided government, we would expect less coalition building when one party controls the White House and the other, Congress, because we would expect a Republican president and a Democratic Congress (or vice versa) to go head-to-head over policy outcomes, resulting in gridlock, not coalition building. Indeed, many political scientists and pundits alike do blame divided government for stalemates and lack of policy change. In this "party matters" interpretation of gridlock, the president bargains with the median of the majority party in Congress; when the two are of different parties, it is difficult to pass legislation to move policy away from the status quo (see Fiorina 1996; Jacobson 1990; Mayhew 1991; Kernell and Cox 1991). According to this interpretation, having a Republican president to the right of the Democratic party medians in the House and Senate, as in the Bush Sr. years, would result in gridlock. On the other hand, it could be expected that gridlock would be broken with the executive and legislative branches under the same party label, as occurred in the 103rd Congress, during the Clinton administration. Democrats would vote with the Clinton proposals rather than vote with the Republicans, and cross-party coalitions would have little role in the passage or defeat of legislation.

But what if gridlock is not solely a party-driven phenomenon? The heterogeneity of preferences among the electorate and in Congress and the complexity of policy areas may be the sources of gridlock regardless of the presence of divided or unified control. In *Divided We Govern*, David Mayhew (1991) has examined gridlock in terms of amount of legislation passed, successful and unsuccessful vetoes, congressional hearings, presidential treaties signed, and appointments approved. Excluding the number of vetoes, he concluded that there is no significant difference in these variables under divided versus unified control. In fact, "[T]he number of laws per Congress varies more *within* universes of unified or divided times than it does between them [emphasis added]" (Mayhew 1991, 76). Therefore, Mayhew's evidence at a minimum indicates that party is not the cause of gridlock and perhaps claims of paralysis are greatly overestimated. Still, we are left in the dark as to the sources of gridlock, if not interparty conflict.

Although Mayhew did not specify a source of gridlock, his work is perfectly compatible with a median-voter account of politics. Regardless of whether the president is a Democrat or a Republican, the policy output will be close to the preference of the median voter in Congress. The median voter need not be of the majority party; the position changes across issue areas. Some Republicans, like John McCain of Arizona, are to the left of some Democrats, like Ernest Hollings of South Carolina, and vice versa. This phenomenon is unlikely to change in a unified government.

When the president is of the opposite party of the majority in Congress, the level of party voting may rise and enforce gridlock. For example, a Republican president might propose cuts in programs that exceed what even southern conservative Democrats desire. The resulting "gridlock" vote not to change the status quo is along party lines. Yet even if the government is unified under a Democratic president, the preferences of the southern Democrats matter, since without them the president cannot win a majority. Thus, by taking policy into account, we can have partisan gridlock *and* unified gridlock.

If members' preferences diverge significantly *within* parties, stalemates may be the result of legislation proposed that is too far from the preferences of the median members in Congress, regardless of their party. In this preference-based interpretation of divided government, cross-party coalitions may play a significant role in policy change for two reasons. First, the heterogeneity of the parties ensures that the majority party in Congress does not necessarily set policy; that is, from issue to issue, preferences vary greatly within the parties. Thus, a cross-party coalition may form a majority to pass a particular presidential proposal unpopular with the majority leadership. Second, under divided government, the majority party in Congress needs the support of some members of the minority party to override a presidential veto.

A Preference-Based Model of Coalition Building

Distinguishing Between Preferences and Party

Members' votes on policy matters are obviously complex decisions, but for our purposes we need to distinguish between preferences and parties. This is not easy. For example, take two policies in the Senate. The roll-call vote is the same for each, 56 Democrats voting in favor and 44 Republicans voting against. In both cases, all members voted their party's position; two identical results occurred, but a closer look at individual preferences tells two very different stories. The preferences are distributed as such in Figure 11.4.

A vote of 56–44 is not surprising in Policy A, nor is it conclusive as to the power of party over members' votes. In this particular case, party happens to be a good measure of individual preferences. An example of such a distribution (though not as clean—a few crossed party lines) may be the partisan division on the vote for motor-voter legislation, with each side capturing an overwhelming majority of members. Was the vote the result of strong party leadership, or did the vote reflect the individual

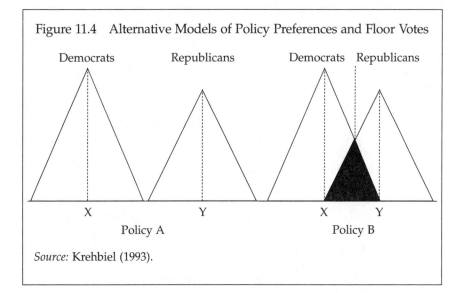

Figure 11.4   Alternative Models of Policy Preferences and Floor Votes

Source: Krehbiel (1993).

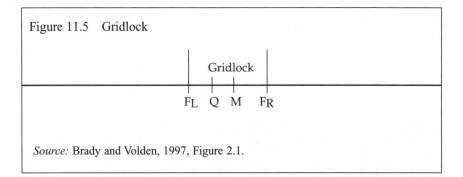

Figure 11.5   Gridlock

Source: Brady and Volden, 1997, Figure 2.1.

preferences of the members? The problem of determining whether party or preference accounts for the vote is illustrated by Policy B. To arrive at the same 56–44 result, some legislators had to vote against their own preferences (as established by the electoral connection) to support the party position. In these policy arenas with more heterogeneous preference distributions, votes cast with respective parties are indicative of strong party leadership, and outside observers will have a hard time distinguishing the motivation behind the two votes.

Preferences and Institutions

Given the strong relationship between members and their constituents and the heterogeneity within American parties,[12] we believe legislators' preferences are critical determinants of political outcomes.[13] By ranking members in terms of their preferences on a continuum from most liberal to most conservative, we can determine which legislators are the critical voters on any given piece of legislation. Moreover, we show that as you add supermajority institutions such as the filibuster and the presidential veto, the critical voter changes and the gridlock region widens.

First we need to determine which legislators are at or near the median. Given the necessity of getting a majority to pass legislation, the critical points in the enactment process are the median of the House (at or about the 218th member) and the median in the Senate (at or about the fiftieth member). In the Senate, however, majority rule is not the only constraint. Some legislation may be blocked by a minority—any one member of the Senate may filibuster a piece of legislation by continuing to debate a proposed bill on the floor. Senate Rule 22 allows for a cloture vote to end the debate but it takes 60 senators, three fifths of the body to end the filibuster. Thus, 41 senators may prevent the majority from enacting legislation by voting against cloture.[14] In such cases, the filibuster pivot—the supermajority point—becomes the critical passage point, not the median-voter position. If the Senate majority party is Republican, the senator at or about the fortieth position is the filibuster pivot. If the Democrats control the Senate, the sixtieth member occupies the filibuster position.

Once we have established the location of the median and filibuster points, we must determine how far away the status quo policy and the proposed legislation are relative to the preferences of these critical voters in Congress. The argument is as follows: If the status quo policy is closer than the proposed policy to the median voters and to the Senate filibuster pivot, the proposed legislation will not pass. Figure 11.5, which is limited to the Senate, illustrates how these constraints create a "gridlock region," that is, the range of status quo policies impossible to move away from. If the status quo policy (Q) is between the filibuster pivots (F), then gridlock will result. The reason for this is that F_L plus 40 senators to the left could successfully filibuster a proposal more conservative than the status quo; F_R plus 40 senators to the right could similarly filibuster a more liberal bill than the status quo.

The U.S. Constitution provides for another constraint: the presidential veto. The support of two thirds of both the House and Senate is required to pass legislation vetoed by the president. Thus, for a bill to become law, it must gain a majority and not be killed by a filibuster or a veto. When we introduce the presidential veto into the model, the gridlock region is extended in both the House and Senate. Figure 11.6 illustrates the possible policy region during a period of divided government in which the president is more conservative than Congress, and the House is more liberal than the Senate (the case in the Bush Sr. presidency). In this scenario, if Congress proposes to move a conservative status quo policy to the left, the president merely needs to gain the support of 34 senators to sustain a veto.

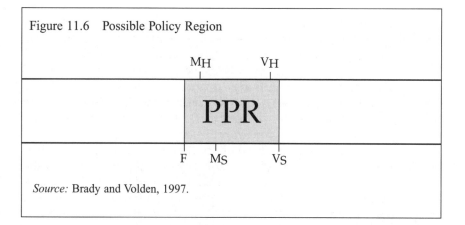

Figure 11.6   Possible Policy Region

Source: Brady and Volden, 1997.

It should be noted that the critical voters may change with elections. New preferences may be introduced with new legislators, resulting in new critical voters. Thus, an election that brings more conservative members to Congress will concomitantly shift the median voter to the right. For example, when an electorate angry over increased taxes and stagflation voted Jimmy Carter out of office in 1980 and voted Ronald Reagan in, along with a Republican-controlled Senate and more conservative seats in the House, the median voter shifted to the right. The shift in preferences and pivotal members moved tax and spending policy from gridlock to a more conservative policy (tax reduction and indexing). There were enough conservative southern Democrats to prevent an effective filibuster, while at the same time they prevented a shift too far to the right from taking place. The result was a new status quo point and a new gridlock region that would require strong bipartisan coalitions to shift tax policy to the left in the subsequent years.

A simple median-voter model can explain political outcomes in terms of legislators' and the president's preferences, and it demonstrates why cross-partisan coalitions are necessary to pass legislation under majoritarian and supermajoritarian institutions.

Coalitions in Unified vs. Divided Control

The preference-based model can be applied to legislation during President Clinton's first term, comprising the 103rd and 104th Congresses. In each case we determine the critical positions of the president, the median voters, the supermajority pivots (veto and filibuster), and the status quo policy relative to the critical legislators. Since members of both parties clearly play a role in whether a bill will become a law, cross-party coalitions are critical in determining which proposals are passed.

The first unified government in 12 years began with high expectations that policy would shift to the left across a wide array of areas. But gridlock was far from eliminated. Clinton faced serious opposition on moving the status quo position, not only on health care but on a range of policies from gays in the military to grazing fees. When the 103rd Congress finished, journalists declared it one of the worst Congresses in 50 years. So much for unified government. After the congressional elections of 1994, divided government returned, and the expectation was that there would be a major policy shift to the right. Republicans pushed through some of their Contract with America, specifically a form of the line-item veto and an end to certain unfunded mandates, and by spring 1995, Speaker Gingrich's and the Congress's popularity ratings soared while Clinton's suffered. By late fall 1995, however, the government was

operating on a continuing resolution after a seven-day shutdown following Clinton's veto of a Republican budget resolution that he deemed too
conservative. In the final analysis, the Republicans in the 104th House
did not achieve their goals. Why the apparent gridlock in *both* these
Congresses—one unified, one divided?

We believe that the median-voter model introduced in the previous
section, which emphasizes legislators' preferences and the importance of
supermajoritarian institutions, can explain political outcomes in both
Congresses. Clinton's first Congress provides a test of the unified government–strong party hypothesis articulated by James Sundquist (1988,
1993) and Lloyd Cutler (1988). If split-party control of government promotes gridlock, as the "strong party" theory predicts, then the first two
years of the Clinton presidency should be characterized by significant
policy change away from the status quo, in contrast to expected stalemates for the last two years under a Republican Congress. But if preferences are important determinants of American public policy, we expect
little difference between periods of unified and divided control and focus
instead on shifts in the median-voter positions in Congress. In the preference-based theory, bipartisan coalitions are expected to influence the
direction of legislation. We compare the predictions of the two theories
concerning the fate of major legislation in the first term of the Clinton
presidency: health-care reform in the 103rd Congress and the budget resolution in the 104th Congress.

Unified Failure: Health-Care Reform in the 103rd Congress

If ever national health care had a chance to be written into law it was
during the Clinton administration. In the 1992 elections, not only did
Clinton promise a universal health-care plan, but *both* Democrats and
Republican members of Congress as well as their challengers called for
the reform of the nation's health-care system. The prospects for a comprehensive health-care policy never looked so good as at the start of the
103rd Congress. But one year later and after much debate and publicity,
health-care reform was officially abandoned without even a vote. By the
midterm elections in 1994, the issue of heath care had all but disappeared
from congressional campaigns. What happened?

According to the "strong party" theory, unified government should
have provided an optimal environment for the enactment of a comprehensive health-care policy—with a Democratic president advocating a
dramatic shift from the status quo and members of a Democratically
dominated Congress bent on reform. Scholars who emphasize the role of
unified party control in facilitating the legislative process focus on the
bargaining between the president and the majority-party median. If such

a model had been accurate, Clinton's health-care agenda should have come to fruition. But such expectations for sweeping change and the amelioration of gridlock under the first unified government since 1980 clearly did not materialize. Analyses based solely on which party controls the executive and legislative branches are inadequate in determining political outcomes, overemphasizing party unity and underestimating the need for cross-partisan coalitions and appeal to the median voters in Congress, regardless of their party label.

We believe health-care reform was a predictable failure in the 103rd Congress.[15] Health-care legislation did not pass because proposals made by President Clinton and members of Congress from both parties were too far from the preferences of critical voters in the House and Senate. A simple median-voter model shows that, in order to win, legislators must appeal to the median voters in the House and to those members who could induce a filibuster in the Senate. Considering both the preferences of legislators and the supermajority institutional arrangements in the Senate, the Clinton plan was doomed from the start.

In order to determine which legislators are the critical voters, we must first rank senators and representatives from the most liberal to the most conservative. We established a left–right continuum for members' preferences by averaging their scores on 18 separate ideologically mixed ratings and then ranked the legislators accordingly. There are many ways to compile a vote-based ideological ranking of members of Congress—a range of groups such as the Americans for Democratic Action (ADA) provide rankings—but the results are similar to ours. That is, the same senators and representatives appear in the median and filibuster positions across rankings. In the 103rd Congress, the median voters in the House and Senate, not surprisingly, are conservative Democrats mainly from southern and border states. Thus, a successful policy—one that can gain a majority of support in Congress—is one that appeals to these conservative or moderate Democrats. In the Senate, however, the threat of a filibuster necessitates an appeal to the right of the median voters, since the sixtieth voter in the 103rd Senate is more conservative than the median. Those senators at or about the filibuster pivot in the 103rd Congress comprise a group of moderate Republicans. In legislation where a filibuster could be utilized, these moderate Republicans in the filibuster position are the critical determinants of a policy's success or failure (Brady and Volden 1997).

The proposals for health-care reform in the 103rd Congress varied in their scope of coverage, cost (who pays for it), and quality of care. Of course, high-quality, low-cost coverage for all Americans would be the outcome preferred by all legislators, but such a proposal would be unrealistically expensive. Health-care reform demands tradeoffs among cost, coverage, and quality. The proposal put forth by the Clinton task force and proposals by members of the 103rd Senate are ranked in Figure 11.7 according to tradeoffs on how many Americans are covered and who is to pay for their care. The most liberal of the proposals is the single-payer plan, which covers all Americans and is paid for by taxpayers. The most conservative, the Gramm plan, does not increase coverage and serves basically as a minimum reform to the insurance industry. The status quo policy—85 percent coverage, Medicare and Medicaid programs, private insurance companies, and emergency access for all—is just to the right of the median voter in the 103rd Senate. It is clear from the position of the status quo relative to the filibuster pivot that any proposal to the left of the median in the Senate had no chance of passing. The Clinton plan of universal coverage funded by employer mandates was far left of the median voters. Thus it is clear from Figure 11.7 why the Clinton proposal failed miserably, never winning more than 30 votes in the Senate.

The greatest chance of a successful health-care reform bill was through the Senate Finance Committee, chaired by Senator Moynihan (D-N.Y.). Given its makeup of moderate Democrats and Republicans—the key to building a majority—the committee was viewed as the most representative of the Senate. But the Moynihan plan, although it sacrificed universal coverage, increased the costs to taxpayers and employers, and so it failed to be a viable contender to the status quo.

Finally, in an attempt to salvage health-care reform in the 103rd Congress, Democratic Senate Majority Leader George Mitchell of Maine put together a bipartisan coalition of moderate Republicans and Democrats led by Senator John Chafee (R-R.I.). The resulting plan increased coverage without requiring employer mandates—an appealing proposal for Senate median voters. The Chafee plan, however, never even

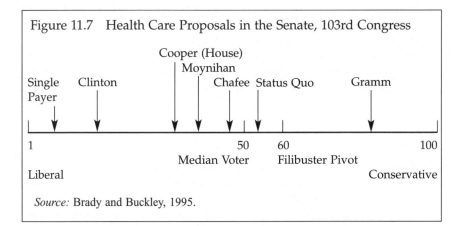

Figure 11.7 Health Care Proposals in the Senate, 103rd Congress

Source: Brady and Buckley, 1995.

made it to the floor. Its failure had as much to do with timing (members were uncertain at this late point in the debate as to the impact of reform on their constituents and consequently on their upcoming reelection campaigns) as with the pro-business filibuster pivots in the Senate. Senators at and around the sixtieth position in the 103rd Senate highly opposed *any* increased cost to small businesses.

Thus, the failure of health-care reform was predictable, if analyzed according to an understanding of members' preferences and institutional constraints. Reform proposals in the 103rd Congress were too far from the median in the House and the filibuster pivot in the Senate. Any proposal that expanded health coverage through substantial increases in costs was destined to fail.[16] Would health-care reform have a chance in the 104th Congress, a divided government? The 1994 elections shifted the median to the right in both the House and Senate. Thus, according to the preference-based median-voter model depicted in Figure 11.7, we would predict that a comprehensive health-care policy would have little chance, but an industry reform at the margin—such as portability or transferability—located to the right of the median might pass. And such a minimal reform *did* pass in divided government—the 104th Congress enacted legislation that guarantees most employees health insurance if they lose or leave their jobs. Thus, as demonstrated in health-care policy, the fate of legislation in Congress is largely determined by median preferences— often the preferences of members of *both* parties.

Gridlock will prevail if the status quo policy is close to or at the same position as moderate members of Congress, regardless of whether control is divided or unified. Presidents who propose policies too far to the left or right of the median preferences in the Congress will fail to see their policies enacted unless they are able to change the proposals enough to accommodate the moderates. Shifts in American public policy are electorally generated: If an election results in a shift of members' preferences to the right or to the left, then policy will change accordingly. The 1994 elections essentially changed the composition of Congress—not only granting the Republicans a majority in both bodies of Congress but introducing a class of conservative freshmen to the House. We turn now to the 104th Congress to assess the effects of this shift of median preferences to the right.

Divided Compromise: Budget Resolution in the 104th Congress

The new Republican majority in the 104th Congress had campaigned on and advocated policies that were to the right of the status quo.[17] The new median voter in both the House and Senate in 1994 was a Republican who favored less government. If majority rule was the only constraint on policy enactment, the Republican agenda would have met little opposition in the 104th Congress. The initial success of the Contract with America attests to the numerous policy areas where new majorities for change were established in Congress. The 73 freshmen Republicans successfully shifted their parties' policies to the right of the status quo across a range of issues, from crime legislation to overhauling the nation's welfare system. Party voting was at the highest level it had been in 50 years, and there was substantial cohesion among congressional Republicans; there was an average party-unity score of 90 percent in 1995 (Jacobson 1997). But by the end of the first session of the 104th Congress, only 2 of the 10 provisions in the Contract had been signed into law. What happened?

One noninstitutional obstacle to the success of the Contract was the more liberal Senate. The Senate either failed to pass, did not act on, or passed a different version of the House legislation pertaining to the Contract. The median voter in the 104th Senate was a moderate Republican to the left of the House median. The institutional obstacles were the presidential veto and filibuster pivots—41 Democrats could tie up the Contract's proposals in the Senate, and 34 Democratic senators could sustain a veto. The combination of institutional and behavioral factors prevented the enactment of much of the Contract. Thus, the American system features supermajority institutions that allow non-majorities, in this case a Democratic president and a Democratic minority in Congress, to extract policy that differs from the majority position. The following section, focusing on the 1995–1996 budget battle between Clinton and the Republican-controlled Congress, illustrates this point.

On November 13, 1995, Clinton vetoed two Republican budget bills, clearly demonstrating his willingness to employ the presidential veto to pull the Republican budget plans to the left. Given the resulting government shutdown and the Republicans' inability to override a presidential veto, both sides compromised on a continuing resolution to keep the government going until December 15. No budget agreement materialized by the extension deadline, as Clinton claimed the Republican spending cuts were too severe in such areas as Medicare, Medicaid, and welfare, and the Republicans blamed Clinton for not putting forth an alternative budget that would balance the budget by 2002. The government therefore shut down for a second time. By January 6, 1996, two proposals reached the negotiating table, one from the executive and one from the Republican Congress, both promising balanced budgets, though based on different economic assumptions. Clinton's proposal—to cut about half of what Republicans proposed to cut in the areas of Medicare, Medicaid, and welfare—differed significantly from the Republican-passed budget. Clinton's plan raised corporate taxes, proposed a $500 tax credit for children, and offered a minimal capital gains tax cut. The Senate and House Republicans began negotiating with conservative and moderate Democrats to find common ground—negotiations that would last until April. But no congressional resolution could beat the president's proposal; yet any move to the left to gain the support of conservative Democrats would ostracize the Republican freshmen. As Clinton's popularity rating climbed and Gingrich's plummeted and as the 1996 elections approached, budget concessions appeared to favor the president. Since the veto point was to the left of the Republican reconciliation bill, the veto pulled the final budget outcome to the left. The freshmen Republicans, responsible for shifting the congressional median to the right, were unable to push their conservative budget plans—tax breaks and entitlement cuts—through the 104th Congress. The filibuster pivot in the moderate Senate and the presidential veto blocked the group of Republicans, emphasizing the importance of members' preferences and the critical role of institutional voters in legislative outcomes (Brady and Volden 1997).

Ironically, Clinton's job became easier under the divided government that resulted from the 1994 elections than it had been in the previous period of unified control, because he no longer had to set the agenda, but rather moderated the Republicans' goals. Democrats in the 104th Congress found the president's position much closer to their own preferences than were the Republican proposals. Thus, congressional Democrats were willing to support Clinton on proposed legislation. Clinton had effectively moved from coalition building in the 103rd Congress to leading a blocking coalition in the 104th. In the 103rd Congress, Clinton could not get policy to shift left from the status quo, which made him appear ineffective as president; in the 104th, he merely blocked rightward shifts and was hailed as a strong leader of his party. Interestingly, all that had changed from one Congress to the next was the position of the median voter.

Coalitions and Marginal Majority Control: The Patients' Bill of Rights in the 107th Congress

Although the 2000 elections ushered in unified Republican control, majority power in the 107th Congress was marginal from the start. The GOP held the advantage in the House by a mere six seats. The Republicans' claim to majority power in the evenly divided Senate rested on the tie-breaking vote of the vice president. Upsetting the precarious balance of power would not take much. Six months into the first session, Jim Jeffords of Vermont abandoned the GOP, handing control of the Senate to the Democrats. Much was made of this sudden return to divided government. Political pundits and the media predicted trouble ahead for Bush's agenda, from his energy proposals to his faith-based initiative.

In his first few months in office, Bush had managed to get a 10-year $1.35 trillion tax cut signed into law and his education initiatives through Congress. Unified government, it had appeared, facilitated the Republican policy goals. But a closer look at the debates over the tax package shows that moderates of *both* parties reined in Bush's initial projected cuts to meet their ideal points. The administration's education initiatives passed both houses only to be stalled in conference committee. Despite the GOP leadership's opposition, campaign finance reform was passed in the Republican-dominated Senate when moderate Republicans broke party ranks to vote with Democrats. In the more conservative House, Speaker J. Dennis Hastert (R-Ill.) postponed indefinitely a vote on campaign finance reform, after losing a critical vote (that structured the rules of debate) to a coalition of moderate Republicans and Democrats. Thus, even under unified government, the critical players in the 107th Congress were the moderate Republicans and conservative Democrats at or about the median in the House and Senate. Without an election to shift the median, the pivotal positions essentially remained the same before *and* after Jeffords's switch.

Nevertheless, press and pundits alike focused on what they believed to be the newfound power of the congressional moderates. Given the slim majorities in the House and Senate, these "unsung centrists" were now the deal makers and deal breakers of the 107th Congress. Moderate Republicans were flexing their political muscles (literally—Congressman Fred Upton, a Michigan Republican, struck such a pose after moderates forced the delay of a vote on Bush's faith-based initiative), challenging the GOP leadership and the Bush administration on a range of issues in what was deemed the "revolt of the moderates" (*Congressional Quarterly,* July 21, 2001, p. 1744). They joined coalitions with Democrats to ban drilling off the coast of Florida and to toughen standards on Mexican trucks entering the United States. They objected to religious organizations receiving federal funds for charitable work unless they adhered to state antidiscrimination hiring laws. Moderate Republicans were certainly enjoying more of the limelight in the 107th Congress; but was this "day of the centrist" (*Congressional Quarterly,* April 7, 2001, p. 768) really anything new? Moderate Republicans pulling a Democratic president more to the right, as in the Clinton years, was perhaps less newsworthy than moderate Republicans pulling their own president to the left. But in both cases the strategic positions for coalition building were the median voters.

Analyses of policy outcomes based on median preferences are complicated by the fact that moderates are a divided lot; their voice in Congress is not a unified one. A member of the House Tuesday Group (moderate

Republicans that meet over lunch once a week) might be pro-affirmative action but not pro-labor; pro-environment but not pro-choice. For example, Representative Sherwood Boehlert (R-N.Y.) generally leads moderates on issues concerning the environment. If moderates hold the balance of power in the 107th Congress, how did Boehlert and a coalition of moderate Republicans and Democrats lose to the Bush administration on the issue of drilling in the Arctic National Wildlife Refuge (ANWR)? This is where an understanding of coalition building is essential. Cross-party coalitions can go both ways. Although many moderate Republicans joined the majority of Democrats on voting against drilling in the ANWR, it was the pro-labor Democrats that tipped the balance in favor of Bush's plan. Although the Teamsters and the Republicans seemed like an odd coalition, their alliance was based on jobs—more drilling means more union jobs. By placing members of Congress on a continuum from left to right, we can capture these important distinctions between members. Determining the fate of a bill requires an understanding of what motivates members at or around the median positions in Congress to join cross-party and intraparty coalitions. Our analysis of health-care legislation in the 107th Congress illustrates this point.

By 2001, the public health-care debate no longer centered on universal coverage as it had the previous decade. The focus shifted to the 190 million Americans with some type of health insurance. With the rapid rise in health-care costs throughout the 1990s (15–20 percent per year), many employers switched to managed care to keep costs down. Consumer concerns now revolved around patients' rights in a managed care system—specifically, protection against health-maintenance organizations (HMOs). Members of Congress from both parties and the president agreed that a patients' bill of rights should delineate general rights of those in managed care—patients should have access to emergency care, specialists, prescription drugs, and an independent medical review of decisions denying coverage. What members differed on, however, was how to amend the 1974 law governing HMOs. According the 1974 Employee Retirement Income Security Act (ERISA), health plans could only be sued in federal court and damages were limited to the cost of the denied care. With more and more Americans in managed care, public pressure was building to change the law that granted HMOs and insurance companies protections from lawsuits—protections enjoyed by no other corporation or individual. Changing the law meant deciding who would be liable when patients were denied care and how much money they would be awarded.

Democrats in the Senate supported the solution proposed by Ted Kennedy (D-Mass.), John McCain (R-Ariz.) and John Edwards (D-N.C.). The bill held HMOs, insurance companies, and employers (those making medical decisions for their employees) liable for denied care, and patients could sue them in state courts (state trial juries award higher damages than the federal courts). Clearly left of the status quo policy, the 1974 ERISA, the Kennedy bill attracted many moderate Republicans in favor of change. But moderate Republicans, the median voters in the 107th Senate, were also concerned about the impact of lawsuits on businesses. Would higher premiums (a consequence of more lawsuits) drive up costs for businesses? If so, could they still afford to cover their employees? The GOP and Bush proposal, which relegated lawsuits to federal courts and capped damages, certainly offered businesses and insurers protections, but it offered moderates little change from the status quo policy. Democrats rallied members to their side with HMO horror stories, while the minority whip, Don Nickles (R-Okla.), called their bill "a knife in the throat of businesses across America" (*Congressional Quarterly*, June 23, 2001, p. 1499). With pro-business (though not necessarily pro–insurance company) Republicans extending from the median to the filibuster pivot in the 107th Senate, a patients' rights bill would need to provide *some* protection for businesses in order to get passed.

A group of moderate Republicans, Olympia Snowe of Maine and Mike DeWine of Ohio, and conservative Democrats, Blanche Lincoln of Arkansas and Ben Nelson of Nebraska, provided the amendment that secured the support of the median voters. The Snowe Amendment allows employers to designate a decision maker (i.e., an insurance company) for all health-care decisions, thereby protecting themselves from lawsuits. Overwhelmingly adopted, the amendment positioned the Democratic-supported bill closer to the pro-business preferences in the Senate. On June 9, 2001, nine moderate Republicans voted with the Democrats for the final passage of the Kennedy-McCain-Edwards bill 59–36.

With its success in the Senate and its popularity in the polls, patients' rights seemed to be gaining momentum. As debate began in the House, it was clear that Americans wanted some form of patients' rights bill. Bush did not want to be the president to veto it; Republicans did not want to be the ones who obstructed it. With election 2002 looming, members were eager to bring something home to their districts. Speaker Hastert promised a vote before the August recess; exactly what members would be voting on was less certain. The House version of Kennedy-McCain-Edwards, sponsored by Greg Ganske (R-Iowa), Charlie Norwood (R-Ga.), and John Dingell (D-Mich.), had passed in similar form in 1999 with the support of 68 Republicans. But many members had voted for the legislation knowing full well it would die before reaching the desk of President Clinton. Now, with patients' rights already through the 107th Senate, a Republican president threatening to veto Ganske-Norwood-Dingell, and with an election only one year away, many of the median voters were reevaluating their positions.

Many moderates who were summoned to the White House during the height of debates stood firm in their support of the Ganske bill. Bush and the GOP were pushing for an alternative plan, a bill sponsored by Congressman Ernie Fletcher (R-Ky.) that was similar to Bush's proposal in the Senate. Concerned over the lack of votes for the Fletcher bill and the potential success of the Ganske bill, Bush continued to threaten a veto. Whereas a *cross-party* coalition had pushed patients' rights through the Senate, a coalition *within* the Republican party was needed to pass patients' rights in the more conservative House. Bush would need to make compromises to moderate Republicans to avoid a politically embarrassing outcome. House moderates would need to move closer to the president's position to avoid a presidential veto and change the law in time for the next campaign. Breaking away from his cosponsors, Republican Charlie Norwood brokered a deal with the president. Bush allowed for HMOs to be sued in state courts; Norwood agreed to lower ceilings on damages. Only 6 of the 30-plus moderate Republicans in the House voted with Democrats against the Bush-Norwood proposal; three conservative Democrats voted with the Republican majority to pass the amendment 218–213. The intraparty coalition of Republicans cleared the way for passage of patients' rights in the House on August 2, 2001, by a vote of 226–203.

Postscript

The terrorist attack of September 11, 2001, brought in a "rally-round-the-flag" period of bipartisanship. However, by mid-November the old differences between Democrats and Republicans were back again; specifically, the parties disagreed over whether airline inspectors should be federal or private employees and they disagreed over the economic stimulus package. The disagreements were predictable: House Republicans favored private inspectors and tax cuts as the way to stimulate the economy while Democrats favored federalizing the inspectors and extending unemployment benefits as the centerpiece of the stimulus package. And, as was the case in much of recent legislation, the centrist Republicans and conservative Democrats were where compromise had to occur if legislation was to be passed. Indeed it was often the president himself who had to act as an entrepreneur in order to break the gridlock of House-Senate differences. In short, as we have argued, congressional parties, preferences, supermajority institutions, and the presidency continue to interact in a myriad of ways making American politics a ceaseless maneuvering for majority coalitions, which vary from issue to issue.

Notes

1. The same held true of the Republican party, which was divided on the gold vs. silver question prior to 1896 and on the question of welfare and government management of the economy in the post-Franklin D. Roosevelt period.

2. In the following section, we rely on the work of Cooper (1975).

3. Even Poole and Rosenthal (1997) show a second dimension on roll-call voting that captures differences within the parties.

4. Before the adoption of the secret, state-printed Australian ballot in 1889–1891, parties printed and distributed their own ballots. These party ballots listed all of the party's candidates from the president to local offices. Voters who wanted to split their ticket and vote for an opposing party's candidate for a particular office would have to scratch out the party's candidate and write in the name of the challenger.

5. It should be noted that this year is artifactual in that measures of the personal vote require that members retire; thus the personal vote that first shows in 1964 surely was a 1950s phenomenon not noticed until the mid–1960s.

6. This approach to measuring incumbency advantage provides two benefits. By focusing on a single district and a set of adjacent elections, it largely controls for district characteristics. Differentiating an incumbent performance from an open-seat performance removes from gross incumbency advantage the portion due to partisan advantage, as reflected by the party's performance in an open-seat contest. The remainder is the net personal advantage enjoyed by the incumbent, above and beyond that available by virtue of the partisan or party organizational strength of the district itself. It is this concept of personal incumbency advantage on which most of the incumbency literature and the related work in the congressional literature implicitly hinges.

7. If we use a somewhat more rigorous test for the existence of personal incumbency advantage, such that both slump and surge occur in the expected direction and both equal or exceed their respective standard errors (though hardly a stringent test by the usual statistical standards), the pattern is even more distinct. This standard was not met even once until 1966, and in every election since then, both slump and surge have been more than twice their standard errors. Personal incumbency advantage, a fluctuation that figures so prominently in the congressional literature of the last 20 years, scarcely predates that literature.

8. These data were taken from Alford and Hibbing (1983) and Brady, Gaines, and Rivers (1994).

9. This does not contradict the Cox and McCubbins (1993) claim that parties have a need to organize across districts for electoral reasons. Rather like them, we believe that in a weaker party era other factors matter.

10. In the American system, interest groups have a better chance to affect policy than do comparable special interests in other countries. Part of the reason is that in these countries political parties can protect members from special interests by bundling policies and controlling nominations. For example, in Britain, a

group like the National Rifle Association could not affect public policy as readily as it does in the United States. Within limits, British political parties control the nomination of members. Thus, they can ensure that the electorate never sees a candidate who favors gun control. Voters in Britain can choose between a party that favors policies A, B, C, D, and E and a party that favors V, W, X, Y, and Z. If the voters favor A, B, C, D, and Z, they will likely choose the first party. Because of the primaries in the United States, however, the parties cannot protect members from interests that favor Z. Thus, the National Rifle Association is a powerful force in American politics, whereas it would not be so in other countries. In the United States, members of Congress must balance each interest in their district—in part because they are unprotected in primaries.

11. See Cox and McCubbins (1993) for reasons why parties still matter.

12. For a formal version of this model, see Krehbiel (1992).

13. There is a major dispute in the literature on parties over how to understand their significance. Cox and McCubbins (1993), Rohde (1988), and Aldrich (1995) are on one side, and Krehbiel (1992) is on the other. Concerning the relationship between preferences and party, Krehbiel's view, in extreme form, is that party is the mere aggregation of induced preferences. Thus, when parties are separated, as in Policy A, we call them strong; when they overlap, as in Policy B, we call them weak (see Figure 11.4). Roughly speaking, Cox and McCubbins, Rohde, and Aldrich see parties as more than aggregations of preferences. The parties tie together voters, elections, institutions, and strategy. For example, Cox and McCubbins argue that party leaders dispense favors such as committee assignments as rewards for party loyalty. We cannot resolve these differences here (or perhaps anywhere), but for our purposes it is enough that Cox and McCubbins for their reasons, and Krehbiel for his reasons, would agree that parties are at present weaker than they used to be. Thus, preferences matter—especially preferences at the point where decisions will be made.

14. See Binder and Smith (1997) on the impact of Senate filibusters on major legislation.

15. For an extension of our argument, see Brady and Buckley (1995).

16. The failure of heath-care reform legislation in the 103rd Congress has generated a number of books. The two best, we believe, are by Skocpal (1996) and Johnson and Broder (1996). Skocpal argues that Clinton's proposal failed because it was sidetracked by other legislation; namely, it took a back seat to NAFTA. Such an interpretation is understandable but difficult to test. Johnson and Broder provide good details of the heath-care debate, but their conclusion that the system is in disrepair remains ideological, not theoretical.

17. Much of this section is based on information from Brady and Volden (1997).

12

Partisan Presidential Leadership: The President's Appointees

G. CALVIN MACKENZIE

Introduction

Politics is about control. Who controls the policymaking process and to what end? In a democracy, the legitimate exercise of political power falls to those who win free elections. One of the benefits of victory is the authority to control appointments to executive offices that are not filled by election but that contribute substantially to the determination of public policy.

Throughout much of American history, political parties have served as wholesalers in this democratic process. In choosing a president, the American people also choose his political party to run the executive branch. From 1800, when Thomas Jefferson's election signaled a transfer of power from the Federalists to the Democratic Republicans, until 2000, when George W. Bush's election ended eight years of Democratic control of the executive branch, parties have been a primary conduit for the translation of electoral victories into public policies. As the election of Jefferson portended the appointment of Democratic Republicans and their policy preferences, so the election of George W. Bush heralded the appointment of Republicans and their policy preferences.

To the casual observer, not much has changed since Jefferson's time. The tides that sweep into government after each election are party tides, carrying in the new president's partisans, carrying out the partisans of the old. But that surface appearance masks a set of important changes in the role that political parties now play in the staffing of presidential administrations and in appointments to the federal judiciary. Although party is still the glue that seems to hold administrations together, this glue's consistency is much thinner than ever before and its holding power is greatly reduced. What endures is the party label; what has changed is the meaning of the label and the influence of the party organizations in presidential personnel decisions. Elections are still about control, but now more than ever before they are about policy control, not party control.

Here I examine the changes that have occurred in party impacts on federal executive staffing in the past century.[1] It begins with a look at the pre–New Deal experience, after which I explore the New Deal and postwar evolution. Then I will try illuminate the reasons for the change in party role and influence, and to explain the impact of that change on the governing process.

Parties in Government: Staffing the Executive Branch

The Birth of Parties

The Constitution and the debates from which it sprang anticipated no role for political parties in staffing the government. In fact, of course, the Framers of the Constitution did not very seriously contemplate the emergence of political parties, nor did they envision a government of such size that positions could not be filled by the president's personal acquaintances. There was little need for them to worry about the details of the appointment process, for indeed they had not worried very much about the details of the executive or judicial branches.

The Framers seemed to believe that a single person—the president— would make wiser personnel choices than any collective body sharing the appointment power. And although they established the Senate's right of advice and consent as a check against defective appointments, they thought they had created a process which the president would dominate. As Alexander Hamilton pointed out in the *Federalist* paper no. 76, that was their clear intent.

> [O]ne man of discernment is better fitted to analise [sic] and estimate the peculiar qualities adapted to particular offices, than a body of men of equal, or perhaps even of superior discernment.
>
> The sole and undivided responsibility of one man will naturally beget a livelier sense of duty and a more exact regard to reputation. He will on this account feel himself under stronger obligations, and more interested to investigate with care the qualities requisite to the stations to be filled, and to prefer with impartiality the persons who may have the fairest pretensions to them. . . . [I]n every exercise of the power of appointing to offices by an assembly of men, we must expect to see a full display of all the private party likings and dislikes, partialities and antipathies, attachments and animosities, which are felt by those who compose the assembly. The choice which may at any time happen to be made under such circumstances will of course be the result either of a victory gained by one party over the other, or of a compromise between the parties. . . . In the first, the qualifications best adapted to uniting the suffrages of the party will be more considered than

those which fit the person for the station. In the last the coalition will commonly turn upon some interested equivalent—"Give us the man we wish for this office, and you shall have the one you wish for that." This will be the usual condition of the bargain. And it will rarely happen that the advancement of the public service will be the primary object either of party victories or of party negotiations. (Cooke 1961, 510–511)

In filling appointive positions, George Washington relied—about as the framers had anticipated—on people of whom he had personal knowledge. Thomas Jefferson, Henry Knox, Edmund Randolph, and Alexander Hamilton filled the cabinet slots; Thomas Pinckney was appointed ambassador to Great Britain and Gouverneur Morris to France; John Jay became the first Chief Justice of the United States. Washington's circle of acquaintances was large and the number of positions he needed to fill was small.

When required to fill federal positions of primarily local importance, like customs collectors or postmasters, he found it convenient to defer to the judgment of senators from the relevant states. This practice quickly acquired the veneer of custom when the first Senate rejected Washington's appointment of Benjamin Fishbourn to be naval officer for the port of Savannah, Georgia. Fishbourn was fully qualified for the post, but the two senators from Georgia preferred another candidate and succeeded in convincing their colleagues to reject the Fishbourn nomination (Mackenzie 1981, 93). Hence was born the concept of "senatorial courtesy" whereby senators are granted significant influence over presidential appointments within their home states. (When parties later emerged, the courtesy was usually granted only to senators of the president's party.)

Although most of Washington's appointees shared his views on important issues of the day, there was little sense of them and him as members of the same political party. Even as disagreements began to emerge on policy matters—the Jay treaty and the financing of state debts, for example—they produced cleavages that only slowly formed into lasting factions. Washington sought men of experience and judgment to aid him in running the government. He paid some attention to geographical balance. But any political litmus test he might have applied was informal and primitive.

That changed rather rapidly, however, after Washington's retirement and the election of John Adams. With Washington gone, politics became more bare-knuckled and political factions hardened. Adams's appointees took on a clearly defined political coloration: Only Federalists need apply. On the eve of his departure from government and the transfer of power to the Jeffersonians, Adams sought to pack the government with Federalist appointments to many lower-level positions. Jefferson and his secretary of state, James Madison, tried to block these midnight appointments. The

Supreme Court, in the great case of *Marbury v. Madison*, permitted them to do so. The battle was joined, and appointments would forever after be a chief prize of partisan politics.

The Spoils System

Partisan control of presidential appointments reached its zenith with the election of Andrew Jackson in 1828. His approach to appointments came to be known as the "spoils system" following the old adage that "to the victor belong the spoils." In the case of victors in presidential elections, the primary spoils were federal jobs.

In truth, Jackson did not invent the spoils system nor was he the first president to put it into practice nor were the vast majority of federal positions subject to it. But Jackson was so vigorous in using his appointment powers to place his own loyalists in visible government offices and so brazen about doing so that his presidency has usually been seen as a watershed in the development of federal personnel practices. It was all the more noteworthy, perhaps, because it resulted in a significant change in the kinds of people who staffed the federal government. Earlier presidents, in seeking fit candidates for office, had often turned to members of the country's wealthier families, and through the first six presidencies there was a distinct upper-class cast to the executive branch. The turn toward popular democracy that Jackson's election signified found expression in his appointees, many of whom had little wealth or education.

To political observers of the time, this suggested not only that Jackson intended to sweep out incumbent officeholders in favor of his own supporters but that political loyalty was to be the principal measure of fitness for office. Jobs in government began to be viewed as rewards for political services to the successful candidate.

Not coincidentally, this was a period of intense partisanship in American politics. Parties were becoming national political organizations and began to hold quadrennial national nominating conventions. Connections among partisans at local, state, and national levels were becoming tighter. The trickle of immigration was also just beginning and would soon turn into one of the great floods in human history. As politicians sought the support of these new groups, increasing numbers of recent immigrants were finding work in government offices or party organizations. Before long, pressure began to build to expand the number of government jobs and to make as many of them as possible available for political appointment. The state and local political machines were growing and they developed hearty appetites for government jobs (see White 1958; Van Riper 1958; Fish 1904).

One consequence of these political developments was that government jobs were becoming an increasingly valuable currency. Political leaders and members of Congress began to contest with the president for control over the appointment process. Presidents came to realize that a well-timed appointment of a political supporter of a member of Congress or a party boss could often produce votes for legislation in Congress. Trading of this sort took place in earnest.

This was also a time when United States senators were chosen by their state legislatures, not by direct election. Since most of those senators were beholden for their offices to the leaders of their party, not to the people directly, they were eager to assist in whatever way they could to acquire federal government jobs for party members in their states. This only added to the pressure to treat the appointment process as a supplement to party politics rather than a mechanism for attracting the country's most talented people into the public service. Political credentials were usually more valuable in seeking a federal job than talent or administrative experience.

Not surprisingly, the quality of the federal service during most of the nineteenth century was, at best, uneven. A great many positions were filled by appointees—sometimes called "spoilsmen"—who lacked any apparent substantive qualifications. The government survived this, in part at least, because it was not engaged in many activities that required significant technical or management skills. In fact, most of the technical specialties that now exist in government agencies were unknown in the nineteenth century: astrophysics, econometrics, environmental analysis, and so on.[2] The principal preoccupations of government in the nineteenth century were the conduct of a small number of routine functions that required little skill or experience: delivering the mail, collecting customs duties and taxes, building roads and canals. In many cases, a political hack could do these jobs about as well as anyone else. What was good for the party, therefore, was not always terrible for the government.

Nevertheless, the spoils system began to produce the seeds of its own destruction. The principal failing, of course, was that many of the people employed by the government were either the most talented nor the most qualified available. In many cases, in fact, they were totally without qualifications other than their political connections. The spoils system was also a hungry monster, a constant source of pressure for the creation of new government jobs, to provide for more political appointments and to lighten the burden on officeholders so that they could devote more of their time to political activities.

The spoils system also invited corruption of all sorts because appointees were constrained by no sense of the honor of public service nor confined by any ethical notions of holding a public trust. They had their jobs because their party had won an election and attained political power. And, as long as they held that power, there were few real limits on how they could exercise it. Knowing that their horizon only extended to the next election, appointees were also driven to take advantage of their offices as hastily as they could, for they might soon be out of a job. If the sun was to shine only briefly, they felt compelled to make hay all the more quickly.

Another troubling aspect of the spoils system was the pressure it put on the president to devote substantial amounts of time to filling low-level positions in the federal government. Presidents in the nineteenth century had none of the elaborate White House staff structure that exists today. There was no one to whom they could delegate responsibility for handling patronage matters. Thus many hours were consumed brokering conflicting demands for appointments to individual offices. A story about President Lincoln suggests the plague-like quality of these pressures. The White House was a public building for much of the nineteenth century and there were few restrictions on access to the main lobby. Job seekers often came there hoping for a moment or two with the president to plead their case. Lincoln found it very uncomfortable to pass through the lobby on the way to his office because that often set off a flurry of such pleading. Once, when he was suffering from a bad cold, he said to his secretary as he was about to enter the lobby, "Now, at last I have something I can give them."

The Creation of the Civil Service

Efforts to reform the personnel staffing process of the federal government appeared as early as the 1850s. They gathered steam after the Civil War. Rutherford B. Hayes was elected president in 1876, having campaigned for civil service reform. He made little headway against congressional resistance, however, during the next four years. His successor, James A. Garfield, had been a supporter of reform while serving in Congress. He was assassinated four months after his inauguration—in the legend of the time, by a "disappointed federal job seeker"—and reformers used his slaying as evidence of the rottenness of the spoils system and the acute need for reform. Two years later, in 1883, Congress passed the Pendleton Act, which created the federal civil service system.

This was hardly the death of the spoils system. Civil service protection spread slowly among government jobs. The majority remained subject to political appointment for years yet to come. Some categories continued to be filled through political appointment until well into the twentieth century. Local postmasters, for example, remained political appointees until 1970. And even the most vigorous of the reformers recognized that

Table 12.1   Growth of the Federal Civil Service System

Year	Total Civilian Employment	Percentage of Civilian Employees Under the Merit System
1821	6,914	
1831	11,491	
1841	18,038	
1851	26,274	
1861	36,672	
1871	51,020	
1881	100,020	
1891	157,442	21.5
1901	239,456	44.3
1911	395,905	57.5
1921	561,142	79.9
1931	609,746	76.8
1941	1,437,682	68.9
1951	2,482,666	86.4
1961	2,435,804	86.1
1971	2,862,894	84.1
1981	2,947,428	58.7
1991	3,138,180	56.4
2000	2,878,800	---

Source: Harold W. Stanley and Richard G. Niemi, *Vital Statistics on American Politics,* 5th ed. (Washington, D.C.: *Congressional Quarterly* Press, 1995), p. 250; U.S. Department of Commerce, *Statistical Abstract of the United States, 1996* (Washington, D.C.: Government Printing Office, 1996), p. 345; Congressional Budget Office, *Changes in Federal Civilian Employment: An Update* (Washington, D.C.: Government printing Office, 2001), pp.16–17. Under the Postal Reorganization Act of 1970, postal employees were moved from the merit system to "excepted service." In 1995, there were 845,393 postal employees.

some positions would always be political in character and thus could never be blanketed under the coverage of a merit-based civil service. But a significant change began in 1883, and it would continue to spread in the century that followed, as Table 12.1 indicates.

The Pendleton Act and its subsequent refinements accomplished several things. First, it set the principle that government jobs should be open and available to all citizens and should be filled by those who successfully demonstrate that they are best qualified for the position. Second, it established the policy that examinations were the best and most objective way to determine those qualifications. Third, it provided civil servants with protections against political removal and established a pattern of continuity: civil servants would continue in office even as the presidency changed hands. And fourth, to supervise this system and protect its neutrality from politics, the act created a Civil Service Commission whose membership would have to reflect a degree of partisan balance.[3]

Growing out of this success of the reform movement was a new question, one that has continued to be debated into our own time. Once the principle was established that some positions in the government should be filled on the basis of merit, not politics, then arguments ensued about where the line should be drawn. Which positions should be granted civil service protection and which should continue to be treated as political appointments? The spread of civil service protection indicated in Table 12.1 suggests that a steadily growing percentage of federal offices have been placed outside of the political stream. But what of those left unprotected by the merit system? How were they to be filled? And by whom? That is the topic of the rest of this paper.

Presidential Appointments in the Twentieth Century

1900–1932

Except that a slowly increasing number of government jobs were coming under the coverage of the civil service, the appointment process in the first third of the twentieth century varied little from what it had been in the second half of the nineteenth. The positions outside the civil service were still filled by a process in which political parties played an important role, and appointments were still viewed as a reward for political services.

This is not to suggest that all presidential appointees lacked substantive qualifications for federal service. Many of those who had been party activists had also built impressive records of public service and would have merited high-level positions even without party sponsorship. Names like Charles Evans Hughes and William Jennings Bryan would have appeared on most lists of highly qualified people eligible for cabinet or other top positions in government. And presidents also retained the latitude to select some appointees who had no significant record of party service, whose primary qualification was their talent or experience. In this category were people like Josephus Daniels (Secretary of the Navy, appointed by Woodrow Wilson), Andrew Mellon (Secretary of the Treasury, appointed by Harding), and Henry Stimson (Secretary of War, appointed by Taft, FDR, and Truman; and Secretary of State, appointed by Hoover).

But partisan pressures in the appointment process were ever-present. In putting together their cabinets, for example, presidents felt constrained to select people who represented different factions or regional elements in their party (Fenno 1959, 78–88). In this sense, Woodrow Wilson's cabinet was not very different from Abraham Lincoln's. Though strong-willed and independent leaders, both felt compelled to respect partisan concerns in staffing the top positions in their administrations.

Throughout this period, the national party organizations played an important role in identifying candidates for presidential appointments. In fact, it was quite common for the head of the president's party to hold a position in the cabinet, usually as postmaster general. This made sense, not only because the Post Office Department had the greatest demand for patronage appointments, but also because a cabinet post provided a vantage point from which the party leader could work with the president and other cabinet secretaries to ensure a steady flow of partisan loyalists into federal posts throughout the government.

The party role was critical to government operations because there was at the time no alternative source of candidates for appointment. Each cabinet secretary had his own acquaintances and contacts, but few of them knew enough politicians to fill all the available positions in their departments with people who would be loyal to the administration, pass muster with appropriate members of Congress, and satisfy the political litmus tests of party leaders in the states and cities where they might serve. The party could help with all of that.

If some of those the parties brought forward to fill appointive positions were unqualified political hacks—and some surely were—the parties performed valuable functions as well. Many of the appointees who came through the party channel were skilled and qualified. This was by no means merely a turkey trot. More important, partisan control of this process usually guaranteed the construction of an administration that was broadly representative of the elements of the president's party and thus, in some important ways, was in touch with the American people it was intended to serve. Equally important, the parties served as an employment agency upon which the government was heavily reliant. They provided a steady stream of politically approved candidates for federal offices. That was a function of no small significance in a government that lacked any other tested means of recruitment for positions outside the civil service.

1933–1952

Following the pattern of his predecessors, Franklin Roosevelt appointed James Farley, the leader of the Democratic party, to serve as postmaster general and superintend the selection of lower-level appointments in the first Roosevelt administration. Farley directed a patronage operation that bore a close resemblance to those of the previous half century.

Despite the familiar look of FDR's patronage operation, however, changes were set in motion by the New Deal that would have lasting consequences for the staffing of presidential administrations. Three of those deserve attention here.

The first was the very nature of the politics of the New Deal. The coalition that brought Franklin Roosevelt to office was composed of a broad diversity of groups and views. It provided FDR a sweeping victory by drawing support from Americans who disagreed with each other about important matters yet agreed on the need to elect a president of their own party. But the New Deal coalition soon proved as useless for running a government as it had been useful for winning elections. Even with the most delicate kind of balancing act, it was no small task to construct an administration of intellectuals and union members, northern liberals and southern conservatives, progressives and racists. The task was complicated all the more by the intensity of the new administration's efforts, not merely to redirect, but to reconstruct public policy in the United States. It simply could not be reliably assumed that Democratic appointees would fully support all the dimensions of the president's program.

Hence, Roosevelt and his senior advisers began increasingly, in filling key positions in the government, to end-run the Democratic party patronage system. More and more the people closest to the president—James Rowe, Louis Howe, Harry Hopkins, and others—began to operate their own recruitment programs. Typically they would identify bright young men already serving in government or anxious to do so and cultivate them with the kind of ad hoc assignments that prepared them for more important managerial positions. Though these were either lifelong or recently converted Democrats, they often were not people with any history of party activism. It was the passions of the time and their commitment to the New Deal that inspired their interest in politics, not a pattern of service to local or state political machines.

The need for such people grew increasingly apparent as the consequence of a second change wrought by the New Deal. The government was growing. Total federal employment was 604,000 in 1933. By the end of the decade it had nearly doubled. The New Deal seemed to spawn new agencies and programs almost daily. This created a voracious need not merely for people to fill newly created slots, but for skilled managers and creative program specialists to attend to problems as complicated as any the federal government had ever before tackled.

This need for high-quality people had the effect of diminishing the importance of the party patronage system as a source of appointees. It became increasingly apparent that the party faithful did not always include the kinds of people required to operate technical agencies like the Securities and Exchange Commission and the Agriculture Adjustment Administration. So Roosevelt turned to other sources, even occasionally risking the wrath of party leaders in so doing.

A third change in the New Deal years fed the momentum of the first two. That was the growing importance of the White House staff. As the energy of the federal government came to be centered in the presidency—and it did dramatically during the New Deal—the need for more support for the president became increasingly apparent. In 1936, Roosevelt appointed a committee headed by his friend Louis Brownlow to study the organization of the executive branch and make recommendations. The report of the Brownlow Committee described the need for vigorous executive leadership to make a modern democracy work. But it also pointed out that "the President needs help" in this enterprise. It went on to recommend the creation of an Executive Office of the President (EOP) and the creation of presidential authority to appoint a small personal staff to assist in the management of the government (U.S. President's Committee on Administrative Management, 1937). In 1939, the Congress acted affirmatively on most of the recommendations of the Brownlow Committee.

In the past, presidents had had little choice but to rely on their party's patronage operation because they lacked the staff necessary to run a personnel recruitment operation of their own. With the creation of the EOP that began to change. Embedded in the recommendations of the Brownlow Committee was a philosophy of public management that also threatened the importance of party patronage. Political control of the government, in the view of Brownlow and his many supporters in the schools of public administration, had come to mean policy control, not merely party control. It was no longer enough for a president to staff his administration with members of his own party and let them work with co-partisans in Congress to superintend the routines of government. Instead, the president needed managerial support through broader control of the budget, government organization, and personnel selection to move public policy in the direction that he set and that had earned the endorsement of the American electorate.

This gradual evolution in management philosophy clearly suggested the need for the president and his personal staff to play a larger role in recruiting appointees who supported his policy priorities and who possessed the skills and creativity necessary to develop and implement them. In that scheme, government jobs could not be viewed primarily as rewards for party loyalty, and recruitment could not be left primarily to party patronage operations.

None of these changes took place overnight, but they slowly found their way into the operations of the presidency. Loyal Democrats continued to claim positions in the Roosevelt and later the Truman administration. The pressure to fill vacancies with the party faithful did not abate. The Democratic National Committee continued to operate a full-service employment agency. But few of the appointments to important positions came via this route any longer.

The strains on the patronage operation grew more acute after Roosevelt's death. Truman found himself in an odd position. Though a Democrat like Roosevelt, he needed to forge his own identity as president. Members of his party often had difficulty transferring their loyalties from the dead president to the new one, especially since many of them thought Truman several cuts below Roosevelt in stature.

The 1948 election campaign widened the fissures in the Democratic party all the more. The southern wing of the party split off to support the Democratic governor of South Carolina, Strom Thurmond. The so-called progressive wing had its own candidate in Henry Wallace. After winning reelection, Truman found that he had to temper his faith, slender as it already had become, in the ability of the Democratic party to provide candidates for appointment who were certain to be loyal to him and the important policies of his presidency.

Truman did what any reasonable leader would have done under the circumstances. He relied less heavily on candidates recommended by the party and built his own recruitment process. The latter never passed much beyond the primitive stage and the former continued to play an important role. But change was under way, and its full impacts would emerge in the administrations that followed.

1952–1968

Dwight Eisenhower was the least partisan president of the twentieth century, and he came to office with fewer debts to his party than any of his predecessors. Though Republicans had not controlled the presidency for 20 years, Eisenhower's election did not signify the beginning of a flood of old-line Republican loyalists into federal offices. Eisenhower's chief of staff, Sherman Adams, reported that the president was often indignant at what he considered to be political interference in his appointments and that he "avoided giving the Republican National Committee any responsibility for the selection of government officials, a duty the committee would have been happy to assume" (Adams 1961, 125). Charles F. Willis, Jr., an Eisenhower aide who worked on personnel matters, has said that the president "seemed to react against intense political pressure, more than anything else that I noticed, adversely, and I think that his appointments and the people he surrounded himself with at the top level reflected that he considered quality rather than political know-how" (Willis 1968, 28).

Eisenhower did intend to oust as many New Dealers and Fair Dealers as he could, but he sought to replace them with people who subscribed to his own brand of Republicanism. Being a Republican, even a lifelong member of the party faithful, was not enough to get one a job in the Eisenhower administration—as soon became evident to Republicans across the country.

While the new administration worked closely with Republican National Committee Chairman Leonard Hall and did in fact place a number of party loyalists, appointments to top-level positions were much more heavily influenced by a group of the president's close friends. During the 1952 transition, Lucius Clay, Herbert Brownell, and Harold Talbott commissioned the New York consulting firm of McKinsey & Co. to do a study identifying the most important positions in the government. Then, and in the years that followed, they were an important source of suggestions and advice to Eisenhower on matters of government staffing.

The composition of the Eisenhower administration quickly came to reflect the diminished role of the president's party as a source of senior-level personnel. A majority of Eisenhower's first cabinet had no significant history of Republican party activism. The subcabinet looked much the same, drawing heavily on the practical talents of the business and legal communities, with only a scattering of officials whose primary credentials were partisan or political (D. Mann 1965, 293).

Eisenhower's second term marked an even more important turning point in the transition away from party dominance of the appointment process. The 22nd Amendment, limiting presidents to two terms in office, had been ratified in 1951. Eisenhower was the first president to whom it applied, and his reelection in 1956 made him the first president ever to enter a term as a lame duck. Since he could not run again for reelection, there was less incentive for Eisenhower to make appointments with an eye to building partisan electoral support; he was freer than ever to distance himself from patronage pressures.

That freedom was reflected in the significant initiatives that developed in Eisenhower's second term for management of the personnel function by people close to the presidency, not the party. The Eisenhower White House was the first to respond to a modern president's need for centralized control over executive branch personnel by seeking to construct procedures and organizational structures to serve that objective. The position special assistant for personnel management was created and the first elements of a systematic recruitment operation were put in place (Kaufman 1965, 66; Weko 1995).

This momentum toward centralized presidential control of the appointment process and away from reliance on party patronage accelerated in the Kennedy and Johnson administrations. Kennedy, like Eisenhower, had won the presidential nomination by setting up his own organization and capturing the party. His was not a life of deeply committed partisanship nor did he grant the Democratic party organization much credit for his narrow victory in the 1960 election. So Kennedy felt little compulsion to staff his administration with party loyalists to whom he might have had any debt or obligation. From the very start, he and his staff operated their own personnel recruitment operation.

After Kennedy's assassination, Lyndon Johnson continued the practice of operating a White House personnel office. He designated John Macy, then chairman of the Civil Service Commission, to handle presidential appointments as well. Macy expanded the personnel office and began to systematize its procedures, even employing computers to maintain records on thousands of potential appointees.

Under both Kennedy and Johnson, the White House personnel office worked with the Democratic National Committee in varying degrees of co-operation. But the participation of the party was clearly subsidiary. Most of the time the DNC's role was to determine that candidates for appointment selected by the White House would not incur the opposition of party leaders in their home states. The White House also conducted checks with home-state Democratic senators and members of Congress to avoid opposition from them. But, as Dan H. Fenn, Jr., an assistant to Kennedy on personnel matters, said, "The kind of people we were looking for weren't the kind of people who were active in party activities" (Fenn 1976).

These checks came to be known as clearances and they emerged as a routine of the appointment process, providing a role for the party, albeit a limited one. Though party officials were a steady source of suggestions of potential nominees, genuine control over personnel selection had shifted to the White House. This process, which had begun in the early days of the New Deal, accelerated as the size of the White House staff grew. The party ceased to have an initiative role in the appointment process and clearly no longer operated that process as it once had. The party had become a checkpoint and, with but few exceptions, not much more. As Hugh Heclo has indicated (1977), its influence was reduced to the exercise of "'negative clearance'; that is, nursing political referrals and clearing official appointments in order to placate those political leaders in Congress and in state, local, or other organizations who might otherwise take exception" (71). The party no longer drove the appointment process, but its disapproval of an appointment could bring that process to a temporary halt.

1969 and Beyond

The movement to centralize control over presidential appointments reached new levels of sophistication and success in the administration of Richard Nixon and those that followed. Nixon himself never had much interest in personnel selection, but the people to whom he delegated that task tended to be experienced professional managers who saw personnel selection as a critical ingredient in efforts to establish control over the executive branch.

In the years after 1969, the White House Personnel Office (later called the Presidential Personnel Office) became an important component of the White House Office and grew in size. It now routinely employs more than 25 people, and often swells to more than 50 at particularly busy times. Appointment procedures have been systematized and routinized. Computers play an important role in tracking the progress of appointments. And clearances with leaders of the president's party, with relevant members of Congress, with officials in the agency to which an appointment is to be made, and with policy specialists in the administration are regular features of almost every appointment decision (Bonafede 1987; Mackenzie 1981; Weko 1995).

But the most important characteristic of the modern appointment process, and the one that most critically affects the influence of political parties, has been the creation of a genuine and aggressive recruitment or outreach capability within the White House staff. Party influence in appointments remained significant as long as the White House lacked the ability to identify qualified candidates on its own. Then the president and his staff had little choice but to respond to recommendations and suggestions that came in, as the terminology of the time had it, "over the transom." It is an iron law of politics that "you can't beat someone with no one," and of football that "the best defense is a good offense." Both apply in the appointment process as well.

The thrust of most of the contemporary development of White House personnel operations has been to grasp the initiative, to relieve presidents from reliance on external sources for their appointees. Primary among those sources historically was the president's own political party organization, but the successful establishment of a recruiting capability in the White House has left the parties with little remaining control over a function they once dominated.

Parties and Presidential Leadership: An Accelerating Evolution

The years after World War II have been a time of diminishing influence for the national party organizations in the operations of the presidency. This was a trend with prewar antecedents, but its pace accelerated after the war. There is no simple explanation for the change. In fact, it resulted from a confluence of other changes occurring both inside and outside the government in those years. The most important of those are summarized here.

The Game Changed

Party influence was always largest on appointments to positions outside Washington. When an appointee was to serve as customs collector for the port of Philadelphia or postmaster in Butte, local party officials generally had a determining influence in choosing the person to fill the slot. Even though this was technically a presidential appointment, presidents readily deferred to the leaders of their party in the local area. Until relatively recent times, there were tens of thousands of such positions and they were a significant part of the political rewards system for party workers. A person who had spent years as party organizer, poll watcher, and minor officeholder could reasonably expect to cap a political career with appointment to a sinecure as a local official of the federal government.

But what was good for the party was increasingly bad for the delivery of government services. After World War II, largely at the behest of an increasingly vocal public service reform movement, many of these positions were taken out of the patronage stream and placed under some form of civil service coverage. And the reform movement thought the solution was to take some of the politics out of appointments to these administrative offices.

The Number of Important Presidential Appointments Grew

From the beginning of the New Deal onward, the number of senior level positions in the federal government grew. New cabinet departments and independent agencies were added. Old ones expanded as hordes of new programs were created. The bureaucracy thickened and new administrative layers were added to the federal government. Departments that might have had two or three presidential appointees before World War II now have a dozen or more. The Department of Defense, which came into being after World War II, has 46 senior positions filled by presidential appointment. The Department of Education, created in 1979, has 16[4] (Brookings Institution and Pew Charitable Trusts 2000). The broader picture is indicated in Table 12.2.

Many of these new positions required appointees with a high level of technical or scientific competence because they bore responsibility for complex government programs: for example, the under secretary of commerce for oceans and atmosphere, the director of defense research and engineering, the director of the Office of Energy Research. The kinds of people needed to fill these positions were unlikely to be found hanging out at party headquarters on election night.

As a consequence of the growth and increasing sophistication of the government's senior appointive positions, presidents needed to develop

Table 12.2   Growth in Top-Level Executive-Branch Positions,
1961–1998

Position	1961	1993	1998
Secretary	10	14	14
Deputy secretary	6	20	3
Under secretary	15	32	41
Assistant secretary	87	225	212
Deputy assistant secretary	78	518	484
Total	196	809	774

Source: Paul C. Light, *The True Size of Government* (Washington, D.C.:
Brookings Institution, 1999), pp. 170–72.

their own personnel recruitment operations. It became apparent during the New Deal that party channels would simply not be adequate to provide the number and kinds of talented appointees that an increasingly active government required.

That gap between need and supply grew wider in the years that followed. In response, successive administrations developed and then refined their own systems and procedures for staffing the senior levels of the executive branch. Parties had once played a central role in this process. By the end of the second decade after World War II, their role was essentially peripheral. Members of the president's party continued to fill most of the appointed positions, but their identification, selection, and recruitment were conducted at some distance from the formal organization of the president's party.

The Power Situation Changed

As the federal government came to play a larger role in American life, appointees who developed and implemented programs became more powerful. Consider the contrast between 1932 and the present. The federal government in 1932 did *not* provide aid to education, run a national pension system, provide health care for the elderly, fund the national highway system, regulate financial markets, shoot rockets into space, or serve as democracy's policeman around the world. It does all of those things and many more today, and it spends nearly $2 trillion dollars each year doing them.

Management of those programs and of the distribution of the funds they involve affords a great deal of power to presidential appointees. Decisions on who fills those positions matter more than ever before. And the groups in American society affected by the choices made by these appointees have become increasingly unwilling to leave them to purely patronage appointees. They have sought instead to put pressure on presidents to select appointees with the necessary technical skills and experience and with particular policy views. Party loyalty and service have been largely irrelevant to these calculations.

As appointments became more important, parties became less important in filling them. For much of American history, the principal contests for power were outside of government, in elections where the parties were strongest. With the beginning of the New Deal, the power struggle increasingly took place within government, in the modern bureaucratic state where the parties were weakest. When the terrain shifted, the locus of power shifted as well.

The Context of the Appointment Process

Nothing in government occurs in a vacuum. In fact, government is a great social mirror: What happens there usually reflects what is happening elsewhere in society. That is certainly true of the changes that took place in the appointment process during the twentieth century. The influence of political parties diminished in the appointment process because their influence was also diminishing elsewhere. Parties could claim a potent role in presidential appointment decisions only as long as they were able to exert influence elsewhere in American politics—by controlling the candidate nominating process, being able to deliver votes, and maintaining their hegemony over critical political skills. But that too was changing during the middle decades of the twentieth century, as other chapters in this book have amply demonstrated.

Parties lost their primacy as organizers of American political life. Direct primaries took control of the nominating process out of the hands of party leaders and gave it to voters. Candidates devised ways to raise their own money, build their own organizations, do their own advertising. They hired political consultants to provide the kinds of skills that parties had traditionally provided. As fewer Americans identified strongly with the two major parties, it became harder and harder for the parties to deliver votes.

The long-term impact of all of this was that parties had fewer debts to call due in the appointment process. Presidents had less and less reason to feel obligated to their parties and party workers for their own elections, hence less incentive to appoint those workers to federal offices to meet such obligations. Once parties began to lose control of the electoral process, they lost control of the appointment process as well.

Simultaneous with the decline in party fortunes was an explosion in the number of national special interest groups. Counting the number of national interest groups is no small task, but Ronald Hrebenar and Ruth Scott identified 20,643 national nonprofit organizations in 1988, more than double the number that existed in 1968 (Hrebenar and Scott 1982, 8; 1990, 11). This figure, of course, omits profit-seeking corporations, which are themselves increasingly active political entities.

These groups were both much more substantive and much more focused than the major political parties. Typically, they were concerned with a relatively narrow set of policies and they represented the people most directly affected by the shape of those policies. This permitted them to concentrate their attention and political influence on the small number of presidential appointments that mattered most to them. It also allowed them to work closely with the congressional committee and subcommittee chairs who were most interested in those programs and who controlled their appropriations. These were often politically potent combinations that generated considerably more influence over presidential appointments than broad-based, coalition parties were able to generate. In the competition for influence over appointments, interest groups' increasing success often came at the expense of the political parties' influence.

In recent years, identity groups—women, racial minorities, gays and lesbians—have also assumed a more influential role in appointment decisions. The Democratic presidents Carter and Clinton were especially sensitive to the demands of these groups for seats at the table. President Clinton's first administration took shape very slowly, in part because he wanted an administration that "looked like America," with appointments that amply represented the ethnic, gender, and geographical diversity of the country, which came to be known as the "EGG standard" (Twentieth Century Fund 1996, 68–71; Weko 1995, 100–103). The first few months of George W. Bush's administration indicated that Republicans too have acquired a substantial sensitivity to the diversity of their appointments. Bush's initial cabinet appointments included three women, two African Americans, two Asian Americans, and one Hispanic—a long way from Richard Nixon's first cabinet in 1969 which was composed entirely of white males.

The decentralization of power in the Congress also worked against the interests of the parties in the appointment process. During the early decades of the twentieth century, real political power in Congress was concentrated in the hands of a relatively small number of institutional party leaders and committee chairs. Local political bosses and national party leaders regularly worked with them to influence the president's appointment decisions. If the leader of the Democratic National Committee or the mayor of Chicago called Sam Rayburn, the Speaker of the House, and asked him to try to get the president to appoint a particular Democrat to the Federal Communications Commission, it was hard for the president to deny the request. Sam Rayburn was a key factor in determining the fate of the president's legislative program. Keeping him happy was usually much more important than any particular appointment.

But increasingly after mid-century, the party leaders and committee chairs lost their grip on power in Congress. Younger members generated reforms that spread power around, to the subcommittee level in the House and to individual members in the Senate. The political calculus became much more complex and it was much more difficult for local bosses or leaders of the national party organization to use the congressional lever to influence presidential appointment decisions. Individual members of Congress were less beholden and less connected to the national party in any case, having built their own personal political organizations and developed their own sources of campaign funds. Their interest in presidential appointments was much more ad hoc and personal in character: They sought appointments for their friends and supporters and staff members, not for traditional party workers. As parties became less important to the job security of members of Congress, incentives diminished for members to use their influence in the appointment process for purposes broader than their own personal objectives.

So the political landscape underwent broad transitions after World War II. Senior-level appointments were growing more important as national political power moved to Washington. Lower-level appointments were transferred in large numbers to the civil service. The presidency was becoming a larger and increasingly sophisticated institution with management capabilities that had never before existed. The electoral process was no longer the sole realm of political party organizations. Interest groups were springing up everywhere and rapidly gaining political potency. A decentralized Congress was less able and less willing to serve purely partisan interests in the appointment process. Individually and collectively, these changes all served to erode the influence that parties once exercised on the staffing of the executive branch of the federal government.

The Continuing Problem of Political Control

Two important trends have been the dominant themes of this chapter. One is also the dominant theme of this book: that parties are not what they used to be. In virtually every aspect of American political life, organized political parties play a smaller role at the beginning of the twenty-first century than they did during most of the twentieth. That is certainly true, as we have sought to demonstrate, in presidential appointments to administrative positions.

The other trend, more directly relevant to the topic of this chapter, has been the steady and successful effort to isolate public employment from political pressure, to create a federal workforce that is "protected" from the tides of political passion in the country and the electorate. At the beginning of the twentieth century, there were 240,000 federal civilian employees. Of these, more than half were political appointees of one form or another. At the beginning of the twenty-first century, there are 2.9 million federal civilian employees. Of these, only a few thousand are actually filled by political appointment.

This suggests a peculiar but familiar reality: that Americans are suspicious of politics and parties. For many of them, politics is a dirty business, something that can easily mess up government. Hence there has been substantial public support for efforts to depoliticize the personnel selection process in government, to eliminate all the pejoratives: cronyism and nepotism and the spoils system.

But Americans are also highly skeptical of bureaucrats and so they respond positively to campaigning politicians who bash bureaucrats and promise to put government back into the hands of the people. The most popular American politician of recent times, Ronald Reagan, was a master of this. "Government," he said, "is the problem, not the solution."

Hence there exists a kind of public schizophrenia that deeply complicates the task of presidential leadership. Americans want a government that is isolated and protected from the worst aspects of partisan politics. But they also want a government that is not controlled by "faceless bureaucrats," but by elected leaders who will keep it responsive to popular concerns. Those are contradictory goals. How is it possible to have a government that is simultaneously free of politics and under political control? The answer, of course, is that it is not possible. And, as a consequence, conflict between these competing objectives constantly pervades the personnel process.

When parties were the dominant influence in presidential personnel selection, the notion reigned that getting control of the government meant establishing partisan control. The way to implement the will of the electorate was to fill as many positions as possible with members of the president's party. By filling all, or a large number, of federal offices with the president's co-partisans, the government would move in the directions he laid out.

It wasn't a bad theory, except that it didn't work in practice, especially after 1932. It didn't work for two reasons primarily. First, it couldn't work in the United States because of the nature of American political parties.

The large national parties whose candidates won presidential elections were constructed of delicate coalitions. They rarely offered the electorate a very detailed or refined set of policy objectives. Their primary task was to win the elections, and to do that they clung to the center, trimming specifics to develop the broadest possible mass appeal. Even in the most intense periods of party conflict in the United States, it was difficult for most voters to perceive very broad *policy* differences between the parties. Parties provided few meaningful clues to what exactly the government would do if their candidate was elected.

There was thus little reliability in the notion that staffing the government with members of the same party would provide a unified sense of direction under presidential leadership. In fact, members of the same party often disagreed with each other, and with their own president, on a great many matters of policy. In many cases, all they shared was a party label. The spoils system and its successors were a very shaky foundation for getting control of the government through coherent policy leadership from the White House.

Even if American political parties had been more ideologically and substantively unified, the theory would have failed in implementation. Partisan domination of the appointments process was never viewed by party leaders as a system for aiding the president in establishing policy leadership. It was treated as a vehicle for party, not presidential, purposes. In suggesting party candidates for appointment, the principal goal was to sustain the vigor and the regional and ideological balance of the party, not to find loyal or effective supporters of the president's program. Many presidential appointments, as indicated earlier, were controlled by the local party organizations who had little interest in national policy. They sought to get federal jobs to reward their own faithful servants and to prevent the federal government from upsetting their local control.

For both these reasons, party participation in presidential appointments failed to serve the purpose of aiding the incumbent administration in establishing policy leadership over the government. And, as we have seen, American presidents began to reject that participation. Slowly but steadily they found ways to construct their own appointment processes, increasingly distanced from party influence. In the past few decades, party influence on appointments has faded almost to the vanishing point.

Presidents still struggle to "get control of the government." Few of them fully succeed. But no recent American president has sought party help in accomplishing this critical objective. And for good reason. American political parties were rarely very helpful at this when they were relevant and potent. They would be even less valuable today with their potency on the wane and their relevance to the task of governing very much in doubt.

Notes

1. Partisanship in judicial appointments will not be discussed in this chapter because of space constraints. Interested readers are referred to the excellent work that Professor Sheldon Goldman has done on this topic over several decades.

2. It should be noted that a few technical specialties had begun to emerge in the nineteenth century. Many of those were in public health and in agriculture. Even at the height of the spoils system, these positions were often treated as exceptions and were filled by the same people from one administration to the next, without regard to political loyalties.

3. In 1979, the Civil Service Commission was abolished and replaced by two new agencies: the Office of Personnel Management and the Merit Systems Protection Board.

4. The numbers in this paragraph refer to so-called PAS appointments: presidential appointments that require Senate confirmation.

13

Subtle Shifts, Dramatic Days: What the Plate Tectonics of American Politics Say About the Country and Its Future

DAVID M. SHRIBMAN

No election seemed to matter so little, demonstrate so little difference between the candidates, elicit so little voter interest, or spawn so little public debate as the 2000 general election. Then came Election Day. And suddenly, everything changed—as if a magician had snapped his fingers in the childhood dramas of yore. Suddenly the election seemed to matter so much, the voters seemed to care so much, the passion seemed so great, the drama seemed so compelling. Indeed, the important thing about the election of 2000 was that it was two campaigns. The one that began in the snows of Iowa and New Hampshire in January and droned on until the final appeals for votes in early November was remarkable for its lack of impact and implications, for the lack of interest it generated. But the campaign that began with a concession call in Nashville, one that was ultimately retracted and led to fights about chads, to multiple legal maneuvers and appeals, to recounts and recounts of recounts, was remarkable for the way it gripped the nation and the world.

By the time the votes were tabulated and then retabulated, the suits had been filed and appealed, the reporters and spokespeople and commentators had spun and then spun again, the longest election in more than a century started to look like no other election. The election overtime provided an extraordinary exercise in political struggle, not only between former Vice President Albert Gore Jr. of Tennessee and Governor George W. Bush of Texas, but also among the established branches and the various levels of government. Legislators battled the judiciary, local officials battled state officials, state judges were upbraided by federal judges. In the course of all this, almost every individual and institution that touched or was touched by the postelection controversy was tarnished. The election overtime raised questions about the independence and neutrality of the Supreme Court, it raised questions about the legitimacy of the presidency of George W. Bush, it raised questions about the conduct of elections at all levels of government.

Political scientists speak of "critical elections," and by this they customarily mean elections that change the course of history, usually by realigning parties and adjusting centers of power. Almost no one has argued that the victory of Bush over Gore in an election in which the winner won fewer votes than the loser produced anything approaching those sorts of transformations. And yet the election of 2000 may have been a critical election because of how it transformed the country, not the political system. The 36-day ordeal awakened the public to the imprecision of vote counts, alerted it to the fragility of the franchise, shined an unforgiving light into the hidden corners of election law and practice. It reminded Americans, who just 24 months earlier had witnessed only the second presidential impeachment in 13 decades, of some of the hidden corners of the Constitution. It provided new reasons for a electorate weary of politicians to turn even more dramatically from politics. And it stripped both the art form of the presidential election and the institution of the Supreme Court of their senses of mystery and majesty and, perhaps, of some of their power.

The implications of these events are difficult to measure, impossible to predict. Since Vietnam and Watergate, the public's indifference toward and or in some cases contempt for politics has been a hardy perennial of the American cultural landscape. Personal scandals, fund-raising abuses, the peculiar totems and taboos of the capital, all have contributed to a sense of political ennui among many Americans. Surely the long election overtime of November and December 2000 will contribute substantially to that sense of discomfort.

But lost in the struggle and spectacle of the 36-day post-election tussle were several facts so elementary that they have been ignored: Americans beyond Florida voted. The verdict of the voters in many regions and states was not ambiguous. Taken together, the actions of Americans on November 7, 2000, present a fascinating snapshot of the United States and an invaluable roadmap for the future of American politics.

The presidential election may not have been settled until mid-December, but the political nature of the United States was defined in the first week of November. The purpose of this essay is to evaluate the political implications of the voters' decisions on Election Day and to use the 2000 election to sketch the character of a nation that knew itself when the polls closed but had to wait more than five weeks to know whom it had chosen as its president.

The consensus of scholars and commentators alike was that the election left in its wake a nation divided as almost never before. The presidential election ended in essentially a tie, leaving the nation to live within democracy's margin of error. The Senate was divided so closely that the ancient chamber was controlled by the Democrats for the first 17 days of the 107th Congress before reverting to Republican control by virtue of the presence of Vice President Richard B. Cheney in the chair of the Senate president. (Later, the Democrats would regain control after Senator James K. Jeffords left the Republican party and gave his former rivals a one-seat majority.) The GOP's margin in the House was wafer-thin. State legislatures across the country were similarly divided. But the consensus that these splits were a definition of division may be wrong. These splits may instead indicate virtual agreement among the public and politicians on the way to proceed in the early years of the millennium.

Indeed, Gore and Bush conducted a nine-week general election campaign in which their differences were slender. One expressed more skepticism than the other over the role of American peacekeepers in world troublespots. One was more willing than the other to invest private funds in Social Security. One was more eager than the other to consider vouchers in education. But overall the two men agreed fundamentally—so fundamentally that they provided justification for Ralph Nader, the Green party candidate, to argue, as George C. Wallace had done in 1968, that there wasn't a dime's worth of difference between the nominees of the two parties.

For much of the campaign it almost seemed as if the sitting president, Bill Clinton, was more of an issue than any of the proposals proffered by the men who worked so hard to succeed him. Clinton, a former Arkansas governor, so dominated the American political scene that he might have won a third term had he been eligible to seek one. Clinton was beloved by Democrats for ending the dozen-year Republican reign in the White House even as he was loathed by Republicans as a symbol of the permissive values and easy morals of the 1960s. He was destined to preside over the longest period of prosperity in history—and to be the second president in history to be impeached. He spoke eloquently about the moral imperatives of diversity in the public square—and became an emblem of slack morals in his private life. He was elected as a president determined to attack domestic issues—and may have had his greatest impact in foreign-policy issues.

But Clinton could not run again, and the 2000 election was a test of whether the brand of politics that Clinton symbolized in the 1992 election, when he defeated Bush's father, and in the 1996 election, when he defeated the Republican warhorse Robert J. Dole of Kansas, was a permanent part of American politics or merely a passing phenomenon. Clinton spoke from the left and governed from the right. He offered a "New Democrat" philosophy of personal responsibility and economic growth, allowing him to overcome Democratic opposition in his efforts to overhaul the welfare system and broaden free trade, most notably with the North American Free Trade Agreement.

The two principal candidates in 2000 represented opposite sides of the baby-boom coin. Both were from sturdy political families, both were the sons of formidable political figures whose names they bore. Both, moreover, were educated in prominent private high schools and took undergraduate degrees from Ivy League universities. But there remained substantial differences between the two. Bush had held public office for only six years, Gore for most of his life. Bush was curiously unaffected by the antiwar and civil rights movements that for others decisively colored the tone and timbre of their college years in the mid-sixties; Gore was deeply involved in the debates that rocked his time at Harvard. Bush watched his father work as a pioneer building a Republican party in a state where there was none, Gore watched his father vote as a pioneer in (largely) supporting civil rights and opposing the Vietnam conflict in a southern state, Tennessee, with strong traditions of military service and deference to the soldier.

Gore was a Democrat who leaned to the center. Bush was a Republican who married his conservatism with compassion, and thus created an alchemy and a slogan that would make him acceptable to millions of voters who otherwise might be skeptical of an inexperienced candidate whose principal asset was his family legacy and congenial personality.

In the end, Americans voted for Gore but sent Bush to the White House. They expressed their views strongly only to send a muddied message. They created a situation where a Republican president had to reach out more to moderates within his party than to conservatives, where centrists of both parties, men and women who may not have the trust of their party leaders but who may best understand the mood of the nation they seek to lead, were thrust to the center. They produced a mixed verdict that will be dissected for years, the fitting end to an election that itself will be analyzed for generations.

Overall Trends in Voting Behavior

The national political snapshot that was taken on Election Day showed a nation that was enjoying prosperity, was experiencing peace, was satisfied with its prospects and pleased with the promise of America. It showed a nation optimistic about the new technologies that had fueled the economic boom and eager to integrate those technologies, and the gadgets they animated, into their lives. Indeed, change was a pervasive element in modern American life; the Internet grew in less than a decade's time from a military computer network to a behemoth with 800 million pages. By 1998, 42.1 percent of American households had a personal computer.

Table 13.1   Voting Patterns of Selected Key Political Groups
(percentages)

	Democrats		Republicans	
	1996	2000	1996	2000
White voters	44	42	45	54
Protestants	43	42	47	56
Union families	60	59	29	37

Source: Voter News Service.

And yet politics remained all but impervious to change. There were few dramatic shifts in American political behavior. Indeed, an analysis of American politics in the last several years shows remarkably little change, though there are signs of substantially more volatility among minority voters, especially Hispanics, than among whites. In many demographic categories, however, the Democratic candidate, Gore, performed almost exactly as his predecessor, Clinton, did four years earlier. Much of the difference between Clinton's healthy margin over Dole and Gore's slim margin over Bush can be accounted for by the collapse of the alternative-party movement in politics, or at least in the 2000 campaign. In three major indicators of political performance—the Protestant vote, the labor vote and the white vote—Gore's performance matched Clinton's almost precisely, well within the margin of error. In all three areas, however, Bush substantially outperformed Dole.

These findings suggest that one key to understanding the election of 2000 isn't to examine how or why Gore was unable to take advantage of the apparent Clinton legacy of peace and prosperity but instead to recognize that much of the white, Protestant, and labor support that went to Ross Perot and the Reform Party in 1996 went to Bush in 2000 (see Table 13.1). Overall, about two thirds of Perot's voters in 1996 voted for Bush in 2000.

The election revealed a nation that was about evenly divided in peacetime, with both major parties retaining the allegiance of important voting groups. Gore carried women, blacks, Hispanics, Catholics, Jews, working-class voters, abortion-rights supporters, and gays—none of which is remarkable. Bush carried whites, men, upper-middle-class and wealthy Americans, Protestants, abortion-rights opponents, supporters of across-the-board tax cuts and gun-owners—a classic portrait of Republican party supporters in the years following Ronald W. Reagan's presidency. Despite Gore's effort to portray himself as an apostle of high technology, those who get their news over the Internet split about evenly between the two men. Despite Bush's effort to reach out to minorities, he carried only 9 percent of the black vote.

One additional macro trend in American political behavior is worth noting, however. The willingness of Americans with strongly identifiable ideologies to bounce between the parties is in sharp decline. In 1976, a Democratic presidential candidate, Jimmy Carter, won 29 percent of the vote of those who considered themselves conservative. Since then, there has been a marked decline in Democrats' ability to attract the support of conservatives and a similar decline in Republicans' ability to attract liberals' support. The rate of liberal support for a Republican ticket has dropped by half in the last quarter-century, as shown in Table 13.2.

This may reflect an ideological hardening of the two parties' positions, or the development of bona fide two-party politics in the South, but whatever the cause, it is an intriguing feature of the new landscape. Although scholars and analysts have remarked upon the decline of the parties as intermediary forces and organizations of enduring loyalty, Americans in the twenty-first century are voting as if party matters. But party matters now in a far different way than it did a half century ago. Now party identification is more a signal to voters about the nature of the candidates than a signal to the candidates about the nature of the voters. Voters take party identification seriously and, as the table above indicates, increasingly use candidate party identification as a cue for their own behavior.

Faith-Based Politics

A reliable old chestnut of American life at the middle of the last century was the admonition that neither politics nor religion should be discussed in polite society. That notion has completely disappeared. Now politics and religion are equally contentious issues—and, it is important to note, increasingly intertwined.

Religion has acquired dual importance in modern politics, first as an element of the political debate itself and second as an indicator of political behavior. It is the former that represents the most remarkable departure from the modern tradition. Much of early Colonial politics was faith-based; the politics of the Massachusetts Bay Colony and of Colonial Rhode Island, Pennsylvania, and Maryland can be explained almost solely in religious terms, and some of the appeal and much of the rhetoric of Abraham Lincoln two centuries later was rooted in biblical imagery and allusions, both of which were on full display in Lincoln's second inaugural address.

In more recent times, however, politics has been far more secular. Religion has intruded into the political sphere only four times in the past three quarters of a century, each time as a result of Democratic nomination politics: the nomination of Catholics as presidential candidates in

Table 13.2   Changes in "Cross-over" Ideological Voting Patterns (Percentages)

	1976	1980	1984	1988	1992	1996	2000
Conservatives voting Democratic	29	23	17	19	18	20	17
Liberals voting Republican	26	25	28	18	14	11	13

Sources: Voter News Service; Voter Research & Surveys; The New York Times; CBS News.

1928 (Governor Alfred E. Smith of New York) and 1960 (Senator John F. Kennedy of Massachusetts); of a born-again Christian, Governor Jimmy Carter of Georgia, in 1976; and of a Jew, Senator Joseph I. Lieberman of Connecticut, as the vice-presidential nominee in 2000.

Vice President Gore's selection of Lieberman broke one of the last remaining barriers in American culture; for generations, Jewish mothers have told their sons, and later their daughters, that they could have any job in America save one, the nation's highest political offices. With Gore's midsummer choice, that obstacle was swept away. The course of the campaign itself proved the point. The days following Lieberman's selection were full of commentary about the implications of a Jew on a national ticket, much of it rife with speculation about latent or even overt anti-Semitism. Little surfaced. By mid-September, according to a Wall Street Journal/NBC News survey, there were strong signs that Lieberman's religion hardly mattered to Americans; more than three Americans out of four said that nothing about Lieberman's nomination troubled them, itself a finding of great cultural consequence. When the election finally concluded, no major figure suggested either publicly or privately that Lieberman's religion cost the Democrats the White House.

Not that Lieberman's religion was inconsequential politically. It mattered in two ways, one reflecting the general content of the campaign, the other affecting the outcome of the campaign. Overall, the proportion of Jews who supported the Democratic ticket in 2000 (slightly greater than three fourths) was nearly identical to that in the previous two elections. But Democratic strategists swiftly identified Lieberman's value as a campaigner in some specific Jewish regions. Though California and New York, two states with large Jewish populations, were never seriously contested, Florida was from the start an important battleground. The 628,000 Jews who live in Florida account for more than 4 percent of the state's population, a substantial proportion in the state that ultimately decided the election, and that did so by fewer than a thousand votes. Lieberman's presence made Gore competitive in a state that Republicans, the governor being their nominee's younger brother, had counted safely as their own.

Lieberman spoke openly and proudly of his religion, so much so that leaders of an important Jewish group, the Anti-Defamation League, warned him that while candidates "should feel comfortable explaining their religious convictions to voters," there was "a point at which an emphasis on religion in a political campaign becomes inappropriate and even unsettling in a religiously diverse society such as ours." But Lieberman's rhetoric, which consisted mainly of references to Scripture and common Yiddish idioms, was not out of character with the rest of the campaign.

From the beginning, major 2000 candidates spoke with a fresh forthrightness of their religious faith: Gore spoke of a life dedicated to fulfilling the vision of Jesus Christ and Bush identified Christ as the philosopher who influenced him the most profoundly. This accelerated a trend already in train in American politics that had its faint beginnings in the Carter era and stirred more loudly in the Reagan years and thereafter as religious conservatives moved into mainstream politics and assumed greater roles and influence, especially in Republican circles. Indeed, President Clinton, with a taste for gospel sings and a tendency to adopt the rhetorical rhythms of the pulpit, mixed religion and politics as regularly and as powerfully as any president since Carter or perhaps even William McKinley, often to the immense discomfort and distaste of religious conservatives. In 2000, Democrats were determined not to relinquish what party theorists called the "God issue," and so the nominees of both parties spoke more openly and more often about personal faith than in perhaps any other political year in American history.

This prompted a new debate about the role of religion in politics, a debate that would be fueled early in the Bush administration when the president made his faith-based initiative one of his top White House priorities. The combination of the new spirituality of politics and the infusion of government money into social-welfare programs operated by religious organizations assures that religion will continue to be a prominent factor in American politics in the near future and perhaps longer.

Religious factors have, of course, often been vital indicators of political behavior. In recent history, the voting behavior of both Catholics and religious conservatives have been of special interest and importance. Both groups were critical targets in 2000, and important trends emerged from both groups.

Since 1928 and the nomination of the Irish Catholic from Brooklyn, Al Smith, the modern Democrats have regarded their party as the natural home of Catholic voters. Indeed, in only four presidential elections since mid-century—the George McGovern debacle of 1972, the two Reagan elections in 1980 and 1984, and the three-way race of 1992—have Democrats received less than half the Catholic vote (see Table 13.3). In

Table 13.3   Two-Party Division of the Catholic Vote

Election	Democratic nominee	Democrat	Republican
1952	Stevenson (lost)	56	44
1956	Stevenson (lost)	51	49
1960	Kennedy (won)	78	22
1964	Johnson (won)	76	24
1968	Humphrey (lost)	59	33
1972	McGovern (lost)	48	52
1976	Carter (won)	57	41
1980	Carter (lost)	46	47
1984	Mondale (lost)	39	61
1988	Dukakis (lost)	51	49
1992	Clinton (won)	42	37
1996	Clinton (won)	54	37
2000	Gore (lost)	50	47

Sources: Gallup Organization; Voter Research and Surveys; Voter News Service.

one of those contests, Clinton's 1992 victory, the Democrats prevailed among Catholic voters despite their failure to win a majority. An immutable rule of modern politics is that Democrats might lose a presidential election while taking the Catholic vote but they cannot win one without a plurality of the Catholic vote.

In 2000, Gore just managed to win the Catholic vote, but Catholics' support of him fell roughly halfway between the votes Clinton won in his first campaign and second campaigns. What may be more significant is Bush's ability to attract Catholic voters; 47 percent of Catholics supported him, which nearly matched the 49 percent who supported his father in 1988, a remarkable achievement given the furor about Bush's relations with Catholics in the primary season. When the Ronald Reagan landslide of 1984 is put aside, one element of a winning GOP presidential campaign is clear: Successful Republican candidates in the past two decades have won between 47 and 49 percent of the Catholic vote.

The white evangelical Protestants who have become a major force in Republican politics in recent years accounted for a major part of Bush's support; the figures in Table 13.4 indicate that fully 40 percent of Bush's vote came from this group, as opposed to only 13 percent of Gore's vote—lower than Clinton's in either 1992 or 1996. Overall, Protestants accounted for nearly two thirds of Bush's vote and not quite one half of Gore's. But one other important element emerges from survey research undertaken by the University of Akron: Bush's ability to draw votes from the religiously observant. More observant white Christians accounted for more than half

Table 13.4   Religious Groups' Votes as Percentage of 2000 Presidential
Candidate's Coalitions

	Bush	Gore	Percentage of Total Votes Cast
White Evangelical Protestants			
More Observant	32	61	9
Less Observant	8	7	7
White Mainline Protestants			
More Observant	10	5	7
Less Observant	11	8	10
Black Protestants	1	9	10
Hispanic Protestants	1	3	2
Roman Catholics			
More Observant	12	9	10
Less Observant	8	11	9
Hispanic Catholics	1	3	3
Mormons	3	—[a]	2
Other Christians	1	3	2
Jews	1	5	3
Other Non-Christians	—[a]	2	1
Seculars	11	19	15
	100%	100%	100%

Source: National Survey of Religion and Politics conducted by the University
of Akron Survey Research Center.
[a] Indicates less than 1 percent.

of all Bush's support. A narrower but exceedingly important subset of that
group, religiously observant white evangelical Protestants, favored Bush
over Gore by a ratio of more than five to one, far stronger support than they
gave to Dole only four years earlier. Moreover, 57 percent of more observant Catholics favored Bush as opposed to 43 percent favored Gore, even
though Catholics as a whole sided with Gore (see Table 13.5). Bush won
seven eighths of the Mormon vote, another increase over Dole in 1996.

Regional Politics

Americans customarily spend only Election Night looking at political
maps. In 2000, they spent five weeks looking at them, and the terrain be-

Table 13.5   Religion and Politics: How groups voted (in percent)

	Bush	Gore
White Evangelical Protestants		
More Observant	84	16
Less Observant	55	45
White Mainline Protestants		
More Observant	66	34
Less Observant	57	43
Black Protestants	4	96
Hispanic Protestants	33	67
Roman Catholics		
More Observant	57	43
Less Observant	41	59
Hispanic Catholics	24	76
Mormons	88	12
Other Christians	28	72
Jews	23	77
Other Non-Christians	20	80
Seculars	35	65

(Two-party vote only; minor-party votes excluded.)

Source: National Survey of Religion and Politics conducted by the University
of Akron Survey Research Center.

came familiar: Democratic domination along the coasts, Republican domination in much of the rest of the country (see Table 13.6). In terms of
acreage, the Republicans pulled a landslide in 2000. In terms of population, the verdict was quite different.

The 2000 election confirmed several trends that were well under way
before Bush and Gore entered the lists. With the exception of the first
campaign of the first Deep South president of modern times, Carter's in
1976 and Clinton's second campaign, in 1996, when the region split
evenly, 46 percent to 46 percent, the Republicans have dominated modern
presidential politics in the South. Once the sturdiest Democratic redoubt
in the nation, the South has become dependably Republican.

Gore entered presidential politics in 1988 with the hope of breaking
the GOP lock on the South; four years earlier Reagan had defeated former Vice President Walter F. Mondale of Minnesota by almost two to

Table 13.6   Regional Political Breakdown (in percent)

	1996 Election		2000 Election	
	Republican	*Democrat*	*Republican*	*Democrat*
East	34	55	39	56
Midwest	41	48	49	48
South	46	46	55	43
West	40	48	46	48

Source: Voter News Service, *The New York Times.*

one in the South. But Gore had the bad luck of finally winning his party's presidential nomination in the very year in which the Republicans also nominated a southerner. Gore lost the region with 43 percent of the vote to Bush's 55 percent. He even lost his home state of Tennessee. The Republicans' decisive victory in a contest featuring two southerners suggests that the GOP's position in the region remains strong.

For decades the East was a swing region of the nation. Between 1976 and 1988, the region bounced between the parties, neither Republicans nor Democrats gaining an advantage of more than 7 percentage points. In each case, the candidate who won the region also won the election. But in 1992, the region's political character, at least in presidential elections, began to show signs of dramatic alteration when the region gave Clinton a 12 percent advantage—an advantage that soared to 21 percent four years later. Then, in 2000, a year in which the national popular election was basically a draw, the Democrats emerged from the East with a 17 percent advantage—bigger than the Republicans' margin in the South. The result is the emergence of a potential Democratic base in the East that, though carrying a smaller number of electoral votes, could ultimately rival the Republican base in the South.

Though the great splotches of Republican red in the television maps suggested vast GOP power in the midwestern states, election results suggest Democratic potential in that region. Four years ago the Democrats still won the region easily, even though a classic midwestern candidate, Dole of Kansas, headed of the Republican ticket. One major reason: Midwestern population is concentrated in urban areas, which tend to vote Democratic. This year the two parties virtually split the vote in the Midwest, with the Democrats taking the important states of Illinois, Iowa, Michigan, Minnesota, and Wisconsin.

At the same time, the Democrats continued their domination of the Pacific West, taking Washington, Oregon, and California—accounting for 72 electoral votes, or more than a quarter needed to win the election—for the third election in a row. Gore's 54-to-42 percent victory in California, combined with Gray Davis's decisive victory in the 1998 gubernatorial election, left the Republican party in California in especially dire straits and established the region as one of the cornerstones of political power for the Democratic party as it seeks to rebuild after the peculiar election loss of 2000.

The Hispanic Vote

The statistics are unambiguous: There are 30 million Hispanics in the United States, about the same as the number of blacks. The population of Hispanics is growing faster than the population of African Americans. Hispanics almost certainly will be the largest minority group three elections from now. In addition, the proportion of Hispanics who vote is increasing dramatically.

As a result, Hispanics are emerging as an ever-growing force in American politics. But, as with many groups, there is no monolithic Hispanic vote; Hispanics in the United States trace their roots to nearly two dozen different nations and their attitudes and outlook are shaped not only by the countries they or their ancestors left but also by the states in which they settled. Mexican Americans in the Southwest, Puerto Ricans in the Northeast, and Cubans in the Southeast all have different political attributes and different priorities. In short, Hispanics contribute to American diversity and in addition may themselves be the most diverse group in the country. In the 2000 election Gore won Mexican Americans, Dominican Americans, Puerto Ricans, and Americans of Central and South American ethnicity, whereas Bush won the Cuban-American vote decisively.

Hispanics have enormous political diversity as well; about 16 percent of Hispanics are Republicans; 44 percent, Democrats, and the remaining 40 percent, independent. Hispanics gave enormous support to Dwight D. Eisenhower in his two presidential campaigns in the 1950s, the legacy of Hispanic service in World War II. But, as Table 13.7 indicates, Hispanics have been a reliable part of Democratic presidential coalitions for the

Table 13.7   The Hispanic Vote in Presidential Contests (in percent)

	Democrat	Republican
1976	76	24
1980	59	33
1984	62	37
1988	69	30
1992	61	25
1996	72	21
2000	67	31

Source: Voter News Service, *The New York Times.*

Table 13.8   Presidential Gender Gap (in percent)

	Women	Men	Gender Gap
2000	+11 Gore	−11 Bush	22 points
1996	+16 Clinton	−1 Dole	17 points
1992	+8 Clinton	+3 Clinton	5 points

Source: EMILY's List Women's Monitor, Voter News Service.

past quarter century, roughly the period in which Hispanic political power has been in the ascendancy.

In the 2000 campaign, Bush made important inroads into the Hispanic vote despite Hispanics' enormous resentment of the former Republican governor of California, Pete Wilson, because of his immigration policies. But Bush came to his presidential campaign after six years in the governor's office in Austin, where he won friends among Hispanics for his openness and his policies and where he reached across not only ethnic lines but the Mexican border. That paid off. Bush won somewhere between 38 percent and 49 percent of the Hispanic vote in his reelection campaign in 1998 (the figures are still hotly disputed), but either figure is impressive. In 2000, he took 31 percent of the Hispanic vote, 10 percent more than Dole had won four years earlier. His vote in California, where anti-Republican feelings run highest among Hispanics, was 29 percent, nearly matching his nationwide level. One telling statistic: About 50 percent more Mexican Americans voted for Bush in 2000 than voted for Dan Lundgren, the GOP gubernatorial nominee, two years earlier. In Florida, Bush won 79 percent of the Cuban-American vote, getting 90,000 more Cuban-American votes than Dole. In Texas, Bush won 42 percent of the Hispanic vote.

The Bush experience underlines the potential Republicans have for winning Hispanic votes, an important potential source of support for the party. This is an especially important development because Hispanics tend to vote at a higher rate than other groups of Americans, even though only about half of Hispanics are registered to vote. Moreover, Hispanics are concentrated in important political states. The states with the highest numbers of Hispanics are California, Texas, New York, Florida, and Illinois—vital battlegrounds in any election and, together, states that provide more than half the 270 electoral votes needed to win the White House.

Gender Politics

The gender gap, the tendency of men and women to vote in oftentimes starkly different ways, has become a staple of American politics (see Table

13.8). It has also become a mainstay of American political tactics and strategy. Clinton had remarkable success with the female vote, especially among women with jobs outside the home, who gave him 56 percent of their vote in 1996 (Dole won just 35 percent of this group). This success has become a template for other Democratic politicians. Gore intensified the effort to target female voters in 2000, and it reaped rewards, according to a poll (by Garin-Hart-Yang Strategic Research) done shortly after the election. The survey found that 52 percent of women felt that Gore did a better job in reaching out to women voters and addressing their concerns, whereas only 27 percent felt that Bush was better at this.

But the very closeness of the election underscored the implicit danger of a strategy that revolves around an outsized effort to attract voters of one sex: It runs the risk of alienating voters of the other sex—which is precisely what happened in 2000. In that election, women gave an 11-point bulge to Gore, siding with him by a 54 to 43 percent. But men gave a similar 11-point bulge to Bush, siding with him, 53 percent to 42 percent. (The gender gap is slightly more pronounced among older voters, but it shows itself among younger voters as well. It is also slightly more pronounced in the suburbs than in the nation as a whole.) The 2000 gender gap of 22 percentage points exceeded the 17-point gap of 1996. Gore took a marginal advantage out of the gender gap because more women voted in 2000 than men, but the point stands. Gender-gap politics can be perilous politics.

The Gore-Bush race also illuminated other characteristics of modern politics, specifically the potential for a candidate to win voters' support even if his views diverge from theirs. Gore's support among women

Table 13.9   What Women Want in a Candidate

Reasons women give for voting for Gore	*Percentage who give reason*
Agree with his stand on abortion	29
Delivered the right message to women	9
Agree with his stand on women's issues/rights	8
More caring, more concerned about women	8
Agree with his stand on the issues	8
Reasons women give for voting for Bush	*Percentage who give reason*
Agree with his stand on abortion	20
Came across as more honest, more sincere	9
Agree with his stand on the issues	9
Has morals, ethics	8
Like the way he speaks, his presentation, style	6

Source: Garin-Hart-Yang Strategic Research.

came from voters who believed in his agenda, which included support for abortion rights and an emphasis on women's rights, according to the Garin-Hart-Yang poll (see Table 13.9). Bush's support, by contrast, rested on an affinity for his personality and the values he espoused.

Less attention has been paid in recent years to another important but persistent gap, one between married and unmarried voters. Since 1988, married voters generally have sided with the Republican nominee (Clinton and the elder George Bush were in a virtual tie among those voters in 1992). Unmarried voters have sided enthusiastically with the Democrats, creating margins of more than 20 percentage points in the two Clinton elections. In 2000, Gore's had a 19-point advantage over Bush among unmarried voters. The reasons for these divergences are matters of great speculation: Married voters may care more about economic issues, and when economic issues are at the forefront it tends to work to the Republicans' advantage (though not always, as the Clinton years showed). These voters also often have a more conservative outlook. Unmarried voters include gays, who vote overwhelmingly Democratic, and other voters who have less affinity for the pro-family rhetoric of the Republicans. Whatever the reason, the marriage gap is a Democratic problem with potentially greater significance than the gender gap. In the 2000 election, 65 percent of those who voted were married.

Politics Where You Live

Like the Hispanic vote, the suburban vote has been one of the political elements that commentators and political scientists have been monitoring. As the suburbs have grown, so, too, has their importance as a political staging area, and not surprisingly, candidates have shaped their campaign messages to appeal to suburban voters. In the 2000 election, for example, Gore specifically stressed road congestion and sprawl, issues calculated to appeal to people who moved to the suburbs for improved quality of life, only to find their mobility blocked and their lifestyles compromised by development.

So far, neither party has been able to claim the suburban vote. As Table 13.10 demonstrates, suburban voters are open to the appeals of Democrats and Republicans alike. This was not always the case; in the early days of growth outside the core cities, the suburbs were regarded as safely Republican, largely because of the conservative impulse that sent residents from cities and the racial homogeneity that they found there. Much of that has changed, of course; suburbs today are in many ways more diverse than cities, and as they have become so they have become more open to Democratic presidential candidates. In 2000, Democrats carried most of the states with large proportions of suburban

Table 13.10   Party Winning Suburban Vote in Presidential
Election Years

	Suburban Vote (by percent)	
	Party Winner	Margin
1980	Republican	20
1984	Republican	23
1988	Republican	15
1992	Democrat	2
1996	Democrat	5
2000	Republican	2

Source: Voter News Service, The New York Times, CBS News.

voters, including California and New Jersey, often regarded as the text-book examples of suburban politics.

Indeed, figures assembled by the Congressional Quarterly from state election offices show a dramatic erosion of Republican support in suburban areas. For example, in Orange County, California, the younger Bush ran 12 percentage points behind his father's showing a dozen years earlier. In two heavily populated New York State suburban counties, Nassau and Suffolk, the younger Bush's share of the total vote in 2000 was 19 percentage points less than the share his father won in the 1988 election. That can be explained in part by the younger Bush's decision not to campaign in New York, a state that from the beginning was regarded as a Democratic redoubt, but the numbers in four counties in Pennsylvania, where Bush campaigned heavily, are no more reassuring to the Republicans. Bush won 17 percent fewer votes than his father in Delaware County, southwest of Philadelphia; 16 percent less in Montgomery County, northwest of the city; and 14 percent less in both Chester County, west of Philadelphia, and Bucks County, to the north. Bush lost all those counties but one, Chester—the only one of the four to vote solidly Republican in the last three elections.

At the same time, Bush ran far stronger than Dole in rural districts, even though Dole, who represented Kansas, was closely identified with farmers and food producers, and independent oil explorers and refiners. He got 39 percent more votes than Dole in Tyler County, West Virginia, in the northwest corner of the state hard by the Ohio border; 30 percent more in LaSalle parish in central Louisiana; and 27 percent more in Scott County, Arkansas, on the Oklahoma border. Four years earlier, Clinton won the county by a 20 percent margin.

But the urban vote remained staunchly Democratic, as Gore won Detroit with 94 percent of the vote and Baltimore with 83 percent. In St. Louis, the major population center of the sharply contested state of Missouri, Gore won 77 percent of the vote.

The Senior Vote

Since the Reagan years, the Democrats have played the age card in presidential elections, arguing that the party of Franklin D. Roosevelt and the 1935 Social Security Act was the party that could best assure the safety and future of the old-age income supplement that has become so much a part of retirement planning and political strategizing. Clinton played the age card in both of his campaigns and succeeding in both of them. Gore also played this card, and he did win over 50 percent of the senior vote, which Clinton never did. But in 2000, Bush scored higher among older voters than did either of his Republican predecessors (see Table 13.11).

Bush's success with older voters—he won Arizona and, of course, Florida, two states with large numbers of retirees—freed him to pursue his campaign pledge to overhaul Social Security and to privatize a portion of it. Bush's proposal on the stump, and his success at the ballot box, suggested that traditional views of the older vote and of Social Security may need to be overhauled. In the 2000 election, voters 60 and older accounted for only 22 percent of the vote. Voters between the ages of 45 and 59—those nearing retirement and approaching the Social Security years—accounted for 28 percent of the vote. The passing of the current generation of older people may mark the passing of an era in American politics. But the advent of hard economic times, the retirement vulnerabilities underlined by the Enron scandal of 2002, and the approaching retirement of the largest bulge in population, the Baby Boomers, could prompt a revival of the Social Security politics that has been so much a part of the electoral scene for a generation.

They Also Ran

For a bland election, the 2000 contest sure had some colorful elements. One of them was Ralph Nader, the consumer crusader who ran for president on the Green Party ticket, attracted 2 percent of the vote—and possibly denied Al Gore the White House.

Nader drew most of his support from the pool of Americans most of whom otherwise would have chosen Gore. His supporters were liberal, interested in the environment, skeptical of big corporations, worried about sprawl—all classic Gore positions. If Nader had not appeared on the ballot in a number of states, including Florida, Gore would have won the election. In tiny New Hampshire, which Clinton carried twice, Nader won 22,156 votes—votes that if cast for Gore would have been far more than enough to tip the state away from Bush, who took New Hampshire's four electoral votes. That would have given Gore 270 votes and placed Bush at 267. Similar calculations can be made for other states.

Table 13.11   Percentage of Senior Vote Given to Two Main Parties

The Senior Vote (in percent)		
Election	Democrat	Republican
1952	39	61
1956	39	61
1960	46	54
1964	59	41
1968	41	47
1972	36	64
1976	52	48
1980	41	54
1984	41	59
1988	49	51
1992	44	37
1996	49	43
2000	51	47

Source: Gallup Organization, Voter Research and Surveys, Voter News Service.
Note: In all but the 1992, 1996 and 2000 elections the figures above represent voters age 50 and older. In the last three elections, the figure represent voters 60 and older.

Nader argued that his campaign was designed to give a fuller airing to issues on the left, especially topics regarding corporate responsibility, than Gore was willing to provide. He contended, moreover, that broadening the debate for years to come was more important than determining the outcome of the 2000 election. Some Democrats believe Gore would have prevailed in a two-way race, and there is much evidence to support their conclusions. But Bush and Gore did not compete in a two-way race. It is possible, of course, that in a two-way race, Bush would have adjusted his tactics and campaigned in different states, and would have found a different formula to reach the required 270 electoral votes.

The 2000 election suggested that the Reform party, which under Ross Perot's leadership won no electoral votes in 1992 or 1996 but won 19 percent and 8 percent, respectively, of the popular vote in those two years, may be in eclipse. Its nominating procedure was chaotic and calamitous, and with Patrick J. Buchanan as the nominee the party drew but 448,750 votes, or 0.43 percent—a huge fall-off from Perot's earlier showing. The Buchanan showing was particularly dramatic in New Hampshire, where he won the Republican primary in 1996. In 2000 he finished in fifth place, with 2,603 votes. It is too early to conclude that the Reform party is a spent force—there is still a charismatic Reform party governor in Minnesota—but it is clear that the mainstream reform message it communicated with such success, particularly in 1992, can only be successful if it is aimed at a mainstream audience.

And yet the experience of the last third of a century also suggests that alternative parties remain part of the American political scene. George Wallace in 1968, Representative John B. Anderson of Illinois in 1980, and Ross Perot in 1992 and 1996 all roiled the political waters. Indeed, the Perot experience affirms in modern times the historical evidence that third-party campaigns, such as the Populists' in 1892, often inject ideas into the mainstream that are co-opted by the traditional parties. A more recent example: Governor Clinton did not run in 1992 on a platform of balancing the budget; that was Perot's platform. But President Clinton governed as if balancing the budget was a top priority and, later, when he sought to solidify his legacy as president, trumpeted his success with the budget and the economy as one of the signature accomplishments of his two terms.

Conclusion

The 2000 presidential campaign may be destined to be the dullest affair ever examined with the microscope that historians are likely to use. It captivated almost no one until Election Day, and then for an extraordinary five-week overtime it enthralled virtually everyone. For the next several decades and more, it will remain of interest to scholars and will be studied along with the curious elections of 1800, 1824, and 1876 for new insights and new explanations. In the overtime more than in the general-election campaign the character of the competing candidates emerged, the nature of the political system became clear, and the quirks in the mechanics of elections became disturbingly concrete.

To psephologists there are no dull elections, and buried in the entrails of this one are some intriguing notions: The Hispanic vote is still up for grabs. The suburban vote is still up for grabs. The elderly vote is increasingly up for grabs. Indeed, the future of American politics is still up for grabs. The very closeness of the election underlined not the divisions in the nation but the consensus in the country. It underlined the remarkable prosperity of a nation that, until the advent of the New Economy, worried about its competitiveness and, even with the New Economy showing strains, remained the engine of world productivity and innovation and both the principal breeding ground and principal marketplace for new products and new ideas. It underlined, moreover, the opportunities that this land holds for any party that brings ingenuity and energy to the political problems and diplomatic challenges that—the terrorist attacks of September 11, 2001, remind us—could lie just around the corner.

References

Adamanay, David. 1984. "Political Parties in the 1980s." In Michael J. Malbin, ed., *Money and Politics in the United States.* Chatham, N.J.: Chatham House.

Adams, Sherman. 1961. *Firsthand Report.* New York: Harper & Brothers.

Agranoff, Robert. 1972. "Introduction: The New Style Campaigning." In Robert Agranoff, ed., *The New Style in Election Campaigns.* Boston: Holbrook.

Albany Argus. 1846. November 3.

Aldrich, John H. 2000. "Southern Politics in State and Nation." *Journal of Politics* 62: 643–670.

———. 1995. *Why Parties? The Origin and Transformation of Party Politics in America.* Chicago: University of Chicago Press.

Aldrich, John H., and David Rohde. 1997. "Balance of Power: Republican Party Leadership and the Committee System in the 104th House." Paper prepared for the 1997 Annual Meeting of the Midwest Political Science Association, Chicago.

Alexander, Herbert E. 1984. *Financing Politics.* Washington, D.C.: Congressional Quarterly Press.

———. 1979. *Financing the 1976 Election.* Washington, D.C.: Congressional Quarterly Press.

Alford, John, and David Brady. 1989. "Personal and Partisan Advantage in U.S. Congressional Elections, 1846–1986." In Lawrence C. Dodd and Bruce I. Oppenheimer, eds., *Congress Reconsidered.* 4th ed. Washington, D.C.: Congressional Quarterly Press.

Alford, John, and John Hibbing. 1983. "Incumbency Advantage in Senate Elections." Paper presented at the Annual Meeting of the Midwest Political Science Association, Chicago.

Altschuler, Glenn, and Stuart M. Blumin. 2000. *Rude Republic: Americans and Their Politics in the Nineteenth Century.* Princeton: Princeton University Press.

Anderson, Ed. 1999a. "GOP Chief Vows to Go Through with State's Presidential Caucus." *Times-Picayune,* November 18, 6A.

———. 1999b. "LA GOP Decides to Cancel Early-Bird Caucuses." *Times-Picayne,* December 12, A1.

Andersen, Kristi. 1979. *Creation of a Democratic Majority: 1928–1936.* Chicago: University of Chicago Press.

Ansolabehere, Stephen, and James M. Snyder. 2000. "Soft Money, Hard Money, Strong Parties." *Columbia Law Review* 100: 598–619.

Appleton, Andrew M., and Daniel S. Ward, eds. 1996. *State Party Profiles: A 50-State Guide to Development, Organization, and Resources.* Washington, D.C.: Congressional Quarterly Press.

Ayres, B. Drummond, Jr. 1996. "Reform Party's Split Widens with Its Convention at Hand." *New York Times,* August 10, A1.

Babcock, Charles R. 1996a. "Top 'Soft Money' Contributors to Republican Party Committees." *Washington Post,* August 14, A19.

_____. 1996b. "Top 'Soft Money' Donors to Democratic National Party Committees." *Washington Post,* August 19, A21.

Bach, Stanley, and Steven S. Smith. 1998. *Managing Uncertainty in the House of Representatives.* Washington, D.C.: Brookings Institution.

Baer, Denise, and David Bositis. 1988. *Elite Cadres and Party Coalitions: Representing the Public in Party Politics.* Westport, Conn.: Greenwood Press.

Baker, Donald. 1992. "After Surprise of 1988, Va. Skips Super Tuesday." *Washington Post,* March 8, A22.

Baker, Ross K. 1996. "Perspective on Politics: It's Down to Whopper vs. Big Mac." *Los Angeles Times,* August 27.

Balz, Dan, and Ronald Brownstein. 1996. *Storming the Gates: Protest Politics and the Republican Revival.* Boston: Little, Brown.

Banner, James. 1970. *To the Hartford Convention: The Federalists and the Origins of Party Politics in Massachusetts, 1789–1815.* New York: Knopf.

Banning, Lance. 1978. *The Jeffersonian Persuasion: Evolution of a Party Ideology.* Ithaca: Cornell University Press.

Barrilleaux, Charles J. 1986. "A Dynamic Model of Partisan Competition in American States." *American Journal of Political Science* 30: 822–840.

Barry, John. 1989. *The Ambition and the Power.* New York: Viking Press.

Bass, Harold F., Jr. 1998. "Partisan Rules, 1946–1996." In Byron E. Shafer, ed., *Partisan Approaches to Postwar American Politics.* New York: Chatham House.

Baumer, Donald. 1992. "Senate Democratic Leadership in the 100th Congress." In Ronald Peters and Allen Herzke, eds., *The Atomistic Congress.* Armonk, N.Y.: M. E. Sharpe.

Beck, Paul Allen. 1977. "Partisan Dealignment in the Postwar South." *American Political Science Review* 71: 477.

Benedict, Michael. 1974. *A Compromise of Principle: Congressional Republicans and Reconstruction, 1863–1896.* New York: Norton.

Benson, Lee. 1981. "Discussion." In Patricia Bonomi, ed., *The American Constitutional System Under Strong and Weak Parties.* New York: Praeger.

_____. 1961. *The Concept of Jacksonian Democracy: New York as a Test Case.* Princeton: Princeton University Press.

_____. 1955. *Merchants, Farmers, and Railroads: Railroad Regulation and New York Politics, 1850–1887.* Cambridge: Harvard University Press.

Benson, Lee, Joel H. Silbey, and Phyllis F. Field. 1978. "Toward a Theory of Stability and Change in American Voting Behavior: New York State, 1792–1970 as a Test

Case." In Joel H. Silbey, Allan G. Bogue, and William H. Flanigan, eds., *The History of American Electoral Behavior.* Princeton: Princeton University Press.

Berry, Jeffrey M., and Deborah Schildkraut. 1995. "Citizens Groups, Political Parties, and the Decline of Democrats." Paper presented at the Annual Meeting of the American Political Science Association.

Beth, Richard. 1995. "What We Don't Know About Filibusters." Paper presented at the Western Political Science Association meetings, Portland, Oregon, March 15–18.

Bibby, John F. 1998, 1994, 1990. "State Party Organizations: Coping and Adapting to Candidate-Centered Politics and Nationalization." In L. Sandy Maisel, ed., *The Parties Respond.* 3rd ed. Boulder: Westview Press.

———. 1996. *Politics, Parties, and Elections in America.* 3rd ed. Chicago: Nelson-Hall Publishers.

———. 1981. "Party Renewal in the National Republican Party." In Gerald M. Pomper, ed., *Party Renewal in America: Theory and Practice.* New York: Praeger.

Binder, Sarah, and Steven Smith. 1997. *Politics or Principle? Filibustering in the U.S. Senate.* Washington, D.C.: Brookings Institution.

Black, Earl, and Merle Black. 1987. *Politics and Society in the South.* Cambridge: Harvard University Press.

Blumenfeld, Laura. 1996. "The Life of the Party." *Washington Post,* August 13, B1.

Bogue, Allan. 1980. *The Earnest Men.* Ithaca: Cornell University Press.

Bohmer, David. 1978. "The Maryland Electorate and the Concept of a Party System in the Early National Period." In Joel Silbey, Allan G. Bogue, and William H. Flanigan, eds., *The History of American Electoral Behavior.* Princeton: Princeton University Press.

Bolling, Richard. 1965. *House Out of Order.* New York: Dutton.

Bonafede, Dom. 1987. "The White House Personnel Office from Roosevelt to Reagan." In G. Calvin Mackenzie, ed., *The In and Outers.* Baltimore: Johns Hopkins University Press.

Border, John, and Don Van Natta. 2000. "The 2000 Campaign: The Money, the Perks for Biggest Donors, and Pleas for More Cash." *New York Times,* July 30, A1.

Brady, David W. 1988. *Critical Elections and Congressional Policy Making.* Stanford: Stanford University Press.

———. 1973. *Congressional Voting in a Partisan Era.* Lawrence: University Press of Kansas.

Brady, David W., and Kara Buckley. 1995. "Health Care Reform in the 103rd Congress: A Predictable Failure." *Journal of Health Politics, Policy, and Law* 2: 447.

Brady, David W., and David Epstein. 1997. "Intra-Party Preferences, Heterogeneity, and the Origins of the Modern Congress: Progressive Reformers in the House and Senate, 1890–1920." *Journal of Law, Economics, and Organizations* 13: 26.

Brady, David W., Brian J. Gaines, and Douglas Rivers. 1994. "Incumbency Advantage in the House and Senate: A Comparative Institutional Analysis." Paper delivered at the Annual Meeting of the American Political Science Association, New York.

Brady, David W., and Craig Volden. 1997. *Revolving Gridlock.* Boulder: Westview Press.

Brennan Center for Justice at New York University. 2000. "2000 Presidential Race First in Modern History Where Political Parties Spend More on TV Ads than Candidates." Press release, December 11.

Broder, David. 2000. "GOP Scraps Plan to Alter Primary Schedule." *Washington Post,* July 28, A6.

_____. 1996. "Parties Trade Policy for Sentiment." *Washington Post,* August 28, A1.

_____. 1971. *The Party's Over: The Failure of American Politics.* New York: Harper.

Brookings Institution and Pew Charitable Trusts. Presidential Appointee Initiative (a project of the Brookings Institution funded by the Pew Charitable Trusts). Available online at http://www.appointee.brookings.org.

Brown, Clifford W., Jr., Lynda W. Powell, and Clyde Wilcox. 1996. *Serious Money.* Cambridge: Cambridge University Press.

Bruce, Harold R. 1927. *American Parties and Politics.* New York: Henry Holt.

Bruce, John M., John A. Clark, and John H. Kessel. 1991. "Advocacy Politics in Presidential Parties." *American Political Science Review* 85: 1089–1106.

Burnham, Walter Dean. 1982. *The Current Crisis in American Politics.* New York: Oxford University Press.

_____. 1975. "American Politics in the 1970s: Beyond Party?" In L. Sandy Maisel and Paul M. Sacks, eds., *The Future of Political Parties.* Beverly Hills: Sage.

_____. 1973. *Politics/America: The Cutting Edge of Change.* New York: D. Van Nostrand.

_____. 1970. *Critical Elections and the Mainsprings of American Politics.* New York: Norton.

_____. 1965. The Changing Shape of the American Political Universe. 59 *American Political Science Review* 7.

Burns, James Macgregor. 2000. "Retrospective on the 1950 APSA Report, 'Toward a More Responsible Two-Party System.'" Comments made at the Roundtable discussion at the Annual Meeting of the American Political Science Association, Washington, D.C.

Campbell, Angus, Philip E. Converse, Warren E. Miller, and Donald E. Stokes. 1960. *The American Voter.* New York: John Wiley.

Campbell, Angus, and Warren E. Miller. 1957. "The Motivation Basis of Straight and Split Ticket Voting." *American Political Science Review* 51: 293–312.

Campbell, James E. 1986. "Presidential Coattails and Midterm Losses in State Legislative Elections." *American Political Science Review* 80: 45.

Canon, David T. 1990. *Actors, Amateurs, and Astronauts: Political Amateurs in the United States Congress.* Chicago: University of Chicago Press.

Carmines, Edward G., Steven H. Renten, and James A. Stimson. 1984. "Events and Alignments: The Party Image Link." In Richard G. Niemi and Herbert F. Weisberg, eds., *Controversies in American Voting Behavior.* Washington, D.C.: Congressional Quarterly Press.

Chambers, William N. 1963. *Political Parties in a New Nation: The American Experience, 1776–1809.* New York: Oxford University Press.

Chambers, William N., and Walter Dean Burnham. 1975. *The American Party System: Stages of Political Development.* New York: Oxford University Press.

Cheney, Richard B. 1989. "An Unruly House." *Public Opinion* 11: 41–44.

Chubb, James E. 1988. "Institutions, the Economy, and the Dynamics of State Elections." *American Political Science Review* 82: 118.

Clausen, Aage. 1973. *How Congressmen Decide.* New York: St. Martin's Press.

Clubb, Jerome M., William H. Flanigan, and Nancy H. Zingale. 1980. *Partisan Realignment: Voters, Parties, and Government in American History.* Beverly Hills: Sage.

Cochran, John. 1996. "Declaring their Independence in '96." *Greensboro News & Record,* November 3.

Cohen, Richard E. 1992. *Washington at Work: Back Rooms and Clean Air.* New York: Macmillan.

Coleman, John. 1996. *Party Decline in America: Policy, Politics, and the Fiscal State.* Princeton: Princeton University Press.

Committee for the Study of the American Electorate. 1996. *Use of the Media Principal Reason Campaign Costs Skyrocket.* Report. Washington, D.C.: Committee for the Study of the American Electorate.

Committee for Economic Development. 1999. *Investing in the People's Business: A Business Proposal for Campaign Finance Reform.* New York: Committee for Economic Development.

Committee on Political Parties. 1950. "Toward a More Responsible Two-Party System." *American Political Science Review* 44, Supplement.

Congressional Quarterly. 1996a. *Congressional Quarterly Weekly Report* 54: 3225–3232.

———. 1996b. "The Split Campaign: Special Report: Presidential, Congressional Candidates Plot Separate Courses on Way to 1996 Elections." *Congressional Quarterly Weekly Report,* June 29.

Connelly, Joel, and Rebecca Boren. 1992. "State Primary May Be Lonely Affair." *Seattle Post-Intelligencer,* May 15, A1.

Connelly, William, and John Pitney. 1994. *Congress's Permanent Minority?: Republicans in the U.S. House.* Lanham, Md.: Rowman & Littlefield.

Converse, Philip E. 1976. *The Dynamics of Party Support.* Beverly Hills: Sage.

Converse, Philip E., Aage R. Clausen, and Warren E. Miller. 1965. "Electoral Myth and Reality: The 1964 Election." *American Political Science Review* 59: 321.

Converse, Philip E., and Gregory B. Markus. 1979. "Plus ça Change: The New CPS Election Study Panel." *American Political Science Review* 73: 32.

Conway, M. Margaret. 1983. "Republican Party Nationalization, Campaign Activities, and Their Implications for the Political System." *Publius* 13: 1.

Cook, Rhodes. 2001. *The Rhodes Cook Newsletter.*

———. 1996. "GOP Faces Uncharted Terrain in Wake of Buchanan Upset." *Congressional Quarterly Weekly Report,* February 24.

_____. 1991. *Race for the Presidency: Winning the 1992 Nomination.* Washington, D.C.: Congressional Quarterly, Inc.

_____. 1981. "Chorus of Democratic Voices Urges New Policies, Methods." *Congressional Quarterly Weekly Report*, January 17.

Cooke, Jacob E. 1961. *The Federalist.* New York: Meridian.

Cooper, Joseph. 1975. "Strengthening the Congress: An Organizational Analysis." *Harvard Journal on Legislation* 12: 307.

Cooper, Joseph, and David W. Brady. 1981. "Institutional Context and Leadership Style: The House from Cannon to Rayburn." *American Political Science Review* 75: 411–25.

Corrado, Anthony J. 1997. "Party Soft Money." In Anthony Corrado et al., eds., *Campaign Finance Reform: A Sourcebook*, pp. 165–177. Washington, D.C.: Brookings Institution.

_____. 1993. *Paying for Presidents.* New York: Twentieth Century Fund.

Cotter, Cornelius P., James L. Gibson, John F. Bibby, and Robert J. Huckshorn. 1984. *Party Organizations in American Politics.* New York: Praeger.

Cotter, Cornelius, and Bernard Hennessy. 1964. *Politics Without Power: The National Party Committees.* New York: Atherton.

Cox, Gary, and Matthew McCubbins. 1993. *Legislative Leviathan: Party Government in the House.* Berkeley: University of California Press.

Crotty, William. 1984. *American Parties in Decline.* Boston: Little, Brown.

_____. 1983. *Party Reform.* New York: Longman.

Cutler, Lloyd. 1988. "Some Reflections About Divided Government." *Presidential Studies Quarterly* 17: 490.

Dahl, Robert. 1956. *A Preface to Democratic Theory.* Chicago: University of Chicago Press.

Dao, James. 1998. "A Political Kingmaker Takes No Prisoners." *New York Times*, January 18, A23.

_____. 1996. "Party Liberals Hard at Work in Explaining Welfare Stand." *New York Times*, August 29, B9.

Davidson, Roger H., Walter J. Oleszek, and Thomas Kephart. "One Bill, Many Committees: Multiple Referrals in the U.S. House of Representatives." *Legislative Studies Quarterly* 13: 3–28.

Deckard, Barbara Sinclair. 1976. "Political Upheaval and Congressional Voting." *Journal of Politics* 38: 326.

Dodd, Lawrence C. 1979. "The Expanded Roles of the House Democratic Whip System: The 93rd and 94th Congresses." *Congressional Studies* 7: 27–56.

Dodd, Lawrence C., and Bruce I. Oppenheimer. 1977. *Congress Reconsidered.* New York: Praeger.

Donovan, Beth. "Democrats Expect a Tuneup, Not a Complete Overhaul." *Congressional Quarterly Weekly Report*, December 5.

Downs, Anthony. 1957. *An Economic Theory of Democracy.* New York: Harper & Row.

Dresser, Michael. 1999. "State GOP Approves Open Primary." *Baltimore Sun*, May 23, 1A.

Drew, Elizabeth. 1996. *Showdown: The Struggle Between the Gingrich Congress and the Clinton White House.* New York: Simon & Schuster.

_____. 1983. *Politics and Money: The New Road to Corruption.* New York: Macmillan.

Duverger, Maurice. *1964 Political Parties: Their Organization and Activity in the Modern State.* 3rd ed. New York: Harper & Row.

Dvorak, John A. 1995. "Kansas Presidential Primary at Center of Political Minefield." *Kansas City Star,* April 16, B1.

Dwyre, Diana, and Robin Kolodny. 2002. "Throwing Out the Rule Book: Party Financing in the 2000 Elections." In David B. Magelby, ed., *Financing the 2000 Elections.* Washington, D.C.: Brookings Institution.

Eaton, William. "Key Democrats Back Retiree Tax Hikes." *Los Angeles Times,* February 13.

Edsall, Thomas B. 2001. "Interest Groups Are Suiting Up for Tax Cut Battle," *Washington Post,* March 11, A7.

Edsall, Thomas B., and Dan Balz. 1996. "Straightaway Till November, Then a Fork." *Washington Post,* August 26, A15.

Ehrenhalt, Alan. 2000. "Political Pawns." *Governing,* July, pp. 20–24.

_____. 1991. *The United States of Ambition: Politicians, Power, and the Pursuit of Office.* New York: Times Books.

Ehrenhalt, Alan, and Warren E. Miller. 1957. "The Motivation Basis for Straight and Split Ticket Voting." *American Political Science Review* 51: 293–312.

Ellwood, John W., and James A. Thurber. "The Politics of the Congressional Budget Process Re-examined." In Lawrence C. Dodd and Bruce L. Oppenheimer, eds., *Congress Reconsidered.* 2nd ed. Washington D.C.: Congressional Quarterly Press.

Epstein, Leon D. 1999. "The American Party Primary." In Nelson W. Polsby and Raymond E. Wolfinger, eds., *On Parties: Essays Honoring Austin Ranney,* pp. 43–72. Berkeley: Institute of Governmental Studies Press, University of California, Berkeley.

_____. 1989. "Will American Political Parties Be Privatized?" *Journal of Law and Politics* 5: 239.

_____. 1986. *Political Parties in the American Mold.* Madison: University of Wisconsin Press.

Erikson, Robert. 1972. "The Advantage of Incumbency." *Polity* 3: 395.

Federal Election Commission. 2001. "Party Fundraising Escalates." Press release. Washington, D.C.: Federal Election Commission, January 12.

_____. 1995. "Costs of Advertising to Influence Congressional Legislation Allocated to Both Federal and Nonfederal Funds." Advisory Opinion 1992–1995.

_____. 1978. "Allocation of Costs for Voter Registration." Advisory Opinion 1978–10.

Fenn, Dan H., Jr. 1976. Interview with the author, March 26, in Waltham, Mass.

Fenno, Richard F., Jr. 1978. *Home Style: House Members in Their Own Districts.* Boston: Little, Brown.

_____. 1973. *Congressmen in Committees.* Boston: Little, Brown.

_____. 1965. "The Internal Distribution of Influence: The House." In David B. Truman, ed., *The Congress and America's Future.* Englewood Cliffs, N.J.: Prentice-Hall.

_____. 1959. *The President's Cabinet.* New York: Vintage.

Ferejohn, John A. 1986. "Logrolling in an Institutional Context: A Case Study of Food Stamp Regulation." In Gerald Wright, Leroy Reiselbach, and Lawrence Dodd, eds., *Congress and Policy Change.* New York: Agathon.

Fiorina, Morris P. 1996. *Divided Government.* 2nd ed. Boston: Allyn & Bacon.

_____. 1989. *Congress: Keystone of the Washington Establishment.* New Haven: Yale University Press.

_____. 1981. *Retrospective Voting in American National Elections.* Rev. ed. New Haven: Yale University Press.

_____. 1979. *Retrospective Voting in American National Elections.* New Haven, Conn.: Yale University Press.

Fischer, David Hackett. 1965. *The Revolution of American Conservatism: The Federalist Party in the Era of Jeffersonian Democracy.* New York: Oxford University Press.

Fish, Carl R. 1904. *The Civil Service and Patronage.* Cambridge: Harvard University Press.

Fleisher, Richard, and Jon Bond. 2000. "Partisanship and the President's Quest for Votes on the Floor of Congress." In Jon Bond and Richard Fleisher, eds., *Polarized Politics: Congress and the President in the Partisan Era.* Washington, D.C.: Congressional Quarterly Press.

Foley, Michael. 1980. *The New Senate.* New Haven, Conn.: Yale University Press.

_____. 1981. "Federalists and Republicans: Parties, Yes—System, No." In Paul Kleppner et al., eds., *The Evolution of American Electoral Systems.* Westport, Conn.: Greenwood Press.

_____. 1974. "Deferential-Participant Politics: The Early Republic's Political Culture, 1789–1890." *American Political Science Review* 68: 473.

_____. 1971. *The Birth of Mass Political Parties: Michigan, 1827–1861.* Princeton: Princeton University Press.

Francia, Peter L., Rachel E. Goldberg, John C. Green, Paul S. Herrnson, and Clyde Wilcox. 1999. "Individual Donors in the 1996 Federal Elections." In John C. Green, ed., *Financing the 1996 Election.* Armonk, N.Y.: M. E. Sharpe.

Frantzich, Stephen E. 1989. *Political Parties in the Technological Age.* New York: Longman.

Freedman, Paul and Kenneth Goldstein. 1999. "Measuring Media Exposure and the Effects of Negative Campaign Ads." *American Journal of Political Science* 43: 1189–1208.

Gerstenzang, James. 1996. "GOP Hears Lots of Debate, No Unified Voice." *Los Angeles Times,* August 17.

Gienapp, William. 1987. *The Origins of the Republican Party, 1852–1856.* New York: Oxford University Press.

_____. 1982. "'Politics Seem to Enter into Everything': Political Culture in the North, 1840–1860." In Stephen Maizlish and John Kushma, eds., *Essays on American Antebellum Politics, 1840–1860.* College Station: Texas A & M University Press.

Gierzynski, Anthony. 1992. *Legislative Party Campaign Committees in the American States.* Lexington: University of Kentucky Press.

Gierzynski, Anthony, and David A. Breaux. 1998. "The Financing Role of Parties." In Joel A. Thompson and Gary F. Moncrief, eds., *Campaign Finance in State Legislation Elections,* pp. 188–206. Washington, D.C.: Congressional Quarterly.

Godwin, R. Kenneth. 1988. *One Billion Dollars of Influence: The Direct Marketing of Politics.* Chatham, N.J.: Chatham House.

Goldstein, Kenneth, and Paul Freedman. 1999. "Measuring Media Exposure and the Effects of Negative Campaign Ads." *American Journal of Political Science* 43: 1189–1208.

Goldstein, Kenneth, and Jonathan Krasno. 2000. "The Facts About Television Advertising and the McCain-Feingold Bill." Unpublished manuscript. University of Wisconsin-Madison.

Goodhart, Noah J. 1999. "The New Party Machine: Information Technology in State Political Parties." In John C. Green and David M. Shea, eds., *The State of the Parties: The Changing Role of Contemporary American Parties.* 3rd ed. Lanham, Md.: Rowan & Littlefield.

Goodman, Paul. 1964. *The Democratic-Republicans of Massachusetts.* Cambridge: Harvard University Press.

Goodwin, George. 1970. *The Little Legislature: Committees in Congress.* Amherst, Mass.: University of Massachusetts Press.

Goodwin, Richard N. 1996. "Has Anybody Seen the Democratic Party?" *New York Times,* August 25, 33.

Graber, Doris A. 1989. *Mass Media and American Politics.* Washington, D.C.: Congressional Quarterly Press.

———. 1988. *Processing the News.* New York: Longman.

———. 1984. *The Mass Media and American Politics.* Washington, D.C.: Congressional Quarterly Press.

Green, John C., ed. 1994. *Politics, Professionalism and Power: Modern Party Organization and the Legacy of Ray C. Bliss.* Lanham, Md.: University Press of America.

Green, John C., John S. Jackson, and Nancy L. Clayton. 1999. "Issue Networks and Party Elites in 1996." In John C. Green and Daniel Shea, eds., *The State of Parties: The Changing Role of Contemporary American Parties.* 3rd ed. Lanham, Md.: Rowman & Littlefield.

Hall, Richard L. 1996. *Participation in Congress.* New Haven, Conn.: Yale University Press.

Harrie, Dan. 1999. "GOP Votes for Open Utah Primary." *State Lake Tribune,* June 27, B1.

Hays, Samuel P. 1959. *Conservation and the Gospel of Efficiency: The Progressive Conservation Movement.* Cambridge: Harvard University Press.

———. 1957. *The Response to Industrializationism, 1877–1914.* Chicago: University of Chicago Press.

Heard, Alexander. 1960. *The Costs of Democracy.* Chapel Hill: University of North Carolina Press.

Heclo, Hugh. 1977. *A Government of Strangers*. Washington, D.C.: Brookings Institution.

Henneberger, Melinda. 1996. "As Party's Leader, Dodd Hews the Line but with a Credible Touch." *New York Times*, August 28, A14.

Herrnson, Paul S. 2002. "Political Party and Interest Group Television Advertising in the 2000 Congressional Elections." In Kenneth M. Goldstein, ed., *Television Advertising and American Elections*. Upper Saddle River, N.J.: Prentice-Hall.

_____. 2000. *Congressional Elections: Campaigning at Home and in Washington*. 3rd ed. Washington D.C.: Congressional Quarterly Press.

_____. 1998. "National Party Organizations at the Century's End." In L. Sandy Maisel, ed., *The Parties Respond: Changes in the American Party System* 3rd ed. Boulder: Westview Press.

_____. 1994. "Congress's Other Farm Team: Congressional Staff." *Polity* 27: 135.

_____. 1990. "Resurgent National Party Organizations." In L. Sandy Maisel, ed., *The Parties Respond: Changes in the American Party System*. Boulder: Westview Press.

_____. 1989. "National Party Decision-Making, Strategies, and Resource Distribution in Congressional Elections." *Western Political Quarterly* 42: 301.

_____. 1988. *Party Campaigning in the 1980s*. Cambridge: Harvard University Press.

Herrnson, Paul S., and Diana Dwyre. 1999. "Party Issue Advocacy in Congressional Elections." In John C. Green and Daniel M. Shea, eds., *The State of the Parties*. 3rd ed. Lanham, Md.: Rowman & Littlefield.

Herrnson, Paul S., and David Menefee-Libey. 1990. "The Dynamics of Party Organizational Development," *Midsouth Political Science Journal* 11: 3–30.

_____. 1988. "The Transformation of American Political Parties." Paper presented at the Annual Meeting of the Midwest Political Science Association, Chicago.

Herrnson, Paul S., Kelly D. Patterson, and John J. Pitney, Jr. 1996. "From Ward Heeler to Public Relations Experts: The Parties' Response to Mass Politics." In Stephen C. Craig, ed., *Broken Contract? Changing Relationships Between Americans and their Government*. Boulder: Westview Press.

Hoffman, Kathy Banks. 2000. "Union, Minority Votes Called Key to Democratic Gains in Senate." *Milwaukee Journal Sentinel*. December 3, A8.

_____. 1999. "Michigan Democrats Unsuccessfully Ask to Move Up Presidential Caucus." *Associated Press State & Local Wire*, October 22, AM cycle.

Holt, James. 1967. *Congressional Insurgents and the Party System, 1909–1916*. Cambridge: Harvard University Press.

Holt, Michael. 1999. *The Rise and Fall of the American Whig Party: Jacksonian Politics and the Coming of the Civil War*. New York: Oxford University Press.

_____. 1978. *The Political Crisis of the 1850s*. New York: John Wiley.

_____. 1973. "The Antimasonic and Know Nothing Parties." In Arthur M. Schlesinger, Jr., ed., *History of U.S. Political Parties*. New York: Chelsea House.

Hook, Janet. 1996. "Despite Truce, Deep Divisions Remain in Massachusetts GOP." *Los Angeles Times*, August 16.

Hoover, Dan. 1989. "State's Dems Shifting Role." *Greenville Times*, July 2, 1E.

Howe, Daniel Walker. 1979. *The Political Culture of the American Whigs*. Chicago: University of Chicago Press.

Hrebenar, Ronald J., and Ruth K. Scott. 1988. *Interest Group Politics in America*. 2nd rev. ed. Englewood Cliffs, N.J.: Prentice-Hall.

Huckfeldt, Robert, and John Sprague. 1992. "Political Parties and Electoral Mobilization: Political Structure, Social Structure, and the Party Canvas." *American Political Science Review* 86: 70–86.

Huckshorn, Robert J. 1976. *Party Leadership in the States*. Amherst, Mass.: University of Massachusetts Press.

Hurley, Particia A. "Parties and Coalitions in Congress." In Christopher J. Deering, ed., *Congressional Politics*. Chicago: Dorsey Press.

Jackson, Brooks. 1995. "Maine GOP leaders OK primary Plan." *Bangor Daily News*, September 12.

_____. 1988. *Honest Graft*. New York: Knopf.

Jacobson, Gary C. 2000. *The Politics of Congressional Elections*. 5th ed. New York: Longman.

_____. 1997. "Reversal of Fortune: The Transformation of U.S. House Elections in the 1990's." Paper presented at the Conference on Congressional Elections in the Post-World War Era: Continuity and Change. The Hoover Institution, Stanford University.

_____. 1990. *The Electoral Origins of Divided Government*. Boulder: Westview Press.

_____. 1985. "Party Organization and Distribution of Campaign Resources: Republicans and Democrats in 1982." *Political Science Quarterly* 100: 603.

Jacobson, Gary, and Samuel Kernell. 1983. *Strategy and Choice in Congressional Elections*. 2nd ed. New Haven: Yale University Press.

Jacoby, Mary. 1995. "Waiting in Wings, a Kinder, Gentler Lott?" *Roll Call*, March 9.

Jennings, M. Kent, and Gregory B. Markus. 1984. "Partisan Orientations over the Long Haul: Results from the Three-Wave Political Socialization Panel Study." *American Political Science Review* 78: 1000.

Jennings, M. Kent, and Richard Niemi. 1981. *Generations and Politics*. Princeton: Princeton University Press.

_____. 1974. *The Political Character of Adolescence*. Princeton, N.J.: Princeton University Press.

Jensen, Richard. 1981. "The Last Party System: Decay of Consensus, 1932–1980." In Paul Kleppner, ed., *Evolution of Electoral Systems*. Westport, Conn.: Greenwood Press.

_____. 1978. "Party Coalitions and the Search for Modern Values, 1820–1970." In Seymour Martin Lipset, ed., *Emerging Coalitions in American Politics*. San Francisco: Institute for Contemporary Studies.

_____. 1971. *The Winning of the Midwest: Social and Political Conflict, 1888–1896*. Chicago: University of Chicago Press.

Jewell, Malcom E., and Sarah M. Morehouse. 2001. *Political Parties and Elections in American States*. 4th ed. Washington, D.C.: Congressional Quarterly Press.

Jewell, Malcom E., and David M. Olson. 1978. *American State Political Parties and Elections*. Homewood, IL: Dorsey Press.

Johnson, Haynes, and David Broder. 1996. *The System: The American Way of Politics at the Breaking Point*. Boston: Little, Brown.

Jones, Charles O. 2000. "Presidential Leadership in the Government of Parties: An Unrealized Perspective 50 Years Later." Paper presented at the Annual Meeting of the American Political Science Association, Washington, D.C.

———. 1994. *The Presidency in a Separated System*. Washington D.C.: Brookings Institution.

Kaufman, Herbert. 1965. "The Growth of the Federal Personnel System." In Wallace S. Sayre, ed., *The Federal Government Service*. Englewood Cliffs, N.J.: Prentice-Hall.

Kayden, Xandra, and Eddie Mahe, Jr. 1985. *The Party Goes On*. New York: Basic Books.

Keefe, William J. 1976. *Parties, Politics, and Public Policy in America*. Hinsdale, Ill.: Dryden Press.

Kent, Frank R. 1923. *The Great Game of Politics*. New York: Doubleday.

Kerbel, Matthew Robert. 1994. *Edited for Television: CNN, ABC and the 1992 Presidential Campaign*. Boulder: Westview Press.

Kernell, Samuel, and Gary Cox. 1991. *The Politics of Divided Government*. Boulder: Westview Press.

Key, V. O., Jr. 1966. *The Responsible Electorate*. Cambridge: Harvard University Press.

———. 1964. *Politics, Parties, and Pressure Groups*. 5th ed. New York: Crowell.

———. 1961. *Public Opinion and American Democracy*. New York: Knopf.

———. 1956. *American State Politics: An Introduction*. New York: Knopf.

———. 1952. *Politics, Parties, and Pressure Groups*. 3rd ed. New York: Crowell.

Kimball, David E., and Chris T. Owens. 2000. "Where's the Party? Eliminating One-Punch Voting." Paper presented at the Annual Meeting of the Midwest Political Science Association, Chicago.

King, Anthony. 1978. *The New American Political System*. Washington, D.C.: American Enterprise Institute.

Kleppner, Paul. 1979. *The Third Electoral System, 1853–1892: Parties, Voters and Political Cultures*. Chapel Hill: University of North Carolina Press.

Kleppner, Paul, et al. 1981. *The Evolution of American Electoral Systems*. Westport, Conn.: Greenwood Press.

Kolodny, Robin. 2000. "Electoral Partnerships: Political Consultants and Political Parties." In James A. Thurber and Candice J. Nelson, eds., *Campaign Warriors: Political Consultants in Elections*. Washington D.C.: Brookings Institution.

———. 1998. *Pursuing Majorities: Congressional Campaign Committees in American Politics*. Norman: University of Oklahoma Press.

and Diane Dwyre. 1998. "Party-Orchestrated Activities for Legislative Party Goals: Campaigns for Majorities in the U.S. House of Representatives in the 1990s." *Party Politics* 4: 278.

Koopman, Douglas L. 1996. *Hostile Takeover: The House Republican Party 1980–1995*. Lanham, Md.: Rowman & Littlefield.

Kousser, J. Morgan. 1974. *The Shaping of Southern Politics: Suffrage Restriction and the Establishment of the One-Party South, 1880–1910.* New Haven: Yale University Press.

Krasno, Jonathan, and Kenneth M. Goldstein. 2002. "The Facts About Issue Advertising and the McCain-Feingold Bill." In Kenneth M. Goldstein, ed., *Television Advertising and American Elections.* Upper Saddle River, N.Y.: Prentice-Hall.

Krasno, Jonathan, and Daniel E. Seltz. 2000. *Buying Time: Television Advertising in the 1998 Congressional Elections.* New York: Brennan Center.

Krehbiel, Keith. 1992. "Where's the Party?" *British Journal of Political Science* 23:235.

Kuczynski, Alex, and Matthew Purdy. 2000. "The Props Talk Back: Young Performers Mix Bush's Message with Their Own." *New York Times,* August 4.

Kuttner, Robert. 1996. "President and Party: An Uneasy Relationship." *Washington Post,* August 25.

Ladd, Everett C. 1985. "As the Realignment Turns: A Drama in Many Acts." *Public Opinion* 7: 2.

Ladd, Everett C., with Charles E. Hadley. 1975. *Transformations of the American Party System.* New York: Norton.

Lapinski, Daniel. 1999. "Communicating the Party Record: How Congressional Leaders Transmit Their Messages to the Public." Paper presented at the Annual Meeting of the American Political Science Association, Atlanta, Georgia.

La Raja, Ray, and Elizabeth Jarvis-Shean. 2001. "Assessing the Impact of a Ban on Soft Money: Party Soft Money Spending in the 2000 Elections." Policy Issue Brief sponsored by the Institute of Governmental Studies and the Citizens' Research Foundation at the University of California–Berkeley.

Lardner, George. 2001. "For Black Caucus, Big Stake in Soft Money: PAC's Fundraisers, Creation of Think Tank Bring Questions About Disclosure." *Washington Post,* July 21.

Lawrence, David G. 1996. *The Collapse of the Democratic Presidential Majority: Realignment, Dealignment, and Electoral Change from Franklin Roosevelt to Bill Clinton.* Boulder: Westview Press.

Lineberry, Danny. 1995. "Democrats May Let Unaffiliated Vote in Primary." *Durham Herald-Sun,* September 14, C8.

Louisville Journal. 1852. September 8.

Lowi, Theodore J. 1979. *The End of Liberalism: The Second Republic in the United States.* New York: Norton.

Mackenzie, G. Calvin. 1981. *The Politics of Presidential Appointments.* New York: Free Press.

Magleby, David B. 2001. *Soft Money and Issue Advocacy.* Salt Lake City: Center for the Study of Elections and Democracy, Brigham Young University. Available online at http://www.byu.edu/outsidemoney.

_____. 2000. "Election Advocacy: Soft Money and Issue Advocacy in the 2000 Congressional Elections." Report. Salt Lake City: Center for the Study of Elections and Democracy, Brigham Young University.

_____, ed. 2001. *Financing the 2000 Elections*. Washington D.C.: Brookings Institution.

_____. 1998. *Outside Money: Soft Money and Issue Advocacy in the 1998 Congressional Elections*. Lanham, Md.: Rowman & Littlefield.

Maisel, L. Sandy. 2002. *Parties and Elections in America: The Electoral Process*. 3rd ed., Post-Election Update. Lanham, Md.: Rowman & Littlefield.

_____. 2000. "American Political Parties: Still Central to a Functioning Democracy?" In Jeffrey Cohen, Richard Fleisher, and Paul Kantor, eds., *American Political Parties: Decline or Resurgence?* Washington, D.C.: Congressional Quarterly Press.

Maisel, L. Sandy, Walter J. Stone, and Cherie Maestas. 2000. "Quality Challengers to Congressional Incumbents: Can Better Candidates Be Found?" In Paul S. Herrnson, ed., *Hardball Politics*. Englewood Cliffs, N.J.: Prentice-Hall.

Malbin, Michael J. 1975. "Republicans Prepare Plan to Rebuild Party for 1976." *National Journal*, March 1.

Malbin, Michael J., and Thomas L. Gais. 1998. *The Day After Reform: Sobering Campaign Finance Lessons from the American States*. Albany: Rockefeller Institute Press.

Mann, Dean E. 1965. *The Assistant Secretaries: Problems and Processes of Appointment*. Washington D.C.: Brookings Institution.

Mann, Thomas E. 1978. *Unsafe at Any Margin*. Washington, D.C.: American Enterprise Institute.

Mannies, Jo. 1998. "New Bill Puts Missouri Back in Presidential Primary." *St. Louis Post-Dispatch*, May 18, B4.

Marcus, Ruth. 1996. "Corporate Armada Pipes the Party Brass Aboard." *Washington Post*, August 14.

Marcus, Ruth, and Charles Babcock. 1997. "The System Cracks Under the Weight of Cash." *Washington Post*, February 9.

Martinez, Gebe. 1996. "Gay Republicans Draw the Line." *Los Angeles Times*, August 12.

Matthews, Donald E. 1960. *U.S. Senators and Their World*. New York: Vintage Books.

Mayes, Kris. 1999. "State Helps GOP Run Premium." *Arizona Republic*, July 21, B1.

Mayhew, David R. 1991. *Divided We Govern: Party Control, Lawmaking, and Investigations, 1946–1990*. New Haven: Yale University Press.

_____. 1986. *Placing Parties in American Politics*. Princeton: Princeton University Press.

_____. 1974a. "Congressional Elections: The Case of the Vanishing Marginals." *Polity* 6: 295.

_____. 1974b. *Congress: The Electoral Connection*. New Haven: Yale University Press.

_____. 1966. *Party Loyalty Among Congressmen*. New Haven: Yale University Press.

McConnell, Mitch. 2001. "In Defense of Soft Money." *New York Times*, April 1.

McCormick, Richard L. 1986. *The Party Period and Public Policy: American Politics from the Age of Jackson to the Progressives Era*. New York: Oxford University Press.

_____. 1981. *From Realignment to Reform: Political Change in New York State, 1893–1910*. Ithaca: Cornell University Press.

McCormick, Richard P. 1982. *The Presidential Game: The Origins of American Presidential Politics.* New York: Oxford University Press.

_____. 1967. *The Second American Party System: Party Formation in the Jacksonian Era.* Chapel Hill: University of North Carolina Press.

McGerr, Michael. 1986. *The Decline of Popular Politics.* New York: Oxford University Press.

McSeveney, Samuel T. 1971. *The Politics of Depression: Voting Behavior in the Northeast, 1893–1896.* New York: Oxford University Press.

McWilliams, Wilson Carey. 1981. "Parties as Civic Associations." In Gerald M. Pomper, ed., *Party Renewal in America.* New York: Praeger.

Menefee-Libey, David. 2000. *The Triumph of Campaign-Centered Politics.* Chatham, N.J.: Chatham House.

Mercurio, John, and Rachel Von Dongen. 1999. "Robb, Davis Have a Lot Riding on Off-Year Races." *Roll Call,* November 1.

Merida, Kevin. 1996. "Less Diverse a Party Than It Appears: Controlled Images of Inclusion Don't Tell Republicans Whole Story on Race." *Washington Post,* August 15.

Merl, Jean, and Laura Wides. 2000. "Democrats Strengthen Dominance in House Delegation," *Los Angeles Times,* November 9.

Merriam, Charles E. 1923. *The American Party System.* New York: Macmillan.

Miller, Nichals R. 1986. "Information, Electorates, and Democracy: Some Extensions and Interpretations of the Condorcet Jury Theorem." In Bernard Grofman and Guillermo Owens, eds., *Information Pooling and Group Decision Making.* Greenwich, Conn.: Jai Press.

Miller, Warren E. 1992. "The Puzzle Transformed Explaining Declining Turnout." *Political Behavior:* 1–44.

Miller, Warren E., and M. Kent Jennings. 1986. *Parties in Transition.* New York: Russell Sage.

Miller, Warren E., and J. Merrill Shanks. 1996. *The New American Voter.* Cambridge: Harvard University Press.

_____. 1982. "Policy Directions and Presidential Leadership: Alternative Interpretations of the 1980 Presidential Election." *British Journal of Political Science* 12: 299.

Morehouse, Sarah M. 2000. "State Parties: Independent Partnership." Paper presented at the Annual Meeting of the American Political Science Association, Washington D.C.

Nagourney, Adam, and David Barstow. 2000. "G.O.P.'s Depth Outdid Gore's Team in Florida." *New York Times,* December 12.

Nelson, Michael. 1993. *The Elections of 1992.* Washington, D.C.: Congressional Quarterly Press.

Nie, Norman H., Sidney Verba, and John R. Petrocik. 1979. *The Changing American Voter.* 2nd ed. Cambridge: Harvard University Press.

Nichols, Roy F. 1967. *The Invention of the American Parties.* New York: Macmillan.

Oppenheimer, Bruce. 1985. "Changing Time Constraints on Congress: Historical Perspectives on the Use of Cloture." In Lawrence C. Dodd, and Bruce I. Oppenheimer, eds., *Congress Reconsidered.* 3rd ed. Washington, D.C.: Congressional Quarterly Press.

_____. 1981a. "The Changing Relationship Between House Leadership and the Committee on Rules." In Frank H. Mackaman, ed., *Understanding Congressional Leadership.* Washington D.C.: Congressional Quarterly Press.

_____. 1981b. "Congress and the New Obstructionism: Developing an Energy Program." In Lawrence C. Dodd and Bruce I. Oppenheimer, eds., *Congress Reconsidered.* 2nd Ed. Washington D.C.: Congressional Quarterly Press.

Ornstein, Norman J., Thomas E. Mann, and Michael J. Malbin. 1998. *Vital Statistics on Congress 1997–1998.* Washington D.C.: Congressional Quarterly Press.

Ostrogorski, M. 1964. *Democracy and the Organization of Political Parties.* Volume 2: *The United States.* Garden City, N.Y.: Anchor Books.

Owens, John. 1998. "The Return of Party Government in the U.S. House of Representatives: Central Leadership Committee Relations in the 104th Congress." *British Journal of Political Science* 27, no. 2: April.

Patterson, Samuel C., and Gregory A. Caldeira. 1984. "The Etiology of Partisan Competition." *American Political Science Review* 78: 691.

Peltason, Jack W. 1999. "The Constitutional Law of Parties." In Nelson W. Polsby and Raymond E. Wolfinger, eds., *On Parties: Essays Honoring Austin Ranney.* Berkeley: Institute of Governmental Studies Press, University of California–Berkeley.

Petterson, John. 1996. "Kansas Cancels Its April Primary." *Kansas City Star,* February 10, C1.

Phillips, Frank, and Scot Lehigh. 1995. "Regional '96 Primary Date Eyed." *Boston Globe,* February 14, 1.

Polsby, Nelson W. 1983. *Consequences of Party Reform.* Oxford: Oxford University Press.

Polsby, Nelson W., and Aaron Wildavsky. 1997. *Presidential Elections: Strategies of American Electoral Politics.* 9th ed. Chatham, N.J.: Chatham House.

_____. 1984, 1988, 1992, 1996. *Presidential Elections.* 4th ed. New York: Scribner's.

Pomper, Gerald M. 1996. "Alive! The Political Parties After the 1980–1992 Presidential Elections." In Harvey L. Schantz, ed., *American Presidential Elections: Process, Policy, and Political Change.* Albany: State University of New York Press.

_____. 1993. *The Election of 1992.* Chatham, N.J.: Chatham House.

Poole, Keith, and Howard Rosenthal. 1997. *Congress: A Political-Economic History of Roll Call Voting.* New York: Oxford University Press.

Potter, Trevor. 1997. "Issue Advocacy and Express Advocacy." In Anthony Corrado et al., eds., *Campaign Finance: A Sourcebook.* Washington, D.C.: Brookings Institution.

_____. 1997. "Where Are We Now? The Current State of Campaign Finance Law." In Anthony Corrado et al., eds., *Campaign Finance Reform: A Sourcebook.* Washington, D.C.: Brookings Institution.

Price, David E. 1992. *The Congressional Experience.* Boulder: Westview Press.

———. 1984. *Bringing Back the Parties.* Washington, D.C.: Congressional Quarterly Press.

Quirk, Paul J., and Joseph Hinchcliffe. 1996. "Domestic Policy: The Trials of a Centrist Democrat." In Colin Campbell and Bert A. Rockman, eds., *The Clinton Presidency: First Appraisals.* Chatham, N.J.: Chatham House.

Ranney, Austin. 1983. *Channels of Power.* New York: Basic Books.

———. 1978a. *The Federalization of Presidential Primaries.* Washington, D.C.: American Enterprise Institute.

———. 1978b. "The Political Parties: Reform and Decline." In Anthony King, ed., *The New American Political System.* Washington, D.C.: American Enterprise Institute.

———. 1975. *Curing the Mischiefs of Faction.* Berkeley: University of California Press.

Register of Debates. 1826. United States Congress, 19th Congress, 1st Session.

Reichley, A. James. 1992. *The Life of the Parties: A History of American Political Parties.* New York: Free Press.

Remini, Robert. 1951. *Martin Van Buren and the Making of the Democratic Party.* New York: Columbia University Press.

Republican National Committee. 2000. *2000 Chairman's Report to the Republican National Committee.* Washington, D.C.: Republican National Committee.

Ripley, Randall. 1967. *Party Leaders in the House of Representatives.* Washington D.C.: Brookings Institution.

Roberts, Roxanne. 1996. "The New Whirl Order: Away from the Convention Hall, a Full Plate of Republican Party Politics." *Washington Post,* August 11.

Robinson, Michael J. 1981. "The Media in 1980: Was the Message the Message?" In Austin Ranney, ed., *The American Elections of 1980.* Washington, D.C.: American Enterprise Institute.

Robinson, Michael J., and Margaret A. Sheehan. 1983. *Over the Wire and on TV.* New York: Russell Sage Foundation.

Rohde, David W. 1991. *Parties and Leaders in the Postreform House.* Chicago: University of Chicago Press.

———. 1988. "Variations in Partisanship in the House of Representatives: Southern Democrats, Realignment and Agenda Change." Paper presented at the Annual Meeting of the American Political Science Association, Washington, D.C.

Rohde, David W., Norman Ornstein, and Robert Peabody. 1985. "Political Change and Legislative Norms in the U.S. Senate, 1957–1974." In Glenn Parker, ed., *Studies of Congress.* Washington, D.C.: Congressional Quarterly Press.

Rohde, David W., and Kenneth A. Shepsle. 1987. "Leaders and Followers in the House of Representatives: Reflections on Woodrow Wilson's 'Congressional Government.'" *Congress and the Presidency* 14: 111–133.

Roseboom, Eugene H. 1970. *A History of Presidential Elections.* New York: Macmillan.

Rosenstone, Steven J., and John Mark Hansen. 1993. *Mobilizations, Participation, and Democracy in America.* New York: Macmillan.

Rosenthal, Alan, and Cindy Simon. 1995. "New Party or Campaign Bank Account? Explaining the Rise of State Legislative Campaign Committees." *Legislative Studies Quarterly* 20: 249.

Rusk, Jerrold G. 1970. "The Effect of the Australian Ballot Reform on Split Ticket Voting, 1876–1908." *American Political Science Review* 64: 1120–1238.

Sabato, Larry J. 1988. *The Party's Just Begun: Shaping Political Parties for America's Future.* Glenview, Ill.: Scott, Foresman.

_____. 1981. *The Rise of the Political Consultants: New Ways of Winning Elections.* New York: Basic Books.

Sait, Edward M. 1927. *American Political Parties in America.* New York: Century Company.

Schattschneider, E. E. 1975. *The Semisovereign People: A Realist's View of Democracy in America.* Hinsdale, Ill.: Dryden Press.

_____. 1942. *Party Government.* New York: Holt, Rinehart, and Winston.

Schlesinger, Joseph A. 1992. *Political Parties and the Winning of Office.* Ann Arbor: University of Michigan Press.

_____. 1985. "The New American Party System." *American Political Science Review* 79: 1151.

Sellers, Patrick J. 1999. "Leaders and Followers in the U.S. Senate." Paper delivered at the Conference on Senate Exceptionalism, Vanderbilt University, Nashville.

Shade, William G. 1981. "Political Pluralism and Party Development: The Creation of a Modern Party System, 1815–1852." In Paul Kleppner et al., *Evolution of American Electoral Systems.* Westport, Conn.: Greenwood Press.

Shafer, Byron E., ed. 1996. *Postwar Politics in the G–7: Eras and Orders in Comparative Perspective.* Madison: University of Wisconsin Press.

Shafer, Byron, et al. 1991. *The End of Realignment? Interpreting American Electoral Eras.* Madison: University of Wisconsin Press.

Shalope, Robert. 1972. "Toward a Republican Synthesis: The Emergence of an Understanding of Republicanism in American Historiography." *William and Mary Quarterly* 29: 49.

Shanks, J. Merrill, and Warren E. Miller. 1989. "Alternative Interpretations of the 1988 Elections: Policy Direction, Current Conditions, Presidential Performance, and Candidate Traits." Paper presented at the Annual Meeting of the American Political Science Association, Atlanta.

Shaw, Darron. 1999. "The Effects of TV Ads and Candidate Appearances on Statewide Presidential Votes, 1988–96." *American Political Science Review* 93: 345–361.

Shea, Daniel M. 1995. *Transforming Democracy: Legislative Campaign Committees and Political Parties.* Albany: State University of New York Press.

Shogan, Robert. 1996a. "Dole Is Warned of Abortion Fight." *Los Angeles Times,* August 7.

_____. 1996b. "Cracks Appear in Democrats' Unity Facade." *Los Angeles Times,* August 26.

Silbey, Joel H. 1999. *The American Part Battle: Election Campaign Pamphlets, 1828–1876.* Cambridge: Harvard University Press.

_____. 1991. *The American Political Nation, 1838–1893.* Stanford: Stanford University Press.

_____. 1985. *The Partisan Imperative: The Dynamics of American Politics Before the Civil War.* New York: Oxford University Press.

_____. 1977. *A Respectable Minority: The Democratic Party in the Civil War Era, 1860–1868.* New York: Norton.

_____. 1967. *The Shrine of Party: Congressional Voting Behavior, 1841–1852.* Pittsburgh: University of Pittsburgh Press.

Simon, Dennis M., Charles W. Ostrom, Jr., and Robin F. Marra. 1991. "The President, Referendum Voting, and Subnational Elections in the United States." *American Political Science Review* 85: 1117–1192.

Sinclair, Barbara. 2000a. "Hostile Partners: The President, Congress and Lawmaking in the Partisan 1990's." In Jon Bond and Richard Fleisher, eds., *Polarized Politics: Congress and the President in a Partisan Era.* Washington, D.C.: Congressional Quarterly Press.

_____. 2000b. *Unorthodox Lawmaking.* 2nd ed. Washington, D.C.: Congressional Quarterly Press.

_____. 1999. "The President as a Legislative Leader." In Colin Campbell and Bert A. Rockman, eds. *The Clinton Legacy.* Chatham, N.J.: Chatham House.

_____. 1998. "Leading the Revolution: Innovation and Continuity in Congressional Party Leadership." In Dean McSweeney and John E. Owens, eds., *The Republican Takeover on Capitol Hill.* London: Macmillan.

_____. 1995. *Legislators, Leaders and Lawmaking.* Baltimore: Johns Hopkins University Press.

_____. 1992a. "The Emergence of Strong Leadership in the 1980s House of Representatives." *Journal of Politics* 54: 658–684.

_____. 1992b. "Strong Party Leadership in a Weak Party Era—The Evolution of Party Leadership in the Modern House." In Ronald Peters and Allen Herzke, eds., *The Atomistic Congress.* Armonk, N.Y.: M. E. Sharpe.

_____. 1989. *The Transformation of the U.S. Senate.* Baltimore: Johns Hopkins University Press.

_____. 1983. *Majority Leadership in the U.S. House.* Baltimore: Johns Hopkins University Press.

_____. 1982. *Congressional Realignment.* Austin: University of Texas Press.

Skocpol, Theda. 1996. *Boomerang: Clinton's Health Security Effort and the Turn Against Government in U.S. Politics.* New York: Norton.

Smith, Steven S. 1993. "Forces of Change in Senate Party Leadership and Organization." In Lawrence C. Dodd and Bruce I. Oppenheimer, eds., *Congress Reconsidered.* 5th ed. Washington, D.C.: Congressional Quarterly Press.

Smith, Steven S., and Christopher J. Deering. 1990. *Committees in Congress.* Washington, D.C.: Congressional Quarterly Press.

Sorauf, Frank. 2000. "Money, Power, and Responsibility: The Major Political Parties 50 Years Later." Paper presented at the Annual Meeting of the American Political Science Association, Washington, D.C.

_____. 1998. "Political Parties and the New World of Campaign Finance." In L. Sandy Maisel, ed., *The Parties Respond: Changes in the American Party System*. 3rd ed. Boulder: Westview Press.

_____. 1992. *Inside Campaign Finance: Myths and Realities*. New Haven: Yale University Press.

_____. 1980a. "Political Parties and Political Action Committees: Two Life Cycles." *Arizona Law Review* 22: 445.

_____. 1980b. *Political Parties in the American System*. Glenview and Boston: Scott, Foresman/Little, Brown.

_____. 1964. *Political Parties in the American System*. 4th ed. Glenview and Boston: Scott, Foresman/Little, Brown.

Sorauf, Frank J., with Paul Allen Beck 1988. *Political Parties in the American System*. 6th ed. Glenview and Boston: Scott, Foresman/Little, Brown.

Steen, Jennifer A. 2000. "Money Isn't Everything: Self-Financed Candidates in U.S. House Elections, 1992–1998." Ph.D. dissertation, Department of Political Science, University of California–Berkeley.

Stein, Robert 1990. "Economic Voting for Governors and U.S. Senators: Electoral Consequences of Federalism." *Journal of Politics* 52: 29–53.

Stid, Daniel. 1996. "Transformational Leadership in Congress?" Paper prepared for delivery at the 1996 Annual Meeting of the American Political Science Association, San Francisco.

Stonecash, Jeffrey M. 1988. "Working at the Margins: Campaign Finance and Strategy in New York Assembly Elections." *Legislative Studies Quarterly* 13: 477.

Stonecash, Jeffrey M., and Sara Keith. 1996. "Maintaining a Political Party: Providing and Withdrawing Party Campaign Funds." *Party Politics* 2: 313.

Sundquist, James L. 1992. *Beyond Gridlock: Prospects for Governance in the Clinton Years—and After*. Washington, D.C.: Brookings Institution.

_____. 1988. "Needed: A Political Theory for the New Era of Coalition Government in the United States." *Political Science Quarterly* 103: 613l.

Thompson, Joel A., William Cassie, and Malcolm E. Jewell. 1994. "A Sacred Cow or Just a Lot of Bull? Party and PAC Money in State Legislative Elections." *Political Research Quarterly* 47: 223.

Thornton, J. Mills. 1978. *Politics and Power in a Slave Society, Alabama, 1800–1860*. Baton Rouge: Louisiana State University Press.

Torry, Saundra. 1996. "For Both Political Parties, the Bar Tab Is Generous." *Washington Post*, August 19.

Traugott, Michael. 2001. "The 2000 Michigan Senate Race." In David Magleby, ed., *Election Advocacy: Soft Money and Issue Advocacy*. Provo, Utah: Center for the Study of Elections and Democracy, Brigham Young University.

Twentieth Century Fund. 1996. *Obstacle Course*. New York: Task Force on the Presidential Appointment Process, Twentieth Century Fund.

U.S. Bureau of Labor Statistics. 1998. "Consumer Price Index for All Urban Consumers (CPI-U): U.S. City Average, All Items from 1913–present." Washington, D.C.: US-GPO.

U.S. House of Representatives, Committee on Post Office and Civil Service. 1988. *Policy and Supporting Positions*. Washington, D.C.: Government Printing Office.

U.S. President's Committee on Administrative Management. 1937. *Report of the Committee, with Studies of Administrative Management in the Federal Government*. Washington, D.C.: Government Printing Office.

Van Riper, Paul P. 1958. *History of the United States Civil Service*. New York: Harper & Row.

Waldman, Sidney. "Majority Leadership in the House of Representatives." *Political Science Quarterly* 95: 373–393.

Wallace, Michael. 1973. "Ideologies of Party in the Early Republic." Ph.D. dissertation, Department of Public Law and Government, Columbia University.

_____. 1968. "Changing Concepts of Party in the United States: New York, 1815–1828." *American Historical Review* 74: 453.

Walters, Steven. 2001. "Groups Say Election Set Spending Record." *Milwaukee Journal Sentinel*, February 9, 2b.

Wardlaw, Jack. 1999. "Infighting Damages GOP's Focus in State." *Times-Picayune*, November 14, 6A.

Watson, Harry L. 1981. *Jacksonian Politics and Community Conflict*. Baton Rouge: Louisiana State University Press.

_____. 1996. *The Decline of American Political Parties, 1952–1994*. Cambridge: Harvard University Press.

_____. 1991. *The Candidate-Centered Politics: Presidential Elections of the 1980s*. Cambridge: Harvard University Press.

_____. 1986. *The Decline of American Political Parties, 1952–1984*. Cambridge: Harvard University Press.

Watts, Steven. 1987. *The Republic Reborn: War and the Making of Liberal America, 1790–1820*. Baltimore: Johns Hopkins University Press.

Wayne, Stephen J. 1996. *The Road to the White House, 1996*. New York: St. Martin's Press.

Webster, Benjamin A., Clyde Wilcox, Paul S. Herrnson, Peter L. Francia, John C. Green, and Lynda Powell. 2001. "Competing for Cash: The Individual Financiers of Congressional Elections." In Paul S. Herrnson, ed., *Playing Hardball: Campaigning for the U.S. Congress*. Upper Saddle River, N.J.: Prentice-Hall.

Wekkin, Gary D. 1985. "Political Parties and Intergovernmental Relations in 1984." *Publius* 15: 19.

Weko, Thomas J. 1995. *The Politicizing Presidency: The White House Personnel Office, 1948–1994*. Lawrence, Kans.: University of Kansas Press.

White, Leonard D. 1958. *The Republican Era*. New York: Macmillan.

_____. 1954. *The Jacksonians*. New York: Macmillan.

Wicker, Tom. 1996. "The Party Convention: A Must-See No More." *New York Times*, August 11.

Wiebe, Robert. 1967. *The Search for Order, 1877–1920*. New York: Hill & Wang.

Wielhouwer, Peter W., and Brad Lockerbie. 1994. "Party Contacting and Political Participation, 1952–1990." *American Journal of Political Science* 38: 211–229.

Wilcox, Clyde. 2000. *Onward Christian Soldiers: The Religious Right in American Politics.* Boulder: Westview Press.

Wilkie, Curtis. 1995. "Louisiana, Iowa Scramble to Be First with GOP Caucus." *Boston Globe,* December 5, 19.

Williamson, Chilton. 1960. *American Suffrage: From Property to Democracy, 1760–1860.* Princeton: Princeton University Press.

Willis, Charles F., Jr. 1968. Oral history interview with John T. Mason, Jr., March 15, Columbia University.

Wilson, James Q. 1995. *Political Organizations.* Princeton: Princeton University Press.

_____. 1962. *The Amateur Democrat.* Chicago: University of Chicago Press.

Wilson, Woodrow. 1885. *Congressional Government.* Baltimore: n.p.

Wolfensberger, Don. 1992. "Comparative Data on the U.S. House of Representatives." Compiled by the Republican staff of the Rules Committee, U.S. House of Representatives, November 10.

Woodward, Bob, and Ruth Marcus. 1997. "Papers Show Use of DNC Ads to Help Clinton," *Washington Post,* September 18.

Young, Gary, and Joseph Cooper. 1993. "Multiple Referral and the Transformation of House Decision Making." In Lawrence C. Dodd and Bruce I. Oppenheimer, eds., *Congress Reconsidered.* 5th ed. Washington, D.C.: Congressional Quarterly Press.

About the Editor and Contributors

L. Sandy Maisel is the William R. Kenan, Jr., Professor of Government and chairman of the Department of Government at Colby College. Former president of the New England Political Science Association and former chairman of both the Political Organizations and Parties Section and the Legislative Studies Organized Section of the American Political Science Association, Maisel has studied American politics both as a scholar and as a participant for more than a quarter century. His own unsuccessful campaign for Congress is documented in his important study of primary elections, *From Obscurity to Oblivion*. In addition to being the author of numerous articles, Maisel is the author of one of the leading texts on parties and the electoral process, editor of *Jews in American Politics*, general editor of *Political Parties and Elections in the United States: An Encyclopedia*, and series editor of Westview Press's Dilemmas in American Politics series. With Walter Stone and Cherie Maestas, he is currently at work on a study of the emergence of congressional candidates.

John F. Bibby, professor emeritus of political science at the University of Wisconsin–Milwaukee, is the author of *Politics, Parties, and Elections in America* and *Governing by Consent: An Introduction to American Politics*, and the coauthor of *Party Organizations in America*. He and Sandy Maisel have teamed up to write *Two Parties or More? The American Party System*. Bibby is a recipient of the Samuel J. Eldersveld Lifetime Achievement Award, given by the Political Organizations and Parties Section of the American Political Science Association. He has had substantial practical political experience as the assistant to the chairman of the Republican National Committee, director of the House Republican Conference, director of the 1976 Republican Platform Committee, and state party officer in Wisconsin.

David W. Brady is Bowen H. and Janice Arthur McCoy Professor of Political Science and Business in the Graduate School of Business at Stanford University and is also a professor in the Department of Political Science. He has written and cowritten numerous articles that have appeared in leading political science journals. In 1989 Professor Brady's *Critical Elections and Congressional Policymaking* won the Richard F. Fenno, Jr., Prize for the best book published in the area of legislative studies. His two most recent books are *Revolving Gridlock* and *Continuity and Change in House Elections*.

Kara Z. Buckley is currently an affiliate of the Center for Social Innovation at Stanford University's Graduate School of Business. After receiving her Ph.D. from Stanford University, she was an assistant professor of political science at Middlebury College. Her most recent journal article focuses on the history of careerism in the United States Congress, and her research interests include public policy under unified and divided control of the government.

Bruce E. Cain is the Robson Professor of Political Science and the director of the Institute of Governmental Studies at the University of California–Berkeley. His most recent publication (with coeditor Elizabeth Gerber) is *Voting at the Political Fault Line: California's Experiment with the Blanket Primary* (University of California Press, 2002).

Michael Franz is a Ph.D. candidate in political science at the University of Wisconsin–Madison; his dissertation is on the role of interest groups in campaigns. Other research interests include political parties, interest groups, and television advertising, and he has published articles on race and politics in *Social Science Quarterly*.

Kenneth M. Goldstein is the author of *Interest Groups, Lobbying, and Participation in America*. His research on political advertising, voter turnout, survey methodology, and presidential elections has resulted in contributions to over a dozen book chapters and journal articles. He is currently at work on a book on television advertising.

Paul S. Herrnson is director of the Center for American Politics and Citizenship and professor in the Department of Government and Politics at the University of Maryland. His scholarly articles and books—including *Congressional Elections: Campaigning at Home and in Washington; Playing Hardball: Campaigning for the U.S. Congress;* and *Party Campaigning in the 1980s*—focus on congressional elections, political party institutions, and campaign finance. He also has testified before the U.S. Congress, the Maryland General Assembly, and other government agencies on these subjects and related policy issues.

Mark P. Jones is an associate professor in the Department of Political Science at Michigan State University. His research focuses on the ways electoral laws and other political institutions influence elite and mass political behavior. His recent publications have appeared in the *Journal of Development Economics, Journal of Politics,* and *Comparative Political Studies*.

Matthew Robert Kerbel is professor of political science at Villanova University. A former television newswriter for the Public Broadcasting Service, he is the author of four books and numerous articles on the media and politics, including *Remote and Controlled: Media Politics in a Cynical Age* and *If It Bleeds, It Leads: An Anatomy of Television News*.

Ray La Raja earned his Ph.D. degree in political science from the University of California–Berkeley and now teaches at the University of Massachusetts–

Amherst. La Raja writes about party organizations, elections, and campaign finance.

G. Calvin Mackenzie, the Goldfarb Family Distinguished Professor of American Government at Colby College, served as the director of widely cited projects on presidential appointments for the National Academy of Public Administration and the Twentieth Century Fund. More recently he was senior adviser to the Presidential Appointee Initiative at the Brookings Institution. He is the editor of *Innocent Until Nominated: The Breakdown of the Presidential Appointments Process.* His earlier works on presidential staffing include *The Politics of Presidential Appointments, The In and Outers,* and *Obstacle Course.*

Cherie Maestas is an assistant professor of political science at Texas Tech University. She has published articles and book chapters on political ambition, legislative behavior, and legislative elections, and she is a co-principal investigator on the Candidate Emergence Study.

Warren E. Miller was the preeminent scholar of voting behavior of his generation and was Regents Professor of Political Science at Arizona State University at the time of his death. He devoted a significant portion of his career to leading the Center for Political Studies at the University of Michigan and the National Election Studies projects. The oft-cited works he wrote or coauthored include the seminal study of voting in the United States, *The American Voter,* as well as *Leadership in Change; Without Consent: Mass-Elite Linkages in Presidential Politics; Parties in Transition;* and *The New American Voter.*

Megan Mullin is a doctoral student in the Department of Political Science and a research assistant at the Institute of Governmental Studies at the University of California–Berkeley. Her interests include state and local politics, political participation, and policy design and implementation.

David M. Shribman is assistant managing editor and Washington bureau chief of the *Boston Globe.* A graduate of Dartmouth College and a James Reynolds Scholar at Cambridge University, England, where he did graduate work in history, he covered presidential elections and national politics for the *Buffalo Evening News,* the *Washington Star,* the *New York Times,* and the *Wall Street Journal* before joining the *Globe.* In 1995 Shribman won the Pulitzer Prize for Distinguished Reporting of American Politics and Culture.

Joel H. Silbey is President White Professor of History at Cornell University. One of the nation's leading political historians, he has written and edited numerous articles and books on American politics, including *The American Political Nation, 1838–1893* and *The Partisan Imperative: The Dynamics of American Politics Before the Civil War.*

Barbara Sinclair is Marvin Hoffenberg Professor of American Politics in the Department of Political Science at the University of California–Los Angeles. A former American Political Science Association Congressional Fellow and a frequent participant-observer of the Congress, she served as chair of the Legislative Studies Section of the American Political Science Association from 1993 to 1995 and is one of the leading analysts of the internal functioning of our national legislature. Her recent books include *Unorthodox Lawmaking: New Legislative Processes in the U.S. Congress; Legislators, Leaders and Lawmaking*; and *Transformation of the U.S. Senate*, which won both the Richard F. Fenno, Jr., Prize and the D. B. Hardeman Prize.

Walter J. Stone is professor of political science and department chair at the University of California–Davis. He is a former editor of the *Political Research Quarterly,* author of *Republic at Risk: Self Interest in American Politics,* and coauthor of *Nomination Politics.* He has published articles in political science journals on various aspects of the electoral process and is currently writing a book (with Ronald B. Rapoport) on the impact of the Perot movement on major-party change in U.S. politics. He is also co-principal investigator, with L. Sandy Maisel and Cherie Maestas, on the Candidate Emergence Study.

Index

MIRACLE SEASON!

MIRACLE SEASON!

The inside story
of the 1991 Atlanta Braves'
race for baseball glory

BY I.J. ROSENBERG

AND THE PHOTOGRAPHY STAFF

OF THE ATLANTA JOURNAL-CONSTITUTION

Editor: Robert Mashburn
Book design: Mike Gordon
Cover design: Michael Walsh
Layout: Robert Mashburn
Copy editor: Al Tays
Photo editor: Rich Addicks
Photo printing: M. Chris Hunt
Sports editor: Glenn Hannigan
Production: David Powell, Bill Willoughby, Olin Gordon, Chuck Turlington
and the Composing-Camera Color Staff

Published by Turner Publishing Inc.
One CNN Center
Box 105366
Atlanta, Georgia 30348-5366

Additional copies may be ordered by calling (404) 222-2000

This book was produced on Macintosh IIfx computers
using Quark XPress software and a Scitex color system.

First edition

Manufactured in the United States of America

ISBN: 1-878685-20-1

CONTENTS

ACKNOWLEDGMENT

I am grateful to so many people whose contributions to this book have been great. To Glenn Hannigan, who set the idea in motion. To Chris Jennewein and Andy Merdek, who put the deal together. To Robert Mashburn, one of the nation's premier layout editiors. To Al Tays, my editor whose presence is felt on every page and who, like Mashburn, worked well into the night to get this material out for the holidays. To the photography staff of the Journal-Constitution, whose pictures are breathtaking. To photo editor Rich Addicks, who patiently went through 80,000 frames of film, and to Chris Hunt, who printed more than 200 of them. To Mike Gordon, whose design ideas are always fresh.

I want to offer a special heartfelt thanks to AJC Publisher Jay Smith, Editor Ron Martin and Managing Editor John Walter, whose support has always been there for me.

I must also recognize other writers whose material was extremely helpful: Joe Strauss, Steve Hummer, Mark Bradley, Thomas Stinson, Gary Pomerantz and Jack Wilkinson.

There was encouragement from family, friends and co-workers. To name just a few, Charles and Bunny Rosenberg, Miriam and Marvin Botnick, Mike Tierney, Mike Fish, J.C. Clemons, Scott Peacocke, Jim Smith, Bobby Clay and the entire sports desk of the Journal-Constitution.

I offer a special acknowledgment to Furman Bisher, whose many years of sportswriting have been an inspiration.

Lastly, I want to thank the Atlanta Braves, for a season I, and many thousands of others, will never forget.

I.J.ROSENBERG

DEDICATION

To Beth Ann, for her patience and understanding in a season that lasted 203 games.

FOREWORD

The column is still in my machine. I'd had to write it in case the Braves won the World Series that Saturday night in Minnesota.

"Santa Claus came in October. The tooth fairy left a million bucks under the pillow. It's not fool's gold any more.

"It is real. It is real. The Atlanta Braves have reached the end of the yellow brick road after a long and tedious trip . . ." and on it went, like some raving adult's fairy tale.

There was really no trace of sadness within when it was over. In the grim dimness of Atlanta's sports life, now stretched into decades, we had been blinded by a sudden stunning brilliance that burst upon us. The 1991 Braves were as unexpected as an earthquake at Five Points. There was nothing in their track record even to hint a pennant and a World Series.

I recall, and I'm not sure if it was more because of the ignorance or the arrogance of it, that billboard that sneered, "Atlanta Will Never Be A Baseball Town." Let me tell you that baseball didn't begin in Atlanta with 1991, nor when the Braves arrived, nor when the stadium was built.

To know baseball in Atlanta, you had to have a sense of history. You had to have some pipeline that took you back to a grassy dell beneath the railroad tracks, beneath the shadow of the mighty merchandising building across the street, a major stop on the trackless trolley line on Ponce de Leon Avenue. When someone might ask you, not that they care any more, where were the most pennants won in the minor leagues, you'd have won the blue ribbon if you answered, "Ponce de Leon Park."

The Crackers were once a farm club for these very Braves that have taken their place in the hearts of the South. More than anything else, these Braves have restored Atlanta's baseball image, yea, the baseball image of the South, for they represent more than our mere metropolis. They have turned it into their own private "Tomahawk Nation," with apologies to no one.

This is a story of pride and self-respect, of a city brought together as no other event or thing has ever so moved it. There was not a nay in the territory. When the one great scorer comes to tote up the sum of Atlanta's 1991, the story of the year will be the Braves, and this is the telling of it.

FURMAN BISHER

CHAPTER 1

A NEW BEGINNING

It was a beautiful autumn afternoon as the line of convertibles inched its way through downtown Atlanta. Some 750,000, the largest massing in the city's history, lined the streets. Halloween was still two days away, but many revelers wore headdresses and wielded toy tomahawks, and a haunting Indian chant could be heard on every corner.

Imagine, a parade for the Atlanta Braves.

They had turned baseball on its ear, rising from last place in 1990 to win the '91 National League pennant and take the Minnesota Twins to the 10th inning of the seventh game of the World Series before finally falling.

Theirs was no ordinary sports rags-to-riches tale. "Worst to first" was accurate, but insufficient. Yes, the Braves shared with the Twins the distinction of being the first teams in major league baseball to win a division title or pennant after finishing last the year before. And yes, the 1990 Braves had the worst record in the majors. But Atlanta's legacy of losing went back years; they were no trash in the pan. They had finished last four of the previous five seasons. They were considered one of the worst franchises in any sport. They were a joke.

"If you would have told me I'd be riding through downtown Atlanta in a parade, I would have told you you're nuts."

GREG OLSON

Photo: JOEY IVANSCO

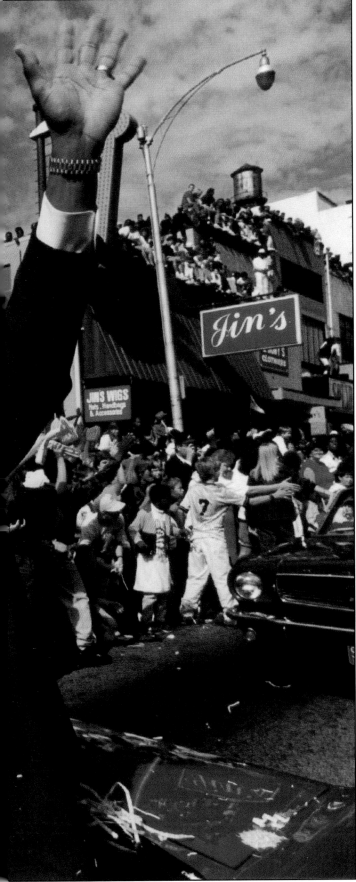

DWIGHT ROSS JR.

JEAN SHIFRIN

An estimated 750,000 chopping, cheering fans swarmed the streets as Terry Pendleton and his teammates rode triumphantly through downtown Atlanta.

Yet here they were, after a fairy-tale season even Grimm might have rejected as too implausible. They had hurled themselves into every abyss they could find, just to see if they could climb out. And sure enough, they could, from a 9½-game deficit to the Dodgers at midseason, from two games behind L.A. with eight to play, from three games-to-two down to Pittsburgh in the NL playoffs.

It was only when they were faced with prosperity, leading the Twins three games to two in the Series, that the Braves finally ran out of miracles. But somehow their final failure only elevated them in their followers' eyes.

And now they were surrounded by hundreds of thousands of worshipers, confetti falling like snowflakes and the crowd sweeping past police lines to surround the cars.

"Imagine if we'd won the Series," said hitting coach Clarence Jones.

It didn't matter. As one of the hundreds of signs lining the streets read: "It's Better to have Chopped and Lost than Never to have Chopped at All!"

Chopped they had. The mimicry of a swinging tomahawk had become the signature rallying cry of an army of fans, and at the games the gesture had become as common as clapping.

Now, as the cars reached their terminus at City Hall, rookie first baseman Brian Hunter looked back wistfully and said, "I wish I could turn around and go through it again."

"There is no feeling in the world like this . . . nothing, no way," said general manager John Schuerholz. "It has to be one of baseball's all-time great stories."

One for which Schuerholz could take credit as author.

A year and 19 days earlier, he had been named general manager of the Braves. A day after quitting the same job with the Kansas City Royals, he had with a straight face told the Atlanta media he intended to turn the Braves into a championship organization. "I've been affiliated with winners all of my life," he said. "I didn't take this job to break that trend."

The reporters had heard this type of talk before. In 1986, new manager Chuck Tanner had promised, "We're going to have a ticker-tape parade in Atlanta." By the time he was fired in 1988, his teams

Crowds flocked to the stadium in record-setting numbers throughout the season, the National League Championship Series and the World Series.

WALTER STRICKLIN

It was only when they were faced with prosperity that the Braves finally ran out of miracles. But somehow their final failure only elevated them in their followers' eyes.

having lost 55 more games than they won, the only parade Tanner could have mustered was one escorting him out of town.

Schuerholz, however, had two things going for him: clothes and credentials.

At 50, he looked much younger. With jet-black hair always perfectly in place, and well-pressed suits often complemented by colorful suspenders, he could have passed for a Wall Street banker. Atlanta Journal-Constitution columnist Steve Hummer described the sartorial Schuerholz as "turned out just right should a board meeting suddenly break out."

Still, the Braves needed more than a sharp-dressed man. What was more impressive was his 23-year record with Kansas City. He promised to rebuild the Braves in the image of the Royals, who had won six American League West titles, two pennants and one World Series and had a gleaming stadium ("Disney World with dugouts," Hummer called it) complete with a huge fountain, appetizing food and good treatment of the customers.

Schuerholz's hiring was a surprise to many. In a quote that would acquire a thick coat of irony a year later when their teams met in the World Series, Twins general manager Andy MacPhail said, "My first reaction, selfishly, would be delight that he's out of our division." Said Braves president Stan Kasten, "Frankly, I'm a little surprised we were able to get someone of this level."

Kasten had begun his search for a full-time general manager in June 1990, when the Braves fired manager Russ Nixon, and then-GM Bobby Cox assumed a dual role. Kasten intended for Cox to hold both jobs only for the rest of the season, and asked him which he preferred to keep. "I told him I like the field better," Cox said.

Despite the success of the Royals, Schuerholz was one of baseball's lowest-paid GMs, with a base salary of $180,000. Kasten's offer — a multi-year contract at more than double that — was enough to make Schuerholz leave Kansas City, though not without at least one regret. He did not wish to be viewed as bailing out on the Royals, whose 1990 record of 75-86 was the second-worst in franchise history. "I really wanted to stay because I believed I could turn that around," he said.

Schuerholz immediately quelled speculation he would bring in his own manager. The decision to keep Cox predated Schuerholz's hiring, but he was comfortable with it. At Kansas City, Schuerholz had eyed Cox as a potential replacement for the beleaguered John Wathan.

While Schuerholz was holding court at Atlanta-Fulton County Stadium, Cox was bedridden at Piedmont Hospital after major knee surgery. The hip-high casts he wore on both legs did not dim his mood. Why should they? The last time he'd been a full-time manager, in 1985, his Toronto Blue Jays had won the American League East.

"Just give me the ballclub," he said. "Once you get the uniform back on, you never want to take it off."

While leaving Cox in place, Schuerholz began bringing in his own front-office staff. He hired his former Kansas City aide Dean Taylor, 39, to be his assistant general manager. Chuck LaMar, 34, was brought from the Pirates to become head of scouting and player development. Bill Lajoie, 56, the former general manager of the Detroit Tigers who had been one of the finalists for the Braves job, became Schuerholz's special assistant.

On Nov. 29, Schuerholz made perhaps his most important addition to the staff when he brought in Ed Mangan from Kansas City. Groundskeepers aren't usually hailed as key figures, but the Atlanta-Fulton County Stadium infield was considered the worst in baseball (the Braves blamed it for much of their defensive ineptitude), and Mangan, 30, was the understudy to the most famous groundskeeper in sports, George Toma. It would be Mangan's job to turn a moonscape playing surface into a field of dreams.

Before Schuerholz could begin bringing new players in, he had to let some old ones go. He ate a $475,000 option on catcher Ernie Whitt, who had hit just .172 after being signed for $1.2 million. He decided not to re-sign third baseman Jim Presley, who had hit 19 home runs but committed a club-high 26 errors. A new infield surface would help the team defensively, Schuerholz reasoned, but a new third baseman would help more.

Schuerholz focused on improving a defense that had made a league-leading 158 errors in 1990. He started at the corners, signing free agents Terry Pendleton (from St. Louis) and Sid Bream (from Pittsburgh) to play third and first, respectively. Then he lured Rafael Belliard, a great-field, no-hit shortstop, away from the Pirates.

Reaction to the moves was mixed. Pendleton and Bream were both 30, both with career averages around .260, and both very good defensively. But the money! Bream got $5.6 million over three years, and that paled against Pendleton's four-year, $10.2 million contract, the biggest in Braves history. And Pendleton was coming off a .230 season, his worst.

"I really don't think they helped themselves with the guy they got," sniffed Presley. But Schuerholz had a feeling, "an instinct," he said, "that Terry would come back strong, real strong."

Schuerholz wasn't through. Lefthander Charlie Leibrandt, whom Schuerholz had traded from the Royals to the Braves after the 1989 season, signed a free-agent contract for a potential total of $11.4 million over four years. Catcher Mike Heath (from the Detroit Tigers) and reliever Juan Berenguer (from the Twins) were the next free agents to join up.

On Jan. 31, Schuerholz persuaded Atlanta Falcons cornerback

DIANNE LAAKSO

"I've been affiliated with winners all of my life. I didn't take this job to break that trend."

JOHN SCHUERHOLZ
GENERAL MANAGER

Deion Sanders, who had been released by the New York Yankees, to accept a minor-league contract. Signing Sanders, who would be available to the Braves until August, when he was due to report to the Falcons, was a risk worth taking, Schuerholz felt. The outfielder had a chance to become the first person to play two pro sports for teams in the same city, and he had loads of potential, including world-class speed. Yet if he didn't make it, Atlanta's $650,000 investment would be a relatively small waste.

But it wasn't Sanders' salary that bothered the skeptics. The seven free agents Schuerholz had signed would earn $9.875 million in 1991; the entire payroll the year before was just $10.8 million. The Braves had a horrendous history of signing the wrong free agents, and Schuerholz's final free-agent signings for Kansas City, pitchers Mark Davis and Storm Davis, had bombed.

Schuerholz was too busy to concern himself with his critics, too busy with his transformation of the franchise.

The club's mascots, Homer the Brave and Rally, were de-emphasized. Comedy character Ernest P. Worrell ("KnowwhatImean, Vern?"), the club's advertising spokesman, was booted. A food court was added in the stadium. Team offices were painted and recarpeted. All male Braves office workers had to wear ties, a change from Cox's open-collar era.

But for all the changes, Schuerholz knew the only significant one would have to come on the field. "Spending more money than anybody else, having more scouts than anybody else, having more minor-league instructors and managers than anybody else doesn't mean a hill of beans," he said. "Having the most focused, having the most disciplined, having the most productive . . . those things matter more to me than having the most."

Come spring training, it would become apparent those were not just empty words.

CHAPTER 2

SPRINGING TO LIFE

Feb. 20, 1991, dawned like any other late-winter day in South Florida — sunny and hot, with a chance of baseball. Spring training was just a day away. Bobby Cox, barefoot in baggy shorts and baseball sleeves, walked into his tiny cinder-block office at Municipal Stadium in West Palm Beach. In one corner was a beat-up bat, in another a pile of statistic sheets. And hanging beside his desk was an Atlanta Braves jersey, "Cox" and "6" on the back.

Cox had not been to spring training as a manager since 1985, but he relished the prospect. He'd had enough of late-night telephone calls for trade talks, enough of contract negotiations. Schuerholz could handle that now. Cox was back to spitting tobacco juice, finding a closer and deciding when to hit and run.

"This is where I want to be," he said. "And I'm not just saying that. Really, I've always been most comfortable with being a manager. Being a general manager was fine, but you can't get the uniform dirty doing that. It's time to get going.

"I'd be lying if I said I wasn't excited. There is no reason to think we can't be a lot better."

JOHNNY CRAWFORD

With all the young players the Braves had, there was plenty for Willie Stargell and the other instructors and coaches to do.

One of the Braves' spring-training priorities was to get the Young Guns — Tom Glavine (on the mound), Steve Avery and John Smoltz — firing again.

JOHNNY CRAWFORD

Cox had turned losers into winners before. In nine years with Toronto and Atlanta, he'd had four winning seasons. And this year, unlike the last one, he could give his full attention to managing.

Over the next several hours, he welcomed the catchers and pitchers as they reported. Most of the faces he knew, but not all.

Heath, the free-agent catcher signed from Detroit, looked in to say hello. He knew Cox from 1977, when they were both with the Yankees organization. "One tough son of a bitch," Cox said admiringly of Heath. "He'll knock your head off if you give him reason to."

Berenguer, the portly reliever sweating profusely after a jog, introduced himself. "Another fiery guy, I've heard," said Cox. "You have to like that. I heard he wants the ball whenever he can get it."

Position players were not due for another five days, so Cox had plenty of time to ponder his club's many questions: Could Berenguer become the closer for a team that had the league's worst bullpen last season? Could Heath take the catcher's job away from last season's Cinderella story, Greg Olson? Could David Justice and Ron Gant be as productive as they had been in 1990? Could first baseman Nick Esasky overcome the vertigo symptoms that threatened a premature end to his career? Who was going to play shortstop?

And perhaps the most important question: Could Cox and Schuerholz work together?

"I'm not going to decide who pinch hits," said Schuerholz. "It's a unique situation — a GM going to manager. It will work."

From the start, Schuerholz made that promise stick. He spent most of his time on the phone in his office, on a cellular model when he was watching games in his seat behind home plate. He was rarely seen in the clubhouse before games. When he met with Cox, it was always after the club's work was done, never interrupting the manager. Occasionally the two would talk in Cox's office late in the day, and Schuerholz frequently shared a beer with Cox and his coaches.

Esasky, who had missed all but nine games of the 1990 season because of vertigo, arrived with his condition not yet cleared up but with doctors' permission to participate fully in workouts. Reporters flocked around his cubicle, and the question, "How are you feeling?" was asked so often it became a standing joke among the players.

Relationships formed. Second-year pitcher Steve Avery was introduced to Sanders, the two destined to become best friends. The most popular items in the clubhouse were Nintendo Gameboys, the handheld computer games ostensibly designed for a far younger market. Several players also had a small black box that would bark obscenities. Reporters were favorite targets of barbs, some good-natured, others, often from Lonnie Smith, not. Tom Glavine placed a Bart Simpson doll above his locker. John Smoltz had his golf clubs in his.

Into this collection of personalities came Justice, the brightest

JOHNNY CRAWFORD

"You put the average person in the street and say 'I want you to sign your name 50 times a day, whenever someone screams at you,' it would get old for them, too."

DAVID JUSTICE, EXPLAINING HIS RELUCTANCE TO SIGN AUTOGRAPHS

light of the dark season of 1990. For his Rookie of the Year season, Justice was rewarded with a $195,000 raise, to $297,000. But he also received a huge amount of publicity, local and national, favorable and unfavorable, and his reaction to this situation became the subject of great debate.

One side said he had changed, that the money and the fame had gone to his head. His critics included some teammates, who asked reporters not to use their names. The two most frequent complaints were that he had started keeping score over who wrote positive things about him and who wrote negative, and that he no longer took time to sign autographs.

Justice defended himself. "You put the average person in the street and say 'I want you to sign your name 50 times a day, whenever someone screams at you,' it would get old for them, too. It does really get old when I sign it for a lot of grownups who are just in it for the investment." About the media, he said, "I just don't like to be misquoted."

Before long, Justice was avoiding autograph seekers by leaving the clubhouse via the back door. It would be a long season for him and the media.

Smith, meanwhile, delighted Cox by showing up weighing 193 pounds, 16 fewer than the previous season, when he became the butt of every fat joke in baseball. "I didn't eat a lot of red meat," he explained, "and I didn't stuff myself on Ding-Dongs."

There were questions about how Smith would relate to Schuerholz, who had released him from the Royals after the 1987 season. The next season, he signed as a free agent with the Braves, and was named Comeback Player of the Year in 1989.

Said Smith, "They didn't treat me fairly in Kansas City, and there are some hard feelings. But everything is cool. You don't see me rocking the boat."

There was little discontent, just the normal fretting by some about job security. Shortstop Jeff Blauser wondered if Belliard's acquisition meant he was going to be traded. Backup second baseman Mark Lemke worried about being sent to the minors.

With all the young players the Braves had, there was plenty for Cox's coaches to do. Pat Corrales and Ned Yost, both former major league catchers, worked with players at that position. Hitting instructor Clarence Jones was a permanent fixture behind the batting cage. But most eyes were on pitching coach Leo Mazzone.

Mazzone, 41, had joined the Braves the previous June, Cox promoting him from the same job in Richmond when Cox replaced Nixon. Under Mazzone, the staff's earned-run average had dropped from 5.25 to 4.58, but even that was the highest figure in the majors. Mazzone's task was to get the Young Guns — primarily Avery, 20,

Glavine, 25, and Smoltz, 23 — firing.

Mazzone focused early on Avery. The lefthander had spent two years in the minors being hailed as the top pitching prospect in baseball, and the previous June, just two years out of high school, he had been placed in the major league rotation. He was not an instant success, going 3-11 with a 5.64 ERA.

"He's going through adversity for the first time in his career," said Mazzone. "I would not think this is the time to jump on him." Smoltz, just three years Avery's senior and a fellow Michigan native, gave him some advice; he was 2-7 when he first came up in 1988. "I told Steve that in the off-season I woke up one morning and realized that I belonged in the majors, and not to worry about what was happening," he said.

While Avery was all business on the field, he had turned into one of the biggest practical jokers off of it. Once he set a reporter's shoelaces on fire. Another time he put shaving cream in a teammate's batting helmet.

The battle to determine who was going to catch was one of the most intriguing of the spring. Both said all the right things to the media, but Olson and Heath were much different in private. Olson was insulted that he was not given the job after being named an All-Star the year before as a 29-year-old rookie, but he had slumped badly in the season's second half.

At 36, Heath had played every position except pitcher in a 13-year major league career that encompassed 1,276 games, all but 65 in the American League. He had many enemies; he never would let his pitchers take abuse.

"There were several times when I got in fights with guys a lot bigger than me," he said. "But that was all right. I wasn't about to take any crap or let them give my pitchers any. I'd go after them."

Schuerholz, meanwhile, was on the phone constantly, trying to trade several players. Blauser's concerns were well-founded; he was on the block. Trade-rumors began to spring up around the Braves. One, published in The National, an all-sports daily, had Oakland A's outfielder Jose Canseco headed for the Braves for Justice, Glavine and a couple of prospects. Schuerholz was furious. "The source that told the National guy that is a liar," he said. "Maybe the reporter ought to seriously consider getting rid of that source."

Kasten, who holds the presidency of both the Braves and the Atlanta Hawks, arrived in West Palm, saying, "I like the way things are going now with the Braves. It's important for the team to see me here, to know that my attentions are with the team."

Not everything was going smoothly, however. Contract negotiations were snagged with Smoltz, the club's best starter the past two seasons. Smoltz wanted a $200,000 raise, to $450,000, but Schuerholz

RICH MAHAN

Most eyes were on pitching coach Leo Mazzone. He focused early on Steve Avery.

was offering only half that. Because he did not yet have three full years in the majors, Smoltz had no bargaining leverage, and Schuerholz exercised his option to assign Smoltz a salary. He settled on $360,000, a raise of $112,500. Upset, Smoltz walked out of camp. He returned two days later, saying, "I just have to get my head straight. I just have to figure this whole thing out so I will be ready for opening day. When I'm on the mound I'll be the same John Smoltz."

At shortstop, Andres Thomas was being given a chance to save his job. Former manager Nixon had labeled him a loser, but Thomas made a promise early in camp: "I've messed some things up, done some things wrong. I've changed. I've matured. I can come back and have a real good season."

The big news early was Sanders. He was hitting, stealing bases. "I've learned more about baseball this spring than ever before," he said. "I'm just listening to everything they say. It's working."

Said Schuerholz, "There are many games and plenty of curveballs to go, but I would have to say that he is playing as well as anybody."

Owner Ted Turner made his first appearance of the spring, escorting Jane Fonda and promising to attend more games during the season. Fonda brought her dog.

A throng of reporters came out to watch a B-squad game, where Esasky was making his first appearance. He singled in his last at-bat, and said, "How about that kind of attention for picking up just one hit?" It would be one of his few bright moments.

Still, it was apparent very early that this team was much improved over the one that had won just 65 games in 1990. Avery, Smoltz and Leibrandt were pitching well. Glavine was having trouble, but he was working on his pitches and not worrying about his ERA. The defense made only nine errors in the first 18 games. The hitting wasn't there yet, but Cox wasn't concerned. That was a common complaint of spring.

Schuerholz briefly considered claiming Bo Jackson, who had been cut by the Royals because of a hip injury. "I've always thought from when this first all started that it wouldn't surprise me to see Bo play again," Schuerholz said of his former player. But Schuerholz did no more than talk to Jackson's doctor.

The final details of the lineup were taking shape. Kent Mercker won the closer's job over Berenguer. And Belliard was moving to the top of the depth chart at shortstop, playing much better than Blauser or Thomas and demonstrating how valuable a good defensive shortstop can be to a pitching staff. Said Smoltz, "He seems to get to everything. He can really get you out of a jam."

Even a negative turned into a positive for the Braves when Lonnie Smith, the starting left fielder, went down with an injury to his left knee. While Smith was packing for Atlanta, Sanders was putting on a

When GM John Schuerholz met with Bobby Cox, it was always after the club's work was done, never interrupting the manager. "I'm not going to decide who pinch hits," said Schuerholz.

JOHNNY CRAWFORD

They were coming home to Atlanta with only one player — second baseman Jeff Treadway — starting in the same position he did in the '90 opener.

show against the Dodgers. With the Braves trailing 4-3 in the bottom of the ninth, he singled home the tying run, took second on the throw to the plate, stole third and scored the winner on a sacrifice fly.

This was enough for Cox. When word came that Smith would have to undergo arthroscopic surgery to repair torn cartilage, Sanders had a spot on the opening day roster. To make room for him, Schuerholz cut outfielder Oddibe McDowell.

Leibrandt was named the opening day starter, Heath his catcher. "I'm not going to pout," said a diplomatic Olson. "I know they brought Mike in for a lot of money. But it's a long season. I'm sure they're going to split it up some."

On April 1, the Braves acquired more outfield help in Montreal's Otis Nixon, giving up catching prospect Jimmy Kremers and a player to be named. Nixon, who had stolen 50 bases in only 231 at-bats in 1990, figured to be primarily a pinch runner and defensive replacement. With the Expos training on the other side of the West Palm complex, he had only a short walk to join his new team. As he crossed the field he said, "Maybe this is a chance for me to do some big things."

Three days later Thomas was cut, ending his stormy relationship with the club in a tearful clubhouse scene.

The next day there would be too much shock for tears as assistant GM John Mullen was found dead of a heart attack in the shower of his West Palm hotel room. Mullen, 66, had been the team's general manager from 1979 to 1985, and had been instrumental in the signing of home run king Hank Aaron.

Mullen's death was especially tough on Cox, who said, "He was a part of us for so long." As a tribute, the Braves would wear Mullen's initials — JWM — on one sleeve.

The final spring game rained out, the team prepared to leave Florida with an exhibition record of 15-12. More important, they were coming home to Atlanta with only one player — second baseman Jeff Treadway — starting in the same position he did in the '90 opener. They were ready to see just how good they were.

CHAPTER 3

PLAY BALL!

T HE BRAVES OPENED THE SEASON WITH THIS MESSAGE to their fans: We are not the bumbling club of old. Others around the league agreed. Cincinnati manager Lou Piniella, who rarely extends a compliment, called the Braves "the most improved team in baseball."

The odds, however, were not with them. The Braves had lost their last three openers, had not had a winning April since 1983 and had gone through 22 straight losing months. Only four National League teams this century had longer losing streaks.

"You can talk all you want, but the whole key is how we start," said Justice. "You can't lose a bunch of games early and then expect to just snap right out of it."

Sanders signed a major league contract a day before the opener for the same money as his minor league deal. "I've got plenty of money," he said. "Playing in Atlanta is the important thing to me."

Everything was new. The field, thanks to Mangan and his crew, looked greener and plusher than it ever had. Sixteen players on the opening day roster hadn't been there at the start of 1990.

The stage was set for a memorable opener against the Dodgers.

The field, thanks to new groundskeeper Ed Mangan and his crew, looked greener and plusher than it ever had.

Otis Nixon carried the base-stealer's little black book, with notes on pitchers' pickoff moves and tendencies. He often added information, but seldom deleted any. Several of the pitchers in the book had long since retired.

Included in the Braves' first sellout crowd since 1987 at Atlanta-Fulton County Stadium was Secretary of Defense Dick Cheney, who was to throw out the first ball. All across America, teams vied for heroes of the Persian Gulf War to ceremonially open their season.

But heavy rains forced postponement of an Atlanta opener for the second straight season. Schuerholz stood in his box shaking his head, saying, "I learned long ago that you can't do anything about the weather."

Because Leibrandt had spent a long time warming up, Cox named Smoltz to start the delayed opener. As the Braves left the stadium that night, pitcher Pete Smith packed for his rehabilitation assignment with Class A Macon.

The one-day delay seemed a bad omen for the Braves. Instead of a sellout, they drew only 18,527. Leaning against the mesh of the batting cage before the game, Sanders was struck on the nose by a foul ball off the bat of pitcher Mark Grant. As every camera on the field focused on the blood pouring from Sanders's nose, it seemed unlikely he would play. But, said Cox later, "I couldn't have scratched him if I would have hit him with a sledgehammer."

This time it was the Dodgers who rained on the Braves, L.A. winning 6-4. Smoltz, who had control problems, took the loss, a portent of things to come. "I was a little nervous," he said, "a little pumped up." On the other side, former Mets outfielder Darryl Strawberry went 2-for-4 with two runs batted in and a run scored in his debut as a Dodger.

Afterward, to a battery of "same old Braves" questions, Bream put the loss in perspective. "Don't read too much into this," he said. "There are still 161 games left."

Twenty-four hours later there were 160 games left, and the Braves were still winless. This time they fell before a familiar tormentor, Ramon Martinez, who beat them 4-2 to run his career record against Atlanta to 6-1 with an 0.87 ERA. Pendleton aggravated an old hamstring injury, something that would bother him for the next month.

The Braves badly needed a victory; they could not afford another start like 1990, when they lost 13 of their first 15. More important, they needed to prove their improvement was no mirage.

"We're grown men and we can handle being 0-2," Cox said as the club headed for Cincinnati and a three-game series with the World Series champion Reds. "We just need to start hitting."

After another rainout, the Braves sent Avery, one day shy of his 21st birthday, out in search of some momentum. Exactly 10 months earlier, he had made his major league debut in this same Riverfront Stadium, but it was not one of his cherished memories. "I was in the dugout in the third inning," he recalled.

Different year, different story. Avery lasted five innings, allowing

FRANK NIEMEIR

"They say I can't hit, but I showed them I'm more than a fielder, more than just a glove."

RAFAEL BELLIARD,
AFTER DRIVING IN 5 RUNS
AGAINST THE CARDINALS

Bobby Cox's philosophy of giving everyone a chance to play was paying off. Said Ron Gant, "It's going to make everyone feel great when we walk out on the field tomorrow."

two runs, and the Braves turned a 6-0 lead into a 7-5 win. It wasn't pretty, but it counted. "It felt good because I didn't get rattled," Avery said. "That was a big step for Steve," Cox assessed.

Bream and Pendleton homered as the Braves finally started to hit. They were running, too, with Nixon and Sanders combining for four steals in three games. Not an overwhelming statistic, certainly, but without either player, the leadfoot 1990 Braves didn't steal their first base until their fifth game. Berenguer picked up the save despite allowing two runs in three innings.

The next day, the Braves won 12-1 and were at .500 for the first time since they split a doubleheader on opening day 1990. Glavine allowed one run in six innings as Cox shuffled his lineup, giving five players their first starts. Among them, Olson had three hits, Lemke two and Blauser one. Nixon had two hits, two stolen bases and two RBIs. The Braves had 16 hits, 25 for the two games, after getting only 12 in two outings against the Dodgers.

Cox's philosophy of giving everyone a chance to play was paying off. Said Gant as the team prepared to return to Atlanta for a six-game homestand, "I've been saying all spring we have the best depth in the National League. It's going to make everybody feel great when we walk out on the field tomorrow."

But only 6,729 showed up on a Monday night for the series opener against Houston, the smallest crowd of the season. First baseman Jeff Bagwell, destined to succeed Justice as NL rookie of the year, hit his first major league home run, a two-run shot off Mercker in the ninth that sealed a 3-1 Astros victory. Mercker was slowly losing his grip on the closer's job.

The Braves split the next two games against Houston, Pendleton coming off the bench the next night, sore hamstring and all, to rescue Atlanta with a three-run double in the eighth. That game, a 10-4 Atlanta win, also included a triple play by the Astros, who also had accomplished the rare feat against the Braves late in 1990.

After a 4-3 loss to the Astros closed the series, the Braves optioned pitcher Paul Marak to Richmond, calling up journeyman catcher Jerry Willard because Olson had a badly bruised hand. In a closed-door meeting with Cox, Marak, the No. 5 starter who hadn't pitched because of rainouts, broke into tears. Disconsolately leaning against his locker afterward, the 25-year-old righthander was barely able to answer questions. He didn't know it, but he would not be back. In Richmond, he began to be rocked regularly by Class AAA hitters.

Two more losses to the Reds preceded a 5-3 win that closed the homestand. After the victory, with his team two games under .500, Cox appeared unusually relieved in his office. His uniform untucked, he said, "I don't usually say this about games this early, but this was a big one."

FRANK NIEMEIR

NICK ARROYO

JONATHAN NEWTON

An opening night sellout was rained out. The Braves lost another sellout to rain later in the season. "I learned long ago that you can't do anything about the weather," said John Schuerholz.

The last place the Braves needed to go now was Dodger Stadium, where they had only a .365 winning percentage over the last 10 years. But Avery wasn't part of that era, and so far, he owned the Dodgers. His 7-1 victory hiked his career record against L.A. to 3-0. "Tonight," he said, "I felt as good as I ever have on the mound." The only thing that came between him and a complete game was a blister that formed on the index finger of his throwing hand and forced him out of the game in the seventh inning.

The Braves also ran into a little gamesmanship from L.A., something few teams had bothered to resort to against Atlanta in a long while. The Dodgers, who had howled in the early '60s when the San Francisco Giants used to do the same thing to L.A.'s premier base-stealer, Maury Wills, softened up the dirt around first base, hoping to slow down the Braves, who had 16 steals in their first 10 games.

"It's an old trick," said Cox, but Sanders, Nixon and Gant, the three primary targets of the tactic, couldn't believe it. Said Sanders, "It's like swimming in quicksand. You can't go nowhere."

They didn't need to, as it turned out. Glavine beat the Dodgers 4-0 for his first shutout since 1989, also against the Dodgers in L.A. "Let's hope this is the beginning of something with this team," said Gant.

The quest to get back to .500 failed in the series finale, as Vienna, Ga., native Kal Daniels had six RBIs, including a grand slam, in an 8-4 L.A. win. Smoltz was the victim, his third loss in three starts.

The winning record finally came in the unlikeliest of places — Houston — as the Braves broke their Astrodome curse, which Cox called "one of the weirdest things I've seen in all my years of baseball," by taking two of three from the Astros. After losing all nine games in Hosuton in 1990, the Braves captured the opener 7-2. The next night it took 13 innings, but a 2-1 Atlanta win left the Braves at 8-7, their first time with more wins than losses since April 23, 1989. It didn't come easy. The Braves had to tie it in the ninth on a two-out walk to Sanders and a Treadway triple, and win it in the 13th on a walk to pinch hitter Glavine and a single by Francisco Cabrera.

Even a 2-0 loss the next day didn't dampen the Braves' spirits. Said Sanders, "I know what people are saying: "Well, the Braves finally got a winning record and they go out and blow it the next day. But that's not the case at all. As long as we keep winning two of three from people, we might play until November. We are for real."

His left knee healed after arthroscopic surgery, Lonnie Smith was activated. But the Braves lost three in St. Louis. Reliever Mike Stanton, who made crucial mistakes in the first two games, walked the three blocks back to the hotel from the clubhouse. The second loss gave the Braves a record of 8-10 in April, 23 consecutive months of losing.

A three-game series with the Cubs at Atlanta produced two wins,

Greg Olson moved into the starting lineup when Mike Heath cut the middle finger on his throwing hand after punching a metal first aid box in anger after striking out.

FRANK NIEMEIR

MIRACLE SEASON!

including Smoltz's first of the season after three losses.

The first win left the Braves 10-10, only a half-game behind first-place Cincinnati and San Diego. It was the closest the Braves had been to a division lead this late in a season since 1983.

They were running wild, with 29 stolen bases, including 11 by Nixon. "This team is able to intimidate with its speed," said Pendleton. "I've never known speed to slump," said Schuerholz.

Nixon, 32, carried the base-stealer's little black book, with notes on pitchers' pickoff moves and tendencies. He often added information, but seldom deleted any. Several of the pitchers in the book had long since retired. Daily, he shared his information with Sanders.

In a 9-2 beating of St. Louis a few nights later, Belliard drove in a career-high five runs with three hits, including two doubles. "They say I can't hit," he said, "but I showed them I'm more than a fielder, more than just a glove." During the game, the wife of Cardinals manager Joe Torre was hit on the head by a foul ball off the bat of Heath and required stitches. The next day Alice Torre was presented a Cardinals batting helmet with a bull's-eye painted on it. Heath sent her flowers.

The next night, when Gant smacked a ball off the "Hank Aaron 715" sign in left for a first-inning home run in a 17-1 romp, Cox felt something special in the dugout. "The whole team perked up when they watched the ball go over," he said. "It was like Ron is back and now we should really get going." Said Gant, who had been avoiding the media for a week, "I didn't want to come back into the lineup until I was ready. Now I'm there for good."

The victory margin tied for the Braves' biggest since 1966, their first season in Atlanta. Belliard had two more doubles and three RBIs, eclipsing in two nights his RBI total (six) of the previous season.

Before the game, Turner made a surprise visit to the clubhouse, "Hey, guys," he said, "nice going. A real baseball team. I was sick of losing. Ya'll don't know what it's like, because you're new ... and good. We'll be playing in October."

Esasky, still trying to overcome his problems with vertigo, came down with a new problem, an eye condition. All his on-field work was called off.

When Philadelphia beat San Diego the next night, the Braves took over first place on a day off, a spot they hadn't occupied this late since 1984. With a 13-11 record, Atlanta led 15-13 San Diego by six percentage points. Upon hearing the news from the West Coast, Gant said, "This is what we've been working for, and I think the rest of the league now realizes we're a good team." He also had a message for Atlantans. "For the last three or four years this city hasn't really been excited about us. That's all changed now."

The Braves flew into Pittsburgh primed for a showdown with the NL East-leading Pirates, but lost 5-2 as Smoltz again had problems.

FRANK NIEMEIR

Sid Bream's seventh-inning grand slam sparked a 9-3 victory over Pittsburgh before a raucous crowd of 32,848. "I've been here awhile now and I've never heard the crowd so loud," said Jeff Treadway.

The only Atlanta highlight was a ninth-inning pinch-hit homer by Bream, who received a standing ovation from the fans of his former club. "It was tremendous," he said, tears in his eyes. "I knew it would really affect me and it did."

Perhaps it inspired the team. The next night the Braves were down 2-1 in the eighth, with Lonnie Smith on base and Gant, hitless in his last nine at-bats, at the plate. "I was thinking don't get down, just try to get the bat on the ball," Gant said. But he did more than that, sending a Doug Drabek pitch into the seats in left for a 3-2 win.

When the Braves won the finale 6-1 behind Avery, whose four victories were already one more than his 1990 total, Pirates outfielder Bobby Bonilla said, "You can see the sparkle in their eyes. They are tired of losing and hungry to win."

In Chicago, pennant fever took a temporary back seat to celebrity-watching. Former Sports Illustrated swimsuit model Carol Alt was on the field for pre-game warmups, and Olson told her it would be best for the team if she sat as far from the field as possible, so the players could keep their minds on the game. But a media madhouse was going on in the broadcast booth, where the Caray family — Harry, 71, Skip, 56, and Chip, 26 — was making history. It was the first time three generations of a family had called the same major league game. Said WGN's Harry of his son, a TBS broadcaster like his grandson, "If I would have known the mess it created, I would never have had him."

The six-game road trip ended with a split, figuratively and literally. The Braves won three and lost three, and in the final game Heath cut the middle finger of his throwing hand after punching a metal first aid box in anger over striking out. Olson would take over the position for a while.

A raucous crowd of 32,824 greeted the Braves in their first game home, a 9-3 pounding of the Pirates. Bream belted a grand slam in the seventh to ignite the crowd. "I've been here awhile now and I've never heard the crowd so loud," said Treadway.

After a 7-2 loss to the Padres on May 22, Sanders was demoted. Sitting in the clubhouse, he asked a local reporter if he was headed for Richmond. When told yes, Sanders replied, "God, I hate that place."

In the next day's paper, though, the top story wasn't the Braves' loss or even Sanders's demotion. It was his arrest.

After leaving the ballpark, Sanders had stopped at a Gwinnett County supermarket to buy thank-you notes for his teammates. He left his black Corvette parked in a fire lane. An officer, who had pulled him over a week before and told him he needed to change his Florida license and tag, recognized the car. A confrontation ensued, ending with Sanders being handcuffed and driven off to jail, charged with disorderly conduct.

After being released, Sanders called a local reporter. "I did nothing wrong, no way," he said. Police maintained that Sanders had been abusive. The next afternoon Sanders held an impromptu press conference outside the stadium to proclaim his innocence, then went into the clubhouse and laid out the thank-you notes in each locker.

To Cabrera he wrote: "Thank you for speaking English so well." To Pete Smith, who was called up to take Sanders's spot on the roster: "Thank you for sending me to Richmond."

The Braves lost three of their next four to the Padres and Giants, finishing the homestand 4-5. But again, they found redemption on the road, sweeping three from San Diego and winning two in a row over from the Giants. Their final record for May was 17-9. Twenty-three months of losing were over.

CHAPTER 4

SAME OLD BRAVES?

THE EUPHORIA OF MAY WAS SOON REPLACED BY THE reality of June, which would prove to be the Braves' worst month of the season. It began with Avery, fighting the flu, stretched out in the training room before his June 1 start in San Francisco. "It will be fine," Cox told Avery. "Sometimes when you don't feel good you have no-hitter stuff."

But Avery's no-hitter ended on his second pitch, his shutout on his second batter. The Giants' 8-2 win halted the Braves' West Coast winning streak at five.

Why were the Braves better on the road (15-8) than at home (10-12)? Justice explained it this way: "There is just a lot more pressure on us at home. We get booed there sometimes and I'm thinking, 'Why is this happening? I think we got a pretty good team.' We're real loose on the road."

Deciding he needed defensive help to back up Bream, whose right knee had undergone several operations, Schuerholz sent Cabrera to Richmond and promoted Hunter, 23, a converted outfielder whom Schuerholz had scouted personally.

> *"There is just a lot more pressure on us at home. We're real loose on the road."*
>
> DAVID JUSTICE,
> ON THE BRAVES'
> 10-12 HOME RECORD

Tom Glavine won eight straight games in the first half, and was the National League's starting pitcher in the All-Star Game.

Said Hunter, "I was really surprised because (roving hitting instructor) Willie Stargell said I probably wasn't coming up until the end of the season."

The Braves lost the finale to the Giants 2-1 to close the road trip 5-2. "Don't get me wrong," said Justice, "I'm happy with the way the week went. It's just we should be going home 6-1."

On their first day home the Braves were off, but the front office was busy with the amateur draft. The Braves picked Arizona State outfielder Mike Kelly with their first choice, the No. 2 overall selection. More good news came later that afternoon as the the Braves swept the National League awards for May. Justice, who hit .381 for the month with five homers and 28 RBIs, was named player of the month. Glavine, 6-0 with a 1.76 ERA, was named top pitcher.

The next night was expected to be a majestic one, with Atlanta icon Dale Murphy making his first appearance at the stadium since his August 1990 trade to Philadelphia. Before the game, Murphy was honored with a highlights video of himself, and an emotional crowd of 30,165 responded by giving him a three-minute standing ovation. Murphy's voice cracked as he told the fans, "I may be a visitor tonight, but Atlanta will always be my home."

The game, won 9-5 by the Braves behind a career-high six RBIs by Blauser, was marred by a brawl. In the eighth inning, Philadelphia's Wally Ritchie brushed Nixon back with his first pitch.

"I told the umpire if he threw at me again I'd go after him," Nixon said.

Ritchie then hit Nixon, who rushed the mound and caught the pitcher with three clean lefts to the back of the head, ripping Ritchie's shirt with his cleats. Said a proud Cox, in a comment he would later be reprimanded for making, "All I know is Otis beat the living daylights out of him. It made me happy." Said Nixon, who was given a four-game suspension, "He deserved it. I'm not that kind of player, but he threw at me."

Hunter hit his first major league homer the next night but made a critical error an inning later as the Braves lost 12-11 in 12 innings. The Braves won the finale 9-4 as Blauser had another home run and four RBIs. For the series, he was 9-for-13 with three homers and 12 RBIs.

Blauser also was one of the most popular Braves in the clubhouse, thanks to a biting wit. His locker was crammed with everything from pin-up pictures to a little male doll capable of dropping its pants on command.

He constantly razzed teammates and reporters. He had become a favorite target of ESPN anchor Dan Patrick, who did morning sports reports for Atlanta radio station 96 Rock. Of course, this was all an act; Blauser's locker was invariably the first place Patrick would go when he covered the Braves.

A gaffe by the Braves' public relations department cost Blauser the NL Player of the Week Award. The staff missed a deadline to call in Blauser's stats to the NL office, so his .500 average, three home runs and 13 RBIs went officially unrecognized. He told public relations director Jim Schultz not to worry about it.

The Braves went to New York and won two of three, capturing their first series at Shea Stadium since 1987. Their most vivid memories, though, were of a Northwest Airlines 757 jet that flew over the stadium a few hours before the game at only 1,000 feet. Said Corrales, one of several coaches and players who ran for cover, "I thought for sure we all had it."

In the second game, Avery, whose batting style Blauser had dismissed as a softball beer league swing, went 4-for-4. More important, he pitched his first complete game of the season in a 6-1 win.

"We all just have to bow down to Steve," said Smoltz. "It's a game a pitcher dreams about." Said Mets manager Bud Harrelson, whose club was limited to five hits, "I'm glad we got two hits in the last inning so we'd out-hit Avery." The next night, Pete Smith earned his first win in a year in a 3-2 Atlanta triumph.

The next stop was Montreal, and the Braves were swept three games, their first such failure all season.

Jeff Blauser was one of the most popular Braves in the clubhouse, thanks to a biting wit. His locker was crammed with everything from pin-up pictures to a little male doll capable of dropping its pants on command.

Charlie Leibrandt
(left) and Sid Bream
called the first team
meeting of the season.
Said Leibrandt,
"We had kind of lost
that cockiness in the
last two weeks or so.
We'd been sort of
tentative."

JONATHAN NEWTON

Dale Murphy was honored when the Phillies came to Atlanta; the night was marred by a bench-clearing brawl ignited by Otis Nixon and Philadelphia pitcher Wally Ritchie.

JONATHAN NEWTON

They claimed former Atlanta pitcher Rick Mahler, who had been released by the Expos, and put him in the bullpen. To make room, they planned to move outfielder Danny Heep, but the handling of the transaction turned into an embarrassing incident. After being faxed to the team's hotel, the papers reassigning Heep to Richmond were mistakenly delivered to Heep's room, instead of assistant GM Dean Taylor's. Heep was not supposed to get the news until after that night's game, had to dress and sit on the bench knowing he was going to be sent down. "Right now my mental approach is mashed potatoes," he said angrily. He later decided not to go to Richmond, accepting his release in hopes that another major league club would pick him up. None did.

In the opener, Glavine's major league leading eight-game winning streak came to an end in a 2-1 loss. On Sunday, Nixon tied the major league record with six stolen bases in a 7-6 loss. "I would trade all those stolen bases and hits for a win," said Nixon, who was asked to send his spikes to the Hall of Fame. "At least a part of me will be in the Hall," he said.

The next night in Philadelphia, old friend Murphy broke Atlanta's heart with an eighth-inning tiebreaking home run. Said Cox, "I guess if anybody was going to hit a home run to beat us, I'd rather it be Murphy." Righthander Tommy Greene, who had pitched the NL's first no-hitter in May, beat his former team and added a homer of his own.

With Heath slumping, Cox went to Olson, who was hitting .282 and had recently thrown out such stellar base stealers as Vince Coleman and Delino DeShields. Said Cox, "Mike gets mad when he doesn't help this team, and he's trying too hard."

After another loss, the Braves took the finale from the Phillies, but not before another ugly incident. Nixon was hit by a pitch in the ninth by Roger McDowell but did not rush the mound. In the bottom of the inning, Glavine threw four halfhearted brushback pitches at Murphy, who happened to be leading off. Glavine was ejected, saying later, "Having Dale up made for a very uncomfortable situation. If it's a different situation, a different hitter, something different might have happened." Said Murphy, "It was like playing dodge ball out there. I don't think Tommy had the same velocity on those pitches that he did the rest of the game."

Overshadowed by the brushback incidents were two developments that would have far greater importance. Bream injured his right knee while rounding third and Justice began experiencing back problems.

Bream and Leibrandt called the Braves' first team meeting of the season before a Sunday home game against the Mets. Said Leibrandt, "We had kind of lost that cockiness in the last two weeks or so that we

David Justice told Bobby Cox he needed time to rest his back. He and Sid Bream both were placed on the 15-day disabled list.

had when we were on the field. We'd been sort of tentative."

Justice missed his third straight start because of his back. He was given a cortisone shot but it didn't help.

In Houston, the Braves lost the opener 1-0 when Pete Harnisch outdueled Glavine again. It was Atlanta's eighth loss in 11 games. Said an unhappy Glavine, "I guess the next time I pitch here I better throw a shutout. . . . It seems like that is the only way I can win here."

Before the series finale against the Astros, Justice told Cox he needed time to rest his back. At the same time, Bream decided to undergo knee surgery. Both were placed on the 15-day disabled list. Sanders and Mike Bell were brought up to replace Justice and Bream. "Sure it's tough," said Cox. "Those are two big guys to lose. But we feel we have guys coming in that can do the job." Cox's optimistic tone didn't mask the fact that Justice and Bream had combined for 20 homers and 85 RBIs. Sanders and Bell weren't likely to keep up that pace.

Sanders's return lightened up the atmosphere, as he recounted tales of the horrors of life in the minors. "Those 4:30 flights and bus rides are awful," he said. "I know when we had two layovers in Atlanta, I was thinking about going AWOL."

A four-game series against the Dodgers in Atlanta gave the Braves a chance to make up ground on L.A., which they trailed by 5½ games. The stadium was packed for Friday night's opening doubleheader, and emotions were high as Jim Gott walked Mercker with the bases loaded for a 3-2 Atlanta win. "I'd rather give up a 500-foot home run than walk a pitcher," Mercker said. "I'm just glad I didn't have to swing." The Dodgers came back to take the nightcap 8-2.

Bream underwent surgery, learning he would be out four to six weeks. The Braves lost again Saturday, 2-1 in 11 innings, and 11-4 Sunday before a national ESPN audience, committing six errors.

"This was a big weekend for us," said Smoltz. "The fans came out and showed their support. Now we have to kick ourself in the butt."

Said Nixon, "We wanted to come out of Houston with some momentum and we did. We didn't do it this weekend, but that is not a reason to say the season is over. It's just time to get things going again."

But a 6-3 loss two nights later in Cincinnati left the Braves 37-37. A year before, a .500 record would have been cause for celebration. Now all it caused was disappointment, for Atlanta had had a winning record since May 5. The Braves split the next two games with the Reds and headed to Los Angeles for three games.

The trip started on a bad note when Friday morning several of the Braves were awakened in their hotel rooms by a small earthquake. Said first baseman Tommy Gregg, "I was thinking either this slump is

FRANK NIEMEIR

Greg Olson and the Braves headed home for the All-Star break under .500 for the first time since May 1 and trailing the Dodgers by 9½ games.

really messing with my mind or this is an earthquake."

The Braves took the opener 4-1 as Glavine locked up the starter's role in the All-Star Game by becoming the first NL pitcher to win 12 games. However, that was the only game of this series that Atlanta would take.

When Smoltz was the loser in the next night's 7-6 loss, it dropped his record to a dismal 2-11. The Braves needed to make a big decision: either send him to the bullpen or the minors, or stick with him? Grimly, he said, "I know my teammates, my manager, my coaches are sick of seeing this. It's not going to happen anymore." The Braves lost their final game of the first half, the 5-3 decision dropping them to 39-40, their first time under .500 since May 1. More important, they were 9 1/2 games behind the Dodgers, and expectations were beginning to retreat.

"I'm not disappointed," said Schuerholz. "I think we have delivered on most of our off-season promises. There have been big strides. ... I think if you asked every player or Bobby they would say we would be better."

On the plane back to Atlanta, Cox talked about several keys for the second half of the season. Primary among them were returning Bream, Justice and Treadway, who had endured a succession of illnesses and injuries, to health. Gant (.239) and Smith (.247) needed to raise their batting averages. The bullpen needed help. Gregg and Heath needed to start hitting.

Glavine was the only Brave headed for the All-Star Game in Toronto, Pendleton snubbed despite his .328 average. But it would be only a short time before Pendleton and the Braves would repay the rest of the league with a second half to remember.

CHAPTER 5

SECOND-HALF SURGE

FOR THE FIRST TIME SINCE MILWAUKEE'S WARREN SPAHN did it in 1961, a Braves pitcher started for the National League in the All-Star Game. There was no arguing with Glavine's credentials. He had a 12-4 record and led the league in ERA (1.98), complete games (six) and strikeouts (108).

His counterpart in the 62nd All-Star Game, played in Toronto, was Minnesota's Jack Morris, and even though the surprising Twins were just percentage points out of first place in the AL West, there wasn't a soul in the SkyDome who thought this was a potential World Series preview.

Glavine was simply thinking about facing the American League's best hitters on national television. "The more you think about it, the more nervous you get," he said the day before the game. "I'm not going to need any help in that department."

But fortified by 11 hours of sleep in his Toronto hotel room, Glavine showed no traces of butterflies. The first hitter he faced, Rickey Henderson, fouled out to first baseman Will Clark. Glavine walked Wade Boggs on four pitches and gave up a single to Cal Ripken Jr., but then struck out AL home run leader Cecil Fielder

"The more you think about it, the more nervous you get. I'm not going to need any help in that department."

TOM GLAVINE,
ON HIS START
IN THE ALL-STAR GAME

and froze Danny Tartabull on a called third strike. In the second inning he struck out Dave Henderson and got consecutive fly-ball outs by Ken Griffey Jr. and Sandy Alomar Jr. Glavine's numbers for two innings read 30 pitches, one hit, no runs, one walk and three strike-outs. He left with a 1-0 lead, but the NL eventually lost 4-2.

That didn't matter to Cox and Mazzone, who watched the game on TV. "He really made me proud," said Cox. "I can't even describe the feeling I had," added Mazzone.

Now it was time to turn attention to the season's second half. Dropping five of seven games to the Dodgers over the last two weeks had convinced many that the Braves were out of the race, and expectations began to focus simply on having a solid second half and finishing above .500. But even that was no lock; the Braves hadn't had a winning second half since 1980 and had won only 41 percent of their post-All-Star break games in the previous 10 seasons.

Schuerholz, however, maintained his optimism. "I think what we have proven to a lot of fans," he said, "is that there is potential here for a real exciting and good baseball team."

Trailing the Dodgers by 9½ games and the Reds by five, the Braves began the second half with a seven-game homestand, four against St. Louis and three with the Cubs. It started off well. Perfectly, in fact, as Avery took a perfect game into the seventh inning of the opener, retiring the first 18 Cardinals batters. He lost the no-hitter when Rex Hudler led off the seventh with a single, but the Braves went on to win 4-1. They first had to survive a St. Louis threat in the eighth, when Avery allowed one run and was replaced by Berenguer with the bases loaded and one out.

As he watched Milt Thompson, one of baseball's top pinch hitters, step to the plate against Berenguer, "I was a nervous wreck," Avery said. "I was watching through my hands."

Thompson hit a 3-and-2 pitch medium deep down the line in left field. Cardinals catcher Tom Pagnozzi tagged up at third, but a throw from Lonnie Smith to Pendleton to Olson completed a double play and ended the threat. "That's a good win for us because it gets us off to a good start in the second half," said Cox. "That's big."

Even bigger was a decision by Schuerholz regarding Smoltz. The general manager suggested that the pitcher consult with a local sports psychologist, Dr. Jack Llewellyn, who had worked with some of the Braves' minor leaguers and had been credited with some success in working with Andres Thomas. "I thought it worked great," Schuerholz said. "We didn't let Andres go because of his attitude. We let him go because he couldn't play anymore."

It worked for Smoltz, too. He went 6⅓ innings to beat the Cardinals 6-2 for only his third win of the season. "When things are going bad, you try everything," Smoltz said. "He gave me some tips and

JONATHAN NEWTON

The Braves drew their millionth fan, something they hadn't done in an entire season since 1987. Said fan No. 1,000,000, Willie Patterson of Decatur, "We had a problem finding parking. I guess it was a good thing."

drills to work on as far as mentally preparing. I thought I could handle these situations, but inside it was eating me up. Now I'm not thinking of anything negative."

At 41-40, the Braves were back over .500 for good.

The optimism generated by Smoltz was tempered by the news that Heath would need surgery to remove bone chips in his throwing elbow. Said Heath, who would miss the rest of the season, "They gave me good money to come over here and I hate to break down." Cabrera was brought up from Richmond, but he would play only sparingly, and Olson would play 76 of the final 83 games.

The next night, the Braves drew their one millionth fan, something they hadn't done in an entire season since 1987. Said Fan No. 1,000,000, Willie Patterson of Decatur, "We had a problem finding parking. I guess it was a good thing."

A few hours later Nixon stole his 43rd base, breaking Atlanta's season record of 42, set by Gerald Perry in 1987, as the Braves won their third straight.

On Sunday, when Glavine completed the sweep with a 2-1 win, Olson quipped, "We whould find a way to keep the Cardinals in town," and Cox was given a two-year extension of his approximately $450,000-a-year contract. Said Schuerholz, "I knew it was the right thing to do." Cox's talks with Schuerholz had been so low-profile that even Cox's wife, Pam, didn't know about them. She learned the news from a televised report. Said Cox, "I think I'm in trouble."

The Cubs halted the four-game winning streak the next night, chasing Pete Smith in the second inning of a 6-4 decision. It was the third time in five starts that Smith had failed to make it past the third inning, and Cox was considering sending him to the bullpen and going to a four-man rotation. But Smith's problems were forgotten a day later, when an 8-5 victory lifted the Braves past Cincinnati into second place, 4½ games behind the Dodgers.

A strange thing had been happening while the Braves were winning five of the first six games of the homestand: the Dodgers and Reds couldn't buy a win. L.A. had lost six straight, Cincinnati eight. Nixon described his feelings upon looking up at the giant message board in center field and seeing that the Dodgers were losing yet again: "I saw it out of the corner of my eye and I got a little giddy, wanted it a little bit more."

According to Cox, the team had never given up on its chances of catching the Dodgers. "To be honest with you," he said, "we thought we could get back into it." Even Cox admitted his surprise the next night, however, as a 12-2 win over the Cubs drew the Braves within 3½ games of the Dodgers. "It's the most amazing week I've ever seen," he said of the seven-day period that had seen the Braves pick up six games on L.A. Amazingly, the Dodgers had gone 0-7 against Montreal and Philadelphia, the two worst teams in the NL East.

Smoltz got the win over the Cubs, but what fans were talking about the next day was the appearance between the sixth and seventh innings of two male streakers, who ran down the left-field line and slid into home plate. "They ought to take those two guys just as they are and put them in an unoccupied cage at the zoo," said a disgusted Schuerholz. Olson, however, had a different idea. "If I had thought twice," he said of the one streaker who dove head-first into home, "I'd have put a nasty tag on him."

While Schuerholz was talking about streakers, he had made a decision about Pete Smith. The pitcher was not going to the bullpen, but to the minors. Schuerholz said he hoped Smith would be ready to return in a month, when the schedule again forced the club to use a fifth starter. "We hope Pete can be the one," he said, "but we're going to look at all of our options." Smith took the demotion hard. He would not return until the roster was expanded in September.

To replace Smith, the Braves called up their hottest minor league hitter, outfielder Keith Mitchell. Mitchell, 21, had hit .344 in 22 games at Richmond after being promoted from Class AA Greenville. He was also known for being a cousin of slugger Kevin Mitchell of the San Francisco Giants. "I just hope I'm around long enough to face him," said Keith. He would be.

FRANK NIEMEIR

"It's the most amazing week I've ever seen."

BOBBY COX,
AFTER THE BRAVES
CUT SIX GAMES OFF
THE DODGERS' LEAD
IN SEVEN DAYS

46

FRANK NIEMEIR

*Ron Gant was
well on his way
to a second straight
season with
30 home runs
and 30 stolen bases.*

On the road now, the Braves beat the Cardinals two out of three in St. Louis. "I don't know what it is with the Cardinals," said Cox as his team concluded its season series with St. Louis, winning nine of 12. "I just know this team is really playing some ball."

Said Pendleton, "I know when I was in St. Louis we couldn't wait for the Braves to come to town. Not too many people are saying that these days."

The winning continued with a 7-3 decision over the Pirates. Smoltz, with his third straight win, benefited from a seven-run fourth inning. "It hasn't happened to me in a long time," he said of the offensive support, "and now it has happened to me in every game in the second half."

The Braves also had two notable visitors at Three Rivers Stadium. Arizona State center fielder Mike Kelly, their top pick in the amateur draft, worked out with them after signing a contract. He told the players, "My goal is to be here by '93." Former manager Chuck Tanner also made an appearance, saying, "You have to like the Braves right now."

That wasn't necessarily true over the next two nights, as the Braves dropped two in a row for the first time since the All-Star break. First Leibrandt lost a 12-3 decision to the Pirates, giving up six runs in 2⅓ innings. "I'm having a tough time right now," he said after failing to reach the seventh inning for the fourth time in his last five starts. "I'm not throwing my fastball where I want to." The Pirates then took the Braves 7-4 as Glavine turned in a rare shaky performance. "I'm just human," he said. "You can't go out there and pitch a great game every time." Added Cox, "Sandy Koufax had his bad nights."

Chicago was the next stop, and again the Braves dropped two out of three. They also became embroiled in a controversy over the severity of Justice's injury. Several teammates had privately questioned his dedication to rehabilitating his back injury. He had been late to the park on several occasions and left early on others. He was not with the club on this road trip, but he learned that TBS broadcaster Skip Caray had used the word "mysterious" in referring to the injury, and he placed an early morning call to Caray's hotel room to complain.

"It makes it sound like I'm faking or like I'm sitting back and doing nothing," Justice said later. "That would be the most ridiculous thing in the world for me to do with the kind of season I was having: hitting over .300 (actually .297), 11 home runs, leading the league in RBIs. When you term an injury 'mysterious,' people think, 'What's wrong with him?' like no one has ever had a pulled muscle before."

Avery won the opener against the Cubs 6-2, his only mistake coming on a ninth-inning home run by Andre Dawson. All the pitcher could think about later was the homer. "When am I ever going to learn to nail down the shutout or complete game?" he said.

"When I was in St. Louis, we couldn't wait for the Braves to come to town. Not too many people are saying that these days."

TERRY PENDLETON, AFTER ATLANTA FINISHED THE SEASON SERIES AGAINST ST. LOUIS WINNING NINE OF 12 GAMES

49

The clubhouse was very quiet. The pattern of not being able to close out road trips was becoming annoyingly apparent.

The game was also the scene of an ugly incident, as several Cubs fans shouted racial slurs at Braves reliever Marvin Freeman, who is black. Freeman ignored them, however, saying later, "They can say stuff like that as long as they are on the other side of the wall. But once they come over, they belong to me, dammit."

During the trip, it was announced that the Braves would switch radio stations beginning with the 1992 season, going from WSB to WGST. This, too, became a source of controversy when Skip Caray learned that WSB had used a seven-second delay on the weekend broadcasts of the Cubs games to ensure there would be no mention of the move on the air. Caray was livid. "It's a shame a great radio station has been reduced to that," he said. "It shows no class."

The road trip ended 4-5, and the Braves, who had cut their deficit to 2½ games, were six back of the Dodgers. The clubhouse was very quiet after the final game in Chicago. The pattern of not being able to close out road trips was becoming annoyingly apparent.

On a nine-game swing through Los Angeles, Houston and St. Louis in April, the Braves won four of five, then dropped three of four. On a six-game trip to Pittsburgh and Chicago in May, the Braves took two of three from the Pirates but lost two of three to the Cubs. Later in the month, they won five in a row — three at San Diego and two at San Francisco, before losing the last two at Candlestick Park. On a nine-day visit to the NL East in June, the Braves won two of three from the Mets, then lost three straight to Montreal and two of three in Philadelphia. "We seem to blow our chances," said Cox.

All they needed, it turned out, was some home cooking, and the longest homestand of the season, 14 games, came at just the right time. First up, the Braves swept a doubleheader from Pittsburgh, cutting L.A.'s lead to 4½ when the Dodgers lost to New York. Glavine won his NL-best 14th game in the opener, and Rick Mahler held the Pirates to one run in six innings as the Braves won the second game 5-3. Both Gant and Sanders saved run with leaping catches, Nixon hit in his 18th straight game and tied the franchise record with 54 stolen bases. The Braves knocked off two good pitchers in John Smiley and Drabek.

After a 10-3 victory in the third game of the series, the fourth was to be the farewell for Sanders, who was due to report to the Falcons. The master of the dramatic, he said goodbye with a three-run homer that helped the Braves overcome a 6-2 deficit. Blauser hit a three-run shot later in the inning to complete an 8-6 win and a four-game sweep.

"This is the first time in God knows how long I feel like I contributed to a team that is winning," said Sanders, who left hitting .193, with four home runs and 13 RBIs.

"Can they win their division?" Pirates shortstop Jay Bell repeated a question about the Braves, who were now 4½ back of the Dodgers. "No doubt about it. All I know is I'm glad we're leaving."

CHAPTER 6

LEADING THE WEST

THE KEY TO THE BRAVES' CHAMPIONSHIP HOPES WOULD not be beating the league's best team's, but whipping the weaker ones. They entered August 26-17 against clubs with winning records, but only 27-29 against those at .500 or worse. They had an immediate opportunity to rectify this situation, however, with all remaining 10 games of the homestand against teams with losing records. The Dodgers, meanwhile, would be on the road for their next 10.

As the Braves prepared to play their 100th game, two of their players stood atop the league batting standings. Both Pendleton and Nixon were hitting .337, four points more than San Diego's Tony Gwynn. Pendleton, who also had 12 home runs and led the NL in slugging percentage (.537), was beginning to be touted as an MVP candidate. Said Gant, "He's brought leadership to the team which we haven't had the last couple of years." Added Blauser, "It seems he always gets the job done. He finds ways to win, and that's rubbed off on us. If I could be half the player he's been this season, I'd be happy."

August, however, did not start on a good note.

As the Braves prepared to play their 100th game, Terry Pendleton and Otis Nixon stood atop the league batting standings.

JONATHAN NEWTON

John Smoltz won six of his first seven starts after the All-Star break, helping the Braves close the gap to 1½ games.

RICH MAHAN

Juan Berenguer pulled a muscle under his right arm. It turned out to be a stress fracture, and his season was over.

Leibrandt was roughed up again, this time 13-3 by the Padres. The veteran lefty had now lost five of his last seven decisions and had fallen to 9-10. He lasted only four innings, allowing seven runs on 10 hits, including a grand slam by Tim Teufel. Mazzone remained optimistic. "To make the run," he said, "we have to get good pitching and he has to play a big part in it. And he will."

That night Bream returned from the disabled list as reliever Jim Clancy, acquired from Houston for two minor-league players, took Jeff Parrett's spot on the roster. Nixon's hitting streak finally ended at 20 games, and his appeal hearing before league president Bill White on his four-game suspension stemming from the Philadelphia brawl was again postponed. "I'm worried now the suspension could come at a crucial time," Nixon said.

The Braves lost their second straight when Andy Benes beat them 3-2. A fifth-inning muff by Padres second baseman Bip Roberts was initially scored a hit for Gant. It was changed to an error two innings later, meaning the Padres were working on a no-hitter, but Benes already had been lifted. In his first at-bat after the scoring change, Gant made it a moot point with his 21st home run. Down 3-1 in the ninth, the Braves loaded the bases with none out, but could score only once.

Watching the game from a hotel room in Pittsburgh was announcer Skip Caray, in the Pennsylvania city to broadcast an NFL exhibition game the next day. "The game ends and I look up and I've thrown crap everywhere," Caray said. "That's great to feel that way."

The Braves halted their skid by taking the final game from the Padres, and just in time, too, since the Giants, winners of 12 of 14, were coming to town. In the 9-7 victory over San Diego, Mitchell, making his first start for the injured Lonnie Smith (groin pull), went 3-for-5 with an RBI and a stolen base. The Braves now trailed the Dodgers by 2½.

Smoltz won the opener 5-2 over the Giants and Pendleton led the Braves to a 10-6 victory the next night with two home runs. "A lot of guys are making a million, $2 million more than me," he said. "But are they having a better season?"

Television viewers noticed something odd during the second game. The A on Blauser's batting helmet was turned upside down. Asked what prankster had done it, he replied, "Me. Thought it might change my luck a little." It did, enough for him to single in the Braves' final two runs. Later he was informed he was out of uniform, so the good-luck charm had to go. "I'll have to find something else to mess

with," he said.

The next night brought a 1-0 loss to Bud Black, but there was good news: a strong performance at last by Leibrandt, whose only mistake in seven innings came on his second pitch, when he gave up Darren Lewis's first major league home run. Said Mazzone, "He's got it back."

The loss was witnessed by baseball commissioner Fay Vincent, who was making his first visit of the season to Atlanta. "I admire what the people have done here," he said. "It is a wonderful story." Reminded that a season before he had expressed concern that the Braves organization seemed more concerned with providing programming for parent company TBS than with putting a quality team on the field, Vincent replied, "I didn't have much doubt that this was a good baseball town. I knew from all my years of working for Coca-Cola here."

An 8-1 loss suffered by Glavine resulted in a split of the series. "You win the first two and you get a little greedy," said Cox. Before the game, Mahler was released. The 38-year-old veteran, who had pitched for the Braves during all or part of the 1979-88 seasons, took the news in stride, even staying to play cards with his teammates before packing up and leaving. Mahler's release made room for the Braves to call up reliever Armando Reynoso, 25, who had been signed as a free agent

Tom Glavine's 18th victory, a 7-5 come-from-behind win over the Mets, brought this response from Los Angeles outfielder Brett Butler: "Their big boy got smoked early today, and that's got to concern them."

FRANK NIEMEIR

MIRACLE SEASON!

out of the Mexican League and was 10-6 with a 2.61 ERA at Richmond. He was to move into Atlanta's fifth-starter role.

The Astros were the final guests of the homestand, and the Braves feasted on the NL West doormats by sweeping three games behind Avery (his sixth straight decision), Smoltz (his sixth win in his last seven decisions), and Reynoso, making his major league debut. The third win brought the Braves within 1½ games of the Dodgers. As reporters gathered around Reynoso in the locker room, Cabrera attempted to interpret for his non-English speaking batterymate. Joked Justice, "Ya'll want me to interpret what Frankie is saying?" Reynoso went six innings, allowing just two hits and no runs. Mercker was placed on the disabled list with a pulled muscle in his rib cage, and Tony Castillo was called up. Castillo had led the club in appearances in 1990, but had spent this season at Richmond.

An 11-game road trip began in San Francisco, where Leibrandt and Black, teammates on Kansas City's 1985 World Series championship team, faced off again. Again it was a pitchers' duel, but this time Leibrandt won 2-1, snapping a personal four-game losing streak. The Braves were supposed to be on the cover of Sports Illustrated that week, but were knocked off by an even more improbable story — ninth alternate John Daly's amazing win in the PGA Championship. Nixon, bothered by a pulled groin, decided to drop his appeal of his four-game suspension.

The next night Keith Mitchell knocked the first pitch of the game over the head of his cousin Kevin and into the left-field seats, igniting a 9-2 victory that lifted the Braves within a half-game of the Dodgers. "The main thing we have to worry about," warned Cox, "is keeping ourselves focused and not worrying about L.A. If we do that, things will take care of themselves."

The master of the dramatic, Deion Sanders said goodbye with a three-run homer that helped the Braves overcome a 6-2 deficit and beat the Pirates 8-6.

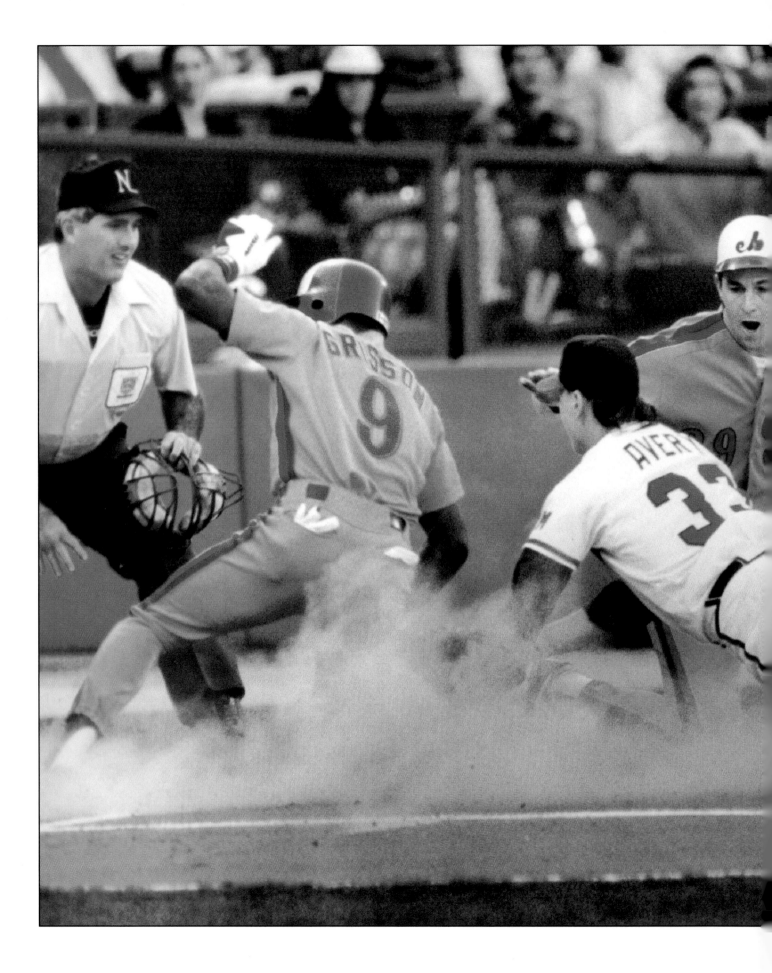

Steve Avery's all-out effort resulted in six straight wins to start the second half.

JONATHAN NEWTON

Avery saw his six-game winning streak stopped in the finale at Candlestick, falling to 0-3 in San Francisco. The Braves now trailed L.A. by 1½ games, but they were mad. The source of their anger was a quote attributed to Strawberry. Asked about the race against the Braves, the Dodgers outfielder said, "I've never been concerned about Atlanta." It would become the bulletin board quote of the year.

"He'd better start rethinking what he said," replied Olson. "The Dodgers have real good pitching and we have good starting pitching. Our bullpen is better than their bullpen. And they're not hitting, and we are knocking it around. We'll see who is talking in October."

The Braves lost the opener in San Diego 1-0 in a duel between Greg Harris and Smoltz, but the big news was that Justice was ready to play again. The Braves sent him to the Class A Macon farm club to test his back. "I just feel like it is probably going to hurt from now until the end of the year," he said. "So if I can play with this pain — and I feel I can play with it — everything will be fine."

While the Braves were beating the Padres 3-2 behind Reynoso, Justice was hitting a home run and driving in three runs in his debut with Macon. But another injury situation was developing. Berenguer had a pulled muscle underneath his right arm, a condition he said happened while he was playing with his kids. It would turn out to be a stress fracture, and his season was over.

As one pitcher faded out of the picture, however, another came into focus. The new closer was 21-year-old Mark Wohlers, called up from Richmond just two days before. He preserved a 2-1 victory for Leibrandt by striking out Tim Teufel with the tying run at third.

After a series-ending loss to the Padres, the Braves headed for Cincinnati. L.A. manager Tommy Lasorda, meanwhile, bemoaned his club's predicament, leading the Braves by just two games. "We've been having our problems," he said. "It's a very simple thing. We're just not operating on all cylinders. We're satisfied we're in first place, of course; it's better than being in second. But we're not doing the job."

Justice's long-awaited return was a quiet performance; he went 1-for-7 as the Braves split a doubleheader. The next night, however, would be remembered as a turning point. With the Braves down by three runs with two outs in the ninth, Cabrera sent the game into extra innings with a three-run homer off reliever Rob Dibble. Justice won it in the 13th with an RBI double, and Castillo survived a two-on, none-out jam in the bottom of the inning.

"I know I was supposed to be going for a home run but I wasn't," Cabrera said after the 10-9 win. "I was glad I could add something to this team, because I have been gone so long."

Justice also felt some redemption. Without him the Braves were 31-22; with him, 33-32. "You see how well they did without me but you don't see how well they did without Sid (Bream)," he said. "There

FRANK NIEMEIR

FRANK NIEMEIR

*Otis Nixon's
58th stolen base
set a Braves
franchise record
in just 98 games.*

JONATHAN NEWTON

MIRACLE SEASON!

Three Braves pitchers produced the National League's first combined no-hitter. Kent Mercker pitched six innings, Mark Wohlers two and Alejandro Pena one.

are a lot of other factors when we win or lose, not just me. I wonder if we lose will it be 'Oh, well, Justice is to blame.' "

The Braves concluded the trip with a 4-1 win, causing Cox to pound his fist on the table in his office and say, "Now that is good road trip." The Braves had finally learned how to close a trip, turning a 4-4 record into a 7-4 one with a three-win finish.

Back home, the Braves opened a seven-game stand by beating Philadelphia on Justice's first home run since coming off the disabled list. Injured pitchers Mercker and Grant were pictured using toy tomahawks to join the crowd in the Tomahawk Chop, the demonstrative cheer that now was sweeping the sports world.

The Dodgers were swept in St. Louis, but the Braves blew two chances to move into first, dropping the next two to the Phillies. They remained one game back. Both teams were becoming adept at rallying from impossible situations. The Braves overcame a six-run deficit to Montreal to win 14-9 as Blauser hit a grand slam, but the Dodgers scored four runs in the ninth to beat Chicago 4-3. "It's going to be some kind of race," said Nixon. "Those Dodgers are unbelievable the way they win games."

The next night, the Braves went into first. "Gotcha! Braves catch L.A." read the headline in the Journal. Leibrandt struck out a career-high 13, and a banner in outfield read, "Worried now, Strawberry?"

Said Dodgers third baseman Lenny Harris, whose club had lost 2-1 to Chicago earlier in the day, "When I go home tonight, I'm going to have a nice dinner with my wife. I stay and think about the Braves, I go crazy."

The upward trend continued with a 3-1 win over the Mets, Glavine's 17th victory, as Pittsburgh knocked off the Dodgers. That night the Braves made a key trade, getting reliever Alejandro Pena from the Mets for Castillo and a minor leaguer to be named. With Berenguer finished, Pena, who merely had to switch locker rooms at Atlanta-Fulton County Stadium, would take over the closer's role.

A 2-0 win over the Mets gave the Braves a two-game margin on the Dodgers, and a 6-1 triumph over the Phillies, in which Avery struck out a career high 10, made it five in a row. Said Phillies manager Jim Fregosi of Avery, "His fastball was 3 feet better than when we saw him in Atlanta."

With the arrival of September, the Braves were able to expand their roster, calling up Pete Smith, shortstop Vinny Castilla, Willard, reliever Randy St. Claire and Bell.

The Braves dropped back into a tie with the Dodgers when Dale Murphy hit a key eighth-inning double and the Phillies won 5-4 in 10 innings while L.A. was completing a three-game sweep of the Cubs. In Montreal, the Braves lost the opener to the Expos but were fortunate that the Cardinals knocked off the Dodgers in 11 innings.

"It's easy to get fired up for the Dodgers and Pirates. It's time to feel the same way about the Expos and Astros. Every game, no matter who it's against, really means the same in baseball."

RON GANT

In a 4-1 win in the second game in Montreal, Smoltz and Olson had a heated exchange over a fourth-inning pitch. Smoltz said he never saw a sign for a changeup; Olson insisted he called it. "I would say there was a much more motivated team tonight," said Lemke. Blauser broke a toe, and Belliard moved in as the starter at shortstop.

The Braves lost the finale in Montreal, dropping a game behind the Dodgers. "Maybe it's good to get Montreal and Philadelphia out of the way," said Treadway.

It was definitely good to get to New York. The Braves swept three from the Mets, and Cox achieved a milestone in the opener, becoming the winningest manager in Atlanta history, with 380 victories. Fifth starter Mercker pitched four scoreless innings, and Pena got the win in a 4-2 victory. Leibrandt earned his fifth straight win the next night, and the Braves overcame a four-run deficit to win the finale 7-5.

They were still a half-game back, and once again a Dodger opened his mouth and gave the Braves something to pin up in the locker room. "They came back and won," said former Brave Brett Butler. "But their big boy (Glavine) got smoked early today, and that's got to concern them." With only four games before the Dodgers came to town, the Braves would remember Butler's words.

The road trip, which had begun 1-3, ended up 5-4. Now the Braves faced two each against the Giants and Padres before the Dodgers arrived. Justice hit two homers in the opener as Smoltz (12-13) came within one game of .500. The next night, Avery pitched a 4-1 victory and the Braves reclaimed first place by a half-game.

The first game against the Padres made history, as three Braves pitchers produced the National League's first combined no-hitter. Mercker pitched six innings, Wohlers two and Pena one. The no-hitter turned on a two-out, ninth-inning call by scorer Mark Frederickson. Darrin Jackson smacked a high bouncer to the left of Pendleton, who lunged at the ball but pulled back at the last moment, unable to make the play. Hit or error? "Error, no doubt about it," said Frederickson. "Basically it was because he (Pendleton) committed to the play. That's why I didn't even look at the replay. Pendleton unwittingly stirred a controversy after the game by claiming he had lost the high bouncer in the stadium lights, which, if true, should have made the play a hit.

Pena got the final out and Nixon, who caught the ball, tossed it into the stands. Realizing his mistake, he retrieved it. Pena inscribed it in these understated tones: "9-11-91, ATL-1, SD-0, Save #8."

When the game ended, Schuerholz was on the phone to his wife. "You guys go into first place last night," she told him, "then pitch a no-hitter tonight. So what are you going to do tomorrow night?"

Easy. Win 5-1, stretching the winning streak to seven and holding the lead at a half-game heading into the season's most crucial series. Bring on the Dodgers.

CHAPTER 7

CHOP TO THE TOP

T HERE WAS ONLY ONE WAY TO MEASURE THE MAGNITUDE of this series, only one opponent with whom to compare the invasion of the despised Dodgers. Tommy Lasorda, meet General Sherman.

Atlanta was acting like a city under siege. Bars stocked up on food and drink. Fans painted slogans on signs and streaks on their faces, gearing for war. And everywhere, there were tomahawks. Thanks to the Tomahawk Chop cheer, an entire cottage industry had sprung to life virtually overnight. The most enterprising of the novelty producers was Paul Braddy, 36, of Peachtree City, a sales manager for a urethane company who was listening to a Braves-Giants game in August when his life was transformed.

"Skip Caray was talking about the Tomahawk Chop," Braddy told Norman Arey of the Journal-Constitution. "He said, 'You know, what we need are some tomahawks or tom-toms or something.'" The rest was marketing history. Braddy whittled a foam tomahawk prototype with an electric knife — "the worst-looking tomahawk you ever saw" — and sold the Braves' concessions people on the idea.

RICH MAHAN

Fans painted slogans on signs and streaks on their faces, gearing for war.

MIRACLE SEASON!

A crowd of 45,769, the Braves' largest of the season, showed up for the opener against Los Angeles. Everyone who was anyone was there.

RICH ADDICKS

Everywhere, there were tomahawks. Thanks to the Tomahawk Chop, an entire cottage industry had sprung to life virtually overnight.

MIRACLE SEASON!

JONATHAN NEWTON

> *"It's the essence of baseball, two top teams battling head-to-head and the fans getting behind it. It will be the same way in Los Angeles when we go there."*
>
> JOHN SCHUERHOLZ

Shortly thereafter, he quit his $60,000-a-year job to become a full-time producer of tomahawks and other sports novelties.

There were tomahawks, yes, but tickets? Native son heavyweight champion Evander Holyfield called ticket manager Jack Tyson and asked for two for each of the three games. Tyson gave him two for Friday night's opener. Tennis star Steffi Graf called at the last minute. Too late. "What am I supposed to say?" asked Tyson.

Media descended from everywhere. "They ought to make a big deal of it," said Schuerholz. "It's the essence of baseball, two top teams battling head-to-head and fans getting behind it. It will be the same way in Los Angeles when we go out there."

Into this highly charged atmosphere came Mike Downey of The Los Angeles Times. In a column published in the Journal-Constitution, he wrote:

The real reason the Dodgers will win their division is their only challenger is ... (I can hardly write this with a straight face) ... Atlanta.

Yes, Atlanta, stronghold of such international athletic powerhouses as the Falcons, Hawks and Braves. ... The unwritten rule of sports continues to be that no professional team based in Atlanta ever wins anything, which is why the hockey team moved to Canada."

Of Justice, Downey wrote: *This is the guy who can't make up his mind whether his first name is Dave, David or Apollo. He thinks a lot of himself. He could give ego lessons to Rickey Henderson.*

Of Lonnie Smith: *I've seen Lonnie catch several baseballs on one hop. Unfortunately, most of them were fly balls.*

You had to give these L.A. people credit for one thing: They sure could provide bulletin board fodder. Schuerholz himself made sure this one went up. But beyond Downey's not-so-subtle digs was a serious question. Could the Braves really beat L.A.? Even in this magical season, they had lost eight of 12 to the Dodgers. But Olson downplayed the significance of that history. "If you asked me right now what happened in those earlier games," he said, "I couldn't tell you."

A crowd of 45,769, the Braves' largest of the season, showed up for the opener. Everyone who was anyone was there, including, of course, Fonda, who inadvertently walked into the men's bathroom. Someone counted 143 banners hanging in the stadium. One of the better ones took a jab at diminutive former Atlanta Hawks coach Mike Fratello, who had taken to hanging out with Lasorda and had even been seen at Dodger Stadium wearing an L.A. uniform in the Dodgers' dugout: "The Braves are going to chop the Dodgers into Fratello-size pieces." Another cited biblical evidence of the Braves' destiny: "Matthew 20:16: So the last shall be first." And one sign held up by a fan poked fun at Lasorda's well-known commercials for a weight-loss program: "I lost 9 1/2 games in only nine weeks! And I owe it all to the Braves plan."

"They sit up in the stands and flip all kinds of fingers at me. I smile and say, 'Lord, help these people. They've got problems.' Fans have to understand that they can't upset me."

DARRYL STRAWBERRY

FRANK NIEMEIR

JONATHAN NEWTON

JONATHAN NEWTON

Safe or out? Tommy Lasorda and the Dodgers got a break when Brett Butler was called safe on this pickoff play at first in Game 2 of the showdown series at Atlanta.

Steve Avery's four-hit, 9-1 victory over the Dodgers improved his lifetime record against L.A. to 4-0, and gave the Braves a 1½-game lead.

FRANK NIEMEIR

MIRACLE SEASON!

How stressful were the three games against the Dodgers in Atlanta? As this fan's reactions demonstrate, emotions ranged from heart-wrenching tension to joyous celebration — all in the same game.

MARLENE KARAS

Rally caps — in four varieties — became the headwear of choice in the Braves' dugout down the stretch. Mark Grant demonstrated the four models.

On the field, the Braves used a Ted Williams-type shift against Strawberry, playing the shortstop on the right side of the infield, leaving only the third baseman on the left side. But it made little difference in the first game. Strawberry went over the shift with a home run, through it with a single and around it twice for two more singles. He drove in two runs and scored two in a 5-2 L.A. victory that moved the Dodgers back into first by a half-game.

Said Strawberry, "If they play me there I'm going to get a lot of hits, because I know they're not going to pitch me inside."

Said Cox, "We definitely didn't pitch to the locations we wanted with him."

Perhaps more disturbing for a team eager to seize the spotlight was that the Braves now had lost in front of five of their six largest audiences of the season.

Glavine suffered his first loss of the season against L.A. in three decisions. "On paper they are not a better team," he said. "But on the field they have been better. Strawberry hurt me."

As Cox left the clubhouse that night, he counseled patience. "It's only one game," he said.

And only one night out of first, for the Braves turned the tables on Saturday with a 3-2 win. It took 11 innings, and four hours and 10 minutes, including a 79-minute rain delay, but Gant finally ended it with a two-out RBI single off Roger McDowell, his 18th game-winning hit of the season. Two innings earlier, Gant had faced the same situation — two out, winning run on third, and grounded into a fielder's choice. This time, he said, "I wasn't going to let a fastball beat me." Said Smoltz, who pitched eight strong innings, "It would have really been tough if we lost. I'm glad we're talking in would-haves. One and a half games behind would have seemed like four. Tomorrow is now a good situation."

Especially with Avery on the mound. His four-hit, 9-1 victory improved his lifetime record against L.A. to 4-0 and gave the Braves a 1½-game lead, and the baseball world left Atlanta wearing its heart on its sleeve for the team with the tomahawk on its chest. Almost overlooked was the fact that, with an 82-61 record, the Braves had clinched their first winning season since 1983.

The biggest blow was a first-inning grand slam by Bream, who hastened a third-inning exit by Ramon Martinez, normally a Braves-killer. Said Avery, now 16-8, "It's ours to win; it's ours to lose."

One key to the two victories was shutting down Strawberry, who went 0-for-7 in the second and third games after going 4-for-5 in the opener. Did the fans get to him? "They sit up in the stands and flip all kinds of fingers at me," he said. "I smile and say, 'Lord, help those people. They've got problems.' Fans have to understand they can't upset me."

The Braves flew to San Francisco for two games with the Giants, the Dodgers home to L.A. for two with the Reds. Fans back East who couldn't stay up past midnight for the results got some bad news the next morning: the Braves had blown a 4-1 lead and lost 8-5, while the Dodgers came from behind twice to win in 12 innings.

But that wasn't the worst of it. Nixon had failed a drug test and was suspended for 60 days. He would miss the rest of the season, including any postseason play, and part of the early 1992 schedule. The Braves had lost the top base stealer in the majors.

Schuerholz heard the news in an early-morning call from Kasten. Nixon, who had been subject to drug testing because of a 1987 arrest when he was in the minor leagues, had failed a test in July but had successfully appealed, claiming the results were faulty.

Nixon's teammates and coaches were stunned. The clubhouse was dead quiet before the game. Nixon had left for Atlanta that afternoon. A reporter ran through the airport with him before his departure, but all he would say was "I really don't have time to talk about this right now. It's something that really hurts." He checked into an outpatient drug rehabilitation unit, remaining in seclusion.

Said Schuerholz, "One thing about it, these guys have already proven to themselves that they can withstand the loss of key guys."

Although Cox told reporters, "This wasn't a major blow," privately he was worried. Nixon had been a major part of the Braves' success. Without him and Sanders, there wasn't much speed left in the lineup. Lonnie Smith had six stolen bases, 66 fewer than Nixon, and was a liability in left field. That point was driven home immediately when his misplay of a two-out fly ball led to two runs in the opener in San Francisco.

As if the Braves hadn't received enough bad news, they learned that Berenguer had a fractured bone in his right arm and would miss the rest of the season. This at least wasn't a shock. He hadn't pitched in five weeks, and Pena and Wohlers were handling the closer's role.

Another night, another loss, and the Braves were out of first. San Francisco 3, Atlanta 2, and Los Angeles 5, Cincinnati 3. Said Dodgers pitcher Bob Ojeda, "It's just wonderful. I knew the series in Atlanta wouldn't be a long-lasting effect."

Arriving in San Diego for two games with the Padres, the Braves held a players-only clubhouse meeting. Bream and Pendleton took charge. "We just needed to relax, be cool and everything would be fine," said Pendleton.

More effective, however, were a 7²/₃-inning effort by Glavine and a five-run first inning as the Braves beat the Padres in the opener 6-4. Helping to produce the first victory of the post-Nixon era was Lonnie Smith, who scored the game's first run after singling and stealing second.

WALTER STRICKLIN

RICH MAHAN

MIRACLE SEASON!

"Nobody, I mean nobody, in this clubhouse is taking anything for granted."

BOBBY COX,
AFTER THE BRAVES
PULLED INTO A TIE
WITH THE DODGERS
WITH 3 GAMES TO PLAY

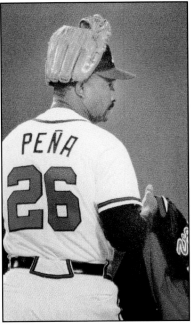

JONATHAN NEWTON

Key players down the stretch included Alejandro Pena, who took over the closer's role, and Terry Pendleton, who was chasing a batting title.

RICH MAHAN

THE 1991 ATLANTA BRAVES

"Ecstasy, pure ecstasy."

GREG OLSON,
AFTER THE BRAVES
RALLIED FROM 6-0
TO BEAT THE REDS 7-6

*Ron Gant came up with big plays in the outfield,
at the plate and on the bases, and became just the
third player with back-to-back seasons with
30 home runs and 30 stolen bases.*

MICHAEL SCHWARZ

JONATHAN NEWTON

WALTER STRICKLIN

From nuns to small children, everyone, it seemed, caught tomahawk fever when they ventured inside the confines of Atlanta-Fulton County Stadium.

FRANK NIEMEIR

JONATHAN NEWTON

MIRACLE SEASON!

The Dodgers also won, beating Houston, and received a boost by winning a coin toss to determine the home field of a playoff game should they end up tied with the Braves. In a conference call involving Schuerholz, Dodgers general manager Fred Claire and NL president Bill White, the Dodgers were allowed to make the call because they were the current first-place team. Claire correctly called heads.

Cox refused to let the news bother him. "All I know is it was a great win," he said.

The Dodgers won again the next night, but the Braves kept pace by beating the Padres 4-2 in 10 innings. The hero? Lonnie Smith, who had three hits, including a homer, drove in two runs and scored the winner. "I hear what they're saying about me, like I don't belong in the lineup," he said. "I'm the bad boy, remember? I can't catch, I can't run, I'm not an offensive threat. I'm not perfect. But I can still play this damn game."

Before the game, Smith, who had spent time in a drug treatment center in the '80s and still undergoes testing, talked about Nixon, who was being savaged by fans and media. "They don't understand," he said. "They're talking about something they know nothing about. They don't know the man and they're judging him. I know what it feels like. I've been there. I've been through more torment than anyone could imagine unless they have been in a war. People come up and say, 'Hey Lonnie, you were an addict, you beat cocaine, you're cured,' I'm still chemical dependent; it's just I haven't used it in the last seven years. Every day is a battle. You are never over it. Let me tell you, the day I'm cured is the day I'm going to my grave."

Down the coast, the Dodgers were waiting.

Fortunately for the Braves, they would open with Avery. And predictably, he tormented the Dodgers again, this time pitching a 3-0 shutout to raise his career mark against L.A. to 5-0. "It's funny," he said. "I still can't figure out why I match up against them so well. The stuff is always there when I throw against them. I just hope it never ends."

Gant hit his 30th homer of the season, joining Willie Mays and Bobby Bonds as the only major league players to have back-to-back seasons of 30 homers and 30 stolen bases. "I had been thinking about it for a while," he said. "It was something I wanted to have. Now I can go back to concentrating on just getting base hits and doing things to help us win."

The next night the Braves took a 1-0 lead into the bottom of the eighth, but errors by Belliard and Pendleton allowed L.A. to tie it, and the Dodgers won it in the ninth on a triple by Juan Samuel. The 2-1 loss put L.A. back in first by a half-game. The seesaw was picking up speed.

"We had been making the plays all night," said Belliard, "then

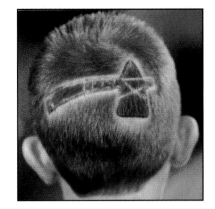

WALTER STRICKLIN

The two mega-series with the Dodgers ended up a wash, each team winning two of three at home. Time was running out on the Braves.

two balls slipped away." Said Butler, "It's a freak thing. Two Gold Glove players making mistakes. I guess we need breaks to beat them."

Actor Tony Danza had been the Dodgers' bat boy in the second game, but he told them he couldn't make it for Sunday's finale because he was throwing a party. Lasorda, however, wouldn't take no for an answer. "We told him we would boycott his show," he said. So Danza returned, and once again the Dodgers won, Martinez and two relievers holding the Braves to three hits in a 3-0 loss. Said Strawberry, "I could tell that some of their hitters were pressing up there. I was like that when I was in my first pennant race."

So the two mega-series with the Dodgers ended up a wash, each team winning two of three at home. A game and a half back again, the Braves headed home for three games with Cincinnati. Time was running out on them. They had only 12 games left, the Dodgers 11.

Schuerholz figured this was no time to stand pat. So he made a surprise move. He tried to get Sanders back from the Falcons. Sanders liked the idea, as long as he wouldn't miss any time with the football club. But the Falcons had yet to be persuaded.

Another former member of the Braves family also wanted to rejoin the club. This was Chief Noc-A-Homa, a.k.a. Levi Walker Jr. Walker, 49, three-quarters Ottawa and one-quarter Chippewa. He had spent 17 years as the team's mascot before being fired in 1986 for failing to show up for engagements. Now he was working as a letter sorter for the U.S. Postal Service in Macon. The Braves, however, refused to budge. They said they weren't interested in dredging up old promotions.

The opener with the Reds was rained out, and the Dodgers hiked their lead to two games by beating the Padres. But once again the big news in Atlanta was Sanders, who signed a contract for the rest of the season. He would practice with the Falcons in the afternoon, then play with the Braves at night. No one could recall a case of another pro athlete playing two sports at the same time. The Falcons were irked at the arrangement, but as long as Sanders fulfilled his obligations to practice and play with them, they were powerless to prevent it. "We're all big Braves fans," said owner Rankin Smith Sr. "We all want them to win. But they handled this Deion thing in an unprofessional manner."

Sanders, who took over the locker of his good friend Nixon ("I asked his permission," he said) also said his decision to play baseball again "is a pretty good sign of what I want to do in the future." Sanders made his debut the next night in the Braves' doubleheader split with the Reds, appearing in both games as a pinch runner. His workday was nearly 15 hours long, as he took a helicopter ride from the Falcons' practice facility in Suwanee to Atlanta-Fulton County Stadium. "It was OK; it was wonderful," he said before finally leaving for his Alpharetta home.

*Even before it was official, Braves fans
made it clear that they knew where
the team would finish in the
NL West standings.*

88

JONATHAN NEWTON

As the Braves played out the final days of the season, fans poured through the turnstiles at the stadium.

FRANK NIEMEIR

MIRACLE SEASON!

As John Smoltz bore down against the Astros, an update from the West Coast sent Braves fans into an early celebration.

FRANK NIEMEIR

After the final out, Greg Olson and John Smoltz met on the mound in a memorable scene. They soon were joined by onrushing teammates.

The previous evening, however, had not been wonderful for Hunter or Mitchell, who both were charged with driving under the influence of alcohol after being involved in separate auto accidents. When they arrived at the park the next night, they were pulled into a room and scolded by Pendleton. Justice, who had been out with the two players at a local nightclub, was also reprimanded by Pendleton, and the two got into an argument. The Braves said Hunter and Mitchell would be fined but not suspended. They were both cheered during the doubleheader, but one sign in the stands read, "We want RBIs, not DUIs."

Both games of the doubleheader went 10 innings, the Braves winning the opener 2-1 and losing the nightcap 10-9. But they picked up a half-game on the Dodgers, who fell to the Padres.

The next night, with an opportunity to draw a half-game closer, the Braves instead fell 8-0, dropping two games behind. For both teams, only nine games remained.

The one positive thing about the shutout loss was the crowd of 42,431, which pushed the Braves over the 2 million attendance mark for only the second time since the franchise came to Atlanta in 1966.

The rest of the schedule had pluses and minuses for both teams. The Braves were looking at a six-game road trip, followed by three at home. The Dodgers had six at home, followed by three on the road. Six of the Braves' games were against Houston, the worst team in the NL, while the Dodgers had six against their most bitter rivals, the Giants.

Both teams opened with wins. Down 2-0, the Braves beat the Astros 4-2 with four runs in the eighth. Bream singled home the tying run with his first hit in 21 at-bats, then Olson knocked in the go-ahead run. "We really saved our butts," the catcher said. L.A., however, beat San Francisco 6-2. Eight games to go, still two down.

That day in Atlanta, hundreds of fans camped outside the stadium for postseason tickets. By 4 p.m., four hours after the windows opened, all 15,000 were gone.

With their 155th game of the season, a 5-4 win over the Astros, the Braves gained ground on the Dodgers for the first time in eight days. The Giants cut the Dodgers' lead to one game with a 4-1 win. Said Blauser, "I think the pressure is back on L.A. We feel pretty relaxed again." For the second straight game, the Braves rallied to win, overcoming a 3-1 deficit in the seventh.

The Braves made it a sweep the next day, beating the Astros 6-5 on Hunter's double in the 13th. But it shouldn't have been that difficult; they had led 5-0 in the seventh. "It's too late to lie," said Cox. "I was nervous." The Braves also made a surprise trade, sending minor league pitching prospect Turk Wendell and pitcher Yorkis Perez to the Cubs for pitcher Mike Bielecki and catcher Damon Berryhill.

In the stands, the Braves' faithful enjoyed the moment along with the players.

JEAN SHIFRIN

FRANK NIEMEIR

*Steve Avery found
the middle of
the celebration,
both on the field
(with Deion
Sanders) and in
the clubhouse
(with Ron Gant).*

MIRACLE SEASON!

THE 1991 ATLANTA BRAVES

*The final day
of the season gave
the players a chance
to relax in the dugout
for the first time
in weeks, as the
regulars rested and
a lineup of reserves
took the field
against the Astros.*

RICH MAHAN

100

Neither new player would be eligible for the postseason, but Schuerholz stressed that this was a trade for the future.

Still, the Dodgers kept winning, beating the Giants 3-2. Six games to go, one down. On to Cincinnati.

Smoltz's first eight pitches in the opener were balls, but with his counselor, Llewellyn, sitting behind the plate, he came back with a curve Olson called "the nastiest I've seen this season," and shut out the Reds 4-0. Sanders flew in after practicing with the Falcons, but never left the bench. The Dodgers also won, beating the Giants 7-2.

Reds reliever Norm Charlton, under a seven-game suspension for intentionally hitting a Dodgers batter on Sept. 9, was reinstated by NL president White, who said that because of the close race, "it is imperative that all teams play with their full complement of players in order to guarantee that the competition is fair." Shaking his head, Cox said, "That's ludicrous." Five games left, one down.

The Dodgers won again the next night, but the Braves were too busy celebrating their own miracle to care. Spotting the Reds a 6-0 lead in the first, the Braves rallied to win 7-6 on a two-run homer by Justice off Dibble in the ninth.

The final day was an afterthought. The Dodgers won, but it was too late. The Braves lost, but it didn't matter.

"Ecstasy, pure ecstasy," exulted Olson as the Braves pounded bats against the tunnel walls on their way from the dugout to the clubhouse.

Glavine's 20th win, a 6-3 decision over the Reds, completed a 6-0 road trip. More important, it lifted the Braves back into a first-place tie as the Padres beat the Dodgers 9-4. In L.A., Lasorda criticized the Reds' performance. Responded Piniella, "We don't have any players. Tell Lasorda to send me a few of his 40 players and I'll be glad to help him out."

Three games to go, Atlanta at home against Houston, L.A. at San Francisco. Reminded that the Braves had won eight straight over the Astros, and the Giants had taken eight of 15 from the Dodgers, Cox remained cautious. "Nobody," he said, "I mean nobody in this clubhouse is taking anything for granted."

Avery brought the Braves within one game of clinching with a 5-2 win as the Giants beat the Dodgers 4-1. Two more Atlanta wins, or one win and one L.A. loss, and the Braves would be champions. Lasorda promised the Dodgers would fight to the end. "You'll see these guys go out there and battle," he said. "You can be sure of that."

But at 5:22 p.m. Eastern time on Saturday, Oct. 5, L.A. was down to its last gasp. That's when Andujar Cedeno's fly ball settled into Justice's glove for the final out in a 5-2 Braves win, and Olson leaped into Smoltz's arms. The Braves had clinched a tie. The real celebration began just moments later, when the Braves and 45,000 fans watched on the stadium's giant television screen as San Francisco second baseman Robby Thompson threw out L.A.'s Eddie Murray to conclude a 4-0 win by the Giants. The division title was Atlanta's.

The final day was an afterthought. The Dodgers won, but it was too late. The Braves lost, but it didn't matter. Cox cleared his bench; not one regular started. The Braves finished 94-68, some 29 wins better than the previous season. Pendleton won the batting title without stepping on the field, hitting .319, but everyone's mind was otherwise occupied.

Pittsburgh and the playoffs were only three days away.

CHAPTER 8

POUNDING STEELTOWN

IN THIS, THE YEAR OF THE TOMAHAWK, KASTEN THOUGHT he had seen everything. But with the team on its way to the airport for the flight to Pittsburgh and the start of the National League Championship Series, the Braves received an honor from a most unlikely source.

Cruising down the Connector south of the city around noon, the Braves' three-bus motorcade came upon a contingent of inmates hacking down weeds by the side of the road. As the buses passed, the prisoners dropped their sickles and saluted with — what else? — the Tomahawk Chop.

"Unbelievable," said Kasten, as the players exploded in laughter. "There is nothing like this. Nothing."

There was more. When they arrived at the airport, the buses went to Concourse B. Several planes taxied past, their pilots chopping in the cockpit windows. One captain merely waved, bringing this response from Kasten: "He must not be from around here." Some 200 Delta employees were lined up to greet the team. As players and personnel were led into the concourse, Indian drums were pounded, joined by an Army band. Fans, crammed behind barricades, screamed and chanted.

At the airport, planes taxied past, their pilots chopping in the cockpit windows.

Fans seeking playoff tickets stayed overnight at the stadium, bringing all manner of creature comforts with them.

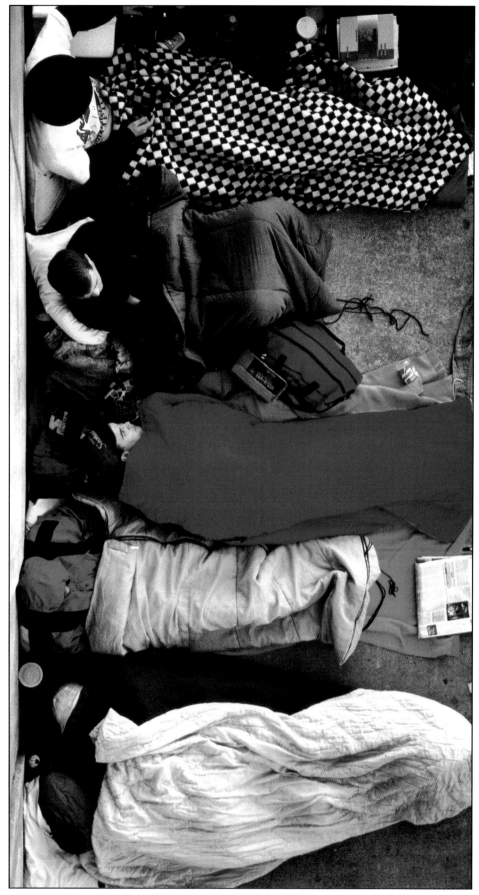

*As players were led
into the concourse,
drums were pounded.
Fans, crammed
behind barricades,
screamed and chanted.*

JONATHAN NEWTON

MIRACLE SEASON!

Game 1: Ron Gant's broken bat typified the Braves' frustration against Doug Drabek and Bob Walk.

"It's just one big party," said Lemke. "I wonder what it's going to be like if we win this thing?"

Even though the Braves had taken nine of 12 from the Pirates during the season, Pittsburgh was established as the betting favorite. The Pirates had postseason experience — they had won the NL East two years in a row now — while the Braves hadn't been to the playoffs since 1982. "Does it bother you being a big underdog?" one reporter asked Glavine. Said another to Olson, "For most of you guys this is your first playoff. Can you handle the pressure?"

Bonds felt they could. "If Terry Pendleton, Sid Bream and Lonnie Smith aren't there, their storybook is over. But because of those three guys, it's going to be one hell of a series."

The best-of-seven series began on a chilly Wednesday night at Three Rivers Stadium in Pittsburgh, and as the CBS cameras clicked on, the Braves' bats clicked off. Doug Drabek and Bob Walk shut them down on only five hits as the Pirates won 5-1. Were the Braves nervous? Said Justice, "It was the first time for a lot of our guys and I could see us being overanxious. But once we got in the third or fourth inning, it was a regular game for us."

By the fourth, however, the Braves were down 3-0. Glavine gave

Opposite:
Greg Olson saw a lot of traffic at home plate in Game 1, but the Pirates would score only 7 more runs the rest of the series.

When the NL playoffs came to Atlanta, fan support was not limited to those at the stadium.

up a solo homer to center fielder Andy Van Slyke in the first inning, giving Glavine a total of 14 first-inning runs allowed in his last seven starts. He gave up a total of four runs in six innings, losing his fourth game in his last seven decisions.

The Braves' only run came in the ninth on a home run by Justice. They might have gotten more but for a fourth-inning gamble that backfired. Lemke led off with a ball that got past Pittsburgh first baseman Gary Redus for an error, rolling down the right-field line. Lemke made second easily, and third base coach Jimy Williams waved him on to third. But right fielder Bobby Bonilla made a perfect throw to shortstop Jay Bell, who relayed to third baseman Steve Buechele to nail the sliding Lemke. Bell compared it to some big plays made the previous year by the Reds in knocking the Pirates out of the playoffs: "It deflates you. I know from what happened last year to us when they (the Reds) made those plays. It changes your outlook."

But Cox wasn't upset. "Somebody had to lose Game 1," he said. "We'll come fighting back tomorrow."

As it turned out, the most significant play of the game was an unsuccessful slide into third, but not Lemke's. Drabek, trying to stretch his sixth-inning RBI double into a triple, was thrown out, stretched a hamstring and had to leave the game. He would not return until Game 6.

The Braves pulled even the next night on a masterpiece by Avery, who allowed six hits and struck out nine in 8 1/3 innings as Atlanta beat former Brave Zane Smith 1-0. After Avery allowed only one putout by an outfielder, Justice said, "I was in right field and I was just there. I should have had a Walkman."

It was Atlanta's first postseason win in eight games. The '69 Braves had been swept in three by the Mets, as had the '82 Braves by the Cardinals. "This first one means a great deal," said Lonnie Smith. "Now we're going home and playing on our own court. And hopefully we can win two of three there."

Offensively, the Braves struggled again. In the second inning they failed to score after loading the bases with none out. They got their only run in the sixth when Lemke scored Justice from second with a two-out bouncer that eluded Buechele at third for a double. Buechele appeared to try to catch the ball and tag Justice in one motion, but failed to do either. Said Lemke, "That's one of the stranger hits I've ever seen."

Lemke also contributed with his glove. His diving, backhanded stop of Bell's bouncer up the middle in the eighth prevented Redus from scoring from second.

Said Cox of Lemke, "He is the original dirt player. He is always at the ballpark and looking for someone to play catch with. He's been a big part of our season."

Game 2: "I was in right field and I was just there. I should have had a Walkman."

DAVID JUSTICE, AFTER STEVE AVERY'S OVERPOWERING PERFORMANCE IN A 1-0 VICTORY

JONATHAN NEWTON

Game 2:
Pirates third baseman
Steve Buechele
appeared to try to catch
the ball and tag David
Justice in one motion,
but failed to do either.

JONATHAN NEWTON

Game 2:
Alejandro Pena wild-
pitched the potential
tying run to third
before striking out
Curtis Wilkerson for
the final out. "Maybe
he is trying to make it
too exciting," said
Rafael Belliard.
"I didn't need
any more of that."

Just what is a dirt player, Lemke was asked. "I just feel like when I go out on the field, I try to give it everything I have," he said.

In the ninth, Avery gave up a leadoff double to Bonilla, but induced Bonds to pop to Belliard at shortstop on a pitch that appeared to be ball four. Cox promptly summoned Pena.

On his second delivery, Pena threw a wild pitch. "Maybe he is trying to make it too exciting," Belliard said later. "I didn't need any more of that."

With Bonilla needing only a fly ball deep enough to bring him home from third, Pena got just what he needed from Buechele — a one-hopper back to the mound for the second out. Now came pinch hitter Curtis Wilkerson. Olson went to the mound to remind Pena that Wilkerson was strictly a fastball hitter. "That's what he's got to hit," replied Pena, "because that's what I'm going to throw him." It was over in an instant. Wilkerson waved at Pena's first two pitches, then decided the third one was low and outside. Bad decision. Strike three. Braves win. Series tied.

Now, said Gant, "they have to come to the Chop Shop."

Said Van Slyke, "Maybe we should all get crewcuts, so the chop won't be a factor. It'll be difficult for us being in a situation like this. They'll be coming at us like it was Custer's last stand."

Indian imagery aside, the Pirates had lost all six games in Atlanta, being outscored 46-21.

"We all realize now that we're at home, it's time to take the upper hand," said Olson. "We've been strong here all year."

The Braves would go with Smoltz, whose major league best second-half record of 12-2 included an 8-0 mark at home, against John Smiley, the Pirates' only 20-game winner. "Fighting the crowd isn't my biggest concern," said Smiley. "It's the lineup you have to face."

Nevertheless, the crowd was impressive; 50,905, the biggest turnout for a Braves home game since the playoffs in '82, showed up for the first postseason game at Atlanta-Fulton County Stadium in nine years. The crowd included celebrities from former President Jimmy Carter and his wife, Rosalynn, who did the chop, to rapper Hammer, formerly M.C. Hammer. But Smiley was right; it was the Braves' lineup that did him in, sending him to the showers after two innings. Said Gant after the 10-3 win, "We knew the bats would come around, and it sure doesn't hurt coming back to this place."

Each of the Braves' first six runs was scored with two outs. Olson not only hit his first home run since Aug. 10, he also stole his third career base. His two-run shot in the first gave the Braves a 4-1 lead. Bream came off the bench and hit his third homer off his former club. Smoltz, bothered by a chest cold, gave up a home run to Orlando Merced on the game's first pitch, but came back to strike out seven in 6 1/3 innings. He also had a hit and a stolen base.

RICH MAHAN

Game 3:
Brian Hunter and the
Braves came up with
key hits, scoring their
first six runs after two
were out.

Bonilla was impressed by the enthusiasm of the crowd, especially the Tomahawk Chop. "When you're at the plate, you do hear that 'THUMP, thump-thump-thump.' I'm going to have to talk to (Florida State football coach) Bobby Bowden."

"You have to start wondering," said Van Slyke, by far the most quotable player on either team, "whether we're a bunch of gaggers."

They weren't, as they would prove the next night when catcher Mike LaValliere won it with a two-out pinch hit in the 10th inning. "I'm not a big momentum guy," Pirates manager Jim Leyland said after the 3-2 win had evened the series at 2-2, "but it certainly was a big game. It's nice to be back even." The Pirates also assured themselves of taking the series back to Pittsburgh.

Game 4 was the first of two forgettable games for Justice, whose throwing error in the fifth inning allowed the Pirates to score the run that tied it 2-2. With two out, Redus singled and Bell blooped a hit in front of Justice in right. Running on the pitch, Redus headed for third. Justice made the throw, but ignored cutoff man Belliard and sailed the ball all the way to third. Well, almost all the way. It short-hopped Pendleton, skipping past and caroming off the cement curb in front of the dugout. Redus scored easily.

Justice defended himself, saying, "I don't need Belliard on that play. It's just a matter of I had an opportunity (to get Redus). There's usually someone that backs up that play there."

Leibrandt said, "I was slow getting over to back up the play."

The Braves had a chance to win it in the ninth when they got a runner to second with two out, but with the pitcher due up, Cox sent Willard in to pinch hit. Willard, who had played in only 17 games for the Braves all season, hitting just .214, popped to first.

Then came the 10th. Two out, runners on first and second. Cox replaced Mercker with Wohlers, bypassing Pena, he said, because "he had pitched two innings last night, and we were only going to use him if we were ahead." Leyland countered by sending up LaValliere, a left-handed hitter, instead of right-handed Don Slaught. After getting two strikes, Wohlers tried to throw a pitch outside, but instead it went down and inside, and LaValliere slapped it into right-center.

The next day, after Turner and Fonda were among 14 people stuck on a stadium elevator for 10 minutes, Justice again cost the Braves a run, this time with his right foot. After apparently scoring in the fourth inning, he was ruled out for having missed third base, and the Braves lost 1-0 to Zane Smith. Now their World Series hopes depended on winning two straight at Three Rivers.

"Nine out of 10 games when you hold the other team to one run you are going to win," said Glavine, who turned in his best performance in more than a month but ended up with his second postseason loss. "It's tough. I know. But by no means is it over."

*Game 3:
Sid Bream and
David Justice were
swinging for the fences
as the Braves battered
Pittsburgh pitchers
for 10 runs.*

Game 4:
Terry Pendleton's
stellar defense
wasn't enough
to keep the Pirates
from pulling even.

FRANK NIEMEIR

Game 5:
The Braves lost 1-0
to Zane Smith.
Now their World
Series hopes depended
on winning two
straight at Three
Rivers Stadium.

Justice had appeared to give the Braves a 1-0 lead in the fourth. He was at second with two out when Lemke singled to left. He stumbled as he approached third, tried to drag his right foot over the base, and hesitated momentarily after rounding the bag, but still beat Bonds' throw to the plate. Bell, however, was standing on third, screaming for the ball. "There was no doubt in my mind," Bell said. "I was there. I was right behind it. I saw it. He missed the base." The ball was thrown to Bell, and umpire Frank Pulli called Justice out. Inning over. No runs.

Again, Justice defended himself. "Usually I touch it with my left foot," he said, "but because of the angle, I touched it with my right. I'm not saying I pounded it. I'm not saying it was very pronounced, but I grazed the bag." Others, however, including Williams, the third base coach, thought he missed it.

The Pirates scored their only run in the fifth when Buechele walked, took second on a single by Slaught and came home on a single by Jose Lind.

In the ninth, with runners at first and second and one out, Cox allowed Lemke to bat against righthander Roger Mason. Cox had left-handed hitting Bream available on the bench, but chose to go with Lemke, a switch hitter, even though Lemke's average was 35 points lower from the left side than from the right. He grounded into a fielder's choice, and the game ended when righthander Blauser hit a soft liner to right. Bream was not happy afterward, but all he would say was, "It's not my job to make that call."

The Braves muffed a chance to score in the second. Just as they had in the second inning of Game 2, they loaded the bases with none out. But Belliard struck out, and Glavine missed the sign for a suicide squeeze bunt on a 2-2 pitch. When he saw Hunter breaking from third, he tried to bunt anyway, but missed on a pitch low and outside. Hunter was a dead duck. Double play, end of inning. Again, no runs.

Cox was skewered on the talk shows the next day, but stood his ground. "I was right in those decisions," he said. "The thing everybody is forgetting is to give Pittsburgh a little credit. They've got some kind of defense and team."

Now the Braves had to turn to Avery again. Said Bream, "I know it sounds old by now, but we've bounced back from a lot of things this season. There is no way we're through." Added Cox, "It isn't like we couldn't have won both (Games 4 and 5)."

Cox called a pregame meeting before Game 6. "I just tried to loosen them up and told them we definitely had the tools to win this thing. I also tried to make them laugh." A Pittsburgh radio station also had laughter in mind when it held a contest for the best Braves joke. The winner said he had just received a telephone call from Justice. What did Justice want, the DJ asked. "He just wanted to touch base."

MIRACLE SEASON!

MARLENE KARAS

The tension of four one-run games in the NL playoffs was almost too much for some fans — but no problem for others.

FRANK NIEMEIR

JONATHAN NEWTON

Game 5:
David Justice beat the
throw home . . . but
he had missed third
base, costing the
Braves a run in a
game they lost 1-0.

Ron Gant stole six bases in the series, a National League playoff record.

MARLENE KARAS

Game 6:
Greg Olson and
Alejandro Pena
celebrate after getting
Andy Van Slyke on
a called strike
for the final out.

RICH MAHAN

Game 7:
All of Atlanta was
watching or listening.
At the Fox Theater,
where "The Phantom
of the Opera" was
being staged, many in
the audience listened
to the game on radio.

Avery and the Braves had the last laugh, however, winning another 1-0 classic to send the series to Game 7. Cox pinch hit for Avery in the ninth, and brought in Pena to finish it. Pena allowed a leadoff single to pinch hitter Gary Varsho, who went to second on a sacrifice bunt. Bell then flied to right, bringing up Van Slyke, the Pirates' final hope. On his second pitch, Pena threw another wild pitch, sending Varsho to third. Pena then threw five consecutive fastballs, and Van Slyke fouled them all off, heightening the tension.

On the eighth pitch, Olson shifted gears. "I thought, 'Hey, let's see what happens if I call a changeup,' " he said. The ball was up in the strike zone, but it didn't matter. Van Slyke was frozen. Umpire Bruce Froemming punched him out.

Avery had now won two 1-0 games, pitching 16⅓ scoreless innings. "I've seen a lot of great pitchers," said Pirates pitching coach Ray Miller, "(Bob) Gibson, (Sandy) Koufax, and if Avery's not up there with them now, he soon will be."

"He's unflappable," said Cox. "He just will not bend. He's got all the qualities to be an All-Star for years to come. He's as good as I've ever seen. I can't say enough about the guy."

Neither could Gant. "We knew all it took was one run the way Avery was pitching and the way our bullpen has been going," he said.

Sharing the spotlight with Avery and Pena was Olson, who broke a 26-inning scoreless streak for the Braves by driving in Gant from second with a two-out double in the ninth. "It's the biggest thing to ever happen to me," Olson said.

Now it came down to the seventh game. Optimistically, Avery pointed out, "The last time I pitched here we came back and scored 10 runs the next day. Let's hope that happens again."

Ten runs were a little too much to ask, but four were just fine. Especially with Smoltz pitching the Braves' second consecutive shutout. Smiley gave up three first-inning runs, including a two-run homer by Hunter, and left after retiring only two batters. Once again Olson concluded the game by leaping into Smoltz's arms, just as he had done after the division-clincher.

Afterward, a practically speechless Turner accepted the championship trophy, saying, "Better late than never."

All Atlanta seemingly was either watching or listening. At the Fox Theater, where the play "Phantom of the Opera" was being staged, many in the audience listened to the game on radio. At the final curtain, star Kevin Gray held up four fingers, indicating the Braves' 4-0 lead after the sixth inning.

The pennant belonged to the Braves, their first since 1958, when the club played in Milwaukee. Said Leyland, "They just dominated us with their pitching. There was no trickery involved. It was just pure power pitching." Indeed, in seven games the Braves had allowed just

11 earned runs in 63 innings for a 1.57 ERA. The Pirates did not score in their final 23 innings. Van Slyke and Bonds finished hitting .160 and .148.

Said Smoltz, "We said all along that you beat the Pirates by keeping Bonds off base. We did that and you didn't hear a whole lot out of the other guys."

Avery was everybody's choice as series MVP — everybody, that is, except himself. "I think if you really get right down to it," he said, "our MVP was Olson and our defense. They just did a great job. We threw the ball in and let them do the rest of the work."

Hunter addressed the pessimism that had preceded Game 6, when the Braves were one loss from elimination. "It looked to many like it might not happen when we came back up here from Atlanta," he said. "But we knew all along we could take it. Now we go to the big party."

Game 7: Brian Hunter's two-run homer in the first inning put the Braves in command.

*Game 7:
John Smoltz
was again on
the mound to
start the Braves'
celebration.*

MARLENE KARAS

*Steve Avery
won the Most
Valuable Player
trophy, but
"our MVP was
Greg Olson and
our defense.
They just did a
great job."*

FRANK NIEMEIR

"It looked to many like it might not happen. But we knew all along we could take it. Now we go to the big party."

BRIAN HUNTER

Ahead was the World Series. The fairy tale wasn't over yet.

Also invited was a team with a similar storyline. In the history of baseball, no team had ever won a pennant after finishing last the year before. Now, in 1991, both the Braves and Twins had done it.

Said Olson, a Minnesota native who had played three games with the Twins in 1989, "It was just fate that the Twins won and finished in last place last year. It was fate that we won and we were in last. Now both of us are in the World Series. It's great for baseball. Everyone going to spring training can now be optimistic."

The Braves headed directly for Minneapolis. Meanwhile, Atlanta went crazy. Thousands danced on Peachtree Street in Buckhead. Traffic was gridlocked, and Braves T-shirts were being sold everywhere.

On the flight to Minnesota, Schuerholz danced in the aisle with Freeman. Kasten kept the trophy in the seat next to him. The plane was decorated with Braves streamers, balloons and banners.

Ahead of them was the World Series. The fairy tale wasn't over yet.

CHAPTER 9

TO THE BRINK

Atlanta Journal-Constitution columnist Mark Bradley called the Braves-Twins matchup the Looking Glass Series. "When the Atlanta Braves wake in the morning and gaze into the bathroom mirror, surely they will see the Minnesota Twins staring back. Throughout the summer and now autumn, these teams have run on parallel tracks.

"Never in this century had a team gone from worst to first, and now two have. These two. Fittingly, they meet in a Series where there's no underdog."

No underdog, maybe, but one distinct advantage. That was the Metrodome, the Twins' House That Roared. Minnesota had won all four previous World Series games played there in 1987. In fact, until Toronto won Game 2 of the '91 playoffs, the Twins were unbeaten at the Dome in seven postseason games. The Braves would have to learn — quickly — how to spot fly balls against the background of the light-colored fabric roof, how to play caroms off the green tarp (the "Trash Bag") in right field, how to deal with high hops off the hard artificial turf, and how to ignore the distracting Homer Hankies waved by the Twins' fans.

Minnesota had one distinct advantage. That was the Metrodome, the Twins' House That Roared.

*Game 1:
Greg Olson braced
for a collision
as Dan Gladden
of the Twins tried
to score.*

FRANK NIEMEIR

Game 1:
Greg Olson lost
his balance, but not
the ball, and Dan
Gladden was out
at the plate.

But mostly, they would have to adapt to the unbelievable noise; when the fans got cranked up it sounded as if a 747 was landing at second base.

The prognosis wasn't good for Atlanta. In '87, when his Cardinals lost all four Series games in the Dome, St. Louis manager Whitey Herzog said, "We could have played in the Dome until Thanksgiving and not won a game." Schuerholz, who was painfully familiar with the Dome from his days with the Royals, said if he had his way, he would "use a nuclear bomb on this place."

Cox decided not to alter his rotation, naming Leibrandt to start the opener against Morris. Many had felt the Braves' manager might open with Glavine and come back with Avery and Smoltz, thus assuring that all three would have at least two starts if the Series went seven games. But Cox expressed confidence in Leibrandt, one of only five Braves with World Series experience.

Another one of those postseason veterans was Lonnie Smith, who had three Series championship rings from three different clubs — Philadelphia in 1980, St. Louis in '82 and Kansas City in '85. After the Braves had hit just .231 against the Pirates, Cox decided that for the games in the AL park, where a designated hitter could be used, Smith would fill that role, Hunter would move to left and Bream would play first. With Minnesota starting three righthanders, Cox wanted Bream in the lineup. "It kind of surprised me," said Hunter, who had played the outfield in the minors but not for the Braves this season, "but I think it's a great move."

The day before Game 1, the Braves tried to familiarize themselves with the idiosyncracies of the Dome in a 90-minute workout. "It makes the Astrodome seem like a piece of cake," Hunter said, ominously. Minnesota center fielder Kirby Puckett offered some advice about the roof. "They play outdoors on grass where they can turn their backs on fly balls and then go back and get them," he said of the Braves. "But they won't be able to do that here. That's one lesson I've learned. Never turn your back."

The national media flocked around Olson, a local hero who had grown up in Minnesota and still had a house in nearby Edina. CBS wanted him to go on its morning show, which required him to be picked up by limo at 5:45 a.m., just three hours after the team plane had landed in Minneapolis. Ever accommodating, Olson agreed. After the show, he returned home to grab a few more hours of sleep, then got up again and went pheasant hunting. "I couldn't have scripted this whole thing better," he said after depositing the heads of two deceased pheasants in the clubhouse garbage. "Am I having a blast? That wouldn't even describe the feeling I have right now. And sleep? Shoot, even if I had time I couldn't."

Before Game 1, a group of Native Americans demonstrated

Game 2: Ron Gant was enraged when umpire Drew Coble called him out after first baseman Kent Hrbek appeared to lift Gant off the base.

MARLENE KARAS

Game 2:
Greg Olson beat this
throw home, but the
Braves fell behind two
games to none.

against the Braves and their fans, especially the use of the Tomahawk Chop. The Indians — they said there were 300 of them; police estimated 150 — carried signs with messages such as "We Are Not Mascots" and "How About The Atlanta Klansmen?" Said Bill Means, the national director of the American Indian Movement, "Do you think people would stand for it if they gave out Jewish yarmulkes (skull caps) and when the other team got a hit, they'd shake the yarmulkes and yell, 'Oy, vey?'

"We're not out to spoil anybody's good time. But when you come to Minneapolis, where there are 50,000 of us (in the state), you have to respect our heritage and our history."

Some Indians sold T-shirts that read "Stop the Chop." Said one, Doug Lemon, of Oneida and Chippewa descent, "I don't have anything against the Braves. I'm from Milwaukee. I was going to pull for the Braves. I don't mind the Tomahawk Chop. But when they started doing that chant I was offended. A lot of our chants have a religious significance."

The word "Braves" was conspicuously absent from a sign outside the stadium that read "Minnesota Twins vs. Atlanta." Inside, where the team names were painted near both foul lines, both clubs' logos were missing — the Braves' tomahawk and the Twins' baseball.

As game time approached, the attention turned to baseball. Cox was repeatedly asked about his decision to start Leibrandt instead of Glavine. "There is no reason, no reason at all, to do anything different," he insisted. But after Leibrandt gave up four runs in four-plus innings and the Braves lost 5-2, few were agreeing with the manager.

Still, the Braves had little success against Morris, reaching him only for a single run in the sixth. Atlanta put its leadoff hitter on base only once in the first seven innings and had only one multiple-hit inning. The four left-handed hitters in the lineup — Treadway, Pendleton, Justice and Bream — went 2-for-11 against Morris.

The deciding blow came in the fifth inning, a three-run homer by Twins shortstop Greg Gagne that finished Leibrandt. "I wish he could have got one (a pitch) in on Gagne," Cox said of Leibrandt, "but he pitched all right." Gagne, the Twins' No. 9 batter, had hit only eight home runs all season.

After the game, Cox admitted the Metrodome would take some time to get used to. "Yes, I guess it's harder to play here," he said. "The roof, the noise, the funny wall, that kind of stuff." Blauser, asked if he had ever played in a louder setting, said, "Well, I played on an airport runway before, but . . . no, really, this has got to be the loudest I've ever played in."

The roof was no factor, except on one foul ball. It landed in the VIP box down the third base line, striking Vincent's daughter, Anne, on the head. She was not seriously hurt.

Gant provided the Braves' only offense, with three hits and both RBIs, but it was far too little.

Game 2 was a chance for redemption for Glavine, who had gone 0-2 against the Pirates. He went eight innings, but once again a shaky first cost him. He gave up a two-run homer to designated hitter Chili Davis, and when he surrendered a solo shot to third baseman Scott Leius in the eighth, the Braves were on their way to a 3-2 loss.

"I'm sure I'm going to hear a lot of garbage about how I haven't won a postseason game," Glavine said afterward. "I've caught an awful lot of flak for the playoff games. People expect me to pitch a shutout every time. If I give up three runs, it's like I'm getting shelled. If that's the case, that's the case."

A typical Dome play hurt Glavine in the first, when Justice and Lemke couldn't communicate on a pop to short right by Dan Gladden. Justice knocked the ball out of Lemke's glove for a two-base error, and three batters later, Davis hit his two-run homer.

Taking some of the spotlight away from Glavine, however, was a play that happened in the third with the Braves down 2-1 and Lonnie Smith at first with two out. Gant drove a hit into left, and Smith beat left fielder Gladden's throw to third. The ball got away from Leius,

*Game 2:
"I'm sure I'm going to hear a lot of garbage about how I haven't won a postseason game. If I give up three runs, it's like I'm getting shelled."*

TOM GLAVINE,
AFTER LOSING 3-2
IN GAME 2

*Atlanta fans showed
they were serious
about the Series and
their disapproval of
Kent Hrbek's tactics
in Game 2.*

and pitcher Kevin Tapani picked it up. He fired it to first baseman Kent Hrbek, trying to catch Gant. Gant made it back safely, but Hrbek, who at 6-feet-4, 250 pounds was four inches taller and 78 pounds heavier than Gant, appeared to pry the Brave's leg off the bag. Umpire Drew Coble said it was Gant's momentum that lifted him off the bag, and called him out. The inning ended with Smith at third and Justice in the on-deck circle.

Gant was enraged. "Everyone in the stands and on TV knew I was on the base," he said. "It was so obvious, the whole stadium saw it. I felt the whole force of him pulling me off the bag. He's twice my size."

Said first base coach Corrales, "He threw him off the base. It looked like a wrestler's move." No coincidence there. As Twins fans already knew, and the rest of America was about to find out, Hrbek had aspirations of becoming a professional wrestler after his baseball days were over. He even had a name picked out — T. Rex, which was inscribed on his shower thongs.

To Coble, however, wrestling had nothing to do with it. "His momentum was carrying him toward the first base dugout," he said of Gant. "When he did that he began to switch feet. He tried to pick up one foot and bring the other down. That just carried him more to the first base dugout."

Again, the odds were against the Braves. Forty-one teams had fallen behind 2-0 in the Series, and only 10 had come back to win. Pendleton reminded doubters that the Braves were no strangers to adversity. "We started the season two games behind (losing the first two to Los Angeles)," he said. "It's a situation we've been in all year long. I don't know if we enjoy doing this or what. But we always seem to be in this situation."

Said Avery, "It's all right because they're expected to win here; there's no secret about that."

"We're going to win at least two in our park," said Hunter. "It would be nice to sweep but we're definitely going to bring it back (to Minnesota)."

Two things favored the Braves as they headed home to Atlanta: their two aces, Avery and Smoltz, would pitch the next two games, and the Twins were a different team away from the Metrodome.

Minnesota had never won a World Series road game, losing three in St. Louis in 1987 and three in Los Angeles in '65. During the season they had hit .302 at home, .259 on the road. Also, because the DH would not be used in the NL park, the Twins would not have Davis in the lineup. Twins manager Tom Kelly, asked about the increased premium on strategy because the pitchers would have to hit, responded sarcastically, "I've lost a lot of sleep worrying about this double-switch thing. To me, it's up there with rocket science."

Game 3: (Next page) David Justice slid home with the winning run in the 12th inning.

FRANK NIEMEIR

FRANK NIEMEIR

MIRACLE SEASON!

Tickets for the first World Series game in Atlanta history were fetching as much as $650 on the black market. But the enthusiasm of some fans was getting decidedly out of hand, as Hrbek reported that he and his family were receiving threatening phone calls, including one to his mother at 3:30 a.m. at her Bloomington, Minn., home. The caller said, "Your son better watch himself in Atlanta, because he's going to get one between the eyes."

As in Minneapolis, there were Indian protestors outside the stadium. Former president Carter defended the Tomahawk Chop, saying, "With the Braves on top, we have a brave, courageous and successful team, and I think we can look on the American Indians as brave, successful and attractive."

Before the game, Cox announced that Glavine would pitch Game 5, replacing Leibrandt. Avery and Smoltz would go in Games 6 and 7, and Leibrandt would be available for long relief. "He could be really effective coming after one of our harder throwers," said Cox. "This has always been an option, and we'll see how it works."

First, however, there was the business of Game 3, and the teams played as if they didn't want it to end. It took four hours and four minutes, the longest night game in Series history, and the teams combined

Game 4: Lonnie Smith leveled Twins catcher Brian Harper, but Harper held on for the out.

JONATHAN NEWTON

Game 4:
The late-night magic
continued for the
Braves as Jerry
Willard lofted a fly
ball to right, and
Mark Lemke raced
toward home . . . then
slid across with the
game-winner in the
ninth inning
(next page).

Photo: FRANK NIEMEIR

THE 1991 ATLANTA BRAVES

to use a Series-record 42 players before Justice slid home in the 12th inning with the deciding run in a 5-4 win.

"I'm not glad we lost," said Kelly, "but it was a hell of a ball-game."

With Avery on the mound, the Braves built a 4-1 lead on homers by Justice and Lonnie Smith. But after Puckett closed the gap to 4-2 with a homer in the seventh, Davis tied it with a pinch-hit two-run homer in the eighth off Pena, who had not blown a save in a Braves uniform in 14 prior opportunities.

In the 12th, with Rick Aguilera pitching for the Twins, Justice hit a one-out single. Hunter flied to center, but Justice stole second. Olson walked, and Lemke, who had just one hit so far in the Series, came to the plate. In the top of the inning, he had misplayed a potential inning-ending double play ball. Was he thinking of getting a hit to redeem himself?

"No," he said later, "but I thought it would be pretty damn good if I did (get the winning hit)."

Aguilera delivered, and Lemke lined the ball into left. Gladden fielded it and fired, but the throw was off the mark as Justice slid home.

"I guess I was looking for a good fastball to hit," said Lemke. "When I got one strike on me, I tried to just hit it somewhere. After I fouled it off, it kind of settled me down. I said, 'Hey, you don't need a home run here. Don't even try to do it.' We really needed this after losing two up there. But when are we going to have a good game where we just break into a big lead and not have to worry about a close game?"

It didn't happen the next night, as Lemke assumed the hero's role once again. This time he tripled and scored the winning run in the ninth on a fly ball by another unlikely hero, Willard, as the Braves won 3-2 to even the Series at two games apiece.

"Everything seems to be pointing our way," said Smoltz, who went seven innings despite still feeling the effects of a stomach virus. "But you know how things go in this game. If there is an easy game from here on out, let me know. I've — everybody has — aged."

The Braves' rally began with the score 2-2 and one out in the ninth. Lemke, who already had two hits, tripled off Mark Guthrie. Blauser was intentionally walked before Kelly brought in a righthander, former Brave Steve Bedrosian. Cox had used his top two left-handed pinch hitters — Treadway and Gregg — so he sent up Willard. Said Justice, "Tonight was the first night I was nervous. Everybody in the dugout was leaning forward, trying to give him some momentum to hit the ball."

Willard did, pushing it high into right field. Shane Mack hurried back, made the catch and threw toward the plate. Catcher Brian Harp-

Game 5:
Ted Turner and Jane
Fonda joined in the
fun as the Braves won
14-5, sparked by
Lonnie Smith's
home run.

JONATHAN NEWTON

caught the ball, whirled and bumped Lemke, but never tagged him. Umpire Terry Tata called Lemke safe, ignoring Harper's histrionics.

The game also featured a botched suicide squeeze by the Twins, an inning where the Braves failed to score despite a single, stolen base, double and walk, and Lonnie Smith's second homer in two games.

Now the Braves' home season was down to one final game. "Hopefully," said Lemke, Atlanta's celebrity-in-the-making, "we won't play as emotionally draining a game as we did the last two nights. You kind of don't have the energy to get too excited."

Finally, he was rewarded. The Braves smashed the Twins 14-5 as Glavine got his first postseason win, and Atlanta was one victory from becoming the capital of the baseball world. Said Olson, "We wanted to end it in grand fashion. I wished I could have stayed out there for five minutes and clapped for the fans. The only thing to do now is go up there and win this thing, and then have a great parade on Tuesday."

Minnesota was more than ready to leave. Said Kelly, "They pounded us around, they beat us fair and square. We have no excuses." Said Hrbek, "I've had enough of Atlanta. The whole team's had enough."

"Maybe it's a good omen," said Puckett, refusing to concede. "We'll do it the same way we did in 1987 (when they trailed St. Louis three games to two but went back to Minnesota and won two straight.

Game 5 was no managerial chess match, just lots of hitting. The Braves mounted an early five-run lead, sending Tapani to the bench in the fifth. The Twins came back in the sixth with three runs, but the Braves pulled away with six in the seventh and three more in the eighth. The 14 runs were two more than the Braves had scored in the first four games of the Series. Said Gant, "Now they know we can score a lot of runs and it puts some pressure on them."

Lemke continued to shine, hitting two triples. Justice had a home run, giving the Braves a 2-0 lead in the fourth. Smith homered for the third straight game, but refused to talk to reporters afterward.

"It's a great feeling," said Glavine, who went $5\frac{2}{3}$ innings for the win. "Now I won't have to sit down and look at the stat sheet and see I was 0-4 in the postseason. Now I can look and see a victory and no one will ask what the score was."

The Braves came back once again. Now it was the Twins who had their backs to the wall. In searching to identify the cause of the turnaround, Grant, who had spent the entire season on the disabled list, pointed tongue-in-cheek to the Braves' system of "rally caps," different ways to wear the hats to produce different results.

The key one, he said, was called "The Shark," in which the back half of the cap is tucked in and the hat worn so the bill is sticking up and facing sideways. "That's when it's time to go for the kill," he said. "We used that in Game 5 and it sure did work."

CHAPTER 10

A SERIES TO REMEMBER

THE BRAVES WERE CLOSING IN ON THE TITLE, BUT ONE player found it difficult to get in the mood for celebrating. That was Justice, who remained irked by the criticism he had received throughout the postseason, even though he was hitting .300 in the Series. He told Journal-Constitution columnist Steve Hummer, "From a team standpoint, this has been a lot of fun. But from a personal standpoint, it's been something else. I feel like I've got 1,000 knife marks in my back."

While Justice attempted to put the criticism behind him, the Braves prepared to fly back to Minnesota. "We expect to go up there and bring the ring home," said Cox.

Minnesota, however, buoyed by its experience of '87, when it rebounded from this same situation against St. Louis, had other plans. "I certainly hope deja vu strikes again," said Hrbek.

Added Puckett, "They left Minnesota down 0-2 and had to sweep here. They did that, so now we have to go back and sweep there. Hopefully, whatever they did here is out of their system. They were raking the ball but hopefully that'll be it for them."

WALTER STRICKLIN

"We expect to go up there and bring the ring home."

BOBBY COX

Game 6:
Rafael Belliard went
flat-out trying to turn
a double play.

The Braves were pinning their hopes on their pitching, for they were 6-0 in postseason games started by Avery and Smoltz. "We only have to play .500 ball the rest of the way to win it," said Glavine. "With John and Steve, I definitely think we're capable of that."

Said Justice, "It means winning just one game. I think we can do that."

Even though they were equally confident in both pitchers, the Braves nevertheless hoped to end it in six, mindful that in the four most recent Series to go the distance, no visiting team had won Game 7. "We made it too close in the playoffs, had to go to that seventh game," said Olson. "Let's do it Saturday. Let's do it in six and go home and celebrate. It's something magical. Now we have to make it complete."

The Game 6 pitching matchup favored the Braves. Avery and Scott Erickson had faced each other in Game 3, but neither was involved in the decision of the 12-inning marathon. Erickson had lasted just 4⅔ innings, giving up four runs, leaving with the Twins down 4-1. Avery went seven innings, giving up three runs. Said Avery, "You dream about getting to pitch a game like this. The last three I've pitched, we were down, we desperately needed the win. I don't look at this as any different."

More than 2,500 fans showed up at Hartsfield International Airport to see the Braves off on their final road trip. Another 1,400 followed them, taking charter planes to Minneapolis.

Game 6:
The noise was
too much, until
John Schuerholz
got earplugs.

Prosperity seemed to affect different members of the Braves in different ways. Before Game 6, several players said they had enjoyed a good night's sleep for the first time in the postseason. Not Schuerholz, though. "I don't know if I can take another day like this," he said.

Braves vice president Hank Aaron, who had avoided the spotlight so far in the postseason, drew a crowd of reporters when he showed up on the field before the game. He said the Braves could have won a championship sooner "if there weren't so many changes over the years."

"We started with free agents," he said, "and then we went back to the kids. Then back to free agents again. We had one general manager, then we had another, so we never were consistent. It's just fortunate that we held onto a few guys like Justice, Glavine and Smoltz. And then Schuerholz got here."

The game did not start well for the Braves. Puckett, hitting just .167 in the Series, doubled in the first to give the Twins a 1-0 lead. Three batters later, Mack got his first hit of the Series for a 2-0 margin. Avery's aura of invincibility was gone. "I didn't have my good stuff," he would say later.

Erickson, meanwhile, held the Braves scoreless through four innings, with a little help from Puckett, who leaped high against the Plexiglas in center to rob Gant of a double that would have scored Pendleton. Pendleton tied it in the fifth on a two-run homer to center that finally silenced the Homer Hanky-waving crowd. Two batters later it appeared the Braves would take the lead when Justice jumped on an Erickson pitch, but his high drive to right bounced off the facade of a skybox, a scant 2 feet to the right of the foul pole.

The Twins re-took the lead in the bottom of the inning on another Puckett RBI, this time a sacrifice fly, but the Braves tied it in the sixth on Gant's bases-loaded fielder's choice that scored Lemke.

The game headed into extra innings with the score tied 3-3. Pena, who had come on in the ninth, retired the Twins in the 10th. Even though he had faced the minimum six batters in his two innings, Cox decided he had had enough. "I think he has only gone three (innings) two times this season," Cox explained. "We got what we wanted out of him, and we can go with him tomorrow if we have to." Said Olson, "If you use the guy more than two innings tonight, if we lose, you can't use him (in Game 7)."

On came Leibrandt, who hadn't pitched since Game 1 and would be making his first relief appearance since 1989. Cox chose the left-hander despite having three righthanders available — Mark Wohlers, Jim Clancy and Randy St. Claire. The leadoff batter was Puckett, a right-handed hitter who had led the majors during the regular season with a .406 average against lefties. Cox defended the decision later, pointing out that Leibrandt had struck out Puckett twice in Game 1.

JONATHAN NEWTON

Game 6:
As Keith Mitchell
watched Kirby
Puckett's 11th-inning
home run,
Charlie Leibrandt
left the field with
his head bowed.

Previous page: RICH MAHAN

JONATHAN NEWTON

Game 6:
"This is a great moment. I'm not usually the guy who hits game-winning homers."

KIRBY PUCKETT

WILLIAM BERRY

MIRACLE SEASON!

WILLIAM BERRY

Game 6:
Back in Atlanta,
fans alternately
cheered and fretted
as the Braves' fortunes
rose and fell
throughout the game.

Game 7:
From the first pitch,
tension was thick.
John Smoltz and
Jack Morris were
in control.

Not this time.

With the count 2 and 1, Leibrandt threw Puckett his signature pitch, a change-up. Normally Leibrandt's change-up moves low and away to a right-handed batter. But this one stayed high and over the plate. "I just kept telling myself to wait until he got one up," Puckett said. "Anything up, I was going to go after."

He did, and sent it rocketing into the stands in left. Mitchell raced back to the wall but could only watch as the ball dropped into the seats.

Twins 4, Braves 3.

Afterward, a dejected Leibrandt sat at his locker in silence. In the Twins' locker room, Puckett was reliving another emotionally draining game. "I feel like I just went 15 rounds with Evander Holyfield," he said. "This is a great moment. I'm not usually the guy who hits game-winning homers."

Said Olson, "We have been getting Kirby out with change-ups the whole Series. Charlie's got the best change-up on the team, but he got the pitch up a little high."

Now it all came down to this: one game, winner take all. "This is a situation I've played out in my mind when I was younger," said Smoltz. "I'll be like a little kid out there." Said Olson, "I'll tell you what, I've jumped into John's arms twice now, all clinching games. We might as well try to make it three times."

Before the game, Braves Hall of Fame pitcher Phil Niekro, manager of their Richmond farm club, addressed the team. "No matter what happens in Game 7," he said, "when you walk off that field, you hold your heads high because you've done something that no (Braves) team has done in 30 or 40 years."

From the first pitch, the tension was thick. Smoltz and Morris, both pitching on three days' rest, were in control. Until the eighth.

The Braves had gotten a runner into scoring position five times, but had not mounted a serious threat. But in the eighth, Lonnie Smith led off with a check-swing single. With Smith running on a 1-2 pitch, Pendleton followed with a drive into the gap in left-center. As Pendleton rounded first and headed for second, he couldn't believe what he saw — Smith was just past the bag at second, hesitant even to take third, let alone score. By the time the Twins got the ball back to the infield, Smith had to stop at third, Pendleton at second.

Why did Smith stop? He refused to talk to reporters after the game, but he later told a Philadelphia Inquirer columnist who knew Smith from his days with the Phillies that he did not know where the ball had been hit. Smith said he was confused by a fake executed by Twins second baseman Chuck Knoblauch, who pretended to field a grounder and flip the ball to Gagne. By the time Smith saw the ball hitting the outfield wall, he had no chance to score.

Game 7:
Steve Avery sat at
his locker for the
last time, while
John Smoltz reflected
on his final start
from a deserted dugout
(next page).

Photo: FRANK NIEMEIR

FRANK NIEMEIR

> *"We had a great season, but believe me, it's very disappointing to get here and not win."*
>
> TERRY PENDLETON

After the game, Pendleton refused to blame Smith, but as he pulled into second, the Braves' third baseman threw up his arms in apparent disgust. "Pendleton asked me at second what the hell Lonnie Smith was doing," Knoblauch said. Told of Pendleton's refusal to criticize Smith, Knoblauch replied, "Pendleton was covering for Smith's butt for not scoring."

Still, there were none out. Gant hit a dribbler to Hrbek at first, and Smith decided against risking a run to the plate. Kelly then ordered Morris to walk Justice, setting up a potential double play with the gimpy-kneed Bream due up next. The strategy worked perfectly, as Bream hit another grounder to Hrbek, who threw home, then took Brian Harper's return peg to end the inning.

The Twins also had a chance in the eighth. Singles by pinch hitter Randy Bush and Knoblauch put runners at first and third with one out and finished Smoltz. But Mike Stanton came in and, after intentionally walking Puckett, got Hrbek to hit a soft liner to Lemke at second that turned into a double play when Lemke caught Knoblauch off the bag.

In the ninth, the Twins threatened again. Davis singled, and Harper laid down a sacrifice bunt. But the ball got past Stanton and Bream for another single, putting runners on first and second with none out.

Stanton pulled a muscle in his back on the play and was replaced by Pena, who got Mack to bounce into a 4-6-3 double play. Pena then intentionally walked Mike Pagliarulo before striking out pinch hitter Paul Sorrento.

Then came the bottom of the 10th.

Gladden led off with a double and went to third on a sacrifice bunt by Knoblauch. Pena then intentionally walked Puckett and Hrbek, hoping for a double play or, at least, a force play at the plate. The outfielders moved in. Jarvis Brown, who had run for Davis in the ninth, was due up, but Kelly instead called on Gene Larkin, who had only three at-bats in the Series.

Said Larkin, "This is what you dream about as a kid — getting into a World Series with a chance to win it.

"I knew a fastball was coming. I just wanted to make contact and hit a fly ball. As soon as I hit it, I knew the game was over and we could relax and enjoy the world championship."

Hunter didn't even bother to chase the fly ball. Gladden, who had scored the first run of the Series eight days earlier, trotted home and stomped on the plate.

Finally, excruciatingly, it was over. Twins 1, Braves 0. By the slimmest of margins, Minnesota was the champion.

While the delirious crowd threatened to blow the roof right off the dome with its cheers, the Braves struggled to accept the truth: There would be no final comeback. Said Cox, "You're talking about a World Series ring. It's the ultimate game." "We had a great season, but believe me, it's very disappointing to get here and not win," said Pendleton, who had been a member of the '87 Cardinals club that had lost to the Twins in the same fashion. Said Justice, "Just one break and we might be the ones celebrating."

In the locker rooms, as perspective began to set in, members of both teams talked about how good — no, great — a Series it had been. It had set records for extra-inning games (three) and for games decided on the final pitch (four).

"If you didn't like baseball, you have to like it now," said Olson. "We've done stuff the hard way all year, and we have come through at the end. Tonight we just fell one run short."

Said Kelly, "Jeez . . . 0-0 for 10 innings. What more could you want? Double plays, bases loaded, first to home. I don't know what you have to do to score a run anymore."

The Braves' loss did not diminish them in the eyes of the nation's media. Rather, they seemed destined to be cataloged with other noble runners-up. Wrote Steve Rushin of Sports Illustrated: "The truth is inelastic when it comes to the 88th World Series. It is impossible to stretch. It isn't necessary to appraise the nine days just past from some distant horizon of historical perspective. Let us call this Series what it

Game 7: "If you didn't like baseball, you have to like it now."

GREG OLSON

is, now, while its seven games still ring in our ears: the greatest that was ever played."

Doug Krikorian of the Long Beach (Calif.) Press-Telegram saw it this way: "The sacred codes of baseball dictate there has to be a winner in the World Series. Too bad. If ever there were two teams in this grand event equally deserving of victory, it would be the Twins and Braves."

And Atlanta Journal Sports Editor Furman Bisher divvied up the title in this manner: "The Atlanta Braves are the World Champions of outdoor baseball; the Minnesota Twins the indoor champions."

Said Puckett, "All I have to say about the Atlanta Braves is that they are a class organization, with some great arms and some great guys. We were the two worst teams in baseball last year, and to achieve what we achieved this year ... it's almost not fair to decide in seven games."

In the morgue-like quiet of the Braves' locker room afterward, Howard Talbot Jr., director of the Baseball Hall of Fame, paid his respects. He also asked Lemke for one of his bats to take to Cooperstown. Lemke had hit .417 in the Series, with four extra-base hits (including three triples), four runs batted in and four runs scored. Said Lemke, who makes his offseason home in Utica, N.Y., "That'll be nice. At first I didn't want to give it up. I wanted it for my own collection. But I figured the Hall of Fame is only 45 minutes from my home, so I can go visit it."

Now there was only one thing left to do — fly home for the parade.

CHAPTER 11

FOR THE FANS

THE SUN HAD NOT YET RISEN WHEN THE BRAVES' DELTA charter jet taxied to the gate after landing at Hartsfield on the morning of Oct. 28. On board was a group of players, coaches and support personnel, all mentally and physically exhausted. The tension of the pennant race and the postseason had finally broken, and their adrenaline was finally used up. But as they made their weary way off the plane one last time, what they saw gave them one more boost, one more reason to smile at the wonder of it all. For there to greet them in the predawn darkness were 5,000 of their faithful — cheering, waving tomahawks and beating drums. This was no loser's reception. As one sign read, "We are the real winners. They still have to live in Minnesota."

Nearly choked with emotion, Cox stepped to the front of the group. "You are all wonderful," he said. "We did all we could do, and we can't do any more."

There would be other celebrations, beginning with the parade. And there were honors to be bestowed. Cox would be named National League manager of the year, Glavine would win the Cy Young Award and Pendleton the MVP trophy.

"You are all wonderful. We did all we could do, and we can't do any more."

BOBBY COX,
TO THE 5,000 FANS
WHO MET THE BRAVES
ON THEIR RETURN
FROM MINNESOTA

Good viewing spots were at a premium for the Braves parade through downtown Atlanta.

Previous page: JOEY IVANSCO

The players went their separate ways. Avery returned to Michigan, where he would marry his high school sweetheart. Olson went back to Minnesota, eager for more pheasant hunting. Cox began cleaning out his garden.

For some, including Lemke, who would have been the Series MVP had the Braves won, the offseason meant winter ball, probably in Puerto Rico. For Schuerholz, it meant a return to his desk and phone, where he would resume trying to improve the club. He found it hard to look ahead, though. "There are so many great things to look back on," he said.

And he was right. So for one last time, player by player, let's punch the rewind button on the highlights tape of the Miracle Season.

Steve Avery: What will be the longest-lingering image? The 18 wins at age 21? The domination of the Dodgers? The two 1-0 wins over Pittsburgh in the NL Championship Series? Or the several pictures of him and Sanders jumping on each other's backs during victory celebrations?

Mike Bell: While playing very little in two promotions from Richmond, his fondest memory came a few hours after his demotion in Chicago, when he was seated in a restaurant next to Madonna. "I can't remember if her hair was that dark red or black," he said.

Rafael Belliard: Cherished for his outstanding defense at shortstop, appreciated for his career season at the plate and valued for his popular presence in the clubhouse, he nonetheless was the victim of one of the season's most heinous (and still unsolved) crimes: Someone stole his Sugar Bear honey dispenser from his locker.

Juan Berenguer: All spring he felt he was the best pitcher for the closer's job. Until he missed the final two months of the season with an arm injury, he was right.

Damon Berryhill: Brought in with pitcher Mike Bielecki in a late-season trade with the Cubs, he batted only once and was not eligible for the playoffs.

Mike Bielecki: He looked sharp in his two regular-season appearances but also could not participate in the postseason.

Jeff Blauser: He contributed a six-RBI game against Philadelphia and a game-winning grand slam against Montreal. His memento-filled locker and sarcasm always attracted a group of reporters.

Sid Bream: He produced on the field, where he had two grand slams, and off, where he became the team's religious leader. He likely would have had a career season if not for the knee injury.

Francisco Cabrera: He will always be remembered for his game-tying homer against Cincinnati's Dibble, perhaps the turning point of the season.

Vinny Castilla: He was used very little after his September callup, but he could be the Braves' shortstop of the future.

Francisco Cabrera will always be remembered for his game-tying home run against Rob Dibble, perhaps the turning point of the season.

Tom Glavine became the Braves' first 20-game winner since Phil Niekro in 1979. He also started in the All-Star Game and won the Cy Young Award.

Tony Castillo: Included in the Pena trade, he was the winning pitcher in the game that featured Cabrera's homer off Dibble.

Jim Clancy: He was frequently blistered by Atlanta fans, but he got the win in Game 3 of the Series, the 12-inning, 5-4 classic.

Marvin Freeman: Before his late-season back injury, he had developed into the club's best middle reliever. He gave members of his fan club his home phone number so they could call him with any questions they had.

Ron Gant: He was second in the league in homers with 32 and stole 34 bases, his second consecutive 30-30 season. His ability to hit in the clutch — 21 game-winning hits — was one of the big reasons for the club's success.

Tom Glavine: The Cy Young winner, he became the Braves' first 20-game winner since Phil Niekro went 21-10 in 1979, started in the All-Star Game and dealt with the bickering when it came time to vote on playoff shares.

Tommy Gregg: Having a disappointing season, he hit just .187 after being the league's top pinch hitter in 1990.

Mike Heath: He started slowly, lost his job to Olson and then missed the rest of the season after elbow surgery.

Danny Heep: Brought in to pinch hit, he was released under circumstances that proved embarrassing to the club.

Brian Hunter: He finished with 12 home runs and 50 RBIs in 97 games after being called up, but may be remembered longest for his DUI arrest.

David Justice: Despite missing almost two months with a back injury, he still finished with 21 homers and 87 RBIs. His only problem came with dealing with the media.

Charlie Leibrandt: One of the nicest players on the team and a quiet leader, he won 15 games but fought periods of inconsistency and was ineffective in the Series.

Mark Lemke: He became a hero in the Series as he led the team in hitting, knocked in the winning run in Game 3 and scored it in Game 4. His work ethic was matched by few of his teammates.

Rick Mahler: His numbers were terrible, but he won a key game in a doubleheader sweep of the Pirates in July.

Kent Mercker: He turned in four strong performances as the fifth starter, including pitching one-third of a no-hitter against San Diego.

Keith Mitchell: Brought up in mid-July, he did a good job filling in for injured Otis Nixon in one stretch but was arrested on a DUI charge the same night as Hunter.

Otis Nixon: He was having the best year of his career until his drug suspension. In 124 games, he broke all of the franchise stolen base records.

Greg Olson: He started the season as Heath's backup but ended up starting 32 of the last 33 games. He had several key hits in the play-offs and became a favorite among the media.

Jeff Parrett: Expected to be one of the club's better relievers, he finished with a 1-2 record and a 6.33 ERA.

Alejandro Pena: Acquired in August, he made good on all 11 of his save opportunities during the regular season, saved three games in the playoffs and was also involved in the no-hitter.

Terry Pendleton: He had a big influence on every player in the clubhouse and is the biggest free agent success Atlanta has ever had. He led the league in hitting after batting only .230 in 1990.

Dan Petry: Like Clancy, he was one of Schuerholz's few failures.

Armando Reynoso: He did not allow a run in his first two perfor-mances as the fifth starter but allowed 18 in his next four.

Deion Sanders: His numbers were not impressive, but he added a lot of spirit in the clubhouse and was Avery's good luck charm.

Doug Sisk: He was shaky in a few games early in the year, then hurt his arm and didn't pitch again.

Lonnie Smith: Few fans will ever forget his baserunning blunder in Game 7 of the Series, but his homers in Games 3, 4 and 5 helped the Braves recover from their 2-0 deficit.

Pete Smith: He was expected to be the fifth starter, but his arm never seemed to heal from surgery.

John Smoltz: He had the best record in the majors in the second half of the season, during which he consulted with a sports psycholo-gist. He pitched both the divison and pennant-clinching games.

Randy St. Claire: Called up from Richmond several times, he joined Petry as the only Braves pitchers not to have a regular-season decision.

Mike Stanton: Perhaps the most consistent pitcher in the bullpen over the entire season, he was effective as a setup man or closer.

Jeff Treadway: He had injury problems throughout the season and lost his position to Lemke in the final weeks of the season and in the postseason. Still, he hit .320 in 106 games.

Jerry Willard: He had only three hits during the season but became a cult hero with his game-winning sacrifice fly in Game 5 of the Series.

Mark Wohlers: Brought up in August after setting the minors on fire, he was part of the no-hitter with Mercker and Pena.

Forty-two players, forty-two stories. And one great season.

Alejandro Pena made good on all 11 of his save opportunities during the regular season and saved three games in the playoffs.

FRANK NIEMEIR

MIRACLE SEASON!

AFTERWORD

BY BOBBY COX

IT WAS DEFINITELY THE GREATEST SEASON OF MY CAREER, a year that was really incredible. A lot of people — the players, my coaches, the fans — made it special. So many really good things happened: when we got into first place in May; when we cut six games off the Dodgers' lead at the beginning of the second half; Cabrera's and Justice's home runs against the Reds; the playoffs and the Series. I don't think there has ever been a postseason like that.

I remember back in spring training when there were so many new faces on that first day. It was a good feeling, a fresh feeling. You never really know what your free agents are going to do; you wonder how much tread is left on those tires. But we felt strongly about ours, and sure enough there was plenty of rubber left. Now everything had to be put together. You could tell from very early on that there was a good feeling in the clubhouse.

And there were the surprises in the spring. I guess the biggest was Deion. He had just stepped out of a football uniform and here he was doing the job in baseball. We thought that either Andres Thomas or Jeff Blauser would be our starting shortstop, but Belliard looked really good. And then we made the trade for Nixon. At that time I didn't think he would be a starter.

We didn't come right out of the gate and win a lot, but we were in first place in May. That was when you could really start to feel the fan support.

"You could tell from very early on that there was a good feeling in the clubhouse."

We then went into a slide before the break, but one thing was for sure: We had made one trip around the league and realized that we could compete with anybody. I told the guys during the All-Star break that there was no reason we couldn't come back, we just needed to make a quick run.

In baseball, you usually look to pick up games slowly, maybe one a week. But in seven days we had taken six games off L.A.'s lead. Just amazing. But at that time I wasn't only worried about the Dodgers, but the Reds too. I really thought the lead would change a lot, maybe among four teams. At that time we started to make some big comebacks.

Cabrera's home run was a big step. The Dodgers series were a lot of fun, but I think we all realized that they were just six games. When we headed on that road trip down two games with nine to play, there was still a lot of confidence. We won it on that trip when we won six straight. When we came home we had three against the Astros, and we knew the Giants always gave the Dodgers tough games. I remember watching that last out in the Dodgers-Giants game on the big screen in center. It was a great feeling watching our players and fans jumping up and down. That is what this is all about.

And then came the playoffs and World Series. Who would have thought it would be that dramatic? We played as well as we could. We just needed another break or two and we would have won it. But it doesn't lessen the accomplishment. The feeling is still great.

There are so many people who deserve so much credit. All the guys in the clubhouse, equipment manager Bill Acree and his assistant, Casey Stevenson, and so on were very helpful. Stan Kasten gave me plenty of support, and the farm and scouting department did a great job. I don't think a manager and GM could work better together than John and I did. I always thought it would work like that. Of course, I have to thank my coaching staff. The Manager of the Year award I received wouldn't have come without them. They all worked so hard. And of course there were the players, some real leaders. I guess the biggest is Terry Pendleton. He is a throwback to the old days. And there's Sid Bream. And how about Steve Avery? All of our pitchers threw in some crucial games, but he came through in the postseason when we needed it most. I would say that is some type of leadership. And on and on. There was my wife, Pam, who stood by me the whole time, and of course my children.

And finally, the fans. I can't imagine any team in the major leagues has ever had the type of support they gave us.

To all, I say from the bottom of my heart, "Thanks for a great season."

No.	Date	Opponent	Score	Winner	Loser	W-L	Pos.	GB
	4/9	Los Angeles	Rained out					
1	4/10	Los Angeles	L 6-4	Belcher	Smoltz	0-1	T2	1.0
2	4/11	Los Angeles	L 4-2	Martinez	Leibrandt	0-2	6	2.0
	4/12	at Cincinnati	Rained out					
3	4/13	at Cincinnati	W 7-5	Avery	Armstrong	1-2	6	2.0
4	4/14	at Cincinnati	W 12-1	Glavine	Browning	2-2	T2	2.0
5	4/15	Houston	L 3-1	Osuna	Mercker	2-3	4	3.0
6	4/16	Houston	W 10-4	Sisk	Hernandez	3-3	T2	2.0
7	4/17	Houston	L 4-3	Portugal	Avery	3-4	5	2.5
	4/18	Off day						
8	4/19	Cincinnati	L 8-3	Armstrong	Glavine	3-5	6	2.5
9	4/20	Cincinnati	L 3-0	Browning	Smoltz	3-6	6	3.5
10	4/21	Cincinnati	W 3-2	Leibrandt	Rijo	4-6	6	2.5
11	4/22	at Los Angeles	W 7-1	Avery	Ojeda	5-6	6	2.5
12	4/23	at Los Angeles	W 4-0	Glavine	Gross	6-6	3	2.5
13	4/24	at Los Angeles	L 8-4	Morgan	Smoltz	6-7	5	2.5
	4/25	Off day						
14	4/26	at Houston	W 7-2	Leibrandt	Deshaies	7-7	4	2.5
15	4/27	at Houston	W 2-1	Sisk	Corsi	8-7	2	1.5
16	4/28	at Houston	L 2-0	Jones	Glavine	8-8	4	1.5
17	4/29	at St. Louis	L 4-3	L. Smith	Sisk	8-9	4	1.5
18	4/30	at St. Louis	L 5-3	Carpenter	Leibrandt	8-10	4	2.5
19	5/1	at St. Louis	W 5-4	Mercker	Perez	9-10	4	1.5
	5/2	Off day						
20	5/3	Chicago	W 5-2	Glavine	Boskie	10-10	3	.5
21	5/4	Chicago	W 4-2	Smoltz	Sutcliffe	11-10	3	.5
22	5/5	Chicago	L 9-6	McElroy	Leibrandt	11-11	T3	1.5
	5/6	Off day						
23	5/7	St. Louis	W 9-2	Avery	B. Smith	12-11	2	1.5
24	5/8	St. Louis	W 17-1	Glavine	Hill	13-11	2	.5
	5/9	Off day						
25	5/10	at Pittsburgh	L 5-2	Smiley	Smoltz	13-12	T1	—
26	5/11	at Pittsburgh	W 3-2	Leibrandt	Drabek	14-12	T1	—
27	5/12	at Pittsburgh	W 6-1	Avery	Palacios	15-12	1	—
28	5/13	at Chicago	W 5-3	Glavine	Boskie	16-12	1	—
29	5/14	at Chicago	L 5-4	Assenmacher	Mercker	16-13	T1	—
30	5/15	at Chicago	L 6-1	Assenmacher	Berenguer	16-14	2	1.0
	5/16	Off day						
31	5/17	Pittsburgh	W 9-3	Avery	Palacios	17-14	T1	—
	5/18	Pittsburgh	Rained out					
32	5/19	Pittsburgh	W 7-1	Glavine	Z. Smith	18-14	2	.5
33	5/20	San Diego	L 7-3	Whitson	Smoltz	18-15	2	.5
34	5/21	San Diego	W 4-1	Mercker	Rosenberg	19-15	2	.5
35	5/22	San Diego	L 7-2	Hurst	Avery	19-16	2	.5
36	5/23	San Diego	L 11-10	Rosenberg	Parrett	19-17	T2	1.5
37	5/24	S. Francisco	W 3-2	Glavine	Righetti	20-17	2	1.5
38	5/25	S. Francisco	L 7-6	Downs	Smoltz	20-18	2	2.5
39	5/26	S. Francisco	L 10-6	Black	Leibrandt	20-19	T2	2.5
40	5/27	at San Diego	W 3-1	Avery	Hurst	21-19	T2	2.5
41	5/28	at San Diego	W 8-6	Stanton	Lefferts	22-19	2	2.5
42	5/29	at San Diego	W 5-1	Glavine	Benes	23-19	2	1.5
43	5/30	at S. Francisco	W 7-2	Smoltz	Downs	24-19	2	.5
44	5/31	at S. Francisco	W 5-2	Leibrandt	Black	25-19	2	.5
45	6/1	at S. Francisco	L 8-2	Robinson	Avery	25-20	2	.5
46	6/2	at S. Francisco	L 2-1	Wilson	Mercker	25-21	2	1.5
	6/3	Off day						
47	6/4	Philadelphia	W 9-5	Glavine	Mulholland	26-22	2	.5
48	6/5	Philadelphia	L 11-12	Akerfelds	Parrett	26-22	2	1.5
49	6/6	Philadelphia	W 9-4	Leibrandt	Combs	27-22	2	1.5
50	6/7	Montreal	L 11-2	Boyd	Avery	27-23	2	2.5
51	6/8	Montreal	W 7-6	Stanton	Burke	28-23	2	1.5
52	6/9	Montreal	W 8-6	Glavine	Gardner	29-23	2	2.5
53	6/10	Montreal	L 7-1	D. Martinez	Smoltz	29-24	2	2.5
54	6/11	at New York	L 2-1	Viola	Leibrandt	29-25	2	3.0
55	6/12	at New York	W 6-1	Avery	Darling	30-25	2	2.0
56	6/13	at New York	W 3-2	P. Smith	Whitehurst	31-25	2	2.0
57	6/14	at Montreal	L 2-1	Gardner	Glavine	31-26	2	3.0
58	6/15	at Montreal	L 2-0	D. Martinez	Smoltz	31-27	2	3.0

No.	Date	Opponent	Score	Winner	Loser	W-L	Pos.	GB
59	6/16	at Montreal	L 7-6	Sampen	Stanton	31-28	3	4.0
60	6/17	at Philadelphia	L 4-3	Williams	Berenguer	31-29	3	5.0
61	6/18	at Philadelphia	L 8-4	DeJesus	P. Smith	31-30	3	6.0
62	6/19	at Philadelphia	W 9-2	Glavine	Mulholland	32-30	3	6.0
63	6/20	New York	L 9-7	Gooden	Smoltz	32-31	3	7.0
64	6/21	New York	W 4-2	Leibrandt	Viola	33-31	3	6.0
65	6/22	New York	L 7-2	Darling	Avery	33-32	3	7.0
66	6/23	New York	W 4-3	Mercker	Whitehurst	34-32	3	7.0
	6/24	Off day						
67	6/25	at Houston	L 1-0	Harnisch	Glavine	34-32	4	7.0
68	6/26	at Houston	W 3-2	Stanton	Clancy	35-32	3	6.0
69	6/27	at Houston	W 3-0	Leibrandt	Portugal	36-33	3	5.5
70	6/28	Los Angeles	W 3-2	Mercker	Gott	37-33	3	4.5
71		Los Angeles	L 8-2	Morgan	Mahler	37-34	3	5.5
72	6/29	Los Angeles	L 2-1	Hartley	Berenguer	37-35	3	6.5
73	6/30	Los Angeles	L 11-4	Hershiser	Smoltz	37-36	3	7.5
	7/1	Off day						
74	7/2	Cincinnati	L 6-3	Armstrong	Leibrandt	37-37	3	8.5
75	7/3	Cincinnati	W 8-6	Avery	Layana	38-37	3	8.5
76	7/4	Cincinnati	L 10-4	Gross	P. Smith	38-38	3	8.5
77	7/5	at Los Angeles	W 4-1	Glavine	Belcher	39-38	3	7.5
78	7/6	at Los Angeles	L 7-6	Hershiser	Smoltz	39-39	3	8.5
79	7/7	at Los Angeles	L 5-3	Martinez	Leibrandt	40-39	3	9.5
	7/8	Off day						
	7/9	All-Star Game						
	7/10	Off day						
80	7/11	St. Louis	W 4-1	Avery	DeLeon	40-40	3	8.5
81	7/12	St. Louis	W 6-2	Smoltz	B. Smith	41-40	3	7.5
82	7/13	St. Louis	W 10-5	Leibrandt	Hill	42-40	3	7.0
83	7/14	St. Louis	W 2-1	Glavine	Tewksbury	43-40	3	5.5
84	7/15	Chicago	L 6-4	Maddux	P. Smith	43-41	3	5.5
85	7/16	Chicago	W 8-5	Freeman	Scanlan	44-41	2	4.5
86	7/17	Chicago	W 12-2	Smoltz	Lancaster	45-41	2	3.5
	7/18	Off day						
87	7/19	at St. Louis	W 8-3	Leibrandt	Hill	46-41	2	3.0
88	7/20	at St. Louis	L 2-1	L. Smith	Stanton	46-42	2	4.0
89	7/21	at St. Louis	W 5-1	Avery	Oliveras	47-42	2	3.0
90	7/22	at Pittsburgh	W 7-3	Smoltz	Z. Smith	48-42	2	2.5
91	7/23	at Pittsburgh	L 12-3	Drabek	Leibrandt	48-43	2	3.5
92	7/24	at Pittsburgh	L 7-4	Smiley	Glavine	48-44	2	4.5
	7/25	Off day						
93	7/26	at Chicago	W 6-2	Avery	Castillo	49-44	2	5.0
94	7/27	at Chicago	L 7-5	Lancaster	Smoltz	49-45	2	6.0

No.	Date	Opponent	Score	Winner	Loser	W-L	Pos.	GB
95	7/28	at Chicago	L 6-2	Bielecki	Leibrandt	49-46	2	6.0
96	7/29	Pittsburgh	W 7-5	Glavine	Drabek	50-46	2	5.5
97		Pittsburgh	W 5-3	Mahler	Smiley	51-46	2	4.5
98	7/30	Pittsburgh	W 10-3	Parrett	Landrum	52-46	2	4.5
99	7/31	Pittsburgh	W 8-6	Smoltz	Palacios	53-46	2	4.5
	8/1	Off day						
100	8/2	San Diego	L 13-3	Hurst	Leibrandt	53-47	2	4.5
101	8/3	San Diego	L 3-2	Benes	Glavine	53-48	2	4.5
102	8/4	San Diego	W 9-7	Avery	Rasmussen	54-48	2	3.5
103	8/5	S. Francisco	W 5-2	Smoltz	Robinson	55-48	2	2.5
104	8/6	S. Francisco	W 10-6	Clancy	McClellan	56-48	2	2.5
105	8/7	S. Francisco	L 1-0	Black	Leibrandt	56-49	2	3.5
106	8/8	S. Francisco	L 8-1	Burkett	Glavine	56-50	2	4.5
107	8/9	Houston	W 7-2	Avery	Deshaies	57-50	2	3.5
108	8/10	Houston	W 4-0	Smoltz	Harnisch	58-50	2	2.5
109	8/11	Houston	W 3-1	Reynoso	Kile	59-50	2	1.5
110	8/12	at S. Francisco	W 2-1	Leibrandt	Black	60-50	2	1.5
111	8/13	at S. Francisco	W 9-2	Glavine	Burkett	61-50	2	.5
112	8/14	at S. Francisco	L 8-3	Wilson	Avery	61-51	2	1.5
113	8/15	at San Diego	L 1-0	Harris	Smoltz	61-52	2	1.5
114	8/16	at San Diego	W 3-2	Reynoso	Bones	62-52	2	1.5
115	8/17	at San Diego	W 2-1	Leibrandt	Hurst	63-52	2	1.5
116	8/18	at San Diego	L 2-1	Benes	Glavine	63-53	2	1.5
	8/19	Off day						
117	8/20	at Cincinnati	L 8-2	Rijo	Avery	63-54	2	2.5
118		at Cincinnati	W 5-1	Smoltz	Sanford	64-54	2	2.5
119	8/21	at Cincinnati	W 10-9	Castillo	Myers	65-54	2	2.5
120	8/22	at Cincinnati	W 4-1	Leibrandt	Scudder	66-54	2	2.0
121	8/23	Philadelphia	W 4-2	Glavine	Mulholland	67-54	2	1.0
122	8/24	Philadelphia	L 6-5	Williams	Castillo	67-55	2	1.0
123	8/25	Philadelphia	L 6-5	Greene	Avery	67-56	2	1.0
124	8/26	Montreal	W 14-9	Wohlers	Sampen	68-56	2	1.0
125	8/27	Montreal	W 3-2	Leibrandt	Nabholz	69-56	T1	—
126	8/28	New York	W 3-1	Glavine	Viola	70-56	1	1.0
127	8/29	New York	W 2-0	Smoltz	Young	71-56	1	2.0
128	8/30	at Philadelphia	W 6-1	Avery	Greene	72-56	1	2.0
129	8/31	at Philadelphia	L 5-0	DeJesus	Reynoso	72-57	1	1.0
130	9/1	at Philadelphia	L 5-4	Williams	Wohlers	72-58	T1	—
131	9/2	at Montreal	L 4-3	Sampen	Glavine	72-59	T1	—
132	9/3	at Montreal	W 4-1	Smoltz	Barnes	73-59	T1	—
133	9/4	at Montreal	L 8-4	Rojas	Clancy	73-60	2	1.0
134	9/6	at New York	W 4-2	Pena	Whitehurst	74-60	2	.5
135	9/7	at New York	W 6-1	Leibrandt	Viola	75-60	2	.5

No.	Date	Opponent	Score	Winner	Loser	W-L	Pos.	GB
136	9/8	at New York	W 7-5	Glavine	Franco	76-60	2	.5
137	9/9	S. Francisco	W 8-3	Smoltz	Black	77-60	2	.5
138	9/10	S. Francisco	W 4-1	Avery	Burkett	78-60	1	.5
139	9/11	San Diego	W 1-0	Mercker	Harris	79-60	1	.5
140	9/12	San Diego	W 5-1	Leibrandt	Hurst	80-60	1	.5
141	9/13	Los Angeles	L 5-2	Morgan	Glavine	80-61	2	.5
142	9/14	Los Angeles	W 3-2	Clancy	McDowell	81-61	1	.5
143	9/15	Los Angeles	W 9-1	Avery	Martinez	82-61	1	1.5
144	9/16	at S. Francisco	L 8-5	Oliveras	Clancy	82-62	1	.5
145	9/17	at S. Francisco	L 3-2	Black	Stanton	82-63	2	.5
146	9/18	at San Diego	W 6-4	Glavine	Bones	83-63	2	.5
147	9/19	at San Diego	W 4-2	Wohlers	Lefferts	84-63	2	.5
148	9/20	at Los Angeles	W 3-0	Avery	Belcher	85-63	1	.5
149	9/21	at Los Angeles	L 2-1	McDowell	Stanton	85-64	2	.5
150	9/22	at Los Angeles	L 3-0	Martinez	Glavine	85-65	2	1.5
	9/24	Cincinnari	Rained out					
151	9/25	Cincinnati	W 2-1	Pena	Power	86-65	2	1.5
152		Cincinnati	L 10-9	Hill	Stanton	86-66	2	1.5
153	9/26	Cincinnati	L 8-0	Rijo	Leibrandt	86-67	2	2.0
154	9/27	at Houston	W 4-2	Wohlers	Mallicoat	87-67	2	2.0
155	9/28	at Houston	W 5-4	Stanton	Hernandez	88-67	2	1.0
156	9/29	at Houston	W 6-5	Clancy	Portugal	89-67	2	1.0
157	9/30	at Cincinnati	W 4-0	Smoltz	Armstrong	90-67	2	1.0
158	10/1	at Cincinnati	W 7-6	Stanton	Dibble	91-67	2	1.0
159	10/2	at Cincinnati	W 6-3	Glavine	Scudder	92-67	T1	—
160	10/4	Houston	W 5-2	Avery	Juden	93-67	1	1.0
161	10/5	Houston	W 5-2	Smoltz	Portugal	94-67	1	2.0
162	10/6	Houston	L 8-3	Harnisch	Leibrandt	94-68	1	1.0

NL PLAYOFFS

No.	Date	Opponent	Score	Winner	Loser	W-L
1	10/9	at Pittsburgh	L 5-1	Drabek	Glavine	0-1
2	10/10	at Pittsburgh	W 1-0	Avery	Z.Smith	1-1
3	10/12	Pittsburgh	W 10-3	Smoltz	Smiley	2-1
4	10/13	Pittsburgh	L 3-2	Belinda	Mercker	2-2
5	10/14	Pittsburgh	L 1-0	Z.Smith	Glavine	2-3
6	10/16	at Pittsburgh	W 1-0	Avery	Drabek	3-3
7	10/17	at Pittsburgh	W 4-0	Smoltz	Smiley	4-3

WORLD SERIES

No.	Date	Opponent	Score	Winner	Loser	W-L
1	10/19	at Minnesota	L 5-2	Morris	Leibrandt	0-1
2	10/20	at Minnesota	L 3-2	Tapani	Glavine	0-2
3	10/22	Minnesota	W 5-4	Clancy	Aguilera	1-2
4	10/23	Minnesota	W 3-2	Stanton	Guthrie	2-2
5	10/24	Minnesota	W 14-5	Glavine	Erickson	3-2
6	10/26	at Minnesota	L 4-3	Aguilera	Leibrandt	3-3
7	10/27	at Minnesota	L 1-0	Morris	Pena	3-4

THE 1991 ATLANTA BRAVES

MARLENE KARAS

Miracle Season!